Practical Drug Enforcement
Procedures and Administration

SERIES IN FORENSIC AND POLICE SCIENCE
BARRY A. J. FISHER, EDITOR

Practical Homicide Investigation: Tactics, Procedures, and Forensic Techniques
Vernon J. Geberth

Friction Ridge Skin: Comparison and Identification of Fingerprints
James F. Cowger

Gunshot Wounds: Practical Aspects of Firearms, Ballistics, and Forensic Techniques
Vincent DiMaio

Practical Fire and Arson Investigation
John J. O'Connor

The Sexual Exploitation of Children: A Practical Guide to Assessment, Investigation, and Intervention
Seth L. Goldstein

Practical Drug Enforcement: Procedures and Administration
Michael D. Lyman

PRACTICAL DRUG ENFORCEMENT
Procedures and Administration

MICHAEL D. LYMAN
Director of Criminal Justice
Columbia College
Columbia, Missouri

CRC Press
Boca Raton   Boston   London   New York   Washington, D.C.

Library of Congress Cataloging-in-Publication Data

Lyman, Michael D.
   Practical drug enforcement : procedures and administration / Michael D. Lyman.
      p.   cm.
   Originally published: New York: Elsevier, 1989
      Includes index.
      ISBN 0-8493-9514-3
      1. Drug traffic--United States--Investigation. 2. Criminal investigation--United States. 3.
         Undercover operations--United States. 4. Narcotic enforcement agents--United States.
         I. Title.
   HV8079.N3L39 1993
   363.4'5'0973—dc20   93-19071
                                                                                          CIP

This book contains information obtained from authentic and highly regarded sources. Reprinted material is quoted with permission, and sources are indicated. A wide variety of references are listed. Reasonable efforts have been made to publish reliable data and information, but the author and the publisher cannot assume responsibility for the validity of all materials or for the consequences of their use.

© 1989 by Elsevier Science Publishing Co., Inc.
© 1993 by CRC Press LLC

No claim to original U.S. Government works
International Standard Book Number 0-8493-9514-3
Library of Congress Card Number 93-19071
Printed in the United States of America   8 9 0
Printed on acid-free paper

Contents

Foreword   ix
Preface   xi
Acknowledgments   xiii
Introduction   xv

PART I
TECHNICAL PROCEDURES FOR DRUG INVESTIGATIONS

1   Case Initiation   3

Selecting the Target   4
Receiving Information   4
Verifying Information   5
Case Preparation   5
Budgeting Resources   7
Other Information Sources   8
Summary   14

2   Undercover Operations   17

Preparing for Undercover Assignments   18
Working Undercover   28
Drug Buy Operations   35
Conspiracy Investigations   47
Forfeiture Sanctions   51
Summary   55

3   **Search and Seizure, and the**
     Collection of Evidence   59
     The Search Warrant   60
     The Mechanics of the Search Warrant   61
     Searching Methods   68
     Warrantless Searches   74
     Strip or Body Cavity Search   77
     Prosecution Strategies and Methods of Proof   78
     Collection and Preservation of Drug Evidence   83
     Summary   90

4   **Drug Identification**   93
     Drug Definitions   94
     Drug Categories   96
     Drug Schedules   97
     Drugs of Abuse   98
     Pharmaceutical Drugs   115
     Over-the-Counter Drugs   121
     Designer Drugs   122
     The Economics of Drug Dealing   123
     Summary   127

5   **Managing Informants**   131
     Types of Informants   131
     Psychological Motivations of Informants   133
     Informant Interviews   136
     Contracting an Informant   137
     Special Informant Problems   143
     The Controlled Drug Purchase   145
     Summary   149

6   **Surveillance Techniques**   151
     Moving Surveillance   152
     Stationary Surveillance   157
     Electronic Surveillance   159
     Summary   170

7   **Special Enforcement Problems**   171
     Marijuana Cultivation   171
     Smuggling Investigations   176
     Smuggling and Prisons   189
     Drug Detection Dogs   190

Pharmaceutical Diversion 191
Medical Practitioners as Suspects 192
The Professional Patient (The Scammer) 195
The Drug Audit 197
Clandestine Laboratories 198
Types of Labs 199
The Laboratory Raid 204
The Crack House Problem 206
Booby Traps 209
Drug Raid Procedures 221
Summary 232

PART II
THE ADMINISTRATION OF THE DRUG ENFORCEMENT UNIT

8 **Theories of Management** **237**

Management Concepts 238
The Open Systems Theory of Management 242
The Behavioral Systems Theory 247
Bridging Theories 250
Performance Management 250

9 **Agency Organization and Structure** **255**

Agency Organization 255
The RISS Projects 264
Records Management 265
The Intelligence Function 270
Intelligence Gathering 271
Charting 274
Fiscal Management 282
The Confidential Funds Account 282
Agent Identification Files 287
Dealing with Outside Agencies 289
Summary 297

10 **Personnel Management** **299**

Personnel Selection 300
Personnel Administration 306
Personnel Risk Management 310
Stress Management 313
Officer Rotation 317

Training Requirements   319
Promotions   321
Disciplinary Procedures   323
Officer Drug Testing   324
Officer Evaluation   327
Summary   329

11   **Drug Enforcement Field Training**   **331**

The Program   331
Selection of a Field Training Officer   332
Role of the Field Training Officer   333
Proposed Program Structure   335
Summary   351

Appendix — A Chronology of Federal Drug Control Policy   **352**
Glossary   **373**
Index   **385**

Foreword

A common problem for law enforcement officers in all 50 states is the increasing specter of narcotics and the additional problems that narcotics have created in the investigations of other crimes. Recent surveys have documented the links between narcotic addiction and crime. Because of the high profits in narcotics, we see gang warfare reminiscent of Prohibition days, and other violent crimes that can be traced back to gang wars and the reduction of intergang competition, which are now everyday occurrences in major cities.

Professor Lyman has brought to bear his education and professional background on this most pressing issue. His professional background — 11 years as a senior narcotics agent with the Oklahoma State Bureau of Narcotics and Dangerous Drugs Control and with the Kansas Bureau of Investigation — enables him to write from the perspective of an experienced field agent.

Part One of this text explains in detail how to initiate a case, either through the use of informants or the information of an alert citizen. The keys to narcotic investigations are the undercover operations and proper selection of personnel. The agents and their assignments, special equipment, and utilization of undercover funds require a different kind of management than the ordinary police investigation.

A major problem for narcotic investigators is paying the informants — how much money for what kind of information. Cover stories and identifications of undercover agents must be kept secure, and the informants must be handled in such a way that the informant does not control or, in effect, manage the investigation.

There appears to be a misconception in the United States that all one needs to become a narcotics agent is a beard, a pair of dark sunglasses, and, in some areas, a pair of white duck pants; in other areas, the white duck pants are traded in for jeans and a pick-up truck with a rifle rack over the back window. This is absolutely not the case, and Professor Lyman has succinctly pointed out the nuances of an investigation and, more particularly, the careful training and on-the-street experience that should be required before an officer is allowed to make an undercover investigation. Surveillance is a learned art, and the proper use of surveillance techniques separates the professional narcotics investigator from the so-called narc on the street, who buys a baggie from the corner dealer and never is able to conduct a major conspiracy investigation.

Part Two of the text focuses on the administration of drug enforcement units and organizations. From the pages on philosophy and theory of management, there is a rich history to be absorbed by the administrator that will enable him to use a mix to handle the day-to-day problems of the organization. There are explanations of the formulation of a drug enforcement organization down to the small drug suppression unit. There are detailed report systems and an excellent explanation of the use of intelligence files and their maintenance.

Drug investigations are sensitive, and confidentiality is crucial to the success of a major investigation. Professor Lyman explains how to recruit and appoint quality investigators for this kind of work. Many administrators believe that the narcotics investigator has certain personality traits that make him or her a high-quality, tenacious agent, and that he or she also has special training needs beyond those of ordinary investigators. This is all carefully brought out in the text.

As law enforcement officers in specialized areas, the abilities of narcotics enforcement supervisors will not only make or break cases, but they can create confusion and low morale at crucial times. For supervisors, there are often difficulties in scheduling investigators and sometimes in guaranteeing their accountability. The main questions are how many cases an investigator should carry at one time and how much money various levels of officers or agents should be allowed to expend on types of investigations. These are timely questions that are discussed and answered in this text.

Whether it is a three-person team or an agency of hundreds of investigators, Professor Lyman has presented a text that has a commonsense, street-wise approach for supervisors and administrators, enabling them to visualize the management of narcotics cases through the writings of an experienced professional.

Tom Heggy
Director
Oklahoma Bureau of Narcotics and
Dangerous Drugs Control (Ret.)

Preface

As a police trainer, I can attest to the fact that there is no such thing as too much police training. Police work deals with human nature, which is always changing and, therefore, constantly poses new challenges every day for the law enforcement officer. The skills learned in basic police training are just that—basic. Much-needed skills require officers to seek continual training to keep up with our criminal counterparts.

The investigation of crimes such as burglary, homicide, and rape have undergone changes over the years, but not to the extent that drug enforcement has. Enforcing drug violations is proactive, and it usually requires the use of undercover operatives, which in itself makes it unique and casts this mode of investigation into a class of its own. Drug enforcement therefore requires extensive and ongoing training for those involved in this type of work.

When I first began my career in drug enforcement in 1974, all I had to base my decision on was the portrayal of undercover police agents in the movies and on television. The realization came quickly that the actual duties of a drug enforcement agent are much different than those of our Hollywood "counterparts."

For me, the initial learning process was somewhat slow, as the only actual investigative training I received was by accompanying more experienced agents on drug buys, surveillances, and raids. Investigative skills were basically learned through trial and error. In those early days many drug-buy techniques were untried and untested, and oftentimes they were attempted by drug agents working alone with no backup.

One does not have to be employed as a narcotics agent to see the impact of drug use and trafficking on society. Law enforcement officers working in all aspects of police work witness, on a daily basis, an array of crimes directly associated with the illicit use of dangerous drugs. Many even lose their lives. A basic understanding is therefore necessary in combating the drug problem, which involves all law enforcement officers in all jurisdictions.

It has been no easy task preparing a text that would be of wide interest to law enforcement officers operating in many different jurisdictions. For example, while researching this book, I spoke with a narcotics agent in Florida who advised me that the only cocaine cases his agency would authorize him to work on were those involving quantities of 10 kilograms or more. I later spoke with a narcotics agent in Kansas and, although kilos of cocaine are occasionally seized there, the agent advised that a 1-ounce cocaine dealer in his jurisdiction is considered a significant violator.

No text could give every investigator all the answers to his or her questions regarding problems encountered in drug enforcement. Any text addressing this subject, however, should offer law enforcement officers from all jurisdictions a suitable guide for the general management of drug investigations and of drug enforcement units as a whole. *Practical Drug Enforcement: Procedures and Administration* is such a text. It addresses contemporary aspects of covert criminal investigation as well as provides the reader with a look at the management of the drug enforcement unit itself. This text, therefore, is offered as a guide to law enforcement officers in their criminal investigations. The goal of the text is to promote thought toward different methods of detecting and capturing drug traffickers, identifying those methods commonly used to avoid detection, and maintaining a cohesive and harmonic working environment for the drug enforcement professional.

Acknowledgments

It would be impossible to attempt a project of this nature without the collective expertise of many qualified and dedicated law enforcement professionals. This text is therefore a tribute to all who helped in its preparation, and proper recognition is in order for the following law enforcement agencies who provided assistance in its final preparation: The U.S. Drug Enforcement Administration; The U.S. Marshals Service; The Federal Bureau of Investigation; The U.S. Bureau of Alcohol, Tobacco and Firearms; The U.S. Customs Service; The National Institute of Drug Abuse; The International Narcotic Enforcement Officers Association; The National Institute of Justice; The Bureau of Justice Assistance; The Oklahoma Bureau of Narcotics and Dangerous Drugs Control; The Arkansas State Police; The Kansas Bureau of Investigation; The Missouri Bureau of Narcotics and Dangerous Drugs; The Missouri Highway Patrol; The Missouri Task Force on the Abuse, Misuse and Diversion of Prescription Drugs; The Florida Department of Law Enforcement; The Kansas City, Missouri, Police Department; The Columbia, Missouri, Police Department; The Oklahoma City Police Department; The New York City Police Department; The Dallas Police Department; The Oklahoma County District Attorney's Office; The LaClede County Sheriff's Department (Lebanon, Missouri).

Those individuals who specifically lended a hand in the production of this text are gratefully acknowledged below.

Special Agent Dave True of the U.S. Bureau of Alcohol, Tobacco and Firearms; Director Tom Heggy and Senior Agent Dave Dagg of the Oklahoma Bureau of Narcotics and Dangerous Drugs Control; Ernest L. Sjoblom, Director of the Missouri Bureau of Narcotics and

Dangerous Drugs; Sergeant Rod Combs of the The Arkansas State
Police; Bureau Chief Lewis Wilson and Special Agent Ralph Garcia
of the Florida Department of Law Enforcement; Assistant District
Attorney Richard Wintory of the Oklahoma County District Attor-
ney's Office; Prosecutor Joe Moseley of the Boone County, Missouri,
Prosecuting Attorneys Office; Detective Mike Himmel and Sergeant
Chris Egbert of the Columbia, Missouri, Police Department; and Ms.
Rita Walther for her artwork and illustrations. I would also like to
extend a special thanks to Series Editor Vernon Geberth for his
support and assistance in making this text a part of the Elsevier
Series in Practical Aspects of Criminal and Forensic Investigations.

Introduction

During the past decade, the public has been inundated with statistics and horror stories of the war against drugs and drug abuse, but it seems that such stories have failed to motivate enough people to curb drug-related activities. If anything, the public is becoming more and more tolerant of the dangers of illicit drugs and its accompanying violent criminal behavior. Drugs saturate all levels of society, and stories involving drugs and drug busts constantly prevail in both electronic and print media. No one group seems to be immune from the perils of abuse.

Obviously, drug trafficking is a lucrative criminal activity. It is worth an estimated $89 billion annually when costs such as law enforcement, drug treatment, prevention, corrections, drug-related crime, loss of productivity on the job, and accidents are considered. Illicit drug consumption is now so widespread that it touches most families, neighborhoods, businesses, and most other corners of our society. Crimes committed by professional criminals also reflect the severity of the problem. For instance, in 1986 the National Institute of Justice revealed that two out of three inmates serving time in state correctional institutions admitted that they were under the influence of drugs when they committed the crimes for which they were later convicted.

The magnitude of the illegal drug trade is growing despite widespread public awareness campaigns and drug enforcement strategies, both of which have seemingly failed to retard its growth. To date, the so-called war against drugs reflects an atmosphere of one-upsmanship: drug enforcement techniques have become increasingly sophisticated to keep up with advanced drug trafficking techniques, and vice versa. In 1988, for example, the street price of cocaine was at its lowest point since the mid-1960s (averaging, in some areas, $10,000 for a kilogram of cocaine, which was down from the traditional $70,000 figure). Accordingly, since 1982, the nation's consumption of cocaine has nearly doubled. In addition to the rise in cocaine use, heroin is experiencing a strong comeback on both the East and West coasts for the first time in 15 years.

Adding to the frustration is the realization that the number of drug-related homicides is soaring in our major cities. More and more police officers are being targeted for murder every year by drug dealers who are becoming less reluctant to use deadly weapons against them. Many drug dealers are superbly organized and have hundreds of thousands of dollars at their disposal for sophisticated equipment, high-priced attorneys, bribes for corrupt judges and cops, and bail to keep them out of prison and on the streets.

The problem is somewhat exacerbated by the fact that entry into the market is relatively easy, thereby making the drug trade an equal opportunity employer for all. Members of the law enforcement community are constantly faced with the challenge of change within their own arena. Perennial problems such as rising officer attrition rates, ongoing training needs, and adequate funding for drug enforcement projects and equipment still haunt most concerned government agencies. Other quandaries are perpetuated by influences outside the law enforcement area such as the overabundance of drug cases burdening our state and federal court systems and the placement of convicted offenders within a penal system that is already grossly overcrowded.

Despite this, however, federal and local governments have realized that their first responsibility is the apprehension and prosecution of those responsible for the manufacturing and distribution of illicit substances. Drug enforcement policy continues to be shaped by well-established beliefs. First is that the control of those drugs that pose the greatest danger to the public should receive the most attention from drug enforcement personnel. Second is the belief that drug abuse by even casual users contributes to the demand for drugs and, therefore, constitutes a significant role in the criminal drug scene. Therefore, in an effort to break the supply and demand cycle, drug enforcement officers must eliminate the demand for drugs by the apprehension and prosecution of all known drug offenders, and maintain concurrent initiatives against sources of supply on both a local and national level.

Practical Drug Enforcement: Procedures and Administration is a resource text that shows the interaction between the management of drug enforcement agencies and investigative techniques. Part I addresses drug enforcement investigation procedures. This section gives the reader a close-up of specific methods used in most drug investigations including drug identification, case initiation, management of investigative resources, and dealing with special enforcement situations. Part II examines management philosophies, the structure of the drug enforcement unit regarding the interaction of line personnel with management, the flow of paperwork, and drug enforcement agent field training.

The drug enforcement initiative is only one segment of the overall solution, which also includes programs aimed at public education, treatment, and corrections. Although it is unlikely that drug enforcement efforts alone will ever abolish the existing drug abuse and trafficking problem in the United States, it is clear that ongoing knowledge of sound drug enforcement practices is essential.

About the Author

Michael Lyman is the Director of the Department of Criminal Justice at Columbia College in Columbia, Missouri. Mr. Lyman was formerly employed as a generalist police trainer and has 11 years practical experience as a narcotics agent with both the Kansas Bureau of Investigation and the Oklahoma Bureau of Narcotics and Dangerous Drugs Control. In his duties as drug enforcement agent, Mr. Lyman was personally involved in hundreds of illicit drug cases; he served in the position of undercover agent and worked in the intelligence and air smuggling units as well as serving as the public information officer for the OBNDDC.

Mr. Lyman's academic background includes a Bachelor of Science degree and Master of Science degree from Wichita State University. He has previously written books in the area of drug enforcement, and in addition to being on the faculty of the University of Missouri–Columbia, he as served on the criminal justice adjunct faculty for the University of Oklahoma in Norman, Oklahoma; Central State University in Edmond, Oklahoma; and Columbia College in Columbia, Missouri.

Practical Drug Enforcement
Procedures and Administration

I

Technical Procedures for Drug Investigations

A common problem encountered in criminal investigation is being able to recall not just a particular technique for use in an investigation, but different investigative techniques over a period of time. All police officers undergo training in many different areas of law enforcement, and in time learn to adapt certain techniques to their particular personality, abilities, and so forth. It is likely, however, that those unsuccessful investigations are so not because an officer was unable to apply learned techniques, but because he or she was unable to remember the right one at the right time. The training process must be continuous, and all officers must try to update their training with new techniques as well as periodically refresh their memory in already learned techniques.

Case Initiation

1

Much of the literature regarding drug investigations labels drug dealing as a "victimless crime." Perhaps it cannot be generalized that all crimes have victims, but it is becoming evident that drug manufacturing and trafficking does in fact have many victims. It should be remembered that the victims of narcotics transactions are frequently removed from the act itself. For example, a short list of actual and passive victims includes:

People who experience drug overdoses, of contaminants in impure drugs, or diseases related to drug use

Victims of crimes against persons (such as assault, robbery, rape, and murder) or crimes against property (such as burglary and auto theft)

Taxpayers who must foot the bill for the increased police protection, court costs, and penitentiary facilities necessitated by increased drug-related crime

Citizens whose insurance rates rise because of drug-related crimes (auto theft, burglary, larceny, robbery, insurance fraud) and drug-related medical costs (accidents, illnesses, long-term disabilities)

Employers who must deal with on-the-job, drug-related accidents, their effects on consumer and employee safety, and their overall effects on costs and productivity

In proactive investigations (such as narcotics and other vice crimes) the actual crime itself has not yet been committed, so there is usually no victim or complainant yet identified in the case. At times cases are seemingly handed over to agents on the proverbial "silver platter" because of reliable informant information, or timely investigative leads provided by other law enforcement agencies. Frequently, however, narcotics agents must initiate their own cases with few initial leads. Officers must therefore become inventive when focusing on a particular suspect or criminal organization.

Selecting the Target

Due to the immensity of the drug abuse problem, it is logical to assume that just about anybody can be suspected as a drug user or drug dealer in any given community. Moreover, restrictions in manpower and money make it impossible for law enforcement agencies to investigate all suspected drug dealers in a particular area. It is, therefore, the responsibility of the investigating officer to make a determination as to the specific type of investigation, and it should be emphasized that the target, regardless of what or who it is, should be a specific one. Such a determination is based on several factors, including: 1) the size of the drug enforcement unit; 2) the availability of equipment, money, and agency jurisdiction; and 3) target input from the community (public pressure).

Priorities for target selection should also include:

Type of drug being trafficked

Weight of drugs (grams, ounces, or kilos)

Level of violator (street dealer, wholesaler, etc.)

The initiation phase of drug investigation involves locating and identifying leads that the investigator may follow up. The key word is *information*. Information about people, places, and organizations provides leads that help identify patterns of illicit drug activity. The making of a drug case involves several distinct stages within the initiation phase, each of which might supply the investigator with dependable investigative leads at the onset. Some of these methods include interviewing informants, conducting covert surveillance, and collecting intelligence on criminals. In addition to these techniques, investigators should consider other methods of case initiation as discussed below.

Receiving Information

There are many sources that can provide information about illegal drug activity to the investigator. One of the most beneficial sources is confidential informants (or CIs). Informants may be persons facing criminal charges who wish to provide information in exchange for a lesser sentence or a reduction in criminal charges, or the informant might be a concerned citizen who offers information to the police out of a sense of civic duty (see Chapter 5). Other valuable sources of information include leads from other law enforcement officers and agencies. These sources include officers both in the investigator's own department and in other jurisdictions who have knowledge about criminal activity in a given area (see Fig. 1 – 1).

It is the investigator's responsibility to evaluate the usefulness of any information received. The investigator must be able to judge the probable truthfulness and reliability of the information given, because information is often based on either guesswork or exaggeration. Moreover, the investigator must always remain cognizant of the motives of those who furnish information.

Verifying Information

Once information is received and its source is evaluated, the verification phase begins. Independent verification of information must be conducted separately from the source itself in order to ensure its accuracy. Three investigative methods are usually considered for this task:

1. *Surveillance:* Monitoring narcotics suspects through observation can be an effective tool in verification. When actual criminal acts are not likely to be observed through surveillance, any corroboration of existing data may help substantiate suspected criminal activity.
2. *Use of informants:* Even though the officer's initial information might have been received from an informant, the use of a second informant might be beneficial in verification. This would apply only if the second informant is in a position to acquire information where undercover officers cannot be utilized.
3. *Other sources:* Finally, the use of internal and external sources of the department may possess much needed information for investigators. These include arrest records, intelligence files, drug-buy reports, and other reports and files within the investigator's department.

Case Preparation

Because of the complexity of criminal organizations, the wide variety of suspects, and conflicting jurisdictional considerations that arise in drug cases, a thoroughly prepared case is imperative for successful prosecution. The uniqueness of drug investigations is commonly distinguished by the unconventional (but effective) prac-

```
┌─────────────────────────────────────────────────────────────────────────┐
│        CITY POLICE DEPARTMENT              File: _____     │
│        INFORMATION  REQUEST                Date: _____     │
│                                                                           │
│ AGENT OR AGENCY REQUESTING INFO: ─────────────────────────────────────    │
│                                                                           │
│ Name and any identifying numbers ──────────────── RACE ────── SEX ────    │
│                                                                           │
│ ADDRESS ──────────────────────────── DOB ────── PHONE ──────              │
│                                                                           │
│ ANY OTHER INFORMATION ───────────────────────────────────────────────    │
│                                                                           │
│ AIRCRAFT # ─────────────────────────────────── TAG # ──────               │
│                                                                           │
│ TELEPHONE # ───────── PRESCRIBER INFORMATION ───── TOLLS ──                │
│         S.D.E.A. ☐    CRIMINAL RECORD IN-STATE   ☐   ADDRESS CHECK ONLY ☐  │
│         N.C.I.C. ☐    CRIMINAL RECORD OUT-STATE  ☐   UTILITY CHECK ONLY ☐  │
│         N.I.N.A  ☐    DRIVERS LICENSE IN-STATE   ☐   CHATTEL MORTGAGE   ☐  │
│         C.N.I.N. ☐    DRIVERS LECENSE OUT-STATE  ☐   CORPORATION COMM   ☐  │
│         R.I.S.S. ☐    N.A.D.D.I.S. CHECK         ☐   F.A.A. CHECK       ☐  │
│         E.P.I.C. ☐                                   OTHER             ☐  │
└─────────────────────────────────────────────────────────────────────────┘

  AGENT OR AGENCY REQUESTING INFO: ───────────────────────────────────────

  INFORMATION RETURNED: ─────────────────────────────────────────────────
  ─────────────────────────────────────────────────────────────────────
  ─────────────────────────────────────────────────────────────────────
  ─────────────────────────────────────────────────────────────────────
  ─────────────────────────────────────────────────────────────────────
  ─────────────────────────────────────────────────────────────────────
  ─────────────────────────────────────────────────────────────────────
  ─────────────────────────────────────────────────────────────────────
  ─────────────────────────────────────────────────────────────────────
  ─────────────────────────────────────────────────────────────────────
  ─────────────────────────────────────────────────────────────────────
  ─────────────────────────────────────────────────────────────────────
  ─────────────────────────────────────────────────────────────────────
  ─────────────────────────────────────────────────────────────────────

  SEARCHED BY: ───────────────────────────────
```

1–1   Information Request form to be submitted to dispatcher, records clerk personnel, etc.

tice of police undercover work, as well as other specialized techniques that have been adapted by many investigators. Despite the unusual methodology occasionally practiced by drug investigators, a system and procedures must be developed to eliminate "trial and error" investigative tactics.

Most drug investigations focus on a target. This might be an individual, an establishment, or an organization with suspected involvement in illicit drug activity. Different targets will call for different investigative measures. For example, if the target of an investigation is a nightclub, the investigator should ask him- or herself the following questions: What drugs are allegedly sold at the establishment? Who are the owners and do they have a criminal history that might support suspicions of drug trafficking? Can the establishment be penetrated by informants or undercover officers for intelligence gathering and making criminal contacts? Answers to these questions may give the investigator ideas on how best to approach the investigation.

If, on the other hand, the target is a suspected drug dealer, other questions should be asked: Is the suspect a dealer or user? If the suspect is a dealer, on what level does he or she operate (i.e., street level, mid-level, higher)? Is the suspect considered dangerous, and if so, why? Might the suspect be willing to become an informer? Again, answers to these questions will give the investigator a measure as how to approach the investigation in terms of equipment, manpower, and funds for drug purchases.

Budgeting Resources

It is at this stage in case preparation that a determination must be made as to whether or not a drug purchase from a suspect will result in an immediate arrest (buy – bust) (see Chapter 2). This will dictate whether or not surveillance officers, uniformed officers, or special tactics will be necessary.

When budgeting available resources for the drug case, various items must be considered. It would be a good idea to create a checklist of resources. The checklist should include:

1. *Financial resources:* Drug investigations are expensive regardless of how they are administered: the costs are built into agent and staff salaries, office administration (i.e., typing and filing), and the purchase or investigative equipment. Unit managers will concern themselves with most of this, but the case officer should consider other possible expenses: cash for drug purchases or informant payments, rent for a house or apartment used for observation, use of a specialty vehicle, or the need for a "flash-roll" (see Chapter 2).

2. *Manpower:* It should be acknowledged from the beginning that additional manpower will be required for cases involving extensive surveillance. This is an area that requires close supervision: much valuable time can be wasted on unworthy investigations, and agents brought in to assist in unproductive surveillances may

be forced to "back-burn" their own case loads. In addition, adequate manpower should be accounted for in the event an informer or undercover agent makes any undercover contacts. A minimum of three cover or surveillance agents should be deployed to assist in every undercover contact.

3. *Investigative equipment:* As mentioned, unit managers should have responsibility for acquiring equipment to be used in the investigation. During the case preparation phase, however, case officers should make an assessment of the unit's available equipment and determine whether other specialized equipment should also be considered: body transmitters, receivers, tape recorders, video recorders, body armor, weapons, listening devices, etc. In the event that a conspiracy investigation is anticipated, binoculars, night viewing devices, pin registers, cameras, and radio scramblers might also be considered.

Other Information Sources

Traditionally, local police agencies have the capabilities to possess more valuable criminal intelligence than any other outside law enforcement agency. This information, however, is generated from a variety of sources that may or may not be considered reliable. In this phase of the investigation, the drug unit's own department is the most likely starting point for the collection of a criminal intelligence base. When looking at a particular suspect, establishment, criminal organization, or area, the following sources of information should be queried:

1. *Police intelligence reports:* These reports might be indexed by several methods: suspect name, address, geographical location, or type of suspected criminal activity.
2. *Incident reports:* These reports are case reports containing records of offenses and minor incidents, which are most likely filed in a general record section.
3. *National Crime Information Center (NCIC) records:* This source of information should not be overlooked. It contains valuable information on an individual's criminal history: types of offenses for which he or she has been arrested, convictions, location of arrests and/or convictions, aliases, and other special information.
4. *Field interview (FI) cards:* These cards are commonly filled out by patrol officers while investigating suspect activity in their districts. If filed and indexed properly, retrieval of information may prove beneficial in future investigations.
5. *Traffic citations:* The traffic ticket, although generally considered a record of a minor offense, may be helpful when attempting to

locate identifiers on a particular suspect. Not only does it provide the suspects' name, address, and date of birth, but it also gives the suspect's physical description, vehicle description, and the location and time of citation.

6. *Fingerprint files:* These files should contain physical descriptions and the criminal histories of previously arrested suspects.

7. *Arrest records:* These records will also contain valuable personal information of previously arrested suspects. Specifically, the information will include name, address, associates, employer(s), relatives, and former addresses (states and cities).

8. *Warrant file:* Again, this file will help investigators locate specific identifiers of a suspected offender. Because specific information is required for the issuance of arrest warrants, the warrant file is a valuable resource for investigators.

Outside Law Enforcement Agencies

After examining police records within the investigator's own department, other police agencies should also be queried. In this process, investigators should not only check agencies within their own jurisdictions but identify outside police jurisdictions where the suspect might have lived or worked. If the suspect has ever been processed by law enforcement in these areas, those agencies will also provide valuable arrest and conviction information (criminal history). To aid the investigator in locating these jurisdictions, an investigator can examine the suspect's former arrest records, relatives' names and addresses, military service duty stations, etc.

Federal agencies should also be contacted in this phase of the investigation. There are 32 federal agencies that are involved in drug enforcement. The six agencies listed below, however, are more likely to have local criminal information than others.

1. *The Drug Enforcement Administration (DEA):* The DEA is the primary federal drug enforcement agency in the United States. With 121 district offices across the country and 61 offices abroad, the DEA possesses criminal and intelligence information on thousands of convicted and suspected drug traffickers. Especially helpful are the DEA's massive computer systems. The El Paso Intelligence Center (EPIC), for example, furnishes information on smuggling and drug production and trafficking trends. Additional information is compiled on top level traffickers and organizations operating in the United States and abroad. EPIC is accessible 24 hours a day and staffed by agents from the DEA, the FBI, the IRS, the U.S. Marshals Service, the Bureau of Alcohol, Tobacco and Firearms (ATF), and the U.S. Customs Service.

2. *The Federal Bureau of Investigation (FBI):* In January 1982 the FBI was granted concurrent jurisdiction with the DEA to conduct drug investigations. Additional expertise offered by the FBI is the investigation of organized crime organizations, financial investigations, and white-collar crime, all of which is useful in the investigation of drug offenses.

3. *The Internal Revenue Service (IRS):* The IRS is located within the Department of the Treasury. Large-scale drug traffickers and money-laundering activities are targeted by the IRS Financial Investigative Task Force, who focus on reports of financial transactions filled by banks and other institutions.

4. *The Bureau of Alcohol, Tobacco and Firearms (ATF):* The ATF is very active in investigating drug-related criminal activity such as gun-running and arson.

5. *The U.S. Customs Service:* The Customs Service is most active in interdiction investigations activities involving international drug smuggling.

6. *The U.S. Marshals Service:* The U.S. Marshals, operating under the Department of Justice, conducts full criminal investigations, and it is heavily involved in the investigating of outlaw motorcycle gangs and forfeiture of property.

Other Criminal Justice Agencies

The next step is to identify sources of information within the criminal justice system other than law enforcement agencies. These agencies will include:

1. *Probation and parole offices:* Because the corrections function of probation and parole requires strict supervision of convicted suspect's activities, it is also an excellent source for current information regarding the associates, residences, and employment of suspected offenders.

2. *Court records:* Criminal proceedings are a matter of public record, and examining these may give new information to the investigator. Court records include criminal, civil, and juvenile proceedings with which the suspect may have been involved, as well as records pertaining to real estate deeds, grants, mortgages, or powers of attorney. Information on certificates of marriage (which include names of bride and groom), divorce decrees (which include the names of the plaintiff and the defendant, the date of separation, and the names of children), wills, births and deaths, bankruptcy papers, etc.

3. *Prosecutor's records:* At times the records of the prosecutor may be of value because they provide a compilation of a suspect's

encounters with local police. These records will also give investigators the names of law enforcement agencies which have dealt with the suspect in the past.

Public Service Agencies

Once criminal justice agencies have been checked by the investigator, an examination of other government agencies may be advantageous. These agencies may also give information about the suspect's previous whereabouts and background.

The state department of motor vehicles: The name of this agency will vary from state to state, but they should provide extremely valuable information for the investigator. Again, specific information regarding the type of vehicle registered, number of vehicles, and their descriptions should be available.

Social service agencies: Social service agencies are good sources of information about a suspect's current residence and employer. Obtaining information through these agencies may require a court order, depending on the individual regulations of each agency.

Medical examiner's office: The medical examiner's office records will give next-of-kin information of deceased individuals. Although not a common source of information, this could still prove beneficial in some circumstances.

City or state licensing departments: If the suspect is employed at a liquor-serving establishment, city or state regulations may require him or her to be on record as possessing a license to operate a liquor serving establishment or to serve liquor. In other cases, different licenses may be obtained for a variety of purposes.

Tax departments: Tax departments will have the names of payers of property taxes, legal descriptions of property, and the names of former owners of property.

The department of highways or roads: Maps of cities showing correct street numbers, alleys, rights of way, locations of drains, sewers, or utility conduits.

The health department: Local health departments will have birth certificates, records of communicable diseases, and immunization records.

The sanitation department: The sanitation department should have landlord's names or subscribers to service.

The board of education: Board of education records will contain teachers' biographies, personal background information, education (location), and student's records.

Private Sector Sources

Finally, in the private business sector of the community, there exist many sources of information that can offer the investigator countless leads. The willingness of these organizations to cooperate with the police may be a stumbling block for investigators because their cooperation is strictly voluntary. The professional manner in which the officer conducts the investigation may have a direct bearing on the degree of cooperation received. Frequently, a particular officer within the unit or department will over time develop a close working relationship with employees in a certain company, such as the telephone or electric company. This relationship should be taken advantage of because many of these companies will not provide information without first being presented with a subpoena or court order. Although the acquisition of these legal instruments should not be considered a difficult task, it could still bog down the overall progress of an investigation. The particular private organizations most helpful in criminal investigations are discussed below.

The Telephone Company

If the suspect's phone number is acquired, subscriber information may be obtained to help determine to whom the phone is registered. Conversely, a suspect's phone number can also be learned if only a name is known, thereby revealing an associated address. Additional leads include the acquiring of the suspect's phone tolls (a list of outgoing long-distance phone calls) may be requested. This usually requires a subpoena, but it enables investigators to order past long-distance phone tolls and will reveal the number called, date placed, city called as well as the time and length of each call.

In addition to acquiring a suspect's long distance toll calls, local numbers called can also be documented with the use of a device called a pen-register. This device looks much like a office adding machine and is affixed to the suspect's telephone line. The pen-register records (on a tape readout) information such as the date and time of outgoing calls, the number called, the length of call, the times of incoming calls, and off-hook times.

The use of a pen-register will probably require a court order, which should include a clause requesting "technical assistance" from the phone company to show the officers how to set up the machine properly. This process involves identifying specific wires within the phone system which are color coded (binders and pairs), and ascertaining where both the suspect's phone lines and the lines of the investigating agency are located (the appearance) so a bridge can be made.

It is sometimes possible to locate the pen-register in an undercover apartment or sometimes even in the police department itself. This devise requires little supervision or maintenance on the part of investigators, and only has to be occasionally monitored to retrieve the tape readout, which shows each day's telephone activity. Some expense is required to lease a line from the telephone company for the period of time the investigation is underway.

Public Utility Companies

This is a beneficial source for identifying suspected offenders whose residence is known. Information from the public utility company will show who is on record as being responsible for paying the bill. It is common for a suspect to live at a certain location, but the utility bills are registered to a different party (perhaps an associate or live-in girl- or boyfriend). It is also possible for the water, gas and electric bills to be registered to several different people at the same residence, thereby identifying numerous possible associates.

Banks

At times it may be difficult to identify a particular bank used by the offender. If this can be accomplished, however, much useful information can be acquired: checking accounts, savings accounts, auto loans, personal loans, IRAs, or certificates of deposit. A subpoena is usually required.

Credit Agencies

It is common for many people to make purchases with credit cards. A check of the major credit cards should be undertaken to establish a suspect's credit holdings. Personal information such as address, employer, relatives, and personal references can be obtained as well as a list of items purchased and from where. In addition, the credit bureau will be aware of many of the suspects' sources of credit. Again, this will require a court order or subpoena, but it is well worth the time.

Telegraph Companies

It is common for drug dealers to use wire services to transport funds and messages to associates. If this can be identified through informants or surveillance, the telegraph company might have information needed by the investigator regarding time and amount of transaction.

Other Sources

Other techniques also may be used to find information regarding suspected drug trafficking activity; they are limited only by the agency's legal restraints and the officer's imagination. Included in these options are:

1. *Undercover intelligence:* Officers may choose to develop investigative leads by working undercover. If the drug enforcement section has an intelligence unit, this function could be performed by them; however, any undercover officer could accomplish the task. The objective here is to collect intelligence covertly without effecting any arrests or in any other way becoming identified (see Chapter 2).
2. *Trashing:* In the case initiation phase, it might be advantageous to acquire the suspect's discarded trash to produce possible investigative leads. Although a tedious undertaking, trashing can produce evidence of crimes (through discarded materials such as glassware and chemicals), or information about associates (through discarded phone bills or mail).

   As of this writing, trashing is a lawful technique provided the breaking of any laws does not have to be accomplished to physically acquire the trash. The courts have held that a suspect has no reasonable expectation of privacy in the trash he or she has thrown away (abandoned property), and therefore no warrant is required. Officers are also protected under the Open Fields Doctrine (*Oliver v. United States*, 1984).

Summary

The case initiation phase of an investigation plays a significant role in the manner in which the investigation will proceed. There are numerous sources of information on suspects who have criminal records (as well as those who do not), which range from law enforcement agencies to public utility services. With proper identification of various information sources, drug violations can be documented without the use of undercover techniques or the use of informants. A suspect's close association with other convicted drug dealers, traffic to and from his residence (including descriptions of persons and vehicles), or other extenuating factors will give probable indication of a suspect's involvement in the illicit drug trade.

It must be determined at the onset of every investigation whether sufficient funding and other necessary resources will be available to support a lengthy undercover investigation or whether prompt arrests in the investigation are to be expected. Other considerations are whether or not informants will be used and to what extent (Chapter 5).

Investigators must also be cognizant of information sources that will provide continuing information on the locations of suspects as well as personal background and criminal history. Officer safety should be kept in mind through all phases of case initiation, as occasional covert duty is sometimes required of investigators. In keeping with this premise, undercover contacts with suspects should only be attempted after every target suspect has been identified and thoroughly investigated. Often these goals can be achieved through the examination records as well as through personal contacts with other law enforcement agencies who might have independent knowledge of the suspect.

Suggested Readings

Abadinsky, Howard, *Organized Crime*, 2nd ed. Chicago, IL: Nelson Hall, 1986.

Dintino, Justin J., *Police Intelligence Systems in Crime Control*, Springfield, IL: Charles C. Thomas, 1983.

Harney, Malachi L., *The Narcotic Officer's Handbook*, 2nd ed. Springfield, IL: Charles C. Thomas, 1975.

Schultz, Donald O., *Police Operational Intelligence*, 3rd. ed. Springfield, IL: Charles C. Thomas, 1973.

Ware, Mitchell, *Operational Handbook for Narcotic Law Enforcement Officers*. Springfield, IL: Charles C. Thomas, 1975.

Undercover Operations

2

Selling illicit or controlled drugs without a license is illegal in all fifty states. Other laws govern the distribution, transfer, possession, possession with intent to distribute or by any other means conduct business involving illicit or controlled drugs. These laws have been passed in an effort to reduce drug consumption and thereby reduce drug-related crime (see Fig. 2–1).

As with other crimes, the investigation of illicit drug offenses may be conducted by techniques that range from the traditional to the unconventional. The technique of using undercover agents to infiltrate criminal groups has been considered an investigative staple for many years, and its success as one of the most effective methods of obtaining credible, first-hand criminal intelligence and physical evidence speaks for itself. However, even in the law enforcement community the duties of undercover personnel are probably the least understood of any criminal investigation procedure. The use of undercover agents poses critical problems for police agencies, police managers, and prosecutors with regard to manpower, training, funding, specialized equipment, and other resources. In some agencies, procedures for undercover work may be clearly and explicitly documented; in others, procedures may be unique to each case, creative, and untried. In either case, undercover investigations must be carried out in strict compliance with agency policy and with local legal restrictions.

In this chapter we will consider the undercover assignment itself and what is required and expected of both the drug enforcement unit as a whole and individual unit agents. It is impossible to recommend one procedure that would be appropriate to all units and jurisdictions. In drug enforcement, there are vast differences in the procedures, restrictions, and requirements that govern federal, state, county, and municipal agencies. In addition, there are drastic operational differences between larger and smaller agencies. Because of these disparities, it is only possible to present a general outline for the use and management of undercover personnel. The systems and procedures discussed below should be modified to meet the individual needs of each law enforcement agency or unit.

Preparing for Undercover Assignments

Undercover work is defined as assuming a fictitious identity and associating with known or suspected criminals for the purpose of collecting information about or evidence of criminal activity. All undercover work is dangerous. It requires that officers establish a "cover story" (which may be "blown" at a critical time), and that they associate closely with individuals who may be armed, unpredictable, or perhaps mentally unstable.

Personnel

Given the inherent dangers of undercover work, the selection and training of personnel must be meticulous. Consideration must be given to the particular goals (and resources) of the unit, the officers' personalities, their professional backgrounds, and their physical and mental conditions. In addition, proficiency with firearms, good reporting skills, and the ability to use cool common sense under stressful conditions must be carefully weighed (see Chapter 11). Because of concern for officer safety and the increasing potential for agency liability, the days of undercover officers working the streets under minimal supervision are over.

Those being considered for undercover assignments should be disabused of television and movie stereotypes. Undercover work is not a glamorous job affording the agent with endless expensive meals, luxurious sports cars, and unheard-of electronic gadgetry. Conversely, it is also not a duty that requires the officer to isolate him- or herself from family and friends and become a drug-using martyr. Most undercover work consists of a brief meeting between the agent and a suspect, an exchange of dialogue, and a transaction — usually a drug purchase. "Deep-cover assignments" — assignments that require agents to operate with minimal protection over much longer periods of time — are not as widely used and require specialized training.

Although required to work one-on-one with a suspected drug dealer, the undercover officer must also realize that both his or her

2-1 (A&B) Photos depicting a rural Florida homicide crime scene (A) and the remains of three drug suspects (B) who were murdered, covered with lime, and buried in a pit. (Photo courtesy of the Florida Department of Law Enforcement.)

safety and the overall success of the investigation require equal participation by all unit members. All roles for unit personnel (undercover contact, surveillance, raid and arrest) are equally important. Even though every officer within the unit must maintain his or her

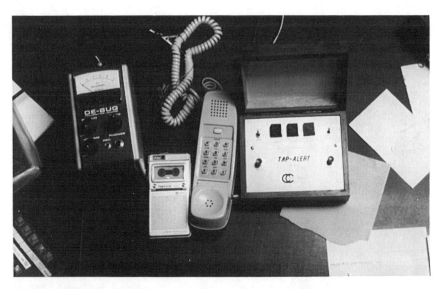

2-2   Devices found in a drug trafficker's residence which are used to detect wire-taps or "RF" signals from concealed transmitters. (Photo courtesy of the Florida Department of Law Enforcement.)

own case load, each officer should regard the overall mission of the unit as the effort of a team rather than one individual.

The Roles of the Officers

There are two general roles for officers to perform within a drug enforcement unit. The *undercover officer* contacts individuals or infiltrates establishments or organizations suspected of illicit drug trafficking or other criminal activities. Usually, such contacts are possible because the officer's appearance, mannerisms, dress, and overall demeanor are similar to those of the suspect. Much time and money are spent in carefully cultivating the officer's ability to function effectively in this capacity; the true identity of the undercover officer should therefore be protected at all times.

The *support officer* (sometimes called an intelligence, cover or tactical officer) is a plainclothed officer who works with the drug unit, but not in an undercover capacity. The support officer assists undercover officers by observing drug transactions in which they (or informers) are involved. Support officers also participate in drug raids at the culmination of an investigation, interview arrestees, and perform other functions within the unit that would otherwise jeopardize or expose the cover of the undercover agent.

Obviously, drug enforcement organizations differ in their resources, methods, procedures, and philosophies. The operational distinctions between undercover and support officers may not be feasible in some agencies. In such circumstances, officers may be required at different times to perform both functions.

Undercover Equipment

To approach any covert investigation effectively, the first order of business is to determine what equipment is necessary to the investigation and to issue it to each agent as soon as he or she is assigned to the unit. The choice of equipment will, of course, vary according to the agency's financial resources, the size of the unit, and the type of assignment. However, when considering equipment purchases, careful thought should be given to its purpose and user, its usefulness, and its durability. Undercover investigators, for example, will require equipment different from that given to support officers. Also, equipment assigned to an agent might be regularly carried with him or her in an assigned vehicle. Therefore, it may experience much wear and tear from being bounced around in the trunk of a car or in the back of a van, or it may suffer from drastic changes in weather conditions (especially in older vehicles, which may leak).

Vehicles

Generally, each vehicle owned by the agency should be assigned a separate number, and a maintenance and repair file should be kept. The kinds of vehicles the agency should own and the equipment the vehicles should contain depend upon how they are used.

Support Officer Vehicles

Unit vehicles for support officers should be generally nondescript: two-door sedans in plain colors such as tan, white, grey, or dark blue. (Exotic or expensive sports cars might be advantageous in short-term undercover assignments, but they will also be easily remembered — "burned" — by nervous or attentive suspects during any moving surveillance.) Unit commanders should consider using vehicles other than standard passenger cars: foreign cars, pick-up trucks, vans, campers, or older cars.

Vehicles should also be assigned to match the driver. For example, a more expensive car should be assigned to an appropriately dressed agent; a sports car should be assigned to an agent who fits the role of someone who typically drives one. If local laws permit it, seized vehicles (if in good condition) are a great asset: they can provide a constant source of plausible vehicles for the unit.

Vehicles assigned to support officers should *not* be used by undercover personnel. Support officers' vehicles need to be outfitted differently than those assigned to undercover officers. These vehicles should have more standard "police-type" gadgetry, which benefits them — but which would "burn" an undercover agent. All support officer vehicles should be equipped with a set of "kill-switches." These are standard toggle switches (usually mounted in the glove box) that are wired so that a single headlight, the tail lights, or brake lights can be turned off. This is beneficial in night-time surveillances to change the appearance of a vehicle when suspects view them through the rear-view mirror.

Undercover Officer Vehicles

As mentioned, vehicles used by undercover agents should not contain the kinds of equipment used by support officers. Undercover vehicles must be kept "clean." Drug dealers will frequently be inside the vehicle while negotiating with the undercover officer. It is common for suspects to examine the agent's vehicle for possible radio wires or hidden microphones, to check the vehicle registration, or to search for personal effects. *Anything* the suspect finds in the vehicle should be an item placed there purposely (e.g., a checkbook, mail) to support the officer's cover story.

As mentioned, many agencies use seized vehicles — especially for undercover work. Others purchase or rent cars for undercover agents. The obvious benefit of a borrowed or rented vehicle is that it can be returned to the lender after the investigation is over, thus enabling officers to have different vehicles for each assignment.

Radios

Police radios, if installed in a vehicle, should be hidden from view. Many agencies place the radio itself in the trunk and the radio head where it can be concealed from inquisitive suspects (e.g., in the glove box). The radio antenna should also be nondescript. Antennas resembling those for standard AM–FM radios ("Dick Tracy antennas") or magnetic-mount, CB-style antennas should be considered. Portable two-way radios, which can be plugged into a cigarette lighter, can also be used. They have the advantage of allowing an officer to remove the police radio from the inside of the vehicle if he or she must assume an undercover role.

Hand-held radios are yet another essential piece of equipment for the support officer. They are useful during surveillances conducted away from the car and during raids and arrests. They are also expensive, however, and may not be available to every agent. If it is necessary to check walkie-talkies in and out, or to assign them to particular agents, procedures should be established to ensure that they will be returned, serviced, and available whenever needed.

Regardless of what radio system is used, frequency scramblers

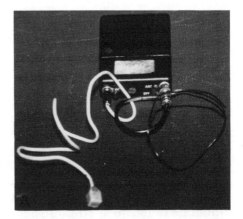

2–3 (A&B) A concealable voice transmitter (A) is commonly used by undercover officers in conjunction with the receiver and briefcase cassette recorder.

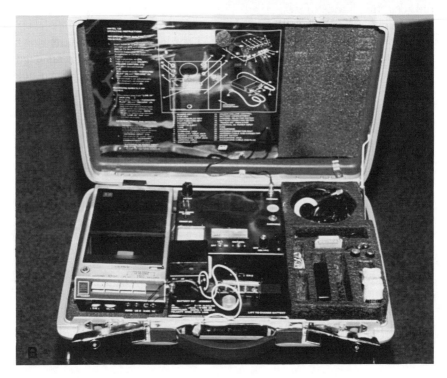

(encoders) should be installed on every radio. This device literally scrambles the transmitted voice of the officer, and only other radios with scramblers (and the correct scrambler code) can decipher the transmission. This is important because of the increasing number of drug traffickers who use programmable police scanners to monitor law enforcement activities.

Tape Recorders

The use of tape recorders is essential in most covert operations. Recorders can be used to tape field notes, undercover contacts, or telephone conversations (with a suction-type induction coil). Ideally, the tape recorder should be small and be equipped with a remote control or an extended microphone lead. These features can be found in many mid-sized recorders. Be sure, however, that the record selected does not have a "warning beep" to indicate the end of a tape.

Because many drug traffickers now use "RF" (radio frequency) detectors to identify hidden tape recorders used by undercover officers (Fig. 2-2), the drug unit should consider removing the erase head (which emits an RF signal) from the recorder. Even though tapes cannot be re-recorded after the head is removed, its removal greatly reduces the chance of detection. The cost of this procedure is usually less than $100 per recorder, and it is money well spent.

Before tape recorders are purchased, unit managers should note what kind of transcription machines the unit's secretarial staff use. The advantages of using compatible equipment (i.e., tape recorders and transcription machines that use the same size tape) is obvious, and it is easily guaranteed if all unit equipment is purchased at the same time. All drug enforcement units should require that every taped undercover and telephone contact be transcribed for later use in court proceedings.

Undercover Identification

Another essential piece of "equipment" is adequate undercover identification. The undercover name chosen by the officer should be one he or she will respond to instinctively. In order to avoid confusion under stressful conditions, it is often a good idea for an undercover agent to use his or her given first name with a fictitious last name.

The first piece of identification to obtain is a driver's license. This is usually acquired through the state department of motor vehicles; most often it requires a letter from the agency's chief executive officer addressed to the head of the department of motor vehicles.

Second, gasoline credit cards should be issued to the undercover agent in the same name as is on the driver's license. If this is not feasible, the credit cards should bear the name of a fictitious company. (*Note:* If a company name is used, it should be worked into the agent's cover story.) Some agency supervisors may require agents to purchase gasoline at a particular gas or service station in order to avoid accounting nightmares or other unforeseen complications later on.

Third, it is imperative that unit managers obtain fictitious social security numbers for all undercover personnel in case agents seek undercover employment. The process may take two or three weeks, so unit commanders should plan ahead. The application criteria for state and local agencies is as follows:

1. The Social Security Administration (SSA) can only provide fictitious (cover) social security numbers in instances in which there is specific legal authority (e.g., state law, a standing court decision, agency regulations) that permit the agency to engage in undercover law enforcement activities and to use false identification in furtherance of their lawful functions.
2. All requests from an agency for cover identity social security numbers should be channelled through a designated agency liaison office for approval and control.
3. Social security numbers issued under these arrangements must only be used in connection with the undercover officer's official duties and only to the extent necessary to carry out the agency's lawful functions.
4. Any social security cards issued for undercover law enforcement activity must be returned to the Office of Assessment at the end of the undercover assignment. A cover letter explaining whether or not the social security number was used in an employment situation should accompany the returned card. If the card was so used, the cover letter should contain sufficient detail about the employment (name, address, gross salary, period of employment) so that the SSA may adjust their records.
5. Although earnings may be reported for the undercover agent during the operation, these earnings would generally not be covered for social security purposes inasmuch as a valid employer-employee relationship would not exist in most cases. When the operation is completed, the SSA will delete any existing records.

Weapons

The type of personal handgun carried by agents is usually an individual choice. Most law enforcement agencies, however, require officers who carry weapons in addition to those issued by the department to qualify with them individually before being permitted to carry them in service. Both revolvers and semiautomatic handguns (see Fig. 2 – 4) have distinct advantages, which should be weighed by each agent. The usual considerations are those of concealability, comfort, and stopping power.

In the event an investigation results in a shooting, unit officers should request the assistance of tactical officers who are trained in SWAT-type maneuvers. (Obviously, this option may not be available to officers in emergency situations, and in some jurisdictions such assistance may not be available.) Depending on the structure of the department, a tactical assault team should also be used when a raid or other tactical situation is anticipated. Use of such a unit, trained in the use of assault weaponry, may reduce the likelihood of an agency's liability in the event of a shooting.

If a department does not have a tactical unit, each officer in the unit must be adequately trained in the use of both handguns and long guns. Two long guns in particular should be considered for use by support officers in the unit: a 12-gauge shotgun and a rifle (.30 – .30, .223 caliber, etc.). Depending on the circumstances in which support officers find themselves, they may need to be experienced with both types of weapons. In the case of raids on residences or buildings, a shotgun might offer maximum protection. In raids on marijuana fields, clandestine laboratories, or other rural operations, however, a rifle might be necessary in the event of an ambush. These two weapons may be carried in the support officer's assigned vehicle in case needed. Fully automatic weapons, concussion grenades, tear gas, and other weaponery might also be necessary in different circumstances; each requires specialized training.

Officers must be properly qualified with the use of each issued weapon. Such qualification should take place throughout the year on a regularly scheduled, "in-service" training basis. Weapons training should prepare the agent for all street circumstances including day and night shooting, strong/weak hand shooting, shoot – don't-shoot techniques, and barricade and prone qualifications from 5 to 25 yards. It is also recommended for agencies to train officers regularly in "red-handle" shooting exercises. This is a practical and realistic type of training in which special training weapons are actually loaded with special ammunition that shoots cotton projectiles.

Other Equipment

Standard Issue Police Equipment

The issuance of basic police equipment is also necessary for arrest, raid, and tactical situations. This equipment should include:

Body armour (lightweight and heavy-duty)
Raid jackets and hats (marked with the word "POLICE")
Sam Brown belt with holster, speed loaders, and handcuff case
Flashlight with auto-charger
Handcuffs (both metal and plastic flex-cuffs)
First aid kit
City and state maps
Binoculars

Special Equipment

Some specialized equipment is also necessary for special circumstances. Because much of this equipment is rare and may be extremely expensive, it may not actually be issued to each support officer but may instead be available through an equipment check-out procedure. If the latter is adopted by the drug unit, a log should be maintained showing dates, times of the equipment's use, the names of officers using the specific equipment, and the maintenance schedule (dates and types of service performed). Depending on the assignment, other types of equipment are commonly used to insure an agent's cover (Fig. 2–3). This equipment includes:

A 35-mm camera and special lenses (e.g., 500-mm telephoto, wide-angle, and zoom), special film (e.g., infra-red), and flash attachments
A Polaroid camera with a light bar and extra film
Night viewing devices
Video cameras with attachments
Concealed body transmitter with receivers (plus extra batteries if required)
Hard-line room transmitters ("spike-mikes")
Vehicle tracking devices ("bumper beepers")
Battering ram (for tactical units)
Bolt cutters
Tear gas guns (for tactical units)
A bull horn

Other equipment (to be kept in support officer's vehicle) should include:

Evidence bags
Evidence tape, duct tape, or masking tape

Drug field test kit (*note:* evidence bags, tape, and testers should also be kept in undercover officers' vehicles in a bolted down, locked strong box to prevent tampering or theft)

Blank forms: consent to search, informant statement, Miranda warning cards (rights waiver), suspect statement, evidence submittal forms, prisoner personal history form

Extra undercover license plates (in and out of state)

Portable scales for weighing small quantities of drugs

A three-day change of clothes.

Working Undercover

The Cover Story

A prerequisite for assuming an undercover role is to establish a cover story for the undercover operative. Simply defined, the cover story is a fictitious story that the agent will convey to suspects concerning his or her background: name, address, home town (or area), and employment. Other details may be included, but it is a good idea to keep the cover story simple in case the agent must deal with inquisitive drug dealers.

The cover story should fit with the area and people involved with the investigation. When an officer chooses to associate him- or her-

2–4   Photo of an automatic weapon cased with bullets, a scope, and silencer, found on a drug raid. (Photo courtesy of the Florida Department of Law Enforcement.)

RECEIVED FOR CASH OR OTHER ITEMS		

RECEIPT FOR CASH OR OTHER ITEMS

TO: *(Name, Title, Address)*

DISTRICT OFFICE	CASE NUMBER
	DATE

I hereby acknowledge receipt of the following described cash or other item(s), which was given into my custody by the above named individual.

AMOUNT OR QUANTITY	DESCRIPTION OF ITEM(S)	PURPOSE *(If applicable)*

RECEIVED BY *(Signature)*	NAME AND TITLE *(Print or Type)*
WITNESSED BY *(Signature)*	NAME AND TITLE *(Print or Type)*

2–5   Form used for transferring funds between agent personnel.

self with a particular town or area, it should be one with which the officer is already familiar in case he or she later meets someone from that area. Officers should remember: A partial truth makes the best lie.

When claiming a place of employment, the officer should choose one that cannot be easily checked out by suspects. (This is more of a problem in rural areas because people are more likely to know each other in small communities.) It may be desireable to choose an out-of-town place of employment that requires a lot of travel, or it may be advantageous to present a fictitious job in which the officer is self-employed (and therefore more difficult to verify). Whatever story is chosen, the officer should be provided with the business cards, customized stationery, credit cards, checking and savings account books, and other supporting credentials necessary to corroborate it. Moreover, the officer should be familiar with the profession chosen for the cover story for the same reasons he or she should be familiar with a purported home town.

The officer's appearance and mannerisms should also fit the cover story. If the officer is claiming to be an oil-field worker, it might be out of character for the officer to be seen after hours in an expensive business suit. Conversely, if the officer's cover story is that of a financier for a big-money drug deal, then expensive clothing might be more appropriate. It might also be necessary for an undercover officer to wear expensive jewelry to help convince sellers of the cover story. (Jewelry can sometimes be borrowed from local stores for short periods; however, the safety and security of the jewelry are the responsibility of the undercover officer.) (Fig. 2 – 5).

Protecting the Undercover Officer's Cover

Once the cover story has been established, the undercover officer is somewhat committed to it. Certainly the basics — name, home town, vocation — cannot easily be changed without jeopardizing both the officer's safety and the integrity of the investigation. Even if changes are not necessary, however, the undercover officer must be able to detect and withstand attempts by suspects or their associates to test and invalidate the officer's cover story.

Typically, suspects will barrage the officer with questions in an attempt to catch a lie or an inconsistency in the cover story. If they are successful (or think they are), the suspects will usually attempt to frighten or intimidate the officer into either admitting he or she is an undercover agent, or abandoning the investigation out of fear for personal safety — sometimes banding together to do so.

Panic is the undercover officer's worst enemy. Officers must realize that (a) paranoia is common among drug dealers, and (b) no matter what suspects say they know about the agent, many times they are just attempting to bluff the officer into an admission for which they have no proof. If the officer keeps the cover story general, most questioning and suspicion should be overcome. Moreover, if the officer has been properly trained and responds to the suspects according to his or her training, a bond of trust may develop between the officer and suspect, which can pave the way to a successful investigation.

A state narcotics agent was assigned to investigate drugs in a small military town. The first night he worked undercover, he decided to go play pool at a local night spot where Detective Clark, the agent's contact on the local police department, had told him there was a lot of drug activity, and where the agent could probably make some drug contacts. The agent arrived at the club and immediately walked toward the pool table area of the tavern. While waiting his turn at the pool table a young black GI sat next to the agent and said, "Hey man I need to talk to ya about your assignment. I know you don't know me but there's a problem, Clark sent me." The agent, not knowing the man, denied knowing anything about an assignment or anyone named Clark. The GI persisted in trying to convince the agent that the detective sent him to deliver an important message, but the agent did not give in. Finally the man said, "Sorry man, I was just checking you out to see if you were cool. I've got some dynamite coke for sale if you're interested."

Drug traffickers use a variety of methods to expose undercover police agents. Even though good field training should prepare undercover personnel for most of them, not every confrontation can be anticipated. Undercover personnel should remember that most questions about the cover story are bluffs, and they should remain calm and confident, discounting the challenges presented without appearing scared, intimidated, or timid (see Chapter 11). Officers should also be aware that traffickers can be quite tricky and cunning when trying to expose a possible police infiltration. They may, for example:

Attempt to intoxicate the officer in the hope that he or she will say something inconsistent with the cover story while under the influence of alcohol

Use prostitutes, girlfriends or boyfriends, or associates to attempt to seduce the officer: in so doing, the upper torso will be felt for body mikes, the waist area for weapons, and pockets for police credentials or anything else indicating an association with police work

Ask the officer questions about the cover story when the suspects already know the answers: the suspects hope to observe nervousness and awkwardness on the part of the officer

Ask the officer to furnish drugs to a friend or associate

Ask the officer to consume drugs furnished by the suspect

Attempt to learn information about the officer's family (spouse, children, other relatives, friends) so that the officer's story can be more easily verified

Ask the officers to perform various illegal acts

Attempt to rummage through the officer's car or personal belongings in order to locate police-related material or information showing that the officer was lying about the cover story

Ask the undercover officer excessive questions to see how many he or she is willing to answer before becoming suspicious

Infiltration

Once a cover story is established, a methodical process of infiltration must then take place. It's during infiltration that a relationship is established between the officer and the suspect. Frequently, officers find it difficult to meet or establish any rapport with the suspect without the help of an informant. In some cases, however, informants may cause more trouble for the officer and the investigation than they are worth; therefore, their use should be carefully considered (see Chapter 5). Infiltration requires inventiveness and originality on the agent's part because he or she might have to create his or her own opportunity to speak with the suspect. For example:

A suspected drug dealer was living alone in a trailer court. Surveillance had shown that he was somewhat of a recluse and did not go out to taverns at night where agents could possibly meet him. In the front of his trailer, however, there was a 1963 Chevrolet Corvair with a for-sale sign. A quick-thinking undercover officer noticed the vehicle and did some homework on the value and history of the Corvair, knowing that it was a collector's item. The agent then approached the suspect in his home under the pretense of purchasing the vehicle. This was a good lead-in to meet the suspect: it created an environment of social interaction and an acquaintanceship was formed. After a half hour of car talk, the agent was invited inside the suspect's house to inspect some additional paperwork on the vehicle. Once inside, the agent observed scales and a water pipe on the coffee table. The conversation then turned to drugs, and a subsequent purchase was made.

Once contact is made between the officer and the suspect, the suspect's confidence must be gained as soon as possible. An officer can best accomplish this by learning of an interest of the suspect's which the officer can then discuss: jobs, the opposite sex, local bars, motorcycles, cars, drugs, and so on. Contacts must be regularly attempted throughout the investigation to maintain a rapport with the suspect.

When working without an informant, it might be necessary to canvas a target area. The undercover officer can expedite the investigation by reviewing intelligence on targeted suspects and locations; concentrating on areas with high incidences of drug traffic might provide investigative leads. Typical starting places might be bars, nightclubs, or taverns, which can be an excellent source of intelligence for UC officers. A lot can be learned by just being present: generally people do not have a reasonable expectation of privacy when "openly" conversing in public places such as a bar. The UC agent can simply overhear otherwise private or guarded information about suspects: their names, types of criminal activity, places of employment, and their vehicles. Once the officer learns such information and if it appears that the information might be useful in showing criminal activity, it should be promptly documented in intelligence reports. It is the lack of properly generating such intelligence reports that accounts for the loss of much valuable criminal information to the unit.

It should be noted that although bars, nightclubs, and taverns can be lucrative sources of information, officer safety is greatly reduced in these settings. If two undercover officers are available, it is a good idea to assign both of them to a particular tavern, but working independent of each other. This accomplishes two things: it gives both officers additional back-up, and it provides each officer the chance to identify different suspects and criminal groups operating in the tavern.

If it is decided that a tavern is to be infiltrated, the undercover officer has several potentially good targets to consider. The initial people contacted may not be offenders themselves, but instead might be people who know those who are. Without being too aggressive, the undercover officer might consider befriending one of the following people in the bar:

The bartender: Bartenders may or may not be involved in criminal activity, but they will most likely know of any criminal activity occurring and who is responsible

Waitresses: Waitresses, too, are frequently aware of dealers and users alike operating in the bar

Bar regulars: Regular customers in a tavern might possibly be good players to befriend; they, too, often know which of those frequenting the bar might also be involved in criminal activity

Sometimes an informant will arrange a drug transaction and a "first-time" meeting between a dealer and the undercover officer. In this case, the seller will have some degree of suspicion about the officer and some initial questioning should be anticipated. It is at this point in the investigation that the officer should remember a few significant guidelines.

First, the officer should not let the suspect question him any more than if the roles were reversed. Some questioning is understandable, but it can become excessive. If this occurs, the officer should deal with it the best way possible, perhaps by acting angry and advising the seller that he's asking too many questions — that the deal is either on or it is not. This should help convince the seller that the officer is aware of what the suspect is attempting, and is not willing to be manipulated. Undercover officers will find that subsequent transactions are usually much easier because the dealer feels confident in that he has not been arrested as a result of dealing with the officer.

Second, while working a bar, an officer might purchase drinks or pay for pool and video games in order to start a conversation with a suspect. However, officers must carefully abide by established policy regarding the consumption of alcoholic beverages while on duty. Most law enforcement agencies permit officers to consume liquor while working undercover, but because an officer's judgement may be impaired and because he or she might become less likely to remember necessary facts, this must be done with discretion. In addition, in case it becomes an issue in court later, the officer should drink as little as possible in order to avoid attacks on the officer's credibility by defense attorneys (see Chapter 11).

Third, if the undercover assignment takes the officer to the suspect's house, in addition to taking additional safety precautions, recognize that this is a good opportunity to learn new information about the suspect. The officer should mentally map out all entrances, exits, and windows, which the suspect may use for escape during a raid. The officer should mentally note the number on the telephone, which might furnish a lead to the name of a new associate later. Discretely observing mail laying out in the open may also reveal the names of associates. Last, noting the presence of controlled substances and their hiding places may be useful later when obtaining a search warrant or conducting a raid.

Fourth, officers should remember that the practice of lying and deceiving is common for drug dealers. If the officer gets caught in a lie, he or she should never become prematurely paranoid and fearful that his or her cover has been blown. The officer should react with disinterest, or perhaps even laugh it off for the suspect's benefit. It is best to try to justify the lie by claiming that he or she "doesn't want too many people knowing too much about my personal business." The suspect will most likely identify with and respect such an explanation.

Drug Buy Operations

Although there are many methods of accumulating evidence on drug traffickers, the drug buy is one of the most reliable. Because drug enforcement is proactive rather than reactive and because the undercover officer is personally involved with the suspect, opportunities to purchase drugs as evidence frequently present themselves in an undercover investigation. The purchase of drugs by the law enforcement officer is unique because the officer actually participates in the crime itself. Such participation in criminal acts is lawful provided prosecutors can show that the suspect was predetermined to commit the act without the participation of the officer. This is done by documenting a suspect's "criminal intent" through recorded conversations and the actions of the suspect.

Preparations

For all drug purchases, the unit should have an established policy requiring officers to completely identify the suspect before the buy operation. If the officer fails to do this, subsequent meetings between the officer and suspect may never take place, resulting in an open case showing an expenditure of funds with no leads to make an arrest. Suspect identification should include:

1. Full legal name
2. Identifiers (date and place of birth, and Social Security number)
3. Address
4. Criminal history
5. Known associates (including friends, partners, ex-wives and girlfriends)
6. Full vehicle description

The drug buy should be strategically planned to serve a particular purpose in the investigation. For example, an investigator may first wish to learn more about the seller's supplier, and additional purchases may be required to accomplish this. Conspiracy investigations necessitate multiple purchases. In other circumstances, however, a straightforward "buy–bust" operation may be best. Multiple purchases from suspects without a specific need will only lengthen the investigation, waste agency funds, and expose officers to unnecessary risks. Moreover, if the suspect is later convicted, the sentences incurred from several different purchases may end up being served concurrently rather than consecutively anyway.

The narcotics buy operation involves an "agent" — either an undercover police officer or an informant — who makes the buy or purchase from the dealer. Though this may sound quite basic or simple, it is not. The narcotics buy operation is the most potentially dangerous, "tricky," and unpredictable of any police investigative technique. There are many variables involved, any one of which might create a new complication during the delicate and dangerous interplay between police agent and dealer*:

1. The behavior and personalities of both the agent and dealer are unpredictable.
2. The conditions of the "set" (the location where the sales are taking place) are unpredictable.
3. The required movements of the police back-up team trying to maintain surveillance and react to actions of the dealer and/or the undercover agent cannot be planned.
4. Both vehicular and pedestrian traffic can affect both observation and movement of the back-up team.
5. Weather conditions can also affect observation and movement.
6. The conditions given by the dealer to the undercover agent under which he or she will complete the deal are never fully controllable (although they are somewhat negotiable). The undercover agent must have options available and these options must be realistic.
7. There may be mechanical breakdowns or equipment failures: back-up autos may break down, transmitting difficulties may occur, or batteries may go dead. In addition, certain areas are "radio dead zones," where transmissions are impossible.
8. Erratic actions by the dealer, and/or evasive methods taken by the suspect to avoid surveillance may make the "tail" or effective observation impossible.
9. Third-party situations may arise unpredictably: (a) The dealer's connection or supply runs out. (b) Someone fouls up on the proposed meeting time. (c) An unexpected police action by other police officers unaware of the "buy" operation; this can occur against the suspect, the undercover officer, or both (see Chapter 11).
10. The dealer or his people may rob the undercover officer (the

---

*See Vernon J. Geberth, "Narcotic Buy Operations," *Law and Order Magazine*, 1979.

"rip-off"). This is the most dangerous situation that can occur during a drug buy operation, and only the undercover can determine how to handle it. Even with a predetermined trouble signal, the first few seconds of the crisis fall upon the undercover agent. Another situation under this category, although not as dangerous, is the "beat" package, whereby the undercover is sold a phony or "dummy" bag. Short of examining the contents, which is nearly impossible to do effectively in front of the suspect, there is little the undercover can do. However, immediately after discovering the "beat," the undercover officer (with a back-up team) should make it his or her business to get back to the dealer and make his "beef"; the same goes for a "short" package (one that weighs less than the agreed upon amount). This is what a dope dealer would do, and the undercover agent should do the same.

Hazards

Dangerous circumstances may arise at any time during drug buy operations. Many of these circumstances can be avoided; many are unforeseeable. Because of this, a strict time limit must be given to each arranged drug deal. This way, support officers will know when to check on the safety of the undercover officer. If this is necessary, support officers may have to use inventive ways to check on the status of a drug deal without actually identifying themselves (prior planning is necessary for this tactic). However, on those occasions when the officer is not out of the residence within the predetermined time period, it might be necessary for back-up officers to storm the residence and make any necessary arrests.

The Buy–Walk Procedure

The buy–walk is a drug purchase for which an immediate arrest is not planned and the suspect keeps the money. There are good reasons why this is considered both a productive and nonproductive investigative practice. An agency conducting a lengthy undercover investigation will soon find that if an arrest is made immediately after each drug purchase, the undercover officer's identity will rapidly become known. Therefore, in order to protect the cover of the officer and to enable the investigation to net numerous suspects at the culmination of the investigation, the buy–walk method can be used. The agency then sets a specific date to conduct a coordinated raid during which suspects can be arrested through the use of "buy–busts." At the same time arrest warrants are then served on other suspects who have been identified earlier in the investigation, and search warrants are served on residences containing known stashes of drugs.

The chief advantage of the buy – walk practice is that many investigative leads can be developed when buying drugs from suspects: places of residence and employment may be observed, associates may be identified and observed, and the existence of organizations can be documented by investigators. Other benefits of the buy – walk method are that small drug purchases enable investigators to have the drugs analyzed for purity, and that with each drug purchase, larger quantities can be negotiated to help identify suppliers farther up the distribution ladder.

The biggest drawback to the buy – walk investigation method is that it is expensive. The cost of continuous drug purchases may become quite substantial over an extended period of time. Additional investigative expenses include the officers' salaries (including overtime), and incidental expenses, such as expense for working the street and taverns (food, drinks, bar cover charges), gasoline, and vehicle expenses. To help defray these expenses, many agencies are pursuing restitution from the defendant to recover the expenditures made during the investigation (drug – buy money, laboratory fees, overtime, etc.).

Another major problem associated with a buy – walk investigation is the suspects' transience. Over a period of time, suspects may relocate several times and be difficult to find at the end of the investigation. In a buy – walk investigation, one of the support officer's duties is to keep track of suspects as they may move from place to place so that they can be quickly located when the investigation is concluded and warrants are finally issued. The record keeping in buy – walk investigations may be time-consuming and tedious, and in investigations involving several suspects, could be almost overwhelming. This is why the length of a buy – walk investigation should be carefully considered; it may even be determined by a support officer's ability to keep track of the suspects during the investigation.

The Buy – Bust Procedure

The buy – bust procedure is to purchase drugs from a suspect and immediately place him or her under arrest. Because of the necessary physical proximity between the suspect and officer, this is considered one of the most hazardous duties performed by drug enforcement officers. It is because of this eminent danger that all "busts" must be meticulously planned and arrangements should be made in anticipation of any possible problems. It is not uncommon in buy –

bust situations, for suspects to be armed and to attempt to kill the undercover agent at the time of the arrest. When the suspect resorts to violence in a drug arrest situation, he or she will sometimes claim the action was self-defense — that he or she was not aware that the agent was a police officer and that the killing was an attempt to protect his or her own life. This is why undercover and support officers should be prepared to properly document every buy – bust operation to show that the arrest was properly conducted and that the officer did, in fact, properly identify him- or herself.

In buy-bust operations it is also necessary for the undercover officer to make early arrangements with back-up officers regarding when the actual arrest will take place. In most drug buys, an actual delivery of the drugs might be required to successfully prosecute the suspect, so back-up officers might need to time their arrival on the scene just after the undercover officer gives the proper signal. This will give the undercover officer time to follow through with the needed elements of the transaction. Once the transaction is complete, the signal is given. This can either be a visual signal (such as taking off hat), or a audio signal (such as using a specific word in the officers conversation). Using this system, the length of time between the back up officers arrival on the scene and the time the signal is given can be predetermined.

On the evening of a drug raid, a narcotics agent had arrested an individual, who then agreed to become an informant and introduce the agent to his cocaine supplier. After a series of telephone calls, a cocaine deal was arranged: 4 ounces for $8000. The supplier agreed to come to the informant's house to meet with the undercover agent.

The supplier soon arrived at the informant's house and said he would have to go to a second location and get the cocaine. The agent argued with the supplier and was able to convince the supplier to let the agent ride along with him to meet the individuals who were furnishing the cocaine. The agent was thinking that he could arrest all of the players at the same time (and seize numerous vehicles), all from one transaction. The agent asked the supplier the location of where they were going, but the supplier would not say. The agent felt confident, however, that the four surveillance vehicles observing and monitoring him would have no trouble following him in the supplier's car.

The informant, the agent, and the supplier all left in the supplier's vehicle. Unbeknownst to the agent, the surveillance vehicles lost sight of him and, because of a recent snowfall, were unable to track the vehicle. The back-up team could hear the conversations of the agent through the body mike the agent was wearing, but they could not visually locate him. After about 15 minutes, the back-up team could hear the agent meeting with the dealers inside a residence. The agent, still believing that the back-up team was just outside the door, drew his weapon and placed the suspects under arrest. A scuffle then ensued between the agent and his four arrestees, and the agent was knocked to the floor. The surveillance officers, by luck, recognized the supplier's vehicle parked on a sidestreet. By observing the footprints in the snow from the vehicle to a house, the officers stormed the house and probably saved the agent from being killed. *Moral:* Don't change locations in the middle of the deal!

The buy–bust is also considered to be an extremely useful enforcement tool for investigators because it is much more cost effective for departments operating on modest budgets. Actually, the undercover officer needs only to display cash to the suspected drug dealer and receive drugs from him to complete the commission of the crime.

The Location of the Buy

There is no "ideal" location for all undercover drug transactions because every drug deal is different and all drug deals are dangerous. As mentioned, many factors may affect the outcome of the transaction. For each drug buy operation, however, basic questions should be asked:

1. Can surveillance adequately cover the undercover officer?
2. Does the location offer the officer maximum safety?
3. Was the location chosen by the officer, the informant, or the suspect?
4. In case of a violent altercation, is it likely that innocent bystanders will be hurt?
5. In case of trouble, how soon can support officers arrive on the scene?

The first priority in any undercover drug transaction is *officer safety.* More times than not, this variable will be the determining factor in deciding the location of the transaction. Another important consideration is whether or not the transaction is a buy–walk or a buy–bust, as both have unique considerations when determining the location of the drug deal. Let's now examine the different types of locations for the drug transaction.

Outdoor Locations

If the purchase is a buy – walk, the degree of danger associated with it is greatly minimized. This is especially true if it is the second or third buy: the suspect will feel more comfortable dealing with the officer.

Good outdoor locations might be shopping center parking lots or crowded city parks. In these locations surveillance officers can get closer to the officer and blend in with the surroundings. Officers should never agree to meet at a location suggested by the suspect: the suspect may employ countersurveillance to look for police, or the suspect may be planning a rip-off. By contrast, a poor outdoor location might be a shopping center parking lot during the middle of the night: surveillance officers would have a difficult time staying near the agent because the stores are not open and little public commotion is taking place.

When an immediate arrest is planned resulting from the drug purchase (buy – bust), officers should make some crucial considerations. Unlike a buy – walk operation, a public place is not a good idea. There will be armed officers (and perhaps armed suspects), and the possibility of gunplay should be taken into account. A busy parking lot would increase the likelihood for an innocent bystander getting shot during the arrest.

An isolated location, however, is not the best solution either; it will be difficult for surveillance officers to get near to the scene of the deal. A good compromise might be a location adjacent to a shopping center parking lot where there is minimal traffic. The location should have good visibility and access from the street to allow back-up officers access to the arrest location.

Indoor Locations

Such locations pose different problems. Once an officer enters the residence of a suspect, the officer's level of protection is considerably reduced. Suspects feel more at ease on their own turf, and they will be more inclined to ask the undercover officer more questions. In addition, suspects might even require agents to consume some quantity of drugs before the transaction can be completed. The officer must bluff his or her way out of this predicament: such behavior is usually against policy, and will reflect poorly on the case, the officer, and the agency. Exceptions would be, of course, situations in which the officer is facing immediate danger to his or her life by not taking the drugs. Proper field training is the key to best dealing with these circumstances (see Chapter 11).

A rookie narcotics agent was assigned to investigate drug dealing by juveniles at a local video arcade. After a week or so, the agent began purchasing small quantities of heroin from a 15-year-old dealer. A surveillance team was observing one particular transaction with the kid when an older white male entered the arcade and appeared to deliver something to the kid. Surveillance then followed the visitor to an apartment complex at which, as it turned out, he managed. After subsequent investigation into the man's background it was learned that the man was the kid's father. A major conspiracy case was then developed, resulting in the seizure of a large quantity of heroin and a huge cache of stolen property.

Another problem associated with the officer conducting the transaction in the suspect's residence, is that the suspect may have others present to check out the officer, or possibly assist in a rip-off. However, an advantage to the deal occurring at the suspect's residence is that probable cause for a search warrant can usually be obtained. In addition, the officer will have an opportunity to observe locations of drugs, and entrances and exits within the residence. Basically, the indoor buy–walk is a good method for criminal intelligence but a risky one for the undercover officer.

Indoor buy–busts are extremely dangerous. Being in the suspect's residence and away from visual contact with surveillance officers minimizes the safety level of the undercover officer. Undercover agents should attempt to draw the suspect out into the open, in most circumstances, so surveillance officers can closer observe the actions of the undercover officer.

Precautions

Even though drug transactions will differ drastically from one another according to their locations, the amounts of drugs and money involved, and the suspects themselves, certain general precautions should be observed in all circumstances. It is easy for undercover officers to get "caught up in the moment" when negotiating for a major deal and forget safety considerations. However, every undercover officer should try to expect the unexpected and observe the following precautions:

Never let the suspect establish the location for the transaction: It could be a set-up for a hijacking.

Never let an informant establish the location for the transaction without the prior knowledge and approval of the informer's control officer (see Chapter 5).

Never change locations for a drug transaction during a drug deal. If a change of location is necessary, the undercover officer should call off the transaction and arrange it for a later time after support officers have been apprised.

Beware of drug transactions at the suspect's residence. In case of an altercation, support officers may have a difficult time entering the residence to assist the undercover officer.

Never agree to conduct a transaction where there are more suspects than undercover officers present. If this occurs, the deal should be called off and arranged at a later time.

Always be aware of innocent bystanders. In case of an altercation with the suspect, have a plan!

Always be cautious during big-money drug transactions.

Planning the Drug Buy

Finally, when planning the drug purchase, it should be remembered that many criminals operate in an organized and regimented fashion in much the same manner as the police. This is evident in cases where there are multiple suspects, each with a specific duty during the transaction, i.e., counter-surveillance, guarding the suspects' residence, etc. To counter these situations officers should consider pre-buy and post-buy planning.

Pre-buy Planning

Much preparation should be undertaken in the planning phases of the drug transaction. Initially, when the buy is being arranged, all conversations between the undercover officers or informers and drug suspects must be recorded. Frequently, a drug deal might be arranged in the early conversations between players, but when the deal finally transpires, little conversation might be made by the seller. Practicing the "record-when-you-can" philosophy should aid the investigator in properly documenting all pertinent conversations.

On the day of the transaction, a "pretext" telephone call should be made by the operative to the suspect for three distinct purposes:

1. to record the voice of the suspect outlining the specifics of the drug transaction: the price of the drugs, what quantity is being sold, and what quality (purity) is being sold;
2. to verify that the drugs are still available at the prearranged and designated time;
3. to determine (if possible) whether the supplier is expected to meet with the dealer prior to the deal.

It is always a good idea for officers to set up surveillance around the location of the arranged drug buy because frequently the dealer will say that he has possession of the drugs when he is actually expecting an associate to deliver them just prior to the deal. If the dealer does not have possession of the drugs at the time of the negotiations, the supplier will likely give ("front") the drugs to the dealer just prior to the time of the transaction (and remain close by). If officers are watching, they can document the delivery of the drugs to the dealer and then follow the supplier to other locations, such as a residence or place of employment.

Another important element in pre-buy planning is the location and documentation of possible countersurveillance (by associates) on the part of the dealer. Countersurveillance is covert observation by criminals to locate police observers in the area of the drug buy, or to assist suspects in a related criminal activity (a rip-off or get-away).

Post-buy Planning

Just as the supplier may have delivered drugs to the dealer just before the transaction, he or she might also be returning after the transaction to pick up his or her share of the profits. In another circumstance, the dealer might leave his residence shortly after the transaction to meet with the supplier and deliver the money owed. Either of these circumstances will make it worthwhile to continue surveillance on the location of the transaction to document new associates (see Chapter 6).

The tactical plan is only a tool or guide to be used in the planning process. It should not become a biblical or administrative panacea for the "paper tiger" type commanders who are neither "street wise" nor adaptable to split-second change and are usually more concerned with "form" and "control" of personnel than with the specific objectives of the investigation. This type of supervisor has been known to use such forms as "cover" in the event that something goes wrong during the investigation, and should not be assigned to "operational-type" commands.

A more realistic approach should be to appreciate the different variables available to the supervisor, choose among alternative actions, develop a "game plan," and then remember: "the only thing that you can be sure of in a narcotics buy is that you cannot be sure about anything." (From Vernon J. Geberth's "Narcotic Buy Operations," *Law and Order Magazine*, 1979.)

The Flash-Roll

A primary goal of the drug enforcement unit is to identify the largest traffickers within a community. Therefore, it is common for undercover agents to work their way up the trafficking ladder to the point where a big-money transaction is necessary to identify a top supplier. In this case, the investigating law enforcement agency must acquire a "flash-roll" to demonstrate to the traffickers that they can afford the drugs. The flash-roll is simply a large sum of money used in undercover drug transactions to show to the dealers (flash) without permitting them to actually take possession of the money. The size of the flash-roll may range anywhere from $5,000 to $100,000; it therefore creates a potentially violent atmosphere because some suspects might consider simply robbing the agent of the currency.

The sources of flash-rolls will vary from jurisdiction to jurisdiction, but if the investigating agency has no specific fund designated for a flash-roll, funds may be borrowed from the city or state treasury, or from local financial institutions willing to loan the money, interest free, on the signature of police officers; sometimes more than one source is pooled to generate enough money for one flash-roll. Ultimately, the law enforcement agency having possession of the roll is totally accountable and responsible for its protection.

As mentioned, violence may result in large money transactions as undercover agents are frequently murdered by suspects for possession of the flash-roll. The following is a checklist of considerations essential before undertaking any transaction using a flash-roll:

1. There should be complete identifiers and criminal history information on all known suspects involved in the transaction.
2. Note whether the suspect has previously been observed with a weapon.
3. If the suspect is claiming to deliver large quantities of a drug that is relatively scarce in the area, a rip-off might be planned by the suspects.
4. Officers must choose the location for the transaction and conduct it on their "turf."
5. Notice any other conditions that might be conducive to a rip-off (this includes the officer's "gut" feelings about the deal).

At some time during the transaction, the officers will be required to show the flash-roll to the suspects. This is necessary to convince the suspects that the officers can afford the drugs in the first place. It is at this point in the transaction where the situation could become violent and the officers should have a contingency plan. The location for the transaction is one of the most significant considerations at this point, and should focus on the following areas of concern:

1. Support officers should have easy access to the undercover agent in the event a rip-off occurs.
2. Support officers should be located so that they have a good van-

tage point to observe suspects entering and exiting the area, or suspects conducting countersurveillance on the transaction.

3. The area should have adequate lighting.
4. In the event of an altercation, any exit points should be easily blocked by the support officers.
5. If a motel room is used as a neutral ground for the transaction, the officers (rather than the suspects) should choose the room, and it should have an adjoining room with a common door for easy access by support officers.
6. All currency in the flash-roll should have its serial numbers recorded prior to the transaction in the event the roll is stolen.
7. In all cases, the undercover officer in possession of the flash-roll should be equipped with a concealed body mike, or any device enabling surveillance officers to listen to the transaction (hard wire, RF room monitor, etc.), so the surveillance team officers can monitor the progress of the transaction.

Sometimes it might be advisable to show the flash-roll to one of the main suspects *without* advance notice. This will catch the suspect off guard and will give the agent the edge because (a) the flash can be conducted at a protected location of the agent's choosing; (b) the agent can have sufficient backup at his disposal; and (c) the suspects should not need to see the money a second time before the transaction; once is enough! In this case, the officer has upheld his or her end of the deal by demonstrating the ability to produce the money. It is then up to the suspects to produce the drugs.

Another method of showing the money is to advise the suspect that the buyer will telephone him when the money is available to show. This will require the suspect to stay home and wait for the agent's telephone call. Officers should then establish surveillance on the suspect's residence and watch for associates coming and going. When the call is made by the undercover agent, the suspect is advised that he will be picked up in ten minutes or so. This short notice will reduce the suspect's time to arrange a rip-off. A second undercover officer then arrives at the suspect's residence (without the flash-roll), and picks up only the suspect. The suspect is then driven to a predetermined location, unknown to the suspect, where agents have established stationary surveillance. The agent driving the vehicle should always be careful to observe mobile countersurveillance. When the suspect arrives, he or she is shown the money and is permitted to count it. In the event the suspect insists that his or her supplier would also have to see the money, a Polaroid picture should be taken with the current day's newspaper in the picture showing the day's date. The photo can then be taken by the suspect to the supplier.

It should be noted here that in any transaction where the officers suspect anything indicating a possible rip-off, the transaction should be called off. The momentum of the case in this phase may create an "ostrich" effect on the part of the undercover agents, causing them to become overly anxious for the buy, and possibly causing careless mistakes.

Entrapment

A common defense for drug cases has traditionally been that of entrapment. In this defense, the suspect claims that he was tricked into the commission of the act. The term entrapment is defined as "the procurement of one to commit a crime that he did not contemplate or would not have committed, for the sole purpose of prosecuting him."

When the defendant claims entrapment, he or she must first admit that he committed the crime before he or she can complain about police misconduct. This requirement alone usually deters a defendant from claiming this defense. Additionally, if the prosecution can show that the suspect was predetermined to commit the crime, this defense cannot be used (see Chapter 3).

An example of entrapment might be an officer claiming to be physically addicted and who needs another quantity of drugs immediately in order to avoid withdrawal. The suspect, in this example, could claim to have procured drugs for the officer out of compassion for the alleged addiction rather than for profit. A good method for avoiding the entrapment defense is to make more than one drug purchase from the suspect (and possibly purchasing different types of drugs). As mentioned, this helps establish the suspect's criminal intent to commit the act by establishing that he or she is conducting a business.

Many suspects mistakenly believe that if an undercover officer lies to them about being a police officer, it constitutes entrapment. In addition, some suspects also believe it is entrapment for officers to record conversations, mark drug purchase money, or use paid informers. All these acts have, however, been upheld as lawful and acceptable investigative techniques.

Conspiracy Investigations

As previously discussed, the undercover drug purchase is an excellent investigative technique allowing an undercover officer the opportunity to observe the violation as it occurs. In such a case the officer's testimony is generally considered the best evidence in the prosecution of the case (especially when backed up with surveillance photos, videotapes of meetings, and phone records). High-level offenders and leaders of criminal organizations, however, are not usually receptive to meeting new people (which would allow informers or undercover officers access to them). In these cases, drug enforcement units should consider undertaking a conspiracy investigation.

A conspiracy is defined as an occurrence when two or more persons enter into an agreement to violate the law and there is a commission of one or more overt acts in furtherance of the agreement. Conspiracy investigations enable law enforcement agencies the means to get at the leaders of criminal organizations who no longer personally handles drug transactions and would otherwise be too well insulated by associates operating on the lower levels of their organization. The law of conspiracy makes each conspirator liable for the actions of others, thus permitting the arrest, prosecution, and conviction of "king pins" for drug sales they did not personally conduct. Investigation of these individuals through conventional investigative channels may prove to be a waste of time, thereby creating the need for a conspiracy investigation.

An enormous amount of overtime and manpower must be invested in a conspiracy investigation. Evidence and documentation must be obtained to link each member of an organization. It is not necessary to show that all conspirators are personally acquainted with each other, but investigators must establish some form of direct or indirect cooperation between suspects. Investigators may, for example, document noncriminal associations between suspects who are also involved with a criminal conspiracy. This noncriminal association can be used to show an acquaintanceship that will aid in proving the overall conspiracy.

The irony of conspiracy prosecutions is that a criminal act does not have to be completed. Additionally, drug trafficking conspiracies might take months to put together because most drug traffickers have more than one customer, thus requiring investigators to take long periods of time to document all essential players in the conspiracy properly.

The Agreement

The first element of a conspiracy investigation is that the agreement between the suspects must be shown. The agreement may take place in many different forms; for example, it could be in writing (not common), through telephone conversations, or through verbal agreements made in person. More commonly, the agreement is inferred from evidence showing the conspirators acted in concert toward an unlawful purpose or confirmed through the testimony of a cooperating co-conspirator.

The initial agreement is usually made between two persons. Others, however, may later join the conspiracy as it progresses. In most cases newcomers to the conspiracy need not know all of the details of the original agreement, only their particular roles. An example would be a smuggling operation, which is planned by two parties. One of the parties later decides to hire a pilot to fly to Mexico, pick up drugs, and return to the United States. In this case the pilot has knowledge of a criminal plan but only has personal knowledge of a portion of it. The pilot in this case is still liable as a co-conspirator in the case because he or she voluntarily joined the original agreement.

The Overt Act

The second step in a conspiracy investigation is to document an overt act on the part of one or more of the conspirators. In the absence of an overt act, even though the agreement to commit the crime has been established, the suspects still have a chance to back out of it. Once an overt act has been completed, however, the offense (the conspiracy) is complete. The overt act must be something done by at least one of the co-conspirators to help achieve the objective of the conspiracy. It may be as seemingly innocent as making a telephone call, purchasing a weapon or even just driving to another conspirator's residence; it could also be a criminal act itself. Basically, the overt act depends, to a great extent, on the agreement itself and the type of crime being planned.

Once a conspiracy investigation is under way, investigators will find that many smaller conspiracies may develop. These will frequently be interrelated, but officers must differentiate between each co-conspirator and the specific conspiracy to which they are associated. The following general guidelines should help illustrate how to link conspirators:

> When larger scale distributors sell drugs to middlemen, knowing that they are middlemen, all may then become members of a conspiracy.
>
> A single sale of drugs does not constitute grounds for a conspiracy between the buyer and seller.
>
> For a drug buyer to become a conspirator he or she must know the conditions of the agreement and be a part of the original agreement.
>
> In order for a vendor of supplies or equipment to be considered a

conspirator, he or she must have knowledge of the unlawful objective of the conspiracy; however, it is not necessary for his or her act to be unlawful.

Types of Conspiracies

A conspiracy may be shown in three different ways; each one has its own peculiarities:

> At 3:00 PM John contacts Steve and advises that he has an ounce of cocaine for sale for $1,800. Steve says he wants to purchase it, but first he needs to go to the bank to get the money. If the investigators can document this agreement, the first step in proving the conspiracy has been accomplished. If Steve then goes to the bank, this action will suffice as the overt act in furtherance of the agreement. In this case, Steve and John can both be arrested and charged with conspiracy. (NOTE: A charge of conspiracy cannot be alleged or substantiated if an undercover agent (or informer) is one of two parties making the agreement.)

The Chain Conspiracy

When substantiating a chain conspiracy, the investigator must show that the goal of the suspect individuals is dependent on the successful participation of each member. In addition, each member of the conspiracy must realize that the success of the scheme is dependent on every other member of the conspiracy. Generally speaking, the chain conspiracy is relatively easy to prosecute, provided investigators can show that the members of the scheme have one common goal (e.g., drug trafficking). Difficulties arise when the members are engaged in a variety of different criminal endeavors and it becomes difficult to show each members participation in one common goal.

The Wheel Conspiracy

A wheel conspiracy is one in which the primary conspirator, called the "hub," makes an agreement with others, who are called the "spokes." In substantiating this type of conspiracy, each of the spokes must be shown to be aware of each other and to know of the others' roles in the scheme. The "rim" of the wheel is the agreement that ties each member to the scheme, and it must be demonstrated by the prosecutor. As one can see, this is considered a difficult method of investigation because a common agreement among all members is difficult to prove. The typical result of a wheel conspiracy prosecution is that the hub is charged with the crimes of the organization based on his individual association with each spoke, and each spoke escapes responsibility for the criminal actions of the other spokes.

The Enterprise Conspiracy

Under federal statutes, an enterprise conspiracy is considered a separate offense, thereby making it a separate crime to agree to participate in an enterprise by engaging in a "pattern of racketeering activity." The enterprise may have numerous criminal activities, so showing a chain is not necessary. The members of an enterprise may not be aware of each other's role in the schemes, and all that needed to be shown is each member's agreement to participate in the organization (enterprise). In this type of conspiracy, at least two acts of racketeering need to be shown. Federal law defines the term racketeering as any of the following activities:

Drug violations

Hobbs Act violations

Loansharking

Mail fraud

Bankruptcy fraud

Mann Act violations (white slavery)

Bribery

Counterfeiting

Embezzlement of union funds

Obstruction of justice

Wire fraud

Prosecution of an enterprise conspiracy can result in massive trials in which everyone charged in the case is present for one criminal proceeding. Juries sometimes have difficulty isolating each defendant and his or her particular charges from the others on trial because an atmosphere of "guilt by association" prevails. As a consequence, convictions obtained at these trials run the risk of being overturned on appeal because of the inability of the prosecution to distinguish between one large conspiracy and numerous smaller ones.

Forfeiture Sanctions

Because drug dealing has created enormous profits for drug dealers, many have accepted the risk of arrest and a long prison term as merely "a cost of doing business." Only by stripping the perpetrator of his or her profits can law enforcement pose a significant deterrent for drug trafficking.

In recent years, laws enabling the law enforcement officers to seize personal property of suspected drug traffickers has in fact accounted for much of the overall success in drug suppression. The 1984 Federal Comprehensive Forfeiture Act (see Appendix) has provided increased authority to seize a suspect's property based on the presumption that

> . . . any property of a person convicted of a drug felony is subject to forfeiture if the government establishes probable cause that the defendant acquired the property during the period of violation, or within a reasonably short period thereafter, and there was no likely source for the property other than the violation.

The Comprehensive Forfeiture Act (and similar state laws) enable officers to seize automobiles, aircraft, vessels, bank accounts, securities, and even real estate holdings and privately owned businesses. Moreover, it also enhanced the penalties of the 1970 Controlled Substances Act, specifically providing for a 20-year prison term and for fines up to $250,000. The Controlled Substances Act itself contains many valuable provisions for seizing a violator's property. The types of property subject to seizure under the Controlled Substances Act (CSA) include

1. All controlled substances
2. Raw materials and equipment
3. Any property use as a container for controlled substances
4. Any vehicles, boats, aircraft used to transport controlled substances
5. Business records, books, computers, or other materials used in violation of the CSA
6. All money or negotiable instruments used for exchange for controlled substances
7. Real property or improvements used to facilitate the commission of violations of the CSA

Under the Controlled Substances Act, for example, if a drug dealer uses his automobile to drive to a location where he is to sell drugs, his car then becomes the conveyance in which the dealer uses to facilitate the crime. The car is, therefore, seizeable under the law. Additionally, if investigators can show that a suspect purchased an automobile with illegal drug revenues, then the vehicle is also subject to seizure. The process of property seizures under federal and most state laws is a civil process rather than a criminal proceeding. In many instances it is possible for a defendant to be acquitted on a felony drug charge and still lose his property.

Sharing Provisions of Federal Forfeiture Laws

Since the passing of the 1984 Comprehensive Crime Control Act, the U.S. Attorney General was given authority to make an "equitable" transfer of the forfeited property. Basically, this divides any property seized in a joint federal and local operation and allows both parties to benefit from seizures. After seizure of the property, a determination is then made, assessing the percentage of involvement of each participating agency, and a proportionate distribution of the assets is then made between the agencies. Listed below are two ways state or local law enforcement agencies may participate in seizure and subsequent forfeiture of property:

1. The state or local agency can join forces with a U.S. Department of Justice agency (FBI, DEA, INS, etc.) in a federal investigation and share any property forfeited as a result of its participation.
2. The state or local agency can request that one of the federal investigative bureaus adopt a seizure it has made and request an equitable share of that property once it is forfeited. This is beneficial when a state forfeiture is not feasible or when a federal seizure would be more advantageous.

> A city narcotics agent and two agents from the Drug Enforcement Administration proceeded to the $250,000 home of a prominent doctor for the purpose of seizing his 1984 Ferrari automobile, from which he had been selling cocaine. At the time of the seizure, the physician had already been indicted on drug charges and was out on bail. The agents served the proper paper work on the doctor, and as they were backing the Ferrari out of the driveway, the unthinking but enraged physician screamed, "You have no right to do this to me. Hell, if you can take my car from me just because I sold dope out of it then why don't you just take my whole goddamn house, too? That's where I had my coke parties." The agents thought about it and based on the doctor's statement . . . they did!

When considering the seizure of property, the FBI and DEA apply two general conditions in the acceptance of a seizure for adoption:

1. There must be a valid prosecutorial purpose in requesting the adoption. Officers should remember that while many state laws

require proof "beyond a reasonable doubt" in seizure cases, federal forfeiture laws require only "probable cause."
2. Property referred for adoption must meet the following minimum monetary requirements:
   Conveyances:
   Vehicles: $2,500
   Aircraft: $5,000
   Vessels: $5,000
   Nonconveyances:
   Real property: $10,000
   All other property: $1,000

The Vehicle Indemnity Form

A frequent problem encountered when seizing a suspect's vehicle is when the seized vehicle is registered to someone other than the suspect. In some cases it might be registered to a friend or relative who may not realize that the vehicle was used for the purpose of dealing drugs. If this is the case, the vehicle must be returned to the lawful owner unless the police can show that the lawful owners had knowledge of the unlawful use of the vehicle. The same applies when the vehicle is being financed by a bank, credit union, or other financial institution. Once seized, it must be turned back to the institution (or the seizing agency must pay off the existing loan in order to lawfully keep the vehicle).

To combat this problem, it is a good practice for investigating officers to use a Vehicle Indemnity form when returning seized vehicles to the lawful owners, banks, or other financial institutions. The Vehicle Indemnity form is used basically to notify the owner that the vehicle was seized during a narcotics investigation and that it is being returned. It also advises the owner that if the same vehicle is loaned out again to the same individual who used it for trafficking drugs, it will be seized and forfeited if the individual is caught a second time. Once advised in this fashion, vehicle owners, especially banking institutions, will seldom return the seized vehicle to the lien holder (see Fig. 2–6).

Similarly, with the widespread use of residential property by drug traffickers, a Real Estate Indemnity form should be considered. This form could be structured basically like the vehicle indemnity form but address the use of property for drug trafficking. A model vehicle indemnity form is featured in this section and should be modified to meet the needs of each jurisdiction (see Chapter 7).

CITY POLICE DEPARTMENT
VEHICLE INDEMNITY AGREEMENT

This agreement is made between _____
                                                    (Name)   (Title)

_____
          (Firm Name)   (Address)
and the City Police Department.

The agreement is made in consideration of the return of a _____

_____
                                              (Description of Property)

registered to _____
                                                  (Name and Address)

used in violation of the Controlled Substances Act, and for the consideration, the receipt of which is hereby
acknoledged:

_____ being the _____
          (Firm or Person Involved)   (Type of Interest)
Of the property as evidenced by a:

_____ dated _____
     (Title, Registration, Contract, Note, etc.)

It is hereby agreed to unconditionally release and hold harmless the City Police Department , its officers, employees
and agents from any and all claims, demands, damages, causes of actions or suits, of whatever kind and description,
and wheresoever situated, that might now exist or hereafter exist by reason of or growing out of or affecting, directly
or indirectly, the seizure or the return of the above described property.

It is further incumbent upon the individual and/or firm to whom the above described property is being released to be
aware of the provisions of state law (statute no.). This section of the state law provides that a claimant of any right of
a seized vehicle may be called upon to prove that such "right, title, or interest was created without any knowledge or
reason to believe that the vehicle, airplane, or vessel was being, or was to be, used for the purpose charged." In the
event you and/or firm choose to authorize the future control of the above described property or any other vehicle,
airplane, or vessel to the individual or individuals causing the seizure addressed in this agreement such vehicle,
airplane, or vessel may be subject to forfeiture for any violation under state law regardless of your and/or your firm's
right, title, or interest.

Executed in triplicate this _____ day of _____ 19 _____.

_____   _____
     (Police Case Number)   (Signature & Date of Person Executing)

                                                            _____
                                                              (Signature & Date of Police Dept. Employee)

                                                            _____
                                                                 (Title of Police Dept. Employee)

IN WITNESS HEREOF, the above signed parties have read and understand fully the terms of this VEHICLE
INDEMNITY AGREEMENT and so state by subscribing their names thereto.

                              Subscribed and sworn to before me this _____ day
                              of _____, 19 _____.

                              _____
                                                   Notary Public

My commission expires: _____

2-6

Summary

The practice of working undercover is a valuable investigative tool, but it should be approached with caution. Undercover work is costly, time-consuming, and dangerous. The deeper undercover one gets, the less safety he or she is afforded. Consequently, many precautions must be observed.

To accomplish the task of working undercover most effectively, the proper investigative equipment is required. This includes equipment to assist the officer in observing and documenting his case as well as equipment to help protect the officer while dealing with criminals. The list of investigative equipment for undercover agents should include: properly equipped vehicles; appropriate weaponry; and undercover identification and recording equipment such as cameras, video tape recorders and cassette recorders.

When working undercover, officers must decide what type of investigation is best suited for the department and community. A lengthy investigation will be more expensive because in buy-walk situations money is spent for drugs and is usually not recovered. If the concept of a lengthy investigation is not feasible, then the practice of conducting buy-busts might be considered. This is an inexpensive way to arrest violators, but the undercover agent's identity is revealed and officers will not be able to work up the drug trafficking ladder much higher than the street level.

Regardless of which method of investigation is pursued, critical attention should be given toward planning the location of the buy. Determining whether the buy is to take place at an indoor or outdoor location may have a direct bearing on the degree of safety available to the undercover officer. Additionally, the status of the drug deal as a small money or big money deal may also be an indicator as to the degree of danger facing undercover personnel.

Those who operate in an undercover capacity may find that they are limited as to how far up the trafficking ladder they can maneuver. If progress is limited in the undercover investigation then other more inventive ways of collecting evidence might be considered. One such method is the use of the conspiracy investigation which enables investigators to target leaders of an organization who would otherwise use associates to insulate them from law enforcement intervention.

Yet another investigative technique that should be considered in all drug investigations is the effective use of federal (and state) forfeiture laws. These effective laws make it possible for law enforcement officers to seize any currency or property that might have been acquired either through the illicit dealing of drugs or from profits made from drug trafficking.

Suggested Readings

Abadinsky, Howard, *Organized Crime*, 2nd ed. Chicago, IL: Nelson Hall, 1986.

Bennett, Wayne W., Hess, Karen M., *Criminal Investigation*, 2nd ed. St. Paul, MN: West Publishing Co., 1987.

Fisher, Barry A.J., *Techniques of Crime Scene Investigation*, 4th ed. New York: Elsevier, 1987.

Geberth, Vernon J., *Practical Homicide Investigation*. New York: Elsevier, 1983.

Harney, Malachi L., Cross, John C., *The Narcotic Officer's Notebook*, 2nd ed. Springfield, IL: Charles C. Thomas, 1975.

Hicks, Randolph D., II, *Undercover Operations and Persuasion*. Springfield, IL, Charles C. Thomas, 1973.

Macdonald, John M., *Criminal Investigation of Drug Offenses*. Springfield, IL: Charles C. Thomas, 1983.

America's Habit, Report to the President and the Attorney General, President's Commission on Organized Crime, U.S. Government Printing Office, 1986.

The Impact, Report to the President and the Attorney General, President's Commission on Organized Crime, U.S. Government Printing Office, 1986.

Search and Seizure, and the Collection of Evidence

3

Any search for illicit drugs must be conducted in accordance with agency policy and procedures, and according to applicable laws. Police search and seizure practices are constantly being analyzed and interpreted by state and federal courts. Perhaps more than any other field of law enforcement, drug enforcement requires specific expertise in this area, and investigators must strive to stay abreast of the many changes in the law.

Warrantless searches will usually be challenged in court. The Fourth Amendment to the Constitution states:

> The right of the people to be secure in their persons, houses, papers, and effects, against unreasonable searches and seizures, shall not be violated, and no warrants shall issue, but upon probable cause, supported by oath or affirmation, and particularly describing the place to be searched, and the persons or things to be seized.

A police search in the absence of a warrant places the burden on the state to show which of the few exceptions to the warrant requirements of the Constitution justified the search. Without a properly executed warrant, even a good-faith seizure by a police officer may result in the suppression of the evidence obtained, and the freeing of an obviously guilty suspect. Conversely, when a warrant has been properly secured, the burden then shifts to the defendant to show that the evidence was illegally obtained. It should therefore be evident that the benefits of securing a warrant far outweigh the advantages of searching without one.

Because there are so many state court precedents regarding search and seizure, and because of the subtle differences in these precedents from state to state, it is impossible to address them all. This chapter must, therefore, address the topic of search and seizure somewhat generally. However, several of the most significant court decisions that pertain to drug enforcement will be reviewed throughout.

The Search Warrant

Because drugs are so easily concealed, investigating officers will often be required to search a suspect's person, residence, or automobile. Evidence obtained from any such search must be gained lawfully, or it will be excluded from consideration during trial (the so-called exclusionary rule; *Weeks v. United States*, 1914). With few exceptions, evidence in criminal cases may be lawfully seized only pursuant to a valid search warrant, and only those items in specified areas, as listed in the warrant, may be taken. Police officers should not shy away from the mechanics of obtaining a search warrant, as it is one of the most effective tools available to the drug enforcement officer: It authorizes the search, it will usually result in a suspect's arrest, and it will expedite the investigation a subsequent case closure.

The Good-Faith Exception: United States v. Leon *(1984)*

Based on information from an informant, narcotics agents in Burbank, California, began investigating Alberto Leon in a suspected drug trafficking operation. Based on information from investigation and surveillance, an affidavit for a search warrant was prepared and reviewed by several assistant district attorneys before a state Superior Court judge issued a search warrant. The defense challenged the validity of the warrant based on the unreliability of the informant and moved to suppress the evidence seized as a result of the search warrant. The District Court and the U.S. Court of Appeals both held that the affidavit was insufficient, but the U.S. Supreme Court supported the prosecution, holding that the exclusionary rule was designed only as a deterrent for the *abuse* of police authority. The court specified that evidence might be excluded if (a) if police officers were dishonest in preparing the affidavit; (b) if the warrant was deficient on its face (e.g., a wrong or missing description of the place to be searched such that no officer could reasonably serve it; or (c) if the magistrate was not found to be neutral.

The practical effect of *Leon* is that any evidence seized through a search warrant is immune from suppression even if the judge signing the warrant was wrong and there was not probable cause to believe that contraband or other evidence would be discovered under the warrant. In addition, securing a warrant also protects the officer from civil liability. Thus, if it is possible for an officer to obtain a warrant, even if there exists a clear exception to the warrant requirement, it should be done.

Search Warrant Checklist

Upon issuance, the warrant must contain the following:

1. The reasons for the request to search.
2. The name of the officer requesting the warrant.
3. The items to be seized.
4. The specific place to be searched.
5. The signature of the issuing judge.

All warrants should be executed promptly. During a search, officers may seize additional items at the location if they are contraband or are similar to the items specified in the warrant, or if they are connected to the specific crime identified in the warrant. Seizing items other than those specified in the warrant is not considered within the "scope of the search" and will likely be excluded from the trial as illegally obtained evidence (see also Chapter 5, Managing Informants).

Search Incident to Lawful Arrest: **Chimel v. California** *(1969)*

Ted Chimel was approached in his home by police officers who possessed a valid arrest warrant for him. The officers then advised Chimel that they wanted to "look around" and proceeded to search the premises without Chimel's permission. After a one-hour search, some coins were located and seized by the officers as evidence in a crime. Although initially convicted, Chimel later appealed the case, which was reversed by the U.S. Supreme Court because the coins were not found lawfully. Although the coins were found "incidental to the arrest," the evidence was excluded because it was not found in plain view and the officers did not have a search warrant to search Chimel's residence, only an arrest warrant. The Chimel decision established that a search made incidental to a lawful arrest must be confined to the area around the suspect's immediate control.

The Mechanics of the Search Warrant

Search warrants can be for the purpose of obtaining anything to help prove the guilt or innocence of suspects in a crime, not just for obtaining contraband. Search warrants generally consist of three parts: (a) the affidavit (the application); (b) the warrant (a court order to search); and (c) the return (itemized list stating the date of the search and a list of all items seized).

The Affidavit

To obtain a search warrant, a search warrant affidavit (application) (Fig. 3–1) must first be properly filled out by the officer (affiant) desiring the warrant. The affidavit must tell the judge three things: what, where, and why.

What Is Being Searched For

The affidavit must fully describe what the officers are searching for and how it constitutes evidence of the commission of a crime. Generally speaking, the following types of property may be searched for and seized pursuant to a search warrant:

Contraband: items that are unlawful for persons to possess under all circumstances (e.g., illicit substances such as heroin, LSD, or marijuana)

Instrumentation of the crime: anything used to facilitate the commission of a crime (e.g., business records, checkbooks, scales, police scanners, etc.)

Weapons

Fruits of the crime: the money earned from drug sales

Mere evidence: Shoes to match footprints, bloody clothing, utility bills (used to show dominion and control of the premises), etc.

The items listed should only be those items the affiant has probable cause to believe will be found, and not simply anything the officer would "like to find." Phrases such as "including but not limited to . . . " should be used to indicate to the judge that some items may be too lengthy to list, or that certain items may be left out.

Where the Search Is to Take Place

This part of the affidavit concerns where it is believed the "what" will be found. The rule of thumb is could anybody, even a stranger in town, take the affidavit and proceed to the correct place? If so, then the location in the affidavit was probably correctly described. Examples of adequate description are:

A residence (or dwelling) located at 1012 Valley Court, which is a one-story, single-family dwelling, red brick with a composition roof and a two-car attached garage on the east side of the structure.

An apartment located at the northwest corner of a building located at 8211 S.E. 33 Terrace, the building being a large single-story dwelling, divided into four apartments.

Apartment number 308 at an apartment complex known as Spanish Gardens Apartments; said complex having several apartment buildings each having a separate street address, apartment 308 being in the building having the street address of 5016 Tomahawk Avenue.

A dwelling located on rural route #5, which is a part of a farm located by traveling north from the intersection of Providence Blvd. and Highway #2 for a distance of 2.3 miles, then turning east on the farm road and traveling west for a distance of 1 mile; said dwelling being identified by a mail box at the road bearing the name of Tom Crawford.

A business located at 2427 N.E. 32 Street, being located in a building which contains many retail businesses, the one to be searched has the name of Ardvarks Head Shop prominently displayed in front.

Why the Search Is to Be Conducted

This section gives the probable cause for the search: It is here that the affiant must tell the judge why it believed the items will be located in the place to be searched. To ensure that the affidavit contains probable cause, the following three requirements should be met:

The affiant must have a good idea of the definition of probable cause.

Facts establishing probable cause must be developed during the investigation.

All facts pertaining to probable cause must be set forth in the affidavit.

The person making application for the search warrant is called the affiant. The affiant may or may not be a law enforcement officer, but if the information for the warrant was from several persons it might be advisable for the officer to be the affiant and designate all of the information he has received in the affidavit. When the officer goes before the judge, it would be advisable to record the testimony so a record of the proceedings will be on file. This can be done by using the judge's court reporter or by simply using a tape recorder. If the latter is used, a transcript should be made of the testimony and filed with the affidavit and warrant. All affidavits should be drafted on the assumption that it will be challenged in court. It should be noted that in the event the affidavit is challenged, the information must either be memorialized on the face of the affidavit or in the form of a recording in order to support the warrant.

An Affiant Checklist

Below is a suggested checklist for information needed from the affiant to show the judge that the affiant has adequate information to justify a search:

A. If no informant is used and affiant is a law enforcement officer:
   1. What is his job?
   2. Did he personally see the items sought?
   3. Where were the items observed?
   4. When were the items observed?
   5. Location of items in structure to be searched?
   6. Who was in possession of the drugs?
   7. How did the affiant recognize the items?
   8. What information was furnished by other officers?
   9. Did defendant make an admission?
   10. What does the affiant know about the defendant?
B. If an informant is used, but is not to be identified:
   1. What is his job?
   2. Is the informant personally known to affiant?
   3. How long did the affiant know the informant?
   4. Is the informant's truthfulness and veracity credible?
   5. When did informant supply information in the past?
   6. Were there charges filed as a result of past information?
   7. Did the informant make admissions against interest?
   8. Did informant observe the contraband?
   9. Where did the informant observe the contraband?
   10. When did the informant observe the contraband?
   11. When did the informant tell the affiant of contraband?
   12. What does the affiant personally know about the defendant?
   13. What does the affiant personally know about the contraband to be searched for?
   14. When did the affiant gain his or her own knowledge about the contraband?
   15. What information did other officers provide the affiant?
   16. Did the defendant make admissions to informant?
C. If an informant is used and the affiant is a law enforcement officer:
   1. What is his job?
   2. Why did informant wish to remain unnamed?
   3. Did the informant make admissions against interest?
   4. Did the informant observe contraband or did defendant make

IN THE DISTRICT COURT OF THE FIFTH JUDICIAL DISTRICT IN AND
FOR:
BOONE COUNTY, MISSOURI

Before _____ Judge, District Court of
Boone County, Missouri

State of Missouri } ss. **Affidavit for Search Warrant**
Boone County

On this _1st_ day of _May_, 19_89_ _Agent Brian Johnson_ being first duly sworn, upon oath deposes and says:

That a certain _Residence_ within said County and State, located and described as follows, to wit:

2304 N.W. 38th Place, Columbia, Missouri located in Boone County being a single family wood frame dwelling facing South, and under the control of Samuel Thomas Lawrence, and wife Dorothy. The garage area of the house is to the West end on the South side. The house is on the North side of the street with tan colored brick along the lower third of the front, while being fenced in, with a chain link fence, around the back yard area.

the same being the _residence_ of _Samuel Thomas and Dorothy Lawrence_ whose more full, true and correct name is unknown to the affiant, there is located certain property particularly described as follows, to-wit:

Controlled substances to include marijuana, Schedule I, LSD, Schedule I, Cocaine, Schedule II, and one fifty dollar bill ($50.00) U.S. currency bearing serial number JO3744496B, and any other records or documents showing illicit business dealings in controlled durgs.

which said property is subject to search and seizure as set out by the laws of Missouri for the following grounds, to-wit:

Violation of the state criminal code controlled substances section RsMo 195.233.

and that the probable cause of the affiant believing such facts exist as follows, to-wit:

1) Your affiant is a sworn police officer with the City Police Department, who has been a full time narcotics investigator for three years and seven months. 2) On April 30,1989 at approximately 1630 hours, officer Johnson purchased one (1) kilo of marijuana for $1500 from Dorothy Lawrence which was contained a black trunk located in the hallway of the residence. 3) On April 30, 1989 at approx. 1945 hours officer Johnson purchased 100 units of LSD for $300 from Samuel Lawrence which he acquired from the freezer area of the kitchen. 4) On April 30, 1989 Samuel Lawrence also displayed approx (1) one ounce of white powder claiming it to be cocaine which was also kept in the refridgerator area of the kitchen.

_____
Affiant

Subscribed and sworn to before me this _1st_ day of _May_ 19_89_

_____
Judge, District Court of
Boone County, Missouri

3-1 Sample Affidavit

admissions to the informant? If observed, how did the informant know the item was contraband?
5. Where was it observed?
6. When was it observed?
7. When did the informant tell the affiant about the contraband?

8. Informant's details of the place to be searched (how many bedrooms, attached garage, where is contraband kept, etc.)
9. Informant's details of defendant's background (job, address, family members, associates, etc.)
10. Has the informant's information been checked out?
11. What does the affiant personally know about the defendant?
12. How and when did the affiant gained knowledge about the contraband?
13. What information did other officers or informants provide the affiant?

The Warrant

The search warrant (Fig. 3–2) basically sets forth the essential elements specified in the affidavit. The affiant must be certain that he is sworn in by the judge prior to the signing of the affidavit. The judge must then sign and date all pages of the affidavit and the warrant.

Execution of the Warrant

Once the warrant has been signed by a judge, most of the officer's problems are over. There are, however, two important errors commonly committed by police officers that could result in the suppression of the evidence seized: (a) the manner in which the warrant is executed; or (b) the improper return of the warrant.

When conducting a search pursuant to a warrant, officers can only do what their warrant says they can do *and no more*. Because of this, officers should pay close attention to the following points

1. *Who may serve the warrant.* Because many search warrant forms are preprinted, they are sometimes "directed" to any sheriff, peace officer, or policeman. The point is that the person who actually *serves* the warrant should be sure his or her jurisdiction is established *on* the warrant; if not, he or she should at least be sure they are "technically" acting under the direction of the person who is authorized to serve the warrant.
2. *The "no-knock" warrant.* This provision does not exist in all states. Officers who do have such a statutory provision available to them must use their discretion during service of the warrant. With no-knock warrants, officers normally must announce their authority prior to entering the residence, and before they can forcibly enter the structure they must be refused admittance by the occupants. If the warrant is not a no-knock warrant, officers can enter only with permission or when the following special conditions prevail:

The announcement would be a useless gesture

The announcement would endanger life

The announcement would subject the property to destruction

The announcement would allow a suspect to escape

3. *Night time service.* Many states require search warrants be served during daytime hours only, unless otherwise authorized by the judge. In this case, if the warrant is served near dusk, then the officers must document exactly what time it was served. The "night time service" scrutiny in these cases usually address the time of entry only and not what time of day or night the premises were actually searched.
4. *Evidence of other crimes.* It is very common for officers conducting a search to observe evidence of other crimes that have not been specified in the original warrant. This is actually a fairly easy problem to solve. First, officers must show that they have a legal right to be in the residence; this would obviously be the case if they are serving a warrant. Second, once officers are in the premises, items that are not obviously contraband (such as guns, TVs, VCRs, etc.) may lawfully have their serial numbers recorded and checked through the National Crime Information Center (NCIC) to determine if they were stolen. This procedure is lawful provided the reading of the serial numbers is performed *before* the item is seized. Once it has been determined that an item was stolen (probable cause), then a second search warrant should be obtained for the item.

The Return

As mentioned, the return of the search warrant is an itemized inventory of all property taken by the officers. The time allowed for officers to return the warrant to the issuing judge will vary from state to state. In most cases, the officer who served the warrant must be the one to return it. The return (Fig. 3–3) should include the following information:

1. The name of the officer who served the warrant.
2. The date the warrant was served.
3. An itemized list of all property seized.
4. The name of the owner of the place searched.
5. The signature of the officer who served the warrant; this is usually signed in the presence of the issuing judge.
6. The signature of the issuing judge and the date of the return. The warrant is then usually left with the judge.

IN THE DISTRICT COURT OF THE FIFTH JUDICIAL DISTRICT IN AND
FOR:
BOONE COUNTY, MISSOURI

BEFORE _____ JUDGE, DISTRICT COURT OF
BOONE COUNTY, MISSOURI

State of Missouri) ss. **SEARCH WARRANT**
Boone County

In the name of the State of Missouri. To any sheriff, constable, marshal, policeman or
peace officer in the County of Boone, State of Missouri.

Proof by affidavit having been this day made before me, by _Agent Brian Johnson_ that there
is probable cause for believing that in the herein described _residence_ is located the
following property particularly described as follows to-wit:

Controlled substances to include marijuana, Schedule I, LSD, Schedule I, and Cocaine, Schedule II, and one fifty
dollar bill U.S. currency bearing serial number: J3744496B

and that the herein described _residence_ should be searched by reason of the following
grounds, to-wit:

Possession of the above described controlled dangerous substances and currency is evidence of violation of the
state criminal code controlled substances section RsMo 195.233.

YOU ARE THEREFORE COMMANDED at any time of day or night to make immediate
search of the _residence_ of _2304 N.W. 38th Place, Columbia, Missouri_ whose more full, true and
correct name is unknown, located and described as follows, to-wit:

a single family wood frame dwelling facing South, and under the control of Samuel Thomas Lawrence, and wife
Dorothy. The garage area of the house is to the West end on the south side. The house is on the North side of the
street with tan colored brick along the lower thrid of the front, while being fenced in, with a chain link fence, around the
back yard area.

for the said property above described, and, if you find the same or any part thereof to
bring it forthwith before me at my office in Columbia, Boone County, Missouri.

Dated this _1st_ day of _May_, 19_89_.

_____
Judge, District Court of
Boone County, Missouri

3-2 Sample Search Warrant

Searching Methods

Safety precautions and tactical methods of approaching the search
location will be discussed in Chapter 7; in this section we will address only the mechanics of searching once the location for the
search has been secured.

SEARCH WARRANT RETURN

Received this writ _____ day of _____,19 __.

Executed the same on the _____ day of _____, 19 __ by going to the within designated place where I found and seized the following property, to-wit:

_____

_____

_____

_____

_____

and brought the same before the within named court.

_____
Sheriff - Peace Officer
Marshal - Policeman

Exceuted the same day on the _____ day of _____, 19 __ by searching the within designated place, where I could find none of the above described property.

_____
Sheriff - Peace Officer
Marshal - Policeman

OFFICERS FEES

Executing writ _____ $ _____

Mileage _____ Miles $_____

Total: $_____

_____
Sheriff - Peace Officer
Marshal - Policeman

3-3 Search Warrant Return form

Regardless of whether the search is broad or narrow in scope, officers should be aware that drugs and associated paraphernalia may be concealed in many different locations within the search area. For this reason, a methodology of conducting a thorough search should be developed and be observed. In accordance with this practice, officers must also remember the "elephant in a matchbox" theory, in that large objects cannot be concealed in tiny areas. If the search is authorized for drugs specifically, however, officers can usually be justified in searching most areas throughout the location. In drug enforcement, most searches will usually take place inside a suspect's residence or other structure. Specific methods must be observed when exercising search authority to minimize confusion. To best accomplish this, search teams should be organized with specific task assignments for participating officers:

1. *The searcher:* The searcher's primary responsibilities are:
   a. to photograph the evidence (photos of the suspects should also be taken whenever possible, as these are admissible as evidence when "mug shots" are not)
   b. to tag the evidence immediately
   c. to seize evidence and to maintain chain of custody (the fewer people in the chain of custody, the fewer people will later be tied up in court)
2. *The recorder:* the recorder's primary responsibilities are:
   a. to direct the search to locate contraband and seizable items showing dominion and control; in addition, the recorder must be able to testify that no authorized person disturbed evidence prior to seizure.
   b. to list what items were seized and where (by using either a notebook or tape recorder). This list will be used for the return of the warrant and when the case goes to court.
   c. to draw a diagram showing the location of items seized and locations of the suspect (or suspects) when entry was made. This should be used in conjunction with photos to reconstruct the search scene when the case goes to court.

Search practices in a drug raid situation differ considerably from other types of search scenes (such as a homicide crime scene) in that certain trace evidence is normally not sought. Officers can therefore concentrate on searching for drugs, related paraphernalia, records or weapons. In a search situation, additional guidelines should also be followed by searching officers. For example, if more than one officer searches the location, the other officers should only visually locate evidence and not physically seize it. Seizing such evidence by more than one designated officer will result in each officer who seized evidence having to appear in court to testify to the chain of custody.

In all cases, officers must have the necessary tools to properly conduct a thorough search. Excuses for not being prepared with the proper equipment will not help once the case goes to court and the search has not been properly documented. The tools necessary are few, but essential:

Tape recorder (with telephone induction coil in case telephone applications are permitted)

Note pad and pencil or pen

Camera with flash, and extra film and batteries (essential)

Evidence bags and boxes

Fingerprinting equipment

Proving Dominion and Control

The two goals of every search are to seize contraband and to establish who had knowledge and control over the contraband. The latter is commonly referred to as dominion and control. To illustrate the problems of establishing probable dominion and control, consider the following common search warrant situation:

> Officers enter a certain house in the execution of a search warrant for cocaine. Upon entering the residence, in the living room there are four adults sitting around the coffee table on which there is a mirror containing a quantity of white powder, a set of triple beam scales and other paraphernalia. There are two bedrooms in the house, and two ounces of cocaine are found in one of them. The cocaine is found in a dresser at one end of the bedroom while at the opposite end there is a waterbed and a nightstand. After interviewing the adults, officers learn that Steve lives there, Dave has been staying there a couple of nights, and Bob and Bill were just stopping by.

In many circumstances, officers would probably arrest all four suspects and charge them with possession with intent to distribute cocaine. However, let's examine what the prosecutor will need to substantiate such a charge. There exist two kinds of possession in drug cases, which are defined as follows:

1. Actual possession (physical control)
2. Constructive possession (the knowledge of the presence of the contraband and the right and power to control its use or disposition)

In the given example, it is obvious that all four suspects had knowledge of the drugs, which already "helps" to establish the elements of constructive possession (knowledge). To obtain a conviction, however, the prosecutor must also show that each individual suspect had the right and power to either use the cocaine or control its use. Power can usually be shown in that a person had used the substance (for example, showing that a person was under the influence of the drugs, white powder on a suspect's nose, etc.). A second method of showing who had power over the drugs is by demonstrating who had control over the premises, which can be shown through the seizure of utility bills, letters, or other records that bear the suspect's name. According to our example, Steve has dominion and control and should be charged with the cocaine. Problems arise, however, when considering what to do with the other three suspects.

Bob and Bill, who "just stopped by," may pose a problem. Both definitely have knowledge of the cocaine, but are merely visitors and their knowledge fails to establish dominion and control over the cocaine. In other words, dominion and control means more than just "being where the action is." Absent a statement or admission from either Bill or Bob incriminating themselves, they probably cannot be charged.

Dave admits to having stayed over for a few nights, but a case might still be difficult to make. Because Dave is living at the residence, even though it is part-time, he still exercises some dominion and control. Therefore, if the cocaine were located in a common area of the house, Dave could probably be charged; however, if the cocaine were located in an area exclusively controlled by Steve (for example, Steve's bedroom), then Dave could not be charged.

When attempting to establish dominion and control, the following items should be sought:

1. *Mail:* This includes utility bills, personal letters, magazines, or other mail bearing the names of the occupants of the residence.
2. *Fingerprints:* Although often overlooked when executing search warrants, fingerprints should be attempted whenever possible on items such as plastic bags, weapons, water pipes, or other paraphernalia.
3. *Photographs:* This includes taking photos of various parts of the residence and property as well as seizing photos taken by the suspects themselves. These will show associates, drugs, weapons, and other facts possibly indicating dominion and control.
4. *Clothing:* This is of particular importance when the occupants of the residence are different sexes and sizes. Clothing can be an easy way to determine who sleeps in which bedroom.
5. *Statements:* The occupants themselves may offer statements that incriminate themselves. Occasionally, testimony provided by other suspects in exchange for leniency will establish dominion and control (see section below).

Search Patterns

Although there are many accepted search patterns commonly used in the search of a crime scene, many of these do not apply to a drug search because minute trace evidence is not being sought. Therefore, this section will only address the two of most common methods of searching the interior of a residence.

The Grid Search Pattern

Considered a common search technique, the grid search pattern requires officers to systematically begin the search at the end of an imaginary grid and work toward the opposite end, repeating the process until the search area is completely covered. This pattern is generally used when attempting to locate "trace" evidence, but can prove effective in looking for drugs within a certain room or area (see Fig. 3–4).

The Zone Search Pattern

This is probably a more applicable method of searching when drug cases are involved. In this pattern, a room or area is sectioned off into quadrants and each quadrant is searched either from end to end or from top to bottom. This method allows officers to concentrate on a particular area before moving on to another area within the structure.

It should be remembered that the objective of the search is not just to seize drugs but also to locate otherwise innocent-looking records that show dominion and control and that will support the seizure of

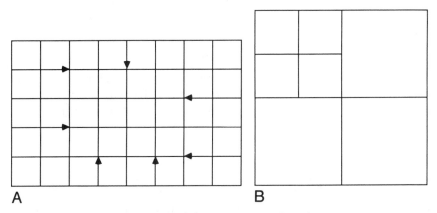

A   B

3–4 (A) Grid Search Pattern. (B) Zone Pattern Search

assets. This is commonly overlooked when there are numerous occupants of a residence in which drugs are found. The regular use of drug detection dogs should also be considered in search warrant cases along with attempts to fingerprint critical pieces of evidence.

Warrantless Searches

As mentioned, occasionally special circumstances will arise in which a warrant is not required under law. The legal exceptions to constitutional warrant requirements commonly observed in drug enforcement are listed below.

Search by Consent

Whenever a suspect gives consent to search, police may do so lawfully, provided the suspect has the authority to do so (e.g., a suspect cannot give consent to search another person's residence). This is especially useful in cases where officers have no legal basis to make a search. Consent searches must be obtained voluntarily where the suspect is free from any official coercion.

It is legal for officers to search on the word of a suspect, but it is a good practice to have him or her sign a consent to search waiver that can be later added to the case file. For the consent to be considered valid, officers must establish that the person giving consent has dominion and control over the area to be searched. This can be established through the seizure of utility bills or other official documents bearing the suspect's name with the necessary address.

In a search by consent, the suspect does not have to be given the Miranda warning or told that he has the right to withhold consent in order for it to be valid. In the event the suspect changes his mind about the search, however, the officers must cease their search, or obtain a search warrant to continue (Fig. 3–5).

Search Under Exigent Circumstances

The case of an emergency, a search may also be conducted without a warrant if probable cause exists. This is normally where a suspect is believed to be destroying evidence (i.e., flushing it down the toilet) while the officers are attempting to obtain a warrant.

Search Incident to Lawful Arrest

Under the Chimel decision, an arrest can be accompanied by a search of the suspect and the immediate area around him or her. This is justified by an officer's right to search the suspect for weapons before being transported to jail. The area around the suspect is searched because it is considered "lunging distance" where a suspect

CITY POLICE DEPARTMENT
<u>**CONSENT TO SEARCH**</u>

DATE _____

LOCATION _____

I, _____, having been informed of my
constitutional right not to have a search made of the premises hereinafter described
without a search warrant and of my right to refuse to consent to such a search, hereby
authorize _____, officers of the
City Police Department, to conduct a complete search of my:

Premises ___

Curtilage ___

Vehicles ___

These officers are authorized by me to take from my premises any letters, papers,
materials, or other property which they may desire, after receipting me for same. I
further state that I am the proper person to give the consent and authorization referred
to herein.

This written permission is being given by me to the above named officer(s) voluntarily
and without threats or promises of any kind.

_____
Signature

WITNESSES:

_____

_____

_____

3-5   Sample Consent to Search form

could conceivably acquire a weapon. When the suspect is arrested
out of a vehicle the "immediate area" is defined as the entire passenger compartment, including closed but not locked containers (*New
York v. Belton*, 1981). In circumstances in which thorough searches
are desired pursuant to an arrest, however, a warrant should be
obtained (*United States v. Chadwick*, 1977).

Searches of Automobiles

The precedent established for warrantless automobile searches is *Carroll v. United States* (1925). This case established that the right to search a vehicle does not depend on the right to arrest the driver, but on the premise that the contents of the vehicle contains evidence of a crime. Because an automobile is mobile and because a person does not enjoy the same right to privacy in his or her car as in the home, warrantless searches are permitted. The automobile search is limited, however, by the amount of probable cause known by the officer. Specifically, probable cause for drugs will authorize officers to search almost anywhere in the vehicle, but if the probable cause is limited to stolen video tape players, for example, the officer is not justified in searching small areas such as the glove box (*United States v. Ross*, 1982).

Other circumstances for a warrantless search of an automobile include vehicle searches where the vehicle is impounded subsequent to the arrest of the driver. Such searches are justified providing the police do not use the arrest as the sole excuse to search the vehicle.

Plain View Searches

Warrantless searches are permitted under the "plain view doctrine" (*Coolidge, v. New Hampshire*, 1971). For a plain view search to be valid, however, three criteria must be met: (a) the officer must be where he is lawfully; (b) the item seized must have been found inadvertently; and (c) the item seized is contraband or would be useful as evidence of a crime (*Texas v. Brown*, 1983).

In a recent plain view case (*Arizona v. Hicks*, 1987), the U.S. Supreme Court held that probable cause is required before moving "suspicious looking" items to record serial numbers (e.g., video cassette recorders or televisions). In this decision, the court held that *moving* an item constitutes a search for the purposes of the Fourth Amendment. The court, in this case, specifically held that the "suspicious" nature of an item, absent probable cause, does not satisfy the requisite of the plain view doctrine. However, the court also held that peering behind items for serial numbers *without moving them* is "not" considered a search.

Limitations on Searches: United States v. Chadwick, 1977

Federal narcotics agents in Boston had developed probable cause to believe 200 pounds of marijuana were contained in a locker due to arrive by train from San Diego. Chadwick and his associates were observed picking up the locker from the depot and placing it in the trunk of Chadwick's automobile. While the car trunk was still open, Chadwick was arrested and the car and locker was seized. One hour later the locker was searched and the marijuana was found. The marijuana evidence was suppressed because the court held that a search warrant should have been acquired for the locker and that the search was not incident to arrest. This was based on the premise that once the suspect was placed into custody, there no longer existed the threat of the suspect trying to obtain a weapon from the locker.

Strip or Body Cavity Search

As discussed in the Chimel case, under certain conditions an individual may be searched without a warrant for weapons. In the event, however, that a suspect is believed to be concealing drugs inside his or her clothing or even within body cavities, certain established procedures must be observed to protect the officer and to avoid violating the suspect's rights. The procedures for conducting strip or body cavity searches should be written explicitly into agency policy, and they may also be prescribed by state law to protect a suspect's rights and to minimize officer liability. In either case, officers should carefully observe the accepted procedures and familiarize themselves with the pertinent laws in their jurisdictions.

Definitions

A *strip search* is defined as the removal or rearrangement of some or all of the clothing of a person so as to permit an inspection of the genitals, buttocks, breasts, or undergarments of the person. This can be accomplished by inspections conducted visually, manually, or by means of any physical instrument.

A *body cavity search* is defined as the inspection of a person's rectum or genitalia, including but not limited to searches conducted visually, manually, or by the use of any physical instrument.

A Model Procedure

1. No person arrested for a traffic offense or an offense that does not constitute a felony may be subject to a strip search or a body cavity search by any law enforcement officer or employee unless probable cause exists to believe that the person is concealing a weapon, evidence of the commission of a crime, or contraband.
2. All strip searches conducted by law enforcement officers or employees will be performed by persons of the same sex as the person being searched.

3. All strip searches and body cavity searches conducted shall be done under conditions of reasonable privacy such that the search cannot be observed by persons other than those physically conducting the search.

4. A body cavity search of any person detained or arrested for a traffic offense that does not constitute a felony, can be accomplished with sufficient probable cause, but only under sanitary conditions and by a physician, registered nurse, or practical nurse licensed to practice in the state.

5. Every law enforcement officer or employee conducting a strip search or body cavity search shall:
   A. Obtain written authorization from a police supervisor within the jurisdiction the strip search or body cavity search is to be conducted.
   B. Prepare a report regarding the strip search or body cavity search including the following information:
      1. Written permission from a police supervisor (as discussed above)
      2. The name of the person searched
      3. The name of the person or persons conducting the search
      4. The time, date and place of the search
      5. The results of the search.

A copy of the report should also be furnished to the individual who was searched.

Prosecution Strategies and Methods of Proof

Although the prosecutor will make the ultimate decision regarding how a defendant is to be charged, initially it is the officer on the search and arrest scene who must collect the necessary items to prove any anticipated charge. Certain tactics, however, may prove beneficial to both the officer and the prosecutor when preparing for a jury trial.

Laws regulating drugs vary widely from state to state, but certain basic elements proving drug trafficking crimes remain the same. Some terms most commonly associated with the prosecution of drug cases will be discussed below, as well as what an officer can best do to prepare a case for prosecution. Once the officer understands prosecution strategies, he or she will be better prepared to collect the necessary evidence required for the court proceeding.

Proof in drug cases can be established by several means. Depending upon what evidence is accumulated by the officers, charges may range from misdemeanor possession, possession with intent to distribute (felony possession), delivery or distribution (definitions depend on the specific criteria set forth by each state's drug laws).

Possession

As mentioned above, there exist two types of possession: actual possession and constructive possession. Actual possession is when controlled substances are removed from the suspect directly or when drugs are thrown to the ground by the suspect. Normally, cases involving actual physical custody are straightforward and seldom present problems at trial. Greater difficulties are encountered, however, in proving a suspect's constructive possession of drugs. Again, the dominion and control of the drugs must be established in these cases. As a reminder, both elements of "knowledge" and "intent" to control must be proven by the prosecution.

Possession with Intent to Distribute (Felony Possession)

The distinction in this category of offense and possession is the term "intent." Intent is defined as the natural and probable consequences of a defendant's actions.

Distribution

Distribution may be defined as dividing, delivering, or sharing other than by administering or prescribing, whether or not for compensation.

Delivering

The definition of "delivering" is the actual attempted or constructive transfer of a controlled substance from one person to another.

Proof of Intent to Distribute

It is generally accepted that if the prosecution proves that the drugs were not for the defendant's personal use, then they were for distribution. To prove intent, several factors should be considered. The investigator's ability to properly identify and document evidence in this area may make the difference between a misdemeanor or felony charge being filed against the suspect. Let's now look at these factors.

Quantity

Frequently the quantity of a drug by itself can determine whether or not a suspect was going to consume all of the drugs by him- or herself. A officer or investigator trained in the area of drug enforcement can testify as an expert witness to establish how many dosage units of the drug were recovered and how that number is inconsistent with personal consumption practices of drug users. (See the list of qualifying questions for prosecutors to establish an officer as an expert witness later in this chapter.) The expert witnesses can greatly enhance the success of a drug case when testimony is given in the following areas:

1. That users of drugs simply cannot afford the quantity that was recovered.
2. The quantity of drugs involved, because of its organic nature (marijuana, cocaine, heroin), would result in moulding or decomposition before a single person could use it. In addition, large quantities of drugs made with ether, such as PCP, would evaporate before a single person could consume them.

Statistics are another good method of relating intent to a jury. For example, agents who testify can relate how many baggies (or joints) could have been made with that quantity of marijuana? How many grams or quarter grams could have been produced from that ounce of cocaine? How many cigarettes (dips) could have been produced from that bottle of liquid PCP?

Quality

The quality of a drug can quickly establish a suspect's intent to distribute a drug. For example, an expert witness (preferably a police chemist) can testify as to the average purity of cocaine usually distributed on the streets of a community. If the cocaine seized is significantly higher than that, it might indicate that a dealer is high enough up the distribution ladder to acquire such high-quality cocaine.

In addition to indicating "position" in the chain of distribution, possession of high-quality drugs shows that the suspect would be able to dilute the drugs by several times, therefore increasing his profit potential. For example, 1 ounce of 80% cocaine could be cut twice, resulting in 3 ounces of 25%–35% pure cocaine. If this were then sold by the gram rather than by the ounce, the profits from the initial investment would triple, or even quadruple.

The Value of the Drugs

When the case goes to court, a blackboard can be used to best demonstrate the enormous amount of money defendants net as a result of drug sales. For example, if an ounce of cocaine sells for $2,000, the expert witness can break down the profit for the benefit of the jurors. Specifically, there are 28 grams in 1 ounce; if the dealer sold the ounce in gram form (based on $100 per gram), he or she would realize $2,800 — or $800 profit over and above the initial investment. If it can be established that the dealer sells quarter-gram quantities, then each quarter-gram might sell for $35 each, thereby netting the dealer $140 per gram and a total of $3,920 for the ounce — a profit of $1,920 from the initial investment.

In addition, if the prosecution can show that the quality of the drugs was high enough to be cut once or twice, then the profit dollar figures listed above could be multiplied two or three times, creating an even larger profit margin and more damaging testimony against the defendant.

Distribution Paraphernalia

Another way of demonstrating the defendant's intent to distribute is to how the presence of items commonly used in distribution. The equipment used will vary somewhat from drug to drug, but its introduction as supporting evidence will greatly enhance the prosecution's chances for a guilty plea. Some common drug paraphernalia are:

Marijuana: Scales, baggies, sifters, scissors, or bowls. Each of these items seems perfectly innocent by themselves, but when examined in combination they create criminal intent.

Cocaine or crack: Scales, bindles (druggist folds), sifters, grinders, cutting agents (such as baking soda, mannitol, lactose, procaine, etc.). Converting cocaine hydrochloride into "crack" will require different materials: small test tubes, glass jars, ammonia, baking soda, razor blades, a heat source (such as candles), coat hangers or knitting needles to loosen the hardened crack from the test tube after cooking, smoking pipes, and acetaline torches or butane lighters for smoking it.

PCP: Small glass bottles (usually brown-colored glass), More or Kool brand cigarettes, ether, droppers, masks, or funnels. PCP is volatile and expensive, averaging around $400 per ounce, or from $10 to $20 per "dipped" cigarette.

Money or Bartering Materials

Drug dealers not only accept money for drugs but frequently pay for drugs with stolen property. Shoplifted items will commonly have price tags still attached to permit the thief an opportunity to return the item to the store for cash, or to establish the basic price of the item when trading for drugs. In either case, all such items should be seized as evidence in the case.

Documents

As mentioned, officers should be on the lookout for not just pieces of mail to establish dominion and control, but business papers, note pads, pieces of paper containing IOUs, etc., to establish intent to distribute (Fig. 3-6).

Surveillance

Surveillance can also establish a defendant's intent to distribute by observing significant numbers of persons entering and leaving the suspect's residence, as well as their length of stay.

Residence Fortification

Because most people do not normally install iron bars, steel door jams, booby traps, attack dogs, and other means of fortification in a residence, investigators may be able to show such items as a method to defeat entry into the residence by police. Many times "residences" are established for the sole purpose of dealing drugs, which can be demonstrated by the lack of "normal" household items such as furniture, food, clothing, or beds. Again, expert testimony will prove valuable in describing the purpose of these conditions.

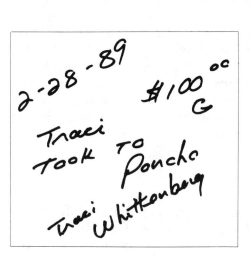

3-6 When searching a suspect's residence, notes such as this will often indicate that the individual is a drug dealer.

Establishing Expert Testimony

As mentioned, the testimony of an expert witness will greatly enhance the prosecution's chances of securing a guilty verdict. In order for an officer to be permitted to testify as an expert in narcotics, the prosecutor must first establish the officer's expertise when he or she first takes the stand. The questioning procedure is basically as follows:

1. Name
2. Occupation (and for how long)
3. Department (and for how long)
4. Narcotics investigation experience (and for how long)
5. Any special training in the field of drug enforcement?
6. What was the officer's training (drug identification, undercover operations, etc.)?
7. How long was the training course?
8. How many hours was the training course?
9. Ever participate in a narcotics investigation before?
10. How many times?
11. Was there an occasion to speak to individuals involved in illicit drug activities?
12. How many times?
13. Ever make arrests of people engaged in illicit drug activities?
14. How many times?
15. Was there an occasion to speak with these people with regard to drug identification and use of illicit drugs?
16. Ever been called upon to testify on behalf of other law enforcement agencies regarding drug users and dealers?
17. How many times?
18. Occasion to be qualified in this jurisdiction as an expert witness?
19. How many times?
20. Did you actually testify?

Collection and Preservation of Drug Evidence

As in all criminal investigations, evidence of the crime will be collected throughout the progression of the investigation. Typically, the purchase of drugs is documented to show that a suspect is dealing drugs, but there is often additional evidence needed to prove a case in court. Normally, defense strategies will focus on attacking the chain of custody of the evidence and/or the credibility of the officer giving testimony. To best avoid complications regarding evidence collection, we will now examine the specific types of evidence most commonly used in documenting an illicit drug case.

Controlled Substances as Evidence

Illicit substances are usually collected by the police in one of two ways: purchase or seizure. In either case, strict rules of evidence should be observed to properly preserve the evidence for prosecution. When drugs are purchased, it is always a good practice to properly record and document a drug transaction to show where the drugs were just prior to being purchased by the undercover officer. Drugs will usually come in four basic forms:

1. *Powders:* cocaine, heroin, and methamphetamine
2. *Liquids:* PCP and injectible Demerol
3. *Tablets or capsules:* LSD and some pharmaceuticals
4. *Plant material:* marijuana, peyote cactus, and psylisyben mushrooms

Once collected, the drugs must be properly marked by the officer who originally acquired them. This is done so that the officer can later identify the evidence in court. These markings should include the officer's initials and the date the evidence was obtained. Normally, these markings are placed on the bag or bindle that contained the evidence. If any other officers handle the evidence or take custody of it outside of the seizing officer's view, they should also mark the evidence, as they have thereby entered the chain of custody and may later have to testify as to the custody of the drugs.

It is also an excellent idea to protect the plastic baggies used by drug dealers because they may contain valuable fingerprint evidence, which can connect the bags to a particular individual. One excellent way of bringing out clear and identifiable latent fingerprints is the use of Superglue fumming, which is a process whereby a small amount of Superglue and petroleum jelly is placed in a container such as a jar lid, which is then placed in a standard empty fish aquarium with the suspect bag. The solution is slowly heated and the aquarium is covered. After about 10–15 minutes, a smoky mist will be produced from the solution and fingerprints will show up on the bag like white paint. This is especially effective in showing associations for conspiracy cases (see Chapter 2).

Once the drugs are properly marked, they should be placed in official evidence containers (envelopes, bottles, etc.), which should be supplied by the department. The purpose of these containers is to preserve the evidence in its original form. Normally, small clear plastic bags are used to contain smaller quantities of powders (an ounce or less). Some drugs, however, such as PCP, LSD, and methamphetamine may contain chemicals that can corrode through a plastic bag; these should be stored and transported in glass containers. Larger paper bags are usually used for wrapping larger quantities. The outside of the bag is also sealed, labeled, and dated. For seized liquids, the original bottle is the best evidence, which is subsequently marked and labeled; care should be taken to insure that the contents of the bottle will not spill while being transported. The bottle should then be placed in either a plastic bag or a larger padded box, which will protect the evidence from being damaged.

After being placed in containers, the containers must also be appropriately marked. Sometimes this can be accomplished by applying evidence labels to the containers with the necessary blanks filled out regarding the name of the seizing officer, date and time of the seizure, location of the seizure, and the suspect's full name and identifiers.

It is a good practice to avoid touching the drugs with bare skin as some substances will absorb into the bloodstream through the skin. To accomplish this, a plastic mitt or glove might be used. If a field test of the substance is desired, the officer should perform this prior to packaging the drugs: any reopening of the evidence after packaging might be construed by defense attorneys as a contamination of the evidence.

The drugs should then be immediately taken to a departmentally designated location where they will be stored until needed for court. This location will vary from department to department, but in most cases it will be the police laboratory. Drugs, unlike many other types of evidence, must undergo chemical analysis to determine that they are, in fact, a controlled substance rather than a noncontrolled lookalike. Once the drugs are signed over to laboratory personnel, it is then their responsibility to maintain and protect the custody of the drugs.

A forensic report is then generated by the laboratory designating the substance as either noncontrolled or as a controlled substance, and its specific type. The report may also advise as to the exact purity or weight of the drugs (quantitative and qualitative analysis), if requested by the investigating officer.

As mentioned, in addition to collecting controlled substances in the search, it will also be necessary for officers to seize related items to show illicit profits, dominion and control of the premises, or to otherwise establish that the suspect was in business as a drug dealer. It is common for searching officers to find large sums of currency during the search. The procedure for seizure of this type of evidence may be set forth in state law, but it is generally seizable if found in close proximity to illicit drugs. As with drug evidence, when money is seized, it should first be photographed in the location where it was discovered. Officers should then carefully count the money in the presence of a second officer (as a witness) to eliminate future allegations of theft of part or all of the money.

The seizure of money is a civil process in which a forfeiture hearing will be held and a determination will be made as to the relationship between the seized item and the offense. Because it is a civil hearing, however, property may be forfeited even if an additional criminal charge is pending or if the suspect has been acquitted of a criminal drug charge. This stipulation, however, may vary from state to state (see Chapter 2).

Photos and Audiovisual Tapes as Evidence

This section discusses the proper handling of tapes and photos as evidence. Chapter 7 will explain the effective use of audiovisual equipment by drug enforcement officers.

It has become evident that photographs and audiovisual recordings are valuable to drug investigations. Certain considerations should be observed, however, when packaging and preserving these items as evidence. Photographs and videotapes have generally been accepted as the best evidence in any drug transaction in which the suspect is observed in possession of the drugs. All photos should be marked with the initials of the officer taking the photo as well as the officer who maintains custody of them. As with drug evidence, the officer's initials and the date of the photo are minimum requirements. In some cases, a brief description of what the photo concerns might be written on the back of the photo if it does not speak for itself. Photo logs may also be prepared, indicating the subject of the photo and any other important aspects of the scene. All photos should be individually indexed with the ongoing case number and filed with the master case file for quick retrieval.

Audio cassettes and videotapes are both an invaluable aid to drug enforcement officers. Like the photo, the recording of a suspect's voice making negotiations for the drug deal, or a videotape of the suspect actually selling drugs is irrefutable evidence in court. Like photos, the officer's initials and date of the transaction must be placed on the tape, and a rigid chain of custody must be maintained and properly documented (see Chapter 2).

Before storing tapes for court, officers must first remove the erasure tabs on the tape, thus preventing the tape from being accidentally erased. When the tape is finally stored, the officer having custody should take care to store it safely (avoid metal shelves) where it will not be erased as a result of being next to any magnetic material or strong RF signals from generators. In addition, tapes should be fast-forwarded and rewound at least once a year and periodically demagnetized to prevent accidental erasures.

The Admissibility of Videotapes as Evidence

It seems increasingly certain that videotaped evidence will be used more and more in criminal drug trials throughout the country. It should be noted, however, that as evidence a videotape is not always as effective as still photos. Actually, videotaped evidence could be compared to oral testimony in that it is transitory in nature. Videotapes, for example, require a monitor before being viewed, as opposed to photos, which can be reviewed at any time.

Some concern exists in the law enforcement community as to a videotape's admissibility in the courtroom. As with a still photograph, a verified videotape (and accompanying sound) is admissible as evidence under the same general set of criteria as a photograph. In verifying the videotape, it is not necessary to show the experience or training of the camera operator, only that the tape clearly and accurately portrays what it is claiming to represent. Because of this, any officer involved in the filming of the subject in question may testify as to the accuracy of its contents, even if the testifying officer did not operate the camera.

In the case of videotapes where the soundtrack is somewhat inaudible, it is permissible for the prosecution to use electronics to enhance the fidelity of the sound for the benefit of the jury. If it is determined that either the sound or the picture is inadmissible for any reason, the unobjectionable mode of the tape can still be used in the court proceedings.

Statements as Evidence

A suspect should not be questioned until the suspect has first been informed of his or her Constitutional rights. In *Miranda v. Arizona* (1966), the U.S. Supreme Court held that a suspect must be read his or her Constitutional rights before questioning and after having been placed in custody. Generally officers should obtain a written statement from the suspect in case he or she later claims that he or she was not properly informed (Fig. 3–7).

A statement is a narrative description of the events leading up to and committed during a crime. Statements are not necessarily confessions, but they may be considered as evidence. When a suspect gives a statement, it should be in his or own words, and the statement itself should be initially taken from the suspect in longhand. The interviewing officer should then be sure the statement is promptly and properly signed by the suspect and a witnessing officer, and then have the statement notarized. Included on the form

<table>
<tr><td>STATEMENT OF RIGHTS AND WAIVER</td><td>CITY POLICE DEPARTMENT</td><td>DATE</td></tr>
</table>

PLACE

NAME   CASE NO. *(If applicable)*

Before we ask you any questions, you must understand your rights. You have the right to
remain silent. Anything you say can be used against you in court or other proceedings. You
have the right to talk to a lawyer for advice before we ask you questions, and to have him
with you during questioning. You have this right to the advice and presence of a lawyer even
if you cannot afford to hire one. In such a case you have a right to have a court-appointed
attorney present at the interrogation. If you wish to answer questions now without a lawyer
present, you have the right to stop answering questions at any time. You also have the right
to stop answering at any time until you talk to a lawyer.

You may waive the right to advice of counsel and your right to remain silent and answer
questions or make a statement without consulting a lawyer if you so desire.

WAIVER

I ☐ have read ☐ had read to me the statement of my rights shown above. I understand
what my rights are and I elect to waive them. I am willing to answer questions and make a
statement. I do not want a lawyer. I understand and know what I am doing. No promises or
threats have been made to me and no pressure of any kind has been used against me. I was taken
into custody at *(time)* _____ ☐ A.M. ☐ P.M., on *(date)* _____,
and have signed this document at *(time)* _____ ☐ A.M. ☐ P.M., on *(date)* _____

WITNESS   SIGNATURE OF PERSON WAIVING RIGHTS

WITNESS

3-7 Statement of Rights and Waiver form

should be a clause stating that the statement was given knowingly
and voluntarily. In addition, interviews should be conducted in a
secluded room with no interruptions.

Statements may also be dictated to a secretary or tape recorded for
transcribing later on a formalized statement form (Fig. 3-8) (this is

CITY POLICE DEPARTMENT
VOLUNTARY STATEMENT

_____
Case #

_____
Date

I _____ am _____ years of age and currently
reside at _____ which is located in the city of
_____.

Statement:

_____

_____

_____

_____

_____

_____

_____

_____

_____

_____

I have read this statement which consists of _____ page(s) and I affirm that it was given
voluntarily and that all facts are truthful and accurate.

This statement was given at _____ (location) on the
_____ day of _____, 19__, at _____ (am) (pm).

_____
Signed

_____
Witness

_____
Witness

3–8   Voluntary Statement form

recommended because most suspects speak clearer than they write). Another method is to take notes from the suspect and have them sign and date the notes, which will later be used as evidence. Suspects frequently tend to ramble on about things not pertinent to the subject at hand. In such an instance, the officer may guide the interview back on track provided he or she is careful not to put words in the mouth of the person being interviewed; videotaping interviews with suspects should definitely be considered.

Summary

The area of police search and seizure is probably one of the most closely scrutinized areas of the profession. It is in this area where a vast potential exists for abuse of authority, which could lead to the freeing of guilty suspects. The drug enforcement professional must, therefore, know the correct procedures for conducting searches, both with and without a warrant.

Searches with a warrant begin with the preparation of the affidavit, which is basically an application for the warrant. The contents of the affidavit are critical and must fully explain the officer's qualifications as the affiant and specify the exact items for which the officer wishes to search. Finally, one of the most commonly neglected areas in affidavit preparation is the complete description of the place to be searched. This should be done so that any stranger in town could locate the place to be searched, leaving no officer discretion in this area.

Once the affidavit is filled out, the warrant itself must then be prepared. Much of the same information is necessary in the preparation of the search warrant, although the warrant itself usually does not require quite as much detail. The affidavit and warrant should then both be signed by a neutral and detached (unbiased) magistrate before execution.

The evidence collected in a drug case may include the drugs themselves, photos and videotapes of the suspect committing criminal acts, drug paraphernalia, and personal records and effects. When considering the search of a suspect or residence, lawful and accepted procedures of search and seizure should be observed to protect the rights of the suspects and integrity of the investigation.

When drug evidence is obtained, officers should take care to protect and document the chain of custody, as this may be an issue when the case goes to court. Evidence (drugs, drug paraphernalia, or audio or videotapes) should be initialed and dated by all who take possession of it after it is acquired. It should then be locked in a storage locker or vault for safekeeping, or (in the case of drugs) transported directly to the police laboratory where chemical tests will be performed for quality (purity) and quantity (weight). Subsequent laboratory test results are also evidence in the case, and the police chemist must be prepared to later testify as to the findings.

In search warrant cases, good search methods are essential because officers are not only searching for contraband but also for articles to show dominion and control over contraband, intent to distribute contraband, and other criminal involvement. All items seized as a result of the warrant must be itemized on the warrant return, which also serves as an inventory of the suspect's property seized. The return should also contain the name of the officer serving the warrant as well as the date and time of its service. The return is then taken back to and signed by the issuing judge (within the statutory time limit), and it is then filed with the court clerk.

During the evidence collection phase, a structured procedure should be established to eliminate confusion and mistakes. This can best be accomplished by assigning two officers to actually work the crime scene: one to direct the search and record the location of evidence, and the other to seize it. Drug evidence may be in any of several different forms, including vegetation, powder, tablets or capsules, and liquid. These substances should all be considered dangerous to the touch, but some may pose additional problems because of their being volatile, corrosive, or otherwise hazardous; they should be handled with care for transportation and storage.

Once the case goes to court, the officer may realize there are many items he or she might have forgotten during the search, which would establish the necessary elements of dominion and control, intent to distribute, and so forth. Such items are essential to refute any defense claims of lack of residency or involvement with illicit drugs, especially if the defendant was only a visitor at the residence. Other types of evidence may also help establish a suspect's criminal intent in a drug case. Such evidence will include photographs, suspect statements, clothing, drug apparatus, etc. The prosecution has the burden of proof in criminal trials and should be adequately prepared to overcome any reasonable doubt in the minds of the jurors.

Drug Identification

4

History shows that mind-altering substances such as opium and marijuana were used as far back as 4000 B.C. Most of the substances now considered modern-day drugs of abuse, however, where synthesized during the second half of the 1800s and the first part of the 1900s. These include drugs such as morphine, heroin, cocaine, LSD, amphetamines, barbiturates and others.

Certainly it should be accepted that different people use drugs for different reasons, some legitimate and some not. Drug use for medical treatment of pain and adverse symptoms is accepted behavior throughout the world. The use of other drugs in religious ceremonies, such as peyote, has sustained a time-honored tradition in some Amerindian cultures throughout the central and northern United States. Most of the current controversy over drug use, however, stems from the arbitrary use of drugs for recreational purposes. A diverse cross-section of our society are constantly at odds with lawmakers over which drugs should be legitimatized and which should remain classified as dangerous substances. Today, even the proponents of recreational drug consumption are ready to admit to the inherent dangers of most popular recreational drugs, but they defend their position by advocating use of these substances under controlled conditions.

In 1986 the National Institute of Justice (NIJ) revealed statistics that helped to clarify many questions about the correlation between recreational drug use and instances of crime. The NIJ declared that according to a nationwide survey of state prison facilities, two out of three inmates admitted to being under the influence of illicit drugs or alcohol at the time they committed the crime for which they were later convicted. It has been determined, therefore, that regardless of whether drugs are acquired legally or illicitly, the likelihood of drug-related crime will remain high. Some experts even predict a higher incidence of crime (in particular, violent crimes) should drugs ever be legalized, due to their greater availability (Fig. 4–1).

Generally speaking, the separate components called upon to combat continued drug abuse are law enforcement agencies, drug education and prevention programs, and drug treatment programs. Regardless of which component might be considered the most effective in the overall drug suppression effort, one fact remains: a comprehensive understanding of the most common illicit drugs available on the street today is essential to formulate policy on control of such substances.

This chapter will address the much-needed area of drug identification in order to better acquaint readers with the specific drugs currently being trafficked and consumed in the United States. Contributing to the confusion are factors such as the changing street names of the drugs, their changing forms of packaging, and fluctuating prices. In some instances drugs have been changed to new forms (such as "crack" from cocaine and "designer drugs"), which possess their own unique and distinctive qualities.

Drug Definitions

When attempting to understand drugs, certain technical terms are commonly used to describe how a particular drug affects the user.

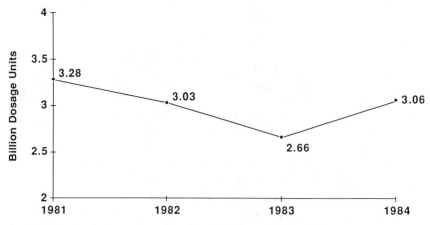

4–1   Dangerous drug consumption in U.S. — 1981–1984.

There are several terms, however, that one should understand:

1. *Physiological Dependence:* This simply means physical addiction, and it refers to drugs that create an actual physical need for a drug. Physiological dependence is defined as an alteration of the normal body functions that necessitates the continued presence of a drug in order to prevent the withdrawal syndrome, which is characteristic of each class of addictive drug.

2. *Psychological Dependence:* This means mental dependence of a particular class of drugs. Psychological dependence is defined as "a craving or compulsion to continue use of a drug because it gives a feeling of well being and satisfaction or to avoid discomfort."

3. *Tolerance:* When individuals regularly use a particular drug, a physiological tolerance frequently occurs. This is seen, for example, in first-time cocaine users who then continue to use the drug regularly. After a period of time, more of the drug is required to give the user the initial effect, which means the user must ingest increasing amounts of cocaine over time. The higher dosages raise his or her chances of blood poisoning, overdose, or other related problems. Tolerance is defined as ". . . the capacity to absorb a drug continuously or in large doses without adverse effects."

4. *Withdrawal:* This term refers to the physical state of an individual who is physically dependent on a particular drug. Those experiencing withdrawal become physically ill and remain that way for days unless the user ingests more of the needed drug. Withdrawal is defined as ". . . a series of symptoms that appear when a drug on which the user is physically addicted is abruptly stopped or severely reduced."

5. *Synergy:* Synergism or synergy is a physical effect resulting from combining more than one type of drug. Problems occur when users experiment with one or more drugs (usually in a "party" or recreational setting), or when alcohol is mixed with drug use, either on purpose or by accident. Overdoses are common, which may result in coma, cardiac arrest, or death. Three different types of synergies exist:

   Antagonistic: When the effects of one or both drugs are blocked or reduced.

   Additive: When the effect is the sum of the effects of each drug.

   Supra-additive: When the effects of the two drugs in combination is greater than it would be if the effects were additive; this is the most dangerous form.

Drug Categories

All drugs, whether classified as dangerous or not, fall into one of four general categories. These categories help classify the various substances so a determination can be made regarding both their physiological and psychological effects on the user.

Narcotics

The term "narcotics" is generally defined as drugs that act on the central nervous system, produce a sleeplike state, and are both physically and psychologically addictive. Narcotic drugs are indispensable in the practice of medicine, but they are greatly abused on the street. Narcotic compounds may be either organic or synthetic in nature. Examples of narcotics are opium, heroin, Dilaudid, and Demerol.

Stimulants

These also affect the central nervous system, but stimulants create a feeling of excitement, greater energy, and alertness. Commonly called "uppers," drugs that fall into this category may or may not be both psychologically and physically addicting. The most potent stimulant is cocaine (formerly misclassified as a narcotic), and it is considered highly physically and psychologically addictive; other stimulants considered addictive are methamphetamine and amphetamine. Noncontrolled stimulants include over-the-counter weight-loss pills, coffee, and many types of soft drinks containing caffeine.

Depressants

In direct contrast to stimulants are depressants. These drugs depress the central nervous system and psychomotor activity, but they do not literally create depression in the user (as the term might imply). In the initial stages, depressant drugs tend to uplift the user's sense of awareness, somewhat similar to a stimulant. Examples of depressants are alcohol, barbiturates, and sedative hypnotics. Many of the drugs listed as depressants create a high potential for physical and psychological dependency.

A subgroup within the depressant category is that of sedatives or sedative hypnotics (the benzodiazepine family). This category usually refers to drugs such as tranquilizers, which are designed to reduce anxiety and tension. Sedatives depress the central nervous system, and in some cases may even cause short-term memory loss. Twelve members of this group of drugs are currently marketed in the United States, and among them are chlordiazepoxide (Librium) and diazepam (Valium) — two of the most widely prescribed drugs in the United States. Both drugs also are characterized by a fairly slow onset and a long duration, and their use may result in psychological as well as physical addiction.

Hallucinogens

These drugs (also called psychoactive drugs) affect the central nervous system and create sensory illusions and perceptual changes in the user. Although not physically addictive, most of these drugs are illegal and only obtainable through illegal sources. Examples of hallucinogens are marijuana, peyote, LSD, and phencyclidine (PCP).

Drug Schedules

The 1970 Controlled Substances Act updated all previously existing federal drug laws and added some organization and direction to domestic drug control efforts (see Appendix). A significant component of this law was the categorization of all dangerous drugs into one of five schedules. These schedules rate drugs from their most dangerous (Schedule I) to the least dangerous (Schedule V). The criteria are outlined below:

Schedule I
1. High potential for abuse
2. No accepted medical use
3. Lack of safety for use under medical supervision
Examples: heroin, LSD, and *cannabis* (marijuana)

Schedule II
1. High potential for abuse
2. Restricted medical use
3. Severe psychological or physiological dependence
Examples: methylphenidate (Ritalin), morphine sulfate, cocaine, hydromorphone (Dilaudid) and phencyclidine (PCP)

Schedule III
1. Potential for abuse less than Schedule II
2. Current accepted medical value in United States
3. Moderate or low physiological dependence with high psychological dependence

Examples: hydrocodone (Tussionex) and benzphetamine (Didrex)
Schedule IV
1. Low potential for abuse relative to Schedule III
2. Current accepted medical value
3. Limited physiological or psychological dependence
Examples: diazepam (Valium), chloral hydrate, chlordiazepoxide
    (Liberium), and pentazocine (Talwin)
Schedule V
1. Low potential for abuse
2. Current accepted medical value
3. Limited physiological or psychological dependence

Drugs of Abuse

Let's now study the specific drugs of abuse most commonly encountered by law enforcement officers in the performance of their duties.

Marijuana (Cannabis sativa)

Marijuana, classified as a Schedule I mild hallucinogen, is one of the most controversial of the illicit substances. It is also the most widely used and abused drug in history. References to marijuana were discovered in a Chinese pharmacology treatise dating back to 2727 B.C. In more recent times, from the mid-1500s to the 1800s the acceptance of "hemp" spread for use in manufacturing rope, clothing, and some veterinary medicines. National legislation in 1937 was passed to control recreational use of the drug, although its use has spread despite these efforts (see Appendix).

The marijuana plant flourishes in all fifty states as well as in most other areas of the world. Much of the marijuana consumed in the United States is smuggled into the country by traffickers from source countries such as Mexico, Colombia, and Jamaica (Fig. 4–4). The plant is easily identified by its dark green, odd-numbered leaf (Fig. 4–2); after maturing it may grow to heights of 12 to 15 feet.

It is the dried "flower tops" of the female plant that are the most desired by users of the drug because the tops contain the highest concentration of tetrahydrocannabinol (THC), the ingredient that gives the user the desired euphoric feeling. Marijuana is harvested from the end of the summer up to the first frost. Dried leaves and flower tops are prepared in ounce, pound, and kilogram (2.2-pound) quantities for distribution. Prices of an ounce of commercial marijuana vary from region to region, but the average range is from $90 to $150; pound quantities may range from $800 to $1,200 (Table 4–1).

4-2 The marijuana leaf is easily distinguishable by its dark green color and saw-toothed leaves.

There are three types of marijuana grown domestically: (a) Indian hemp, (b) commercial, and (c) sinsemilla. Each of these strains varies from one another in quality (THC content) and appearance, as do their retail prices. The most common type of marijuana is the wild-growing Indian hemp or "ditchweed." This is the least sought after by users and dealers because of the low potency of the plant. Hundreds of thousands of Indian hemp plants grow freely in open fields and along fence rows throughout the United States, and it is generally thought of as more of a nuisance than a law enforcement threat. Eradication is somewhat difficult because as Indian hemp reseeds every year, its seeds have been known to lay dormant for up to seven years. It is estimated that Indian hemp has an average THC content of about 0.014%, which is considered extremely low. Because of the low potency of the plant, some traffickers will mix Indian hemp with commercial marijuana and sell it as a high-grade product.

The most common retail marijuana is called "commercial marijuana." This is the most commonly cultivated marijuana by local growers throughout the United States and is the standard type purchased on the street. When grown, commercial marijuana is usually cultivated in small patches of approximately 100 plants each, and the male and female plants are permitted to grow together. (This is significant for reasons discussed in the next section on sinsemilla.) The potency of commercial marijuana is much higher than that of Indian hemp (approximately 4-5% THC). Moreover, it provides the seller a considerable profit, considering that each plant yields an average of one pound of street product.

Finally, the highest-priced and highest-quality marijuana grown in the United States is called sinsemilla, which is a Spanish word meaning "without seeds." Sinsemilla originated in California in the 1960s, and its popularity spread to the rest of the country shortly thereafter. This strain entails more effort in growing as it is a female-only plant with interesting habits. Growers must extract the male plants from the patch before pollination because marijuana has the ability to change its sex overnight. Growers of sinsemilla, therefore, must take care not to permit any newly formed male plants to remain in the patch as they will contaminate the patch (resulting in a lower-quality plant yield). The THC content of sinsemilla ranges from 7-8%, and its street price may be twice that of commercial marijuana (Table 4-1, Fig. 4-3). To many growers the bother of producing the plant is far outweighed by the greater profit potential.

Although marijuana is somewhat consistent in popularity, the street names of the drug may vary from year to year. During the last 10 to 15 years marijuana has been called grass, smoke, weed, pot, reefer, duby, and root (see Glossary).

The Argument Over Legalizing Marijuana

Those who advocate the legalization of marijuana often compare its uses and effects to those of cigarettes, claiming that marijuana is no more harmful. Additionally, proponents of marijuana use often claim that given the violence traditionally associated with marijuana trafficking, if it were legalized there would then be no more enforcement problems. Claims are also commonly made that drug laws are discriminatory and violate the constitutional rights of individuals

Table 4-1 Marijuana Trafficking Indicators, 1983-1986

Marijuana Prices	1983	1984
Commercial grade		
Wholesale (lb)	$ 350.00-$ 600.00	$ 400.00-$ 600.00
Retail (oz)	$ 40.00-$ 65.00	$ 45.00-$ 75.00
Potency (% THC)	2.94%	3.49%
Sinsemilla		
Wholesale (lb)	$1,000.00-$2,000.00	$1,200.00-$2,500.00
Retail (oz)	$ 100.00-$ 150.00	$ 120.00-$ 180.00
Potency (% THIC)	7.74%	6.73%

Source: National Narcotics Intelligence Consumers Committee (NNICC), June 1987.

4-3 Photo of 200 pounds of Turkish hashish seized in Columbia, Missouri. Hashish is a by-product of the marijuana plant and has a much higher THC content than marijuana.

who choose to smoke marijuana rather than drink alcohol or smoke cigarettes.

An intelligent response to this cannot be made without first understanding the pharmacological and physiological effects of marijuana on the human body, and its social and economic effects on the public. With this understanding, people may then be able to distinguish between the genuine concern of informed and educated peo-

Table 4-1 (*continued*)

1985	1986
$ 300.00-$ 600.00	$350.00-$ 700.00
$ 50.00-$ 100.00	$ 45.00-$ 120.00
3.12%	3.67%
$1,200.00-$2,000.00	$800.00-$2,000.00
$ 120.00-$ 200.00	$100.00-$ 200.00
7.28%	7.94%

4-4   Photo of mail bags containing kilos of marijuana which were smuggled into Florida and seized by drug agents. (Photo courtesy of the Florida Department of Law Enforcement.)

ple, and those who advocate the legalization of marijuana out of ignorance, or for selfish and unfounded reasons.

Marijuana's effects on the human body include psychological dependence, some tolerance, and certain undesirable side effects. It affects the user's central nervous system by altering the blood pressure and respiration; it has hypoglycemic effects, which tend to increase the user's appetite; it dilates the pupils, impairs reproductive and endocrine functions, lowers resistance to infection, and promotes bronchitis and asthma. Because marijuana is a mild hallucinogen, it alters coordination and awareness, in particular with regard to space and time. The total marijuana "trip" will last from 3 to 5 hours, and with increasing doses the user may experience hallucinations that may be either pleasant or unpleasant.

One argument commonly offered by proponents of marijuana use is that it should be legalized because tobacco, which also causes both physical and psychological dependence, is accepted by our society. Proponents also claim that marijuana laws are discriminatory for outlawing marijuana and permitting the manufacture and use of tobacco. Tobacco, however, can be smoked while the user goes about other activities and still not pose a threat to himself or others. This is not the case with marijuana, for reasons discussed above. In addition, it is estimated that each marijuana cigarette contains approximately 50 times the tar contained in the strongest nonfilter cigarette, thereby increasing the user's risk of lung cancer considerably.

Another argument commonly levied in favor of legalization of marijuana is the alcohol analogy, which is similar to the tobacco defense. Alcohol is a drug—and a dangerous one at that: it is estimated that there are more than six million people who have mental and physical impairments because of alcohol dependence. Most experts estimate that marijuana has the same potential to produce the same number of impaired individuals if it were legalized. It is therefore somewhat alarming to note the lack of social responsibility commonly displayed by those who advocate the legalization of marijuana use by comparing it to other dangerous substances.

Cocaine (Erthroxylon coca)

Cocaine is the second most widely abused drug (marijuana being the first) in the United States: the number of cocaine users doubled between 1983 and 1988. Principally derived from alkaloid compounds in coca leaves, cocaine was isolated in 1844 and originally thought to be somewhat of a wonder drug for an array of ailments (including morphine and heroin addiction). Up until recent years, much misunderstanding has surrounded the effects of cocaine. The 1914 Harrison Narcotics Act originally miscategorized the drug as a narcotic (although it is now properly listed as a Schedule II stimulant). In all 50 states cocaine in any quantity is illegal to possess by nonregistrants unless a lawful prescription is obtained.

Cocaine is an intense stimulant, it is commonly available in the form of a white powder, and it has undergone considerable changes in its appeal over the last 10 to 15 years. Much misinformation exists about cocaine, and much of it has been disseminated *by* drug users *to* drugs users. The drug acts upon the central nervous system and is generally referred to as "a confidence drug." This basically means that users of cocaine acquire a sense of well-being and achievement, believing that whatever they are doing, they feel they are doing it better than ever before. This premise is unfounded: the drug just makes one "feel" that way. Cocaine also attacks the pleasure center of the brain and fools the brain into thinking that cocaine is every bit as essential to the body as food, water, or sex. This is the underlying danger of the drug. Addicted users of cocaine cannot easily be convinced otherwise.

Since the mid-1980s, researchers have proven that cocaine is every bit as physically and psychologically addictive as heroin. In spite of the sought-after euphoric effects of the drug, the negative effects seem to overshadow these sensations: insomnia, increased heart rate, chronic fatigue, depression, loss of sex drive, nasal bleeding, severe headaches, loss of appetite, increased blood pressure, convulsions, irritability, memory problems, paranoia and death.

The coca plant is somewhat finicky, requiring a special growing climate found only in certain South American countries (Peru, Ecuador, Bolivia, and Colombia along the Andes mountains). Optimal growing conditions can be imitated in a greenhouse, but it takes so many leaves to successfully produce a significant quantity of cocaine hydrochloride that controlled conditions are not usually possible or feasible: 500 kilos of dried leaves produce one pound of cocaine hydrochloride (powder).

Cocaine is usually ingested through the nose by being "snorted" through rolled up dollar bills, straws, or other devices. Generally speaking, one gram of cocaine powder will produce four to six lines of powder for consumption. Once entering the nose, it is absorbed through the nasal membranes, taken into the bloodstream, and then transported to the brain. The euphoric feeling occurs quickly, but it usually wears off in 20 to 30 minutes (a crack high is approximately 8 minutes).

Although at this time cocaine prices in the U.S. are falling, the traditional high cost of cocaine has usually been prohibitive for recreational users and higher yet for those who are dependent. One gram of cocaine will cost a user from $85 to $120 and from $1,500 to $2,500 per ounce. For dependent persons, the weekly cost could range from $1,000 to $3,000. Generally speaking, the purity of street cocaine is between 12% and 30%; this figure, however, will vary greatly from dealer to dealer and region to region (Table 4–2).

Cocaine tolerance can develop quickly. When a user has acquired a high tolerance for the drug, he or she might then choose to inject it. This process is not nearly as common as snorting, but for one who has acquired an appreciable tolerance, injection provides the user with a stronger dose, and creates a more intense high. If the user chooses not to inject the drug, he or she will most likely choose

Table 4–2 Cocaine Trafficking Indicators, 1983–1986

	1983	1984
Cocaine retail purity (%)	35%	35%
Cocaine prices (in thousands)		
Wholesale (kg)	$ 4.005–$ 55.00	$ 40.00–$ 50.00
Retail (g)	$100.00–$125.00	$100.00–$120.00
Laboratories seized (U.S.)	11	21

Source: National Narcotics Intelligence Consumers Committee (NNICC), June 1987.

4-5 Photo of a water pipe and small butane torch commonly used to smoke "crack," an inexpensive, ready-made freebase form of cocaine. (Photo courtesy of the U.S. Drug Enforcement Administration.)

"freebasing." Freebasing is a process in which cocaine is reduced to a liquid solution and then smoked. The process involves diluting the powder with ether or kerosene, creating a potent (and very flammable) solution. The solution is then smoked in a specially designed pipe. Freebasing allows a much larger percentage of the drug to be ingested than snorting. It is considered a way of ingesting an almost pure form of cocaine because many impurities are cooked out during the heating process.

Crack

"Crack" cocaine has gained popularity among cocaine users throughout the country since the mid-1980s. Crack is simply a ready-made freebase form of cocaine. It resembles small pieces of paint chips or soap (Fig. 4–6), it is sold in small quantities for an inexpensive price, and it is nonflammable. Crack is a form of cocaine

Table 4-2 (continued)

1985	1986
50%–60%	55%–65%
$ 30.00–$50.00	$22.00–$ 45.00
$100.00	$80.00–$120.00
33	23

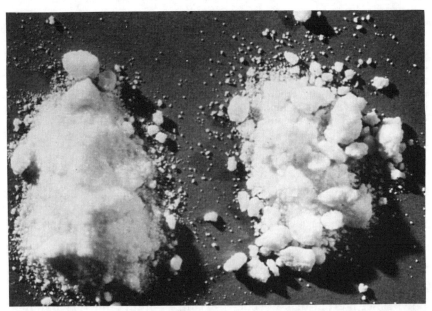

4–6 Powdered cocaine (left) and crack cocaine (right), which is identified by small white chips resembling soap chips and which sells for $5 to $50 each on the street. (Photo courtesy of the U.S. Drug Enforcement Administration.)

that is always smoked (Fig. 4–5), rather than injected or snorted. It is considered to be anywhere from 70% to 90% pure, and it may sell for as little as $10 to $50 per dosage unit (per "rock") on the street. Because of its highly addictive qualities, crack is considered a greater threat to public health than cocaine: conceivably it could be used by first-time cocaine users (rather than those who have developed a tolerance), making the probability of physical addiction and even "sudden death" extremely high. There is a rising public concern about crack because it is cheap enough to allow adolescents and even children to afford the drug.

Crack dealers benefit from the crack form of cocaine not because it is cheaper and more potent, but because it is so addictive. Occasionally users of cocaine hydrochloride may not become physically addicted to the drug, thereby allowing them to use it at will; crack, however, physically addicts the user so much faster that the dealer's repeat business is almost guaranteed.

The methods of converting cocaine to crack are rapidly spreading among dealers throughout the country, which adds to its increased availability on the street. Even though it is a somewhat fragile process, generally it is done as follows:

1. A quantity of cocaine hydrochloride is mixed with an equal quantity of baking soda or ammonia.
2. The powder is then dissolved in water.
3. The solution is first heated and then cooled.
4. As the moisture is dissolved from the solution, the remaining residue dries into crack.
5. After drying, the substance is cut up into small rocks and sold.

Phencyclidine (PCP)

Phencyclidine is another illicit drug that has experienced a constant degree of popularity over the years. Classified as a Schedule II hallucinogen, PCP began as a dissociative anesthetic in 1959, and it was intended for use in surgery. Because of the negative side effects experienced by recovering patients, the use of PCP was almost immediately discontinued. It was subsequently used as a veterinary medicine until 1978, when PCP was outlawed and classified as Schedule II.

PCP is available in two forms: powder and liquid. The powder is white or off-white (angel dust), and it is generally mixed with marijuana or reduced to a liquid solution for smoking. In many areas, however, the popularity of liquid PCP is more common than the powder. The liquid version of the drug looks like a clear or tan-colored water, and it is usually distributed by dealers in small brown glass bottles (which many dealers feel is necessary in keeping direct rays of the sun from diluting the solution). Liquid PCP is commonly called by street names such as "water," "wack," and "jet fuel"; cigarettes dipped in PCP are called "shirms," "shirm sticks," "dips," or "super cools" (see Glossary).

Liquid PCP is usually smoked by dipping a cigarette into the solution and allowing it to dry. Once dry, the cigarette is lit while held away from the user. It will ignite and the user must blow out the flame to begin smoking it. Because of the large concentration of ether in its chemical makeup, PCP is extremely flammable. The ether, however, also makes PCP an easily detectable drug because of its distinctive odor.

Clandestine laboratories are responsible for the manufacture of PCP, and most of these operate in isolated or rural areas where detection is unlikely. PCP seems to be most popular in larger cities or areas of town with an economically depressed economy (much like heroin). It is not considered a drug of the elite (like cocaine once was); many avid recreational drug users deplore the use of PCP while they advocate the benefits of marijuana and cocaine.

From a law enforcement standpoint, probably the most noteworthy feature of PCP is its propensity to create violent and unpredictable hallucinations in users. Because it is essentially an anesthetic, users feel a sense of invincibility because they do not feel pain. In addition, the drug seems to prompt feelings of strength and power, which increase the likelihood of violence among users. This has caused concern among law enforcement officials (see Chapter 7).

Heroin (Diacetylmorphine)

A derivative of morphine, heroin was first discovered in 1874. Like cocaine, heroin was also tauted as a wonder drug, and it was thought to cure opium and morphine addiction. Pharmaceutical companies became so convinced of its beneficial uses that in 1898 the Bayer Company of Germany began commercially manufacturing it. Legal controls began with the 1906 Federal Food and Drug Act and the 1914 Harrison Narcotic Act, which taxed its manufacture, importation, and distribution. Heroin is classified as a Schedule I narcotic under the 1970 Controlled Substance Act.

Heroin is distinguished by its effects on the central nervous system, which cause a depressed feeling and relief from pain. Heroin is highly addictive, both physiologically and psychologically. It is currently estimated that there are between 500,000 and 750,000 heroin addicts in the United States.

Heroin is manufactured in illegal laboratories, primarily in Mexico and Asia. Two Asian poppy-growing regions produce most of the world's heroin supply (Figs. 4 – 7, 4 – 8; Table 4 – 3):

Southeast Asia ("the Golden Triangle"): Burma, Laos, and Thailand.

Southwest Asia ("the Golden Crescent"): Pakistan, Afghanistan, and Iran.

When first produced, heroin is a brown or white powder (Figs. 4 – 9, 4 – 10) (depending on where it is manufactured), which is then smuggled into the United States for distribution. After reaching the U.S., heroin is diluted with adulterants such as baking soda, mannitol, or lactose. These neutral powders enable the dealer to double, triple and even quadruple the quantity of heroin on hand; the result is an average street purity of 3% to 5%. Heroin may sell for $35 to $50 per gram (spoon) and as much as $1,500 to $1,700 per ounce. Although it

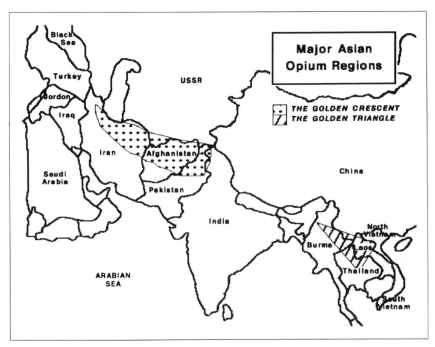

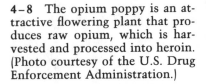

4-7   Map of the Golden Triangle and the Golden Crescent, opium and heroin producing regions.

4-8   The opium poppy is an attractive flowering plant that produces raw opium, which is harvested and processed into heroin. (Photo courtesy of the U.S. Drug Enforcement Administration.)

Table 4–3 Heroin and Morphine Trafficking Indicators, 1983–1986

	1983	1984	1985	1986 (Jan.–June)
Origin (%)				
Southwest Asia	48	51	47	40
Mexico	33	32	39	41
Southwest Asia	19	17	14	19
Retail Heroin				
Purity	4.5%	2.37%	5.3%	2.12%
Prices (mg)	$2.15	$2.37	$2.30	$2.12

Source: National Narcotics Intelligence Consumers Committee (NNICC), June 1987.

may be snorted, it is usually injected intravenously. First-time users might begin sniffing heroin and slowly graduate to skin-popping. Sniffing and skin-popping, however, offer the user no "rush," which is the most sought-after feeling. To experience the rush, users resort to mainlining (intravenous injection). Users become physically addicted in a fairly short period of time.

Once addicted, the user must maintain minimum levels of the drug in his or her system in order to avoid painful withdrawal reactions. If deprived of the drug, within the first 8 to 12 hours the user will experience watery eyes, runny nose, yawning, and excessive perspiration. Peak withdrawal symptoms usually occur within 48 to 72 hours: profuse sweating, extreme depression, and vomiting. Without treatment, the symptoms will run their course and finally

4–9 Photo of Asian White and Mexican Brown heroin. (Photo courtesy of the U.S. Drug Enforcement Administration.)

4-10 Photo of "Black Tar" heroin, a rock type of heroin originating in Mexico. (Photo courtesy of the U.S. Drug Enforcement Administration.)

disappear within 7 to 10 days. It is the obsession to avoid withdrawal that will usually cause many addicts to commit street crimes for cash. Ultimately addicts may ignore matters of personal hygiene, or even food. Conditions of malnutrition and unchecked infectious disease are not uncommon among long-time addicts.

There has been recent attention on heroin addiction because it is typically administered via hypodermic needles. It is common for heroin users to sit in groups of three to five people and share one syringe among them. Unfortunately, it is a very efficient means to share diseases. It has been estimated that almost half of the AIDS (acquired immune deficiency syndrome) carriers are intravenous drug users. To illustrate the magnitude of the problem, in 1987 one out of every 60 babies born in New York City was an AIDS carrier.

Other dangers associated with heroin use include: physical dependence, psychological dependence, tolerance, withdrawal symptoms, disease (such as hepatitis A and B, mononucleosis, and AIDS), lesions and abscesses of the skin (i.e., open, infected sores), pregnancy complications for addicted mothers, and death from overdose.

LSD (D-Lysergic Acid Diethylamide)

LSD was originally discovered in 1938 by two Swiss chemists. It is made from the fungus that forms on rye (the Ergot fungus). Five years after its discovery, Dr. Albert Hoffman (one of its discoverers) ingested some of the drug, which resulted in hallucinations. Subsequently Dr. Hoffman continued his experimentation with LSD and wrote about its effects. LSD was later adapted by the U.S. Army, which experimented with it as a brainwashing agent and truth serum for prisoner interrogations. In 1963 Dr. Timothy Leary, a one-time professor at Harvard University, became a cult figure who praised the effects of LSD. LSD is classified as a Schedule I hallucinogen. Its possession is illegal in all fifty states.

LSD's raw form resembles water—colorless and odorless—thereby allowing application on just about any surface. Typically, LSD comes in three distinct forms: microdot (tiny tablets); blotter acid (Fig. 4–11) (a sheet of paper containing small cartoon characters); and window pane (similar to blotter). In all of its forms, each dosage unit will sell for about $3 to $5, with buyer discounts for larger quantities.

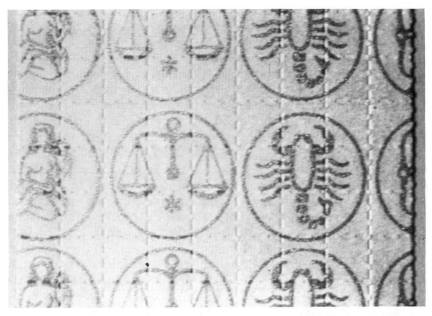

4–11 Photo of "Blotter" LSD, which is usually a cartoon picture containing one drop of liquid LSD. (Photo courtesy of the U.S. Drug Enforcement Administration.)

LSD is one of the most potent drugs known. Its effects are usually felt within an hour. These can last from 6 to 12 hours and are primarily psychological; there are few, if any, physical effects. Under the influence of LSD, the user's perceptions are intensified: colors are brighter, sounds become magnified, and there are distortions of time and space. Both pleasant and unpleasant effects can result from taking LSD (Table 4 – 7): bad trips are frequently described as a nightmare from which there is no escape. Another negative effect is a "flashback": a recurrence of a LSD trip weeks or even months after the last dose was taken. Research has revealed little as to why flashbacks occur.

Methamphetamine

Methamphetamine is classified as a Schedule II stimulant. It is usually sold in the form of white powder. Most methamphetamine users inject the drug into the bloodstream, much like heroin. This causes an almost immediate effect (rush), which usually gives the user a feeling of increased alertness and energy; these feelings may be followed by a sense of paranoia. Beginning in the late 1960s the use of stimulants increased considerably, with many kinds of "speed" available to potential users. Although many different stimulants still are available, methamphetamine seems to have captured a majority of the user market. The 1960s term "speed-freak" is commonly associated with users of methamphetamine and close cousin, amphetamine. Both powders are so similar in chemical make-up that only forensic chemists can tell the difference through chemical analysis.

Chronic "meth" users may be constantly under the influence of the drug for days at a time, resulting in a stimulated physical state but a depressed and worn out mental state. Negative effects of the drug are much the same as cocaine. Users may suffer many diseases associated with the use of unsterile needles and unclean diluents used to cut the drug. Cocaine users sometimes will try methamphetamine as a cheaper substitute (they are both stimulants). Lately, however, the price of methamphetamine is approaching that of cocaine: $75 to $120 per gram and up to $2,000 per ounce (see Table 4 – 4). Street names for meth include crank, crystal, speed and go-fast (see also Chapter 7).

Methamphetamine, like many other drugs, is produced in illegal laboratories throughout the country. Outlaw motorcycle gangs are commonly involved in methamphetamine business: a 1986 Drug Enforcement Administration report claimed that an estimated 40% of the methamphetamine consumed in the United States is manufactured and trafficked by these gangs.

Table 4–4 Selected Dangerous Drug Trafficking Indicators, 1983–1986

	1983	1984	1985	1986
Wholesale prices				
Amphetamine (DU)*	$ 1.50	$ 1.50	$ 1.50	$ 1.50
Methamphetamine (oz)	$1,000.00–$2,000.00	$1,100.00–$2,000.00	$ 800.00–$2,000.00	$1,000.00–$1,800.00
Methaqualone (DU)	$ 2.00–$ 2.50	$ 1.75–$ 2.50	$ 0.50–$ 2.00	$ 0.50–$ 2.00
PCP (oz)	$ 900.00–$1,200.00	$1,200.00	$1,200.00	$1,000.00
LSD (DU)	$ 1.50	$ 1.50	$ 1.50	$ 1.00–$ 2.30
Retail prices				
Amphetamine (DU)	$ 3.00	$ 3.00	$ 3.00	$ 3.00
Methamphetamine (g)	$ 60.00–$ 120.00	$ 60.00–$ 100.00	$ 60.00–$ 100.00	$ 60.00–$ 120.00
Methaqualone (DU)	$ 5.00–$ 8.00	$ 4.00–$ 15.00	$ 3.00–$ 10.00	$ 3.00–$ 10.00
Methaqualone (counterfeit DU)	$ 3.00–$ 5.00	$ 3.00–$ 5.00	$ 3.00–$ 10.00	$ 3.00–$ 10.00
PCP (DU; 100 mg 5% pure)	$ 10.00–$ 15.00	$ 10.00–$ 15.00	$ 10.00–$ 15.00	$ 10.00–$ 15.00
LSD (DU)	$ 3.00–$ 5.00	$ 2.00–$ 5.00	$ 2.00–$ 5.00	$ 3.00–$ 6.00

Source: National Narcotics Intelligence Consumers Committee (NNICC), June 1987.
DU = dosage units.

Pharmaceutical Drugs

Pharmaceutical drugs are drugs that have a legitimate medical use, are manufactured legally, and are most commonly available in tablets, capsules, caplets, and liquids (both oral and injectable). Although drugs in this category are legally made, many of them can only be purchased upon presentation of a lawful prescription; these are termed *controlled drugs*. Controlled drugs serve many legitimate purposes, and include tranquilizers, cough suppressants, appetite suppressants, and painkillers. Drugs that can be purchased without a prescription are called *over-the-counter drugs*, and they, too, have a variety of legitimate purposes: gastrointestinal drugs, cold remedies, analgesics, and antihistamines.

Many users feel that because a drug is legally manufactured, it will then be a safer recreational drug. This is not correct: even medications prescribed by physicians will differ in their effects from patient to patient (even for like ailments) because drug reactions and side-effects differ from individual to individual.

The different types of pharmaceuticals that pose the greatest threat to users typically fall into a few distinct categories.

Narcotics

As discussed earlier, narcotics are both physically and psychologically addicting to the user and have accounted for many overdoses over the years.

Morphine

A derivative of opium, morphine was discovered in 1802 and was named after Morpheus, the god of dreams. Still one of the most potent pain-killers known, morphine is a standard in the medical profession for surgery and related treatment. Morphine is only partially water soluble, so most users acquire it as a white crystalline powder. Users of morphine experience an orgasmic rush (as with heroin), resulting in a dreamlike state (Table 4–6). Morphine abuse can cause nausea, vomiting, sweating, respiratory depression, and death.

Codeine

Codeine was discovered in 1832, and it has been considered to be one of the most effective cough and pain suppressants known. It is also extremely addictive. Many pharmaceutical drugs contain codeine and are much sought after by drug users on the street (Table 4–5).

Table 4–5 Narcotics, Analgesics and Heroin Substitutes and Supplements: Use and Trafficking Indicators, 1983–1986

	1983	1984	1985	1986
Drug-related death				
Pentazocine	28	14	13	20
Hydromorphone	14	13	8	8
Oxycodone	11	14	21	24
Prices				
Pentazocine/tripelennamine (per "set")	$10.00–$12.00	$15.00	$10.00–$20.00	$10.00–$20.00
Codeine/glutethimide (per "set")	$ 6.00–$12.00	$ 7.00–$14.00	$ 7.00–$14.00	$ 7.00–$14.00
Hydromorphone (Dilaudid) (per 4 mg)	$40.00	$40.00	$50.00	$30.00–$65.00

Source: U.S. Drug Enforcement Administration, June 1987.

Table 4-6 Evidence of Drug Abuse

Drug	Physical Evidence	Conditions
Cocaine	White powder, "coke" spoons, water pipes, razor blades, hypodermic needles	Needle marks, excited activity, dilated pupils
Crack	White "rock"-looking chips, crack pipes (clear glass), pellets, small vials	Excited activity, dilated pupils, depression, convulsions
Depressants	Tablets and capsules of different shapes and sizes	Actions resembling drunkenness, slurred speech
Hallucinogens	Eyedroppers, tiny tablets, clear liquid, cartoons on small pieces of paper	Dilation of pupils, unreasonable behavior
Heroin	Brown or white powder, burned spoons with cotton, balloons, razor blades, candles	Needle marks, glazed look, constricted pupils
Marijuana	Roach clips, small pipes, baggies, scales, sifters	Smoke odor, glassy eyes, semiconsciousness
Morphine	Burned spoons, candles, syringes, prescription bottles	Needle marks, constricted pupils, euphoria
PCP	Small brown (1 oz) bottles, More brand cigarettes, odor of ether	Dilation of pupils, hostile disposition
Stimulants	Tablets, capsules and white powder, syringes, tin foil packets, baggies	Restlessness, nervousness, dilated pupils

Dilaudid

Dilaudid is a type of synthetic morphine used mainly for severe pain. It is also extremely addictive. Drug abusers consider it a more attractive drug than morphine because it does not produce morphine's side-effects (such as vomiting and nausea) yet it is much more potent. Dilaudid is produced as green, yellow, and blue tablets (Fig. 4-12), each representing different doses; these may sell for as much as $50 to $60 per dosage unit on the street.

Demerol

Demerol is a synthetic narcotic available in pills or injectable form (Fig. 4-13). It is commonly used in the treatment of moderate to severe pain. Demerol's physical reactions are similar to those of morphine, including physical addiction. Overdose may result in coma or death. Many members of the medical profession have got caught up in the diversion and use of this drug because of its effects and its high street price.

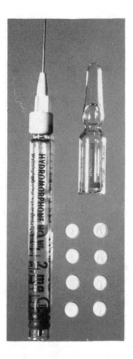

4-12   Photo of Dilaudid in both injectable and tablet form. (Photo courtesy of the U.S. Drug Enforcement Administration.)

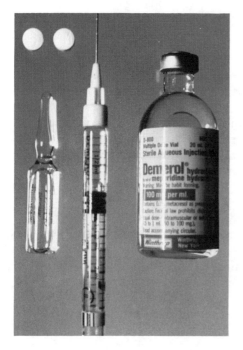

4-13   Photo of injectable Demerol, a popular and highly addictive drug. (Photo courtesy of the U.S. Drug Enforcement Administration.)

Barbiturates

Barbiturates (also termed sedative-hypnotic, or "sleep-inducing") depress the central nervous system. First discovered in 1864, barbiturates are highly addictive, both psychologically and physically; when mixed with alcohol (synergy), they may cause coma or death. According to the Drug Enforcement Administration, the four most sought-after barbiturates are Nembutal (pentobarbital), Amytal (amobarbital), Seconal (secobarbital) and Tuinal (secobarbital and amobarbital combined).

Because barbiturates are so highly addictive, to stop using the drug suddenly (cold turkey) causes such severe withdrawal symptoms that the addict may die. Because of this, barbiturate withdrawal is considered more dangerous than withdrawal from heroin.

Valium

Valium (diazepam) is classified as a sedative hypnotic and falls in the depressant category. Normally used in the treatment of tension and anxiety, Valium can create tolerance as well as a severe physical and psychological dependence. Valium is considered one of the most widely prescribed tranquilizers in the United States and is distributed in white, yellow, and blue tablets (Fig. 4–14).

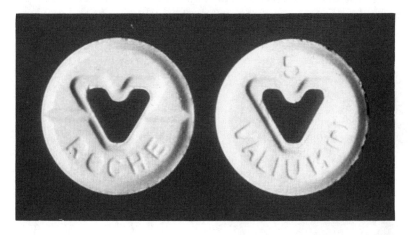

4–14 Close-up photo of a Valium (diazepam) tablet, a widely abused hypnotic sedative and a commonly diverted pharmaceutical drug. (Photo courtesy of the U.S. Drug Enforcement Administration.)

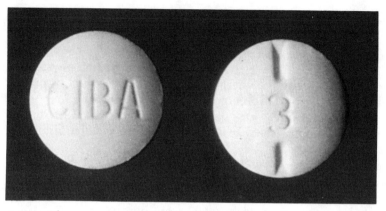

4-15   Close-up photo of Ritalin Hydrochloride (methylphenidate hydrochloride) a commonly abused synthetic stimulant. (Photo courtesy of the U.S. Drug Enforcement Administration.)

Stimulants

These are drugs that stimulate the central nervous system (Figs. 4-15, 4-16). The most commonly abused stimulants are nicotine and caffeine, which are found in cigarettes and popular beverages, respectively. The more potent stimulants (which pose the greatest problems) are controlled under the Controlled Substances Act; they include cocaine, methamphetamine (Desoxyn), and methylphenidate (Ritalin). Users tend to take the drug as a method of staying awake longer or to make themselves feel more productive. Problems emerge when stimulant users take "uppers" in the early part of the day and "downers" at night in order to relax.

4-16   Close-up photo of Preludin (phenmetazine hydrochloride), a commonly abused and powerfully addictive amphetamine. (Photo courtesy of the U.S. Drug Enforcement Administration.)

Table 4-7 Physical Characteristics of Drug Intoxication

Drug	Physical Effects
Cocaine[a]	Walking faster than normal
	Runny nose
	Red or watery eyes
	White powder molecules in nose hairs
	Dilated pupils
	Irritable
Marijuana	Reddening of the eyes
	Cotton mouth
	Delayed reactions
PCP[b]	Illogical or slurred speech
	Difficulty in standing
	Unruliness
	Paranoia
Heroin	Delayed reactions
	Slow walking ("floating")
	Slow speech
	Sweating or scratching
	Dry mouth
	Nodding
	Caked white powder around corners of mouth
	Constricted pupils (pinhole)
LSD	Overstimulated perceptions of reality
	Objects appear brighter to the user
	Overexaggerated reactions to ordinary objects
	Unusual descriptions of the ordinary
	Users may be sad and depressed over something minor in nature
	Bad trips — users feel their body is actually changing or they are dying

[a]When attempting to identify the cocaine user, look for horizontal nystagmus (bouncing eyes); if the officer moves a pen slowly toward the suspect, the eyes will bounce back to looking straight ahead (this differs from alcohol use, where the eyes will most likely cross).

[b]The user can be identified by horizontal nystagmus (the eyes will bounce back and forth). Vertical nystagmous may also occur, which is not common with those under the influence of alcohol. Officers dealing with arrestees should use back-up officers and be prepared for physical confrontations. Remember that PCP is an anesthetic, which minimizes pain in the user.

Over-the-Counter Drugs

Over-the-counter (OTC) medications are yet another source of drug abuse. There are an estimated 350,000 OTC drugs, which may be purchased without a prescription; OTC drugs account for more than $5 billion in sales annually. The most common OTC drugs of abuse are those that contain analgesic, sedative, or stimulant ingredients. The drugs rating highest in abuse are cough syrups, sleeping aids, and appetite-depressants.

Designer Drugs

After 80 years of antidrug legislation and drug control policies designed to crush the supply and demand of illicit substances, law enforcement officials and lawmakers alike witnessed a curve-ball of sorts thrown by drug manufacturers in the mid-1980s: designer drugs. Chemists, highly proficient in their craft, custom-manufactured (designer) drugs that (a) copied the effects of illegal drugs and (b) were in most cases perfectly legal to possess.

The concept is simple enough. When designer drugs were first introduced to the drug scene, the "benefits" (effects and legality) were highly tauted by dealers. In fact, however, designer drugs are more dangerous than the controlled drugs they were patterned after.

MDMA (3,4-Methylenedioxymethamphetamine)

MDMA (or Ecstasy, Eve, Turbo) was the first designer drug to have widespread appeal in the drug-using community. MDMA is not really a new drug; it was first developed in 1914 by Merck as a diet pill, but it was never commercially manufactured. Except for an army research project in 1953, there was no interest in the drug until the mid-1970s when a few studies of the drug were published. Despite no founded data supporting its beneficial uses in psychotherapy, MDMA began to be used by a few psychiatrists as an adjunct to therapy (as was LSD in its early days).

Ironically, MDMA was never produced legally, yet its use was never prohibited either; "sub-legal" chemists manufactured it for recreational users and psychiatrists alike. In the recreational community, word spread rapidly about its euphoric effects; it was billed as a party drug that promoted intimacy, personal insight, and uninhibited interaction between its users. Up until summer of 1985, MDMA was legally sold on the streets and distributed in nightclubs as a "hug drug." It is now classified as a Schedule I hallucinogen, although the psychiatric community continues to lobby for its legalization.

MDMA may be distributed in white powder form sold in paper bundles, or in the form of a tablet or caplet, which is usually white with bluish speckles. The tablets will sell for around $20 each, and are commonly broken in two, permitting users to share one tablet.

China White Heroin (3-Methyl Fentanyl)

"Designer china white heroin" should not be confused with its predecessor by the same name (true heroin). Designer china white heroin was first introduced in southern California in 1979 as real heroin. It was a white powder, packaged in balloons, and cut with lactose (milk sugar), which is also used to cut heroin. China white, however, is synthetic: it is made in a laboratory rather than from opium poppies.

The physical appearance of designer heroin and organic heroin are very close. Designer heroin, however, is more lethal than organic heroin: organic heroin is approximately three times more potent than morphine; designer china white heroin is estimated (conservatively) to be 1000 times more potent than morphine. Adding to its list of dangers are its side-effects such as Parkinson's disease, which affects a majority of its users by crippling or paralyzing all or part of a user's body.

Initially, the frustrating thing about designer drugs such as china white was that once legislation was passed to control it, chemists would add a new molecule to its structure and effectively make it a new drug, which required new legislation (again) to control it. Currently, federal and most state laws control the ingredients (analogs) used in the manufacture of designer drugs rather than listing the finished product under law.

The Economics of Drug Dealing

Many levels exist in the drug trafficking business, from the harvesting of coca leaves, opium poppy gum, or marijuana plants, street-level distribution (generally considered the lowest rung on the ladder). Each participant within this labyrinth is motivated by profit. To understand the profit flow in a particular organization, let us first examine the different players in a typical trafficking cartel.

The Farmers or Land Owners

Those who actually take to the fields and acquire the raw materials do not benefit as much as one might think. Peasants usually do the physical labor; although they are paid more than for legitimate crops, their income is marginal at best. In Thailand, for example, the hill tribes who harvest raw gum opium are extremely poor; although crop substitution has been tried, opium farming has proven to be the most reliable and financially rewarding activity. Similar circumstances exist on the coca plantations in Peru and Bolivia, which supply most of the coca leaves needed by Colombia cocaine manufacturers. In many cases, however, peasant farmers do not actually receive currency at all, but instead use the raw drug material for bartering for food and clothing.

The Transporters

After the raw materials are collected, they are transported from their point of origin to a preliminary area of manufacturing (usually in a nearby country).

The Chemists Laboratory Operators

In the case of cocaine and heroin, raw material must be converted to hydrochloride form (powder) before it can be sold as a finished product. The conversion processes differ with each drug, but each requires a specific type of expertise. When considering profit margin, the chemists are the highest paid players yet in the trafficking chain.

The Distributors (Smugglers)

It should be noted that with each type of illicit drug, there are smugglers operating on behalf of not only the source country, but also the receiving country (frequently the United States). Smugglers operate as couriers for the manufacturers and may use aircraft, ground vehicles, or ocean-going vessels (see Chapter 7). Smugglers are usually well-compensated for their efforts, and take a considerable risk of being arrested or hijacked (ripped-off).

The Specialists

Throughout every large-scale drug transaction there are professionals operating within both the legitimate and illegitimate business community; however, all act on behalf of the illegal drug enterprise. Among the business professionals are attorneys, bankers, real estate brokers, electronics specialists, corrupt police officers and judges, and various ground crews. Depending on the individual's task, the specialist may be one of the highest paid actors within the operation.

It should be noted that the actors listed above will not only operate within the source country, they will also have counterparts operating within the destination country who provide many similar services to the traffickers. In addition, many domestic drug production operations (such as PCP and methamphetamine laboratories and marijuana cultivators) commonly work within a similar infrastructure, but with fewer players and levels.

The Financial Anatomy of Cocaine

A 1988 article on the front page of a major midwest newspaper read:

> A deputy on routine patrol yesterday afternoon noticed an old army ammunition box sitting alongside the road which turned out to contain 13 ounces of 80% cocaine. The 13 neatly wrapped baggies were estimated to have a street value of $100,000, according to a statement made by the county sheriff.

As indicated above, many people make up the trafficking mechanisms of a drug operation (see Fig. 4–17). These players help to determine the cost of the drug in its various quantities. Understanding how prices are determined will aid the unit in estimating the street price of a drug. Many factors affect the prices of illicit drugs, including: the type of drug, its purity (10%, 90%, etc.), its quantity (grams, ounces, pounds, kilos, etc.), and the region where it is sold (East coast, West coast, southwest, etc.).

In the above newspaper excerpt, the $100,000 figure is too high *if* the drug is estimated by sales of ounce quantities. If, however, the drug's street worth is estimated according to sales of gram quantities, the $100,000 figure is a more realistic estimate (see Chapter 10).

As in legitimate industry, commodities purchased in bulk or large quantities will usually provide the purchaser with more product at a cheaper price. Conversely, the smaller the quantity purchased, the higher the price and the lower the quality of the product. To further complicate matters, the prices of illicit drugs vary geographically. For instance, there is a broad diversity between the price of a kilo of cocaine purchased in New York City or Miami and the same kilo purchased in Kansas City or Minneapolis. In this case the kilo may also be purer in quality when purchased at a coastal port of entry, as opposed to one which must travel to the midwest, and which might be cut (diluted) before being sold on the street.

To best illustrate the enormous profit margin generated by the illicit drug business, a hypothetical breakdown of a single kilo of cocaine is shown below:

1. 1 KILO (2.2 lbs)
   Street price: $15,000 – $20,000
   Average purity: 70 – 90%
   If sold in kilo lots and diluted one time, the dealer would then have two kilos (4.4 lbs) at half the purity, selling for a total of $30,000 – $40,000 (approx. $20,000 profit).
   This process continues each time the kilo is diluted, but the overall price of the kilo might remain the same as when originally purchased.

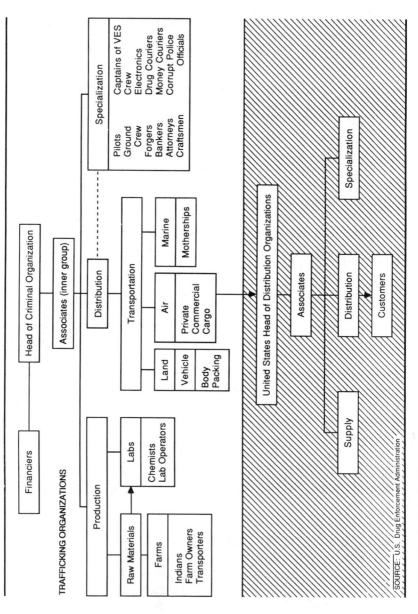

4-17 Typical Colombian cocaine organization.

2. 1 POUND (16 ounces)
   Street price: $8,000 – $11,000
   Average purity: 70 – 80%
   Sold in one pound quantities and cut once, each pound would
   average 30 – 40% purity and would probably sell for the same
   price as the original quantity. As the diluting process continues,
   the pounds multiply and the dealer doubles, triples, and even
   quadruples his original investment.
3. 1 OUNCE (28 gm)
   Street price: $1,200 – $1,800
   Average purity: 40 – 50%
   Each ounce would sell for approximately $1,200 × 16 oz. =
   $19,200. This amount is then doubled to account for the original
   kilo quantity, which would mean a return of $38,400. If one
   calculates the diluting of the cocaine by one, two, or three times,
   the profit figure (if sold in street quantities) could reach $115,200
   from an initial investment of $15,000.
(Note: These figures are extremely conservative. The smaller the
quantities sold the higher the expected profit margin, but also the
higher the dealer's risk of detection.)

Summary

The illicit drug business is an ever-changing one with players on all
levels demonstrating intelligence and creativity. In addition, the
traffickers themselves have resources that exceed those of law enforcement because greater revenues provide greater resources. These
resources often result in new drugs being developed, and new
methods of packaging and distribution (Table 4 – 8). We see this, for
example, in the development of crack and designer drugs, which
have an increased potency and smaller price tag for the consumer.

Marijuana is still the number-one abused drug in the United States,
with cocaine a close second. Drugs such as heroin and PCP prevail
mostly in inner city areas where addiction and crime rates remain
consistently high; for the most part, they are not as widely used as
marijuana or cocaine. Other popular drugs of abuse include LSD,
methamphetamine (which are clandestinely manufactured), as well
as an array of pharmaceutical drugs (usually in the narcotic and
depressant category) such as Dilaudid, Demerol, and Valium, which
are widely diverted from their legal channels of distribution.

A drug's street price may be a direct reflection on its availability,
potency, and source of distribution and manufacture. Police officials

Table 4-8 Controlled Substances; Uses and Effects

Name	Slang name	Chemical or trade name	Source	Classification	Medical use	How taken
Heroin	H., Horse, Scat, Junk, Smack, Scag, Stuff	Diacetyl-morphine	Semi-synthetic (from morphine)	Narcotic	Pain relief	Injected or sniffed
Morphine	White stuff, M.	Morphine sulphate	Natural (from opium)	Narcotic	Pain relief	Swallowed or injected
Codeine	Schoolboy	Methyl-morphine	Natural (from opium), semi-synthetic (from morphine)	Narcotic	Ease pain and coughing	Swallowed
Methadone	Dolly	Dolophine, Amidone	Synthetic	Narcotic	Pain relief	Swallowed or injected
Cocaine/Crack	Corrine, Gold dust, Coke, Bernice, Flake, Star dust, Snow	Methylester of benzoyleogonine	Natural (from coca, NOT cacao)	Stimulant, local anesthesia	Local anesthesia	Sniffed, injected, or swallowed
Marijuana	Pot, Grass, Hashish, Tea, Gage, Reefers	Cannabis sativa	Natural	Relaxant, euphoriant; in high doses, hallucinogen	None in U.S.	Smoked, swallowed, or sniffed
Barbiturates	Barbs, Blue devils, Candy, Yellow jackets, Phennies, Peanuts, Blue heavens	Phenobarbital, Nembutal, Seconal Amytal	Synthetic	Sedative-hypnotic	Sedation, relief of high blood pressure, hyper-thyroidism	Swallowed or injected
Amphetamines	Bennies, Dexies, Speed, Wake-ups, Lid poppers, Hearts, Pep pills	Benzedrine, Dexedrine, Desoxyn, Methadrine, Methamphetamine	Synthetic	Sympatho-mimetic	Relief of mild depression, control of appetite and narcolepsy	Swallowed or injected
LSD	Acid, Sugar, Big D, Cubes, Trips	D-lysergic Acid diethylamide	Semi-synthetic (from ergot alkaloids)	Hallucinogen	Experimental study of mental function, alcoholism	Swallowed
DMT	AMT, Businessman's high	Dimethyl-triptamine	Synthetic	Hallucinogen	None	Injected
Mescaline	Mesc.	3,4,5-trimethoxyphen-ethylamine	Natural (from peyote)	Hallucinogen	None	Swallowed
Psilocybin		3(2-dimethylamino) ethylindol-4-oldihydrogen phosphate	Natural (from psilo-cybe)	Hallucinogen	None	Swallowed
Alcohol	Booze, Juice, etc.	Ethanol, Ethyl-alcohol	Natural (from grapes, grains, etc., via fermentation)	Sedative-hypnotic	Solvent, antiseptic	Swallowed
Tobacco	Fag, Coffin nail, etc.	Nicotiana tabacum	Natural	Stimulant-sedative	Sedative, emetic (nicotine)	Smoked, sniffed, or chewed

? Question marks indicate conflict of opinion. Illicit drugs are frequently adulterated and thus pose unknown hazards to the user.
Source: U.S. Drug Enforcement Administration

Table 4-8 (continued)

Name	Usual dose	Duration of effect	Effects sought	Long-term symptoms	Physical dependance potential	Mental dependance potential	Organic damage potential
Heroin	Varies	4 hr	Euphoria, prevent withdrawal discomfort	Addiction, constipation, loss of appetite	Yes	Yes	No*
Morphine	15 milligrams	6 hr	Euphoria, prevent withdrawal discomfort	Addiction, constipation, loss of appetite	Yes	Yes	No*
Codeine	30 milligrams	4 hr	Euphoria, prevent withdrawal discomfort	Addiction, constipation, loss of appetite	Yes	Yes	No
Methadone	10 milligrams	4 - 6 hr	Prevent withdrawal discomfort	Addiction, constipation, loss of appetite	Yes	Yes	No
Cocaine/ Crack	Varies	Varied, brief periods	Excitation, talkativeness	Depression, convulsions	No	Yes	Yes?
Marijuana	1 - 2 cigarettes	4 hr	Relaxation, increased euphoria, perceptions, sociability	Usually none	No	Yes?	No
Barbiturates	50 - 100 milligrams	4 hr	Anxiety reduction, euphoria	Addiction with severe withdrawal symptoms, possible convulsions, toxic psychosis	Yes	Yes	Yes
Amphetamines	2.5 - 5 milligrams	4 hr	Alertness, activeness	Loss of appetite, delusions, hallucinations, toxic psychosis	No?	Yes	Yes?
LSD	100 - 500 micrograms	10 hr	Insightful experiences, exhilaration, distortion of senses	May intensify existing psychosis, panic reactions	No	No?	No?
DMT	1 - 3 milligrams	<1 hr	Insightful experiences, exhilaration, distortion of senses	?	No	No?	No?
Mescaline	350 micrograms	12 hr	Insightful experiences, exhilaration, distortion of senses	?	No	No?	No?
Psilocybin	25 milligrams	6 - 8 hr	Insightful experiences, exhilaration, distortion of senses	?	No	No?	No?
Alcohol	Varies	1 - 4 hr	Sense alteration, anxiety reduction, sociability	Cirrhosis, toxic psychosis, neurologic damage, addiction	Yes	Yes	Yes
Tobacco	Varies	Varies	Calmness, sociability	Emphysema, lung cancer, mouth and throat cancer, cardiovascular damage, loss of appetite	Yes?	Yes	Yes

* Persons who inject drugs under nonsterile conditions run a high risk of contracting AIDS, hepatitis, abscesses, or circulatory disorders.

are, therefore, faced with a daily challenge to educate themselves regarding all aspects of the different drugs, their prices, and street names in order to better understand and control the problems associated with illicit drugs.

Suggested Readings

Grabowski, John Ph.D. (editor), *Cocaine: Pharmacology, Effects, and Treatment of Abuse.* National Institute on Drug Abuse, NIDA Research Monograph 50, 1984.

National Narcotics Intelligence Consumers Committee (NNICC), *The NNICC Report 1985–1986, The Supply of Illicit Drugs to the United States from Foreign Sources in 1985 and 1986.* June 1987.

O'Brien, Robert, *The Encyclopedia of Drug Abuse.* New York: Facts on File, 1984.

Spotts, James V. Ph.D., *Use and Abuse of Amphetamines and Its Substitutes.* National Institute on Drug Abuse, Research Issues 25, 1978.

Weil, Andrew, *Chocolate To Morphine.* Boston: Houghton Miflin Company, 1983.

Managing Informants

5

Few investigative tools offer as much value to the criminal investigator as the informant. Historically, it is the hard-to-get information rendered by these civilians that has resulted in the successful conclusion of many major cases. The term "informant" refers to many individuals in the community who offer information to the police for any number of reasons. A high percentage of law violators are likely candidates as informers because of their close proximity to crime; with proper handling — which must include accurately identifying their motives — quality criminal cases can frequently be made. Informants may also be respected members of the community who have become aware of criminal activity and who desire to help the police out of a sense of civic duty.

This chapter will address the handling of informants by officers, how to identify informant motives, and how to properly manage different informant – officer relationships. Although there are many types of informants, the United States Drug Enforcement Administration (DEA) offers the following definition: any nonlaw enforcement person who, by reason of his familiarity or close association with criminals, supplies regular or constant information about criminal activities to a police officer. (From *Narcotic Investigator's Manual*, DEA, 1978).

Types of Informants

To begin, there are three general classifications of informants, which should be recognized for better understanding of informant management. They are:

Occasional informants: This informant is one who is used by officers over long periods of time, and who offers information sporadically. This individual participates only when he or she wants to, and will not testify in cases. Occasional informants are often cultivated as a result of becoming acquainted with an officer through a variety of situations. The reliability of this individual is questionable, and the information rendered will usually have to be verified by investigators.

Regular informants: Generally considered a productive informant, the regular informant works frequently with officers over a period of time. This individual is usually considered a reliable source of information who has provided past information that resulted in arrests and convictions. The regular informant's motives vary, but because of the long-established relationship with law enforcement, his or her information is usually reliable.

Arrested informants: The "hammered" informant cooperates with police to escape prosecution for a crime with which he or she has been charged. This individual is usually available for one particular investigation and seldom returns. It is common for the arrested informant to testify against others in exchange for a dismissal or reduction of criminal charges.

Informants can be extremely beneficial during an investigation and their usefulness may outweigh any displeasures the officer may experience when working with them. The principal purposes for using informants are:

- To gain first-hand knowledge of the price and type of drugs on the street, who is dealing, and where is drug dealing taking place;
- To furnish information from sources not readily available to the officer;
- To make covert observations in localities where strangers would be suspected; and
- To conduct undercover negotiations with suspects.

Before considering the proper procedure for interviewing a prospective informant, the specific motives for their involvement should first be identified. This is the first responsibility of the investigator: an informant's motives could weigh heavily against the officer's safety or the credibility of the investigation. Reasons for an individual becoming involved with the police as an informer are offset by their reasons for not wishing to associate with law enforcement. A few of these reasons are dislike by the public; a loss of respect from associates; fear of retribution from other suspects; a loss of self-respect; or a feeling that involvement is not worthwhile.

Psychological Motivations of Informants

As mentioned, the reasons people desire to deal with law enforcement will vary, but in order to avoid any problems in an investigation, the informant's motives should be identified (see Fig. 5-1).

CITY POLICE DEPARTMENT
HISTORY SHEET

Case #_____   Case File No. _____
Soc. Sec. #_____   Date _____
Driver Lic. #_____ Time_____

Name_____A.K.A._____Marital Status _____
Maiden Name _____Former Married Names _____
Address _____Previous Address _____
Telephone _____Lives With _____How long _____
City & State of Birth_____Date of Birth _____Sex _____
Race _____Height _____Weight _____
Scars or Marks_____Glasses.......Yes _____No _____
Drug Used_____Armed: Yes _____No _____Facial Hair _____
Education (years) Elementary_____High School _____College _____Vo. Tech _____
Location of Schools_____
Wife (Maiden Name)_____Address _____

Husband_____Address _____

Father_____Address _____

Mother_____Address _____

Children (Names and Ages) _____

Brothers and Sisters_____

Employed_____ Address _____

Occupation _____Draft Registration No. _____

Military Service Yes_____No _____Branch _____Serial No. _____

Prior Drug Treatment Yes _____No _____Dates (years) _____

Prior Arrest   Place of Incarceration   Dates

Associates_____

Questioned by_____

Place of Interview_____Arresting officers _____

Signed Statement of Rights and Waiver   Yes _____ No _____

5-1 Personal History Sheet

The Fear Motivation

Because the risks are so great and trust is so scarce in the drug trade, potential informers will occasionally assist in investigations out of fear. This may manifest itself in many different ways. As mentioned, an arrested informant may participate because of his or her fear of punishment for a crime. This is generally considered a good "control" motivation for an informant because if he or she fails to perform properly for the officer, the original charges can be filed and the reluctant informant can be prosecuted.

Fear may also stem from a person's fear of retribution from associates who might be at odds with the informer. In this case, a informant's desire to protect his or her own well-being and that of family or friends would also be a strong motivator and could produce good-quality information.

The Revenge Motivation

Although a somewhat questionable motive, the informant who seeks revenge may prove to be well worth the agent's time and effort. The revenge motive may stem from a sour drug deal, anger toward associates who have reneged on drug transactions, profit-sharing disagreements, or other events. Sometimes noncriminal acts will motivate the informer: jealously toward associates, or over disputes involving girlfriends, boyfriends, or spouses.

Officers must identify this motive early in the investigation. The informant might resort to entrapment to achieve his or her goal, or perhaps "heal the breach" with the target of the investigation later on and refuse to continue working with the officer.

The Perverse Motivation

The definition of perverse is "to turn away from what is right." When dealing with an informant with a perverse motivation, the informer has selfish motives other than what have been acknowledged to the officer. For example, the informant may approach police with seemingly good information, when he or she is merely trying to observe the appearance of other undercover officers working in the unit. This is a dangerous motive; because the informant is not trustworthy, his or her true motivation must be detected by officers as soon as possible.

The Mercenary Motivation

A mercenary informant is one who works for the police for financial gain. This individual is not facing criminal charges and may or may not be considered a criminal, but because of his or her personal lifestyle, the informant is in a position to be acquainted with violators. The informant may prove to be extremely effective, but he or she may also become a source of aggravation for the control officer. It is common for the mercenary informant to always want more than he or she is getting. It is also common for a mercenary informant to have another motive (such as revenge or fear) while working with the police.

The Repentance Motivation

This informer desires to repay society for wrongs committed in the past. Although considered a fairly rare motive, it could also be a productive one. However, informers in this class have a tendency to return to criminal behavior after becoming involved as an informant in an investigation.

The Egotistical Motive

An egotistical informer is one who enjoys associating with police officers and is intrigued by police work. As in the case of the mercenary informer, he or she may not be personally involved with criminal activity, but may attempt to infiltrate the criminal element for police. Sometimes this individual can be very productive and ask little of control officers, thereby making this motivation a good one for investigators. Caution should be observed, however, because the egotistical informer is not "hammered," and therefore control may be minimized.

The Unwitting Informant

The unwitting informant is probably the most useful and productive of all. Basically, the unwitting informant is an individual whom the undercover agent befriends during the course of an investigation. The informant, of course, does not realize that the undercover officer is a law enforcement officer; because of this, he or she is willing to provide information and make introductions to other criminal suspects.

Great care must be practiced when working with an unwitting informant. Because he or she is usually in the presence of the undercover officer regularly, suspicions may eventually be aroused if the informant notices that the officer never engages in criminal activity. This can sometimes be remedied by staging a fake drug deal between two undercover officers for the informant's "benefit."

Informant Interviews

The initial interview of the potential informant is critical. It will identify the informant's motives and help the officer determine whether or not the individual is suitable for a professional working relationship. When dealing with informants, the key word is "control": many of them possess strong personalities and may tend to dominate the initial conversation. Once it is determined that a subject should be interviewed, the following basic guidelines should be adhered to:

1. Do not rush the interview, but try to keep the conversation from wandering; be subtle when pressing for details.
2. Sympathize with the informant on any problems he or she may be experiencing; try to build a rapport.
3. Show appreciation for any information rendered, in particular information that is of value.
4. Never belittle seemingly worthless information.
5. Do not try to show the informant how his or her information differs from that from other sources.
6. Take notes or document the conversation as soon as possible.
7. To verify the informant's information or truthfulness, ask about information you already know.
8. Constantly attempt to identify any motives that are causing the informant to render information.
9. Avoid questions that might embarrass the informant.
10. Avoid unnecessary prying into the informant's private affairs.
11. Avoid arguments with the informant.
12. Always keep control of the interview.
13. If two officers are involved in the interview, one should do the talking and the other should take notes.

Great caution should be exercised when working with informants. Officers should be careful not to give out too much personal information: this could result in reducing the effectiveness of the officer's control over the informant or even compromising the safety of the officer and the investigation. In addition, officers should be certain the informant understands that any criminal activity on his or her part will not be tolerated and may result in prosecution. This should not only include violations of criminal law, but also lesser infractions such as traffic violations and public intoxication.

Many informants are deeply involved in a criminal lifestyle, and this will be reflected in their personal morals and ethics. Control officers must be conscious of this and take care not to adopt a similar lifestyle for the sake of cover. For example, many informers are prostitutes who may also be dancers in topless nightclubs. To these individuals, sexuality is business and they may attempt to seduce a male officer in order to exert more control over him during the investigation. This predicament will jeopardize both the integrity of the officer and the investigation, and it will serve to blacken the reputation of the agency.

Contracting an Informant

After the officer has decided to use the informer, basic understandings must be discussed regarding his or her role and actions while working with the officer.

The Method of Payment

No payments are to be made to an informant unless he or she has first been fingerprinted, photographed, and otherwise properly documented. Payments can be made only on a per diem basis, and only if the informant is providing reliable information or services to the department. The specific amount per diem should be established by the officer's supervisor at the beginning so that any future misunderstandings will be avoided. Any money for relocation of the informant after the investigation is over should first be authorized by the officer's supervisor.

Expenditures of Official Drug Funds

Informants should be advised of the consequences of absconding with money issued to them for drug purchases. Drug purchase money should only be used for the purchase of drugs unless otherwise authorized. When issued drug purchase money, the informant must first sign a receipt for the money. This receipt will set forth the responsibility of the informant while in possession of the money. In particular, if the informant steals the money, he or she will be charged with theft and prosecuted. If this happens, the informant should be declared unreliable and removed from the files as a cooperating individual.

Criminal Activity by the Informant

As mentioned earlier, there must be no misunderstanding regarding the expected behavior of the informant. Informants are not permitted to engage in any type of illegal activity, either when with the control officer or not in his or her presence. If the informant is arrested for a criminal offense, he or she must be made to know that working with the police will not provide an escape. Sometimes an informant will tell arresting officers that he or she was committing a crime to maintain the cover. Officers who permit this are risking disciplinary action or even termination.

Policy on Drug Purchases

Because there are so many different types of drug purchases and the circumstances surrounding them are so variable, common policy should be established and understood regarding the informant's role in each of them.

Inside Buys

Drug buys are generally safer if conducted on the street or in a suitably wired undercover apartment. If circumstances require the drug buy to take place in the suspect's residence, an officer should be present to corroborate any activity or statements made by criminal suspects. When informants participate in undercover drug transactions they should always be equipped with a concealed transmitter so surveillance officers can monitor and record the conversation for evidence (see Chapter 2).

Multiple Buys

It is good practice to make more than one drug purchase from a single suspect. Multiple buys help demonstrate that the dealer was in business and that criminal intent existed for the transaction, and could protect the officer against the suspect's use of the defense of entrapment. Multiple buys also help identify or meet the dealer's source of supply (see Chapter 3).

Controlled Buys (Informant Buys)

Although useful in some circumstances, the controlled buy should be avoided whenever possible. In this type of buy, informants usually make direct contact with the dealer and the informant's testimony is subsequently required. Problems also arise when the informant later decides he or she does not want to testify and the case is therefore lost (see section on Controlled Buys in this chapter).

Mutual Agreements and Understandings

Other details of undercover contacts must be worked out before the informant is placed into service.

The Cover Story

As described in Chapter 2, a cover story is crucial to the success of the undercover investigation. Informants may be allowed to suggest a cover story, but the officer should ultimately decide on the details. Both the informant and the undercover officer should be comfortable with the cover story.

Method of Introduction

The way that the informant introduces the agent to the suspect should be discussed before the undercover contact. In some cases the informant might wish to converse with the suspect for a few moments before the introduction, sometimes not. In either case, the method should be discussed in advance in order to avoid confusion and misunderstanding.

Negotiating Amounts

It is a good practice for the informant not to be told in advance what he or she is supposed to buy or how much. Again, entrapment by the informer may be avoided; he or she may simply be out to set up a rival dealer or some other enemy. What drugs to buy and when to buy them should only be established just prior to the transaction. If an earlier meeting is required, officers should record the contact for verification of its legitimacy. Before each drug buy, the informant should be required to phone the suspect (if a phone is available) to reconfirm the drugs to be purchased, the amount, and the quality.

Time of Day

Daylight hours are usually the best time to attempt a drug purchase. Surveillance officers are better able to notice license tags, addresses, and physical descriptions of associates. In addition, surveillance officers can more readily be hidden in traffic to better cover the informant or undercover officer.

Informant Payments

From the outset of the relationship it should be determined how the informant will receive compensation (if any) and what is required to receive it. It is better to pay informants on a per diem basis rather than case by case. Informants also tend to request additional funds for extras such as the telephone bill, auto repairs, or groceries in addition to the agreed-upon payments for services rendered.

Use of Female Informants

Policy should be established regarding the handling of female informants. When male officers are involved, interviews of female informants should only be conducted when at least two officers are present. This will minimize any spurious complaints, which could possibly be lodged against the officers later. Female informants should be searched by female officers to ensure that the informant is not armed. A female informant may prove to be as dangerous to the officer as a male informant; their aggressiveness should not be underestimated (see Chapter 3).

Manipulation of Funds

It is possible that informants might advise the officer that a particular drug sells for a specific price, when in reality it sells for less. In this case, the informant may attempt to "skim" the extra money without the officer's knowledge. If this or any other illegal or unethical manipulation of funds occurs, the informant should be declared unreliable and should not be considered for any future use. Moreover, if there is sufficient evidence, the informant should be charged with theft, embezzlement, or any other appropriate criminal charge.

Statement of Officer–Informant Relationship

An officer must always remain in control of the officer–informant relationship. For this reason, the officer must be careful not to become too friendly; inadvertently revealing personal information about spouse or children may later reduce the officer's effectiveness or control. Moreover, such information may possibly be revealed during the suspect's trial and cause embarrassment for the officer and the agency.

Informant Statements

Once an informant has been approved for use, a cooperating individual (C-I) agreement should be signed and kept on file (Fig. 5–2). This agreement states the conditions under which the informant will continue working with the police. There have been cases in which informants have sued law enforcement agencies for workmen's compensation claims because they considered themselves as employees of the city, county, or state. The C-I agreement, if properly worded, will eliminate such a claim.

After each undercover contact, the informant should provide the officer with a written statement of what occurred, what was said, and what was observed. The informant should sign only the original copy of the statement, which should then be placed in the informant's file; unsigned copies should be placed in the case file for later use in court. In the event the informant is compelled to testify, the

CITY POLICE DEPARTMENT
COOPERATING INDIVIDUAL AGREEMENT

I, _____, the undersigned, state that it is my intent to associate myself, of my own free will and without any coercion or duress, with the City Police Department as a cooperating individual.

As a cooperating individual, I understand and agree that I have no police powers under the laws of the state of (____) and have no authority to carry a weapon while performing my activity as a cooperating individual. Further, I understand and agree that my only association with the the city of (____) is as a cooperating individual on a case-by-case or time-to-time basis as an independent contractor, and not as an employee of the police department. Any payment I receive from the City Police Department will not be subject to federal or state income tax withholding or social security. I understand that it is my responsibility to report any income and also that I am not entitled to either workmen's compensation or unemployment insurance payments for anything I do as a cooperating individual.

In consideration for being allowed to associate with the City Police Department as a cooperating individual, and in consideration for any payment I may receive, I agree to be bound by the following terms and conditions and procedures while so associated.

1. I agree that under no circumstances will I purchase or possess any controlled substances or suspected controlled substances without the direction and control of a police officer and then will make a purchase only with monies supplied by him.

2. I agree not to use or sell, dispense, or transfer any controlled substance except that I may use any controlled substance prescribed to me by a licenced physician.

3. I agree to maintain a strict accounting of all funds provided to me by the City Police Department and I understand that misuse of city funds could be grounds for criminal prosecution against me.

4. I agree not to divulge to any person, except the officer with whom I am associated, my status as a cooperating individual for the City Police Department unless required to do so in court, and shall not represent myself to others as an employee or representative of the City Police Department nor use the department or any of its officers as personal references or as credit or employment references.

5. I understand that any violation of the above listed provisions may be grounds for my immediate removal as a cooperating individual and that any violation of law may result in my arrest and prosecution.

   I understand that association with the City Police Department as cooperating individual may involve strenuous physical activity and may become hazardous to my physical well-being and safety. Nevertheless, it is my desire to associate myself with the department, on an independant contractor basis, as a cooperating individual. I am associating myself with the department in this status freely and without any coercion or duress. In consideration for being accepted as a cooperating individual, I release and discharge the City of (____), the City Police Department and its elected officials, officers, employees, and agents from all claims, demands, actions, judgements, and executions which I may have or acquire and subsequently claim to have against the City for personal injuries and property damage I sustain which arises out of or in connection with my association with the city. I make this release for myself, my heirs, executors, and administrators. Also, I agree not to maintain any action against the City of (____), the City Police Department, or its elected officials, officers, employees, or agents for personal injuries and property damage I sustain which arise out of or in connection with my association with the City Police Department.

_____
Cooperating Individual

_____
Date

WITNESSES:

_____
Officer

_____
Officer

5-2 A cooperating Individual Agreement should always be signed by the CI to avoid problems of informants claiming unemployment and workman's compensation benefits.

original statement will be used as evidence along with his or her testimony.

Protection of Informant Identity

The U.S. Supreme Court has recognized the importance of confidentiality with regard to an informant's identity. An informant's identity should not be disclosed unless absolutely necessary, and then only to the proper parties. Generally speaking, an informant's identity should not be disclosed if it would create an immediate danger to the informer or cut off a reliable source of information. The general rule regarding the protection of an informant's identity was decided in *Wilson v. United States*:

> It is the right and the duty of every citizen of the United States to communicate with executive officers of government charged with the duty of enforcing the laws all the information which he or she has of the commission of an offense against the laws of the United States, and such information is privileged as a confidential communication which the courts will not compel or permit to be disclosed without the consent of the government. Such evidence is excluded, not for the protection of the witness but for the policy of the law . . . however, a trial court must dispose of a case before it. If what is asked is essential evidence to vindicate the innocence of the accused or lessen the risk of false testimony, or is essential to the proper disposition of the case, disclosure will be compelled.

Generally, there are three possible consequences of an officer's refusal to disclose an informant's identity: (a) the court may uphold the officer if there is no harm to the defendant; (b) the court may dismiss the charge against the defendant; or (c) the court may find the officer in contempt of court and have him arrested (see section on The Informant in the Courtroom, below).

The following general guidelines should be observed by all agents to ensure effective management of informants and to ensure officer safety:

Every attempt should be made to keep track of the informant's independent activities.

All informant contacts should be made with consideration for optimum officer safety.

Informants should not be paid until information has been evaluated.

All informant information should be verified when possible.

Prior to any undercover contact, the name of the informant and the location of the contact should be relayed to the police supervisor.

A receipt for informant payments should be acquired when all payments are made.

The Cooperating Individual (C-I) Agreement

The C-I agreement is a necessary ingredient in the informant management process and should be considered by all drug enforcement personnel. Basically, it works like a big league contract: no play, no pay! Good faith efforts don't count in the world of working informants. The only way law enforcement officers can justify to the public for giving an arrested informant a break is to trade charges against him or her for charges against a larger violator. Therefore, the C-I agreement spells out the expectations of the C-I, which include: 1) the objectives (persons to be investigated, type of drugs to be purchased, etc.) and 2) the methods to be used (controlled buys, tape recorded telephone calls, C-I testimony, etc.). Also included are other agreements which release the law enforcement agency from liability in the event of the informant being hurt on duty or even claiming Workman's Compensation or unemployment benefits.

The C-I should be told exactly what he or she will receive if the terms of the agreement are fulfilled and a prosecutable case is furnished. This could be a letter to the sentencing judge, a reduction of charges, relocation of the C-I, etc.

Cooperating conditions may include:

1. The defendant understands that only *results* will help him or her and not simply good faith efforts.
2. The defendant must be truthful and submit to a polygraph examination or urine analysis upon demand.
3. The defendant may be released from his or her obligations whenever they wish. In this case the state will not be bound to their part of the agreement and there will be no retribution against the C-I unless they jeopardize the subsequent investigation.

Special Informant Problems

The Informant with Cold Feet

Occasionally officers will develop an informant, and shortly after they begin working the informant will have second thoughts about the arrangement. This sometimes happens because of fear of retribution from fellow drug dealers. In such cases it is usually best to release the informant (after explaining that the original "deal" is now off). There are three good reasons for officers not to work with informers with cold feet:

1. Frightened informers are seldom productive.
2. Frightened informers may place the undercover agent in danger-ous circumstances by acting nervous or by panicking during drug transactions.
3. Informers may be fearful of participation because of the danger involved, and an informer should have the option not to work.

The Informant and the Target's Right to Counsel

There are occasions when police might wish to use an informer to learn more about a particular prisoner, or after arresting several individuals, place a wire on one of them to learn the defense strate-gies the others might use. It should be remembered that any time a suspect is either in custody or has a case pending against him or her, the target's right to counsel might become an issue. The rules vary from state to state, but the following points generally should be considered:

1. Generally, once a defendant has asked for an attorney, officers cannot use an informant to try to gain information. The infor-mant would be acting on the part of the police, and thereby would be a "police agent." Once the suspect has been read the Miranda Rights and has signed a statement of rights and waiver, however, he or she is fair game for a police informant.
2. The above does not apply, however, in the case of an inmate who approaches the informant with information.
3. Once a defendant has been indicted or charged, the right to coun-sel is "attached." Basically this means that police cannot attempt to get information from the suspect (on the case which he or she is charged) through an informant. This applies even in the case in which the informant is a co-defendant.
4. These requirements do not necessarily prevent police officers from using an informant to obtain information from the suspect on *other* crimes. If the suspect is planning to murder a witness, the informant has a free hand in attempting to obtain as much information on that particular crime as possible.

The Informant in the Courtroom

Investigators should know in advance whether or not the informant will be needed to testify in the case. The best time to prepare for this is while the case is being prepared and not after the arrests have been made. To reduce the likelihood of testimony being required of the informant:

1. Officers should corroborate as much of the informant's testimony as possible with the use of tape recordings, surveillance, and other physical evidence.
2. After each contact with the suspect, a statement should be taken from the informant either in longhand or by a tape recorder for later transcription. Informers, like policemen, must have a means to refresh their memory in the event the case does end up in court. It is usually not satisfactory for the informant to rely on the officer's report, as it could be charged that they are merely memorizing details from the officer's report. In addition, an informant report will lock them into testimony if they later choose not to cooperate in the case or to lie on the witness stand.
3. All monies paid to the informant should be carefully documented in case disclosure is required of the prosecution. Defense attorneys may attempt to show that the informant was paid an enormous amount to "entrap" the defendant. Adequate records, and a proper method of payment will invalidate this defense.

The Controlled Drug Purchase

Frequently, undercover police officers are unsuccessful in infiltrating trafficking organizations, and they must consider other means of penetration. In such cases, police should consider using informants who are already accepted and known by the suspects. To be sure, it is always better for an informant to be used to introduce an undercover agent to the suspects as a trusted friend rather than risk sending the informant undercover to the suspects alone: there is greater informant control and the case will be strengthened by the officer's first-hand testimony. This, however, is not always possible.

If an informant is the only one who can meet and negotiate drug transactions with a suspect, the informant's services can be used in two ways: (a) by making undercover drug purchases for the purpose of later charging the dealer with drug dealing; or (b) by making undercover drug purchases for the purpose of obtaining probable cause for a search warrant of the suspect's residence. Both strategies have distinct advantages and disadvantages. If the drug purchase results in the later arrest of the suspect, the informant will probably have to testify (along with the informant's control officer and any surveillance officers). The defense strategy in this scenario is to attack the credibility of the informant:

Is the informant's testimony truthful?

Does the informant have a motive that would cause him or her to lie?

Does the informant have a history of criminal involvement?

Does the informant now or has he or she ever used drugs?

Has the informant ever been convicted of a criminal offense involving drugs or honesty?

If the answer is "yes" to any of these questions, the defense counsel may have an improved basis for defense of the suspect. Because the defense attorney may cross-examine any prosecution witnesses, some of the above information may be revealed for the purpose of discrediting and impeaching the testimony of the informant. The defense counsel's ultimate goal is to establish reasonable doubt in the minds of the jurors and to therefore seek an acquittal.

If the informant is proven, reliable, and comfortable on the witness stand, then he or she might be successfully used for multiple drug buys. If the informant's reliability is untested, a controlled informant purchase for obtaining probable cause will be more appropriate. In either case, however, a strict procedure for handling the informant must be observed. Following this procedure will ensure that the informant's involvement with the suspect was monitored by case officers in order to minimize possible wrongdoing by the informant. Outlined below is a step-by-step process of conducting a controlled drug purchase.

1. Only use informants who have been established as reliable, either in previous drug purchase operations, or by verifying any information they have rendered.
2. Conduct an in-depth interview with the informant.
    a. Determine his or her knowledge of various drugs in the community, drug prices, drug packaging, and information on drug dealers.
    b. Determine whether or not the informant is using drugs, and if so, what types.
3. A separate statement should be taken from the informant regarding his or her personal knowledge and dealings with the suspect.
    a. What types of drug is the suspect dealing?
    b. In what quantities does the dealer deal?
    c. Is the suspect considered dangerous? (If so, why?)
    d. Does the suspect carry a weapon? (If so, what type?)
    e. Who are the suspect's associates?
    f. Does the suspect live alone or with others?
    g. If employed, where does the suspect work?
    h. What vehicles are involved? (Get descriptions.)
4. Verify the informant's information.

    a. A comprehensive utility check should be conducted by the informant's control officer to determine others who might be living at the residence.

    b. Complete criminal histories should then be acquired on each suspect. This should include teletypes to other jurisdictions for local criminal history inquiries.

    c. State driver's license information should be acquired. Attention must be given to arrests as well as convictions to help profile the suspect.

5. Record the serial numbers of money used for official drug purchases.

    a. Evidence of serial numbers must be incorporated into the case report and used as evidence in the case.

    b. Official funds might later be seized at the suspect's residence as a result of a search warrant. if so, such funds are to be used as evidence in the case.

6. Strip-search the informant.

    a. This must be conducted just prior to the drug buy and should be thorough enough that the officer can later testify that the informant had no illicit drugs concealed on his or her person prior to meeting with the suspect.

    b. If a body cavity search is required, trained medical personnel should be used, not officers (see Chapter 3).

    c. Medical personnel or officers of the same sex must be used to conduct body searches.

7. Equip the informant with a recording device.

    a. A concealed transmitter should be placed on the informant to allow surveillance officers the opportunity to monitor conversations between the informant and the suspect and to record the conversations for evidence.

    b. If a transmitter is unavailable, a small tape recorder should be considered. This is a less satisfactory method because officers cannot monitor the conversation, but a recorded tape of the contact will be available as evidence.

8. Search the informant's vehicle.

    a. The vehicle used by the informant should also be searched by officers for drugs or money.

    b. Once the informant and/or the vehicle is searched, neither should be left unattended until after the drug deal is over. This will ensure that both are "clean."

9. Conduct drug buys in populated and open areas where surveillance teams can be easily positioned and which are familiar to them (i.e., a shopping center parking lot, a bus station, a city park, etc.).

    a. Motel locations should be preselected by officers for accessibility and safety.

    b. Do not allow the informant or the suspect to select the location for the drug transaction.

    c. If a particular location is suggested by the suspect, a second (or third) preselected counter-location should be suggested. Never conduct the deal on the suspect's "turf."

10. Conduct close surveillance of the informant.

    a. The informant must be constantly observed from the time of the strip search to the time he or she meets with the suspect.

    b. To help surveillance officers, the informant must be instructed to drive slowly while using proper turning indicators, and to go directly to a predetermined location. If the location changes during the deal, the informant should call off the transaction.

    c. A set period of time must be given to the informant for the transaction. If the transaction is not completed within a given time, the informant must be advised that officers will assume the informant is in trouble and storm the location.

    d. Officers must carefully log all activities of the informant: times, direction of travel, and any pertinent conversation with the suspect.

    e. The informant should be instructed to speak as little as possible, but should instead ask the suspect questions about the transaction (price, quality and quantity of drugs, future drug transactions).

    f. If possible, the actual exchange of drugs for money should be observed and photographed by surveillance officers.

11. After the purchase, the informant must be instructed to proceed to a prearranged location while officers maintain visual contact. The location should not be the police department in case the informer is followed by the suspects.

    a. The drug evidence should be taken from the informant, initialed by both the officers and the informant, and packaged and preserved according to accepted practices of evidence custody.

    b. All drug evidence should be promptly transported to the laboratory to protect chain of custody and for chemical analysis.

    c. A second strip search should then be conducted for money and drugs retained by the informant.

    d. A statement should be taken from the informant. The statement should include any conversation made with the suspect and locations where additional drugs were observed.

12. If a search warrant is to be obtained, it should be acquired as soon as possible after the last drug purchase (see Chapter 3).

    a. It will be necessary for the police laboratory to expedite the testing of the drugs. Special arrangements might have to be made. If this is not realistic, the drugs will have to be field tested by officers in order to establish probable cause.

    b. Surveillance should be maintained on the location of the intended search in order to identify associates or customers entering or leaving the location.

    c. During the search, drugs, paraphernalia, records, weapons, and money should be seized if it can be shown that they pertain to the case.

    d. Vehicles should be seized if they were used to facilitate any drug trafficking activity or if they were acquired by illegally obtained drug money.

Summary

The informant is potentially a valuable investigative resource for drug enforcement officers. The use of informants in drug investigations must be preceded by a thorough understanding of the motivations that underlie their involvement with law enforcement agencies. These motivations may either benefit or hinder investigators in their endeavors.

Procedures for the cultivation and placement of informants must be understood by all investigative personnel. Proper control and management of the informant must be established at the onset of the investigation, and the informant's role should be well defined. If a task can be accomplished by an undercover officer without the aid of an informant, then it should be considered; an uncooperative or unreliable informant may hinder the progress of the case. There are many circumstances, however, in which informants can provide valuable information on persons, places, and organizations operating within the drug trade.

Agency personnel should take care to use informants in a proper and lawful manner. If they have done so, then the information and evidence obtained through informants will be a significant aid in the successful prosecution of drug traffickers.

Surveillance Techniques

6

There are many purposes to police surveillance in an ongoing criminal investigation. It is clear, however, that within a covert unit this function is essential for the successful completion of most investigations. Specifically defined, surveillance is the surreptitious observation of persons, places, objects, or conveyances for the purpose of determining criminal involvement. Generally, there are three types of surveillance effectively used by law enforcement agencies: moving, stationary, and electronic.

Surveillance is usually undertaken to obtain certain objectives: to obtain specific details of persons and places suspected of drug trafficking; to verify informant information; to collect evidence of crimes; to obtain probable cause for search warrants; to apprehend suspects in the commission of crimes; to prevent the commission of crimes; and to locate persons wanted for a crime.

Surveillance is also probably the most time-consuming and tedious task in law enforcement. One key to a successful surveillance operation is good, reliable intelligence. In addition, the surveillance function itself can also provide invaluable intelligence, which might be unobtainable through other sources. Surveillants (officers assigned to make observations) must be creative in their efforts to observe criminal suspects and activity covertly. Ideally, the surveillant's appearance and mannerisms should blend in with the surroundings to remain inconspicuous. He or she must also remain alert to details and be resourceful and patient throughout the operation.

To best prepare for surveillance, officers must first study police files for any information pertaining to the case: the suspect's physical description; names, addresses and physical descriptions of associates; vehicle descriptions; identifying residence and business addresses; and reviewing any other known areas the suspect frequents. Next, appropriate equipment should be made available to each team; 35-mm cameras with telephoto lenses; binoculars; tape recorders for surveillance notes; night viewing devices; and basic items (such as pens, pencils, notepaper for the surveillance log, and change for pay phones).

After basic information is gathered, the target area should be reconnoitered to determine the vehicles and dress that will be appropriate. The team should also note surveillance vantage points (where officers can best observe the area), street names, one-way streets, dead-end streets, and traffic conditions in order to avoid problems during the operation.

Surveillance should not be assigned to one officer working alone: two sets of eyes and ears are better than one, and tedium is better avoided by teams. A team leader or supervisor should also be present during the surveillance to add cohesiveness and direction to the operation. If the surveillance becomes mobile, a system of communication must be established to reduce confusion and to avoid excessive radio traffic. As surveillances are often lengthy, relief officers are necessary. The supervisor must establish procedures to guarantee that each new shift is apprised of any advancements or changes in the case. The briefing should include the identification of new suspects, vehicles, residences, and locations. Depending on the case, different methods will be employed to best document the actions of criminal suspects.

Moving Surveillance

Mobile surveillance is usually much more difficult to manage than one that is stationary. Mobile surveillance can be accomplished by foot, by vehicle, or by a combination of both. The likelihood of officers being noticed by suspects is greater in mobile surveillances, and back-up officers must be available in order to continue the surveillance without raising the suspicions of the suspects.

One-Man Foot Surveillance

One-man foot surveillance may occasionally be necessary, but it is not generally considered the best method. There is personal risk to the officer, and a single officer has more chances of being detected than do multiple officers. When conducting a one-man foot surveillance, an officer should keep the suspect in view at all times, which means that the surveillant must constantly remain close to the suspect. Pedestrian traffic can afford an officer a certain amount of cover; if the officer is observing the suspect from across the street, he or she must generally stay even with the suspect to avoid loosing him or her when entering buildings or turning down streets.

A suspect who notices a surveillance officer can generally lose him or her without much effort. Officers who sense that the suspect is becoming suspicious should pull off and reestablish surveillance later so as not to "burn" the investigation. The surveillant must also be aware of any countersurveillance employed by the suspect. This is becoming more and more common, and it poses not only a threat to the investigation but, more importantly, to the officer's safety. At times an officer may think he or she has been spotted and overreact in an effort to appear "normal." Overreactions, however, may actually draw attention to the surveilling officer.

The ABC Method

The ABC method uses three officers, and it is considered the best technique for foot surveillance. Officers will find their job much easier and safer with two support officers. A greater variation exists when three officers participate in a surveillance. In this case, one officer can have the point (lead) for a period of time and then periodically trade off with the other officers to avoid detection.

Ideally, the point officer (A) maintains visual contact with the suspect while a second officer (B) maintains visual contact with (A). The third officer (C) will usually walk across the street and watch for the countersurveillance. Occasionally, one officer may be positioned in front of the suspect for variation and if pedestrian traffic is too heavy, all three officers may be positioned on the same side of the street.

Generally, when the suspect is observed approaching an intersection, C (who should be across the street) should lead the suspect and reach the intersection first. By pausing at the corner or crossing the street, C can continue visual contact with and through hand signals inform the other officers of the suspect's actions. If the suspect stops, then A should cross the intersection before proceeding in the same direction as the suspect. If the suspect remains stopped, then both A and B may be forced to continue on ahead of the suspect, relying on C officer to maintain visual contact. Officer C will then have to signal when the suspect moves on. Any time the suspect turns a corner gives the officers chance to rotate positions.

The "Leap-Frog" Method

The leap-frog method uses two surveillance officers. It is not considered as successful as the ABC method because of the time involved, but it can be of some value in locating a suspect's hiding place. In leap-frog, one officer follows the suspect while the other officer moves well ahead, usually on the opposite sidewalk. When the suspect passes, the lead officer moves in behind. The leap-frog method works well inside large stores. When used on the street, it might be easier to facilitate if the suspect takes the same route every day. If, however, the suspect follows a different route daily and officers are not very alert, the suspect will most likely get away.

Generally, if the suspect is believed to be aware of the surveillants, the surveillance should be called off and resumed later. If continued surveillance is deemed necessary, the surveillants should watch for the possible following countersurveillance traps set by the suspect.

1. A suspect can view reflections in a store-front window as a rear-view mirror.
2. A suspect may enter a restaurant, observe who enters behind him or her, and then leave abruptly mid-way through a meal.
3. A suspect may drop a worthless piece of paper to see if a suspected officer picks it up.
4. A suspect may drive the wrong way down a one-way street or make an illegal U-turn to see if anyone follows.
5. A suspect may drive down an alleyway to see if any one follows. This could also be a set-up for a hijacking.
6. A suspect may approach the officer directly and accuse him or her of following or being an officer (see Chapter 2).

When foot surveillance officers need to communicate with one another, small radios may be used. If these are too obvious (or too expensive for the department), a system of hand signals should be used. These signals must be clearly understood prior to the surveillance operation to eliminate confusion; for example: Taking off (or putting on) a hat; tying a shoe; turning up one's collar; placing a newspaper under an arm; or throwing away a newspaper.

Combined Vehicle-Foot Surveillance

If only one car is available, surveillance may be conducted by using both foot and vehicular surveillance. In such cases it is a good idea to place two officers in the car and place it behind and to the right of that of the suspect. The distance behind the suspect's vehicle will vary depending on the amount of traffic in the area. In moderately heavy traffic, it is wise to allow one to two vehicles between the surveillance vehicle and the suspect's car: This creates cover for the officer's vehicle, allowing them to see the suspect without being seen themselves. In rural areas, the suspect must be given a considerable lead so as not to attract attention to the officer's vehicle. This should not pose too much of a problem on the highway, but on section line roads or on small town streets, the risk of detection is much greater.

In night surveillance, the officer's vehicle should not have any distinguishing lights (i.e., bright lights or running lights that can be easily recognized). The same is true for burned-out headlights or parking lights, which might be remembered by the suspect after he or she has seen them once (see Chapter 2).

Multiple Vehicle Surveillance

When the two-car method is used, both cars are normally positioned behind the suspect's vehicle. A variation of this method, which works fairly well, is for one car to follow the suspect on a parallel street while the other stays behind the suspect. The parallel vehicle's job is to arrive at intersections just prior to the suspect so the suspect's direction of travel can be noted and conveyed to the others by radio.

Three cars give the surveillance officers still more flexibility by being able to change positions. When three vehicles are available, the "leap-frog" method is sometimes used: Surveillance vehicles are located along a known route. After the suspect's car passes a surveillant's car, the surveillant then proceeds to pass the suspect at high speed, enabling the surveillant to take up a position beyond the other official vehicles. This allows the officers to keep track of a suspect without actually following him or her. This system does not work when the suspect takes a route unknown to the officers.

In Figure 6 – 1 we see that the "set" is the corner of 81st Street and Amsterdam Avenue. This location can be very effectively covered from the roof observation point. The officers at this location can advise other units of any pertinent information. (Never assign only one man to a roof-top surveillance. Always assign at least two; one to make observations and one to watch the other's back.)

The units are situated where visual observation of the establishment (the bar) can be conducted and at the same time, ready themselves for moving surveillance should it become necessary. If it does become necessary, each vehicle is in position to cover (tail) any direction in which the suspects travel, while the other three units arrange themselves so they can aid the point vehicle in perimeter and parallel observation of the suspect. However, if there is no movement of the suspect by automobile, the mobile units remain stationary and allow the observation units to report back any observations.

The observation truck unit (unit #3) should have been parked at least one hour prior to the time of the transaction in order not to

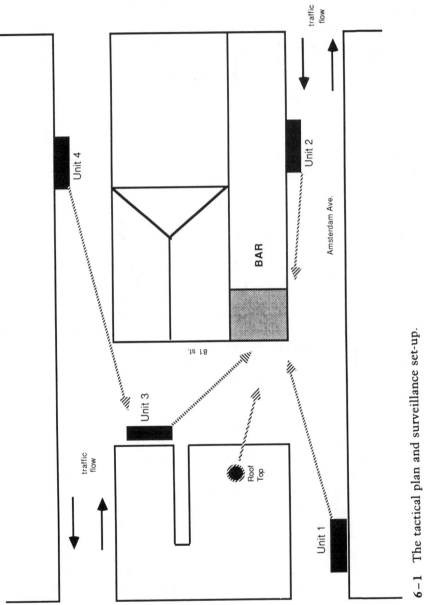

6-1 The tactical plan and surveillance set-up.

arouse suspicions. From the truck, surveillants can watch not only the "set" but they can also attempt to observe the location of the "stash" as well. This unit will be first to arrive on the scene and the last to leave, remaining about an hour after the transaction to observe possible additional suspects and to take photographs of the transaction and the suspects. (The preceding block on the tactical plan was taken, in part, with permission from Vernon Geberth, "Narcotic Buy Operations," Law and Order Magazine, January 1979.)

When surveillance of undercover personnel is anticipated, surveillants must consider several important factors. First, it should be understood that once the undercover officer assumes his or her role in a contact, his or her ability to control the overall safety of the meeting is diminished. Even if the undercover officer is the case agent, he or she will not be able to observe the "big picture." Basically, this means that the undercover officer cannot observe countersurveillance by suspects or new and unforeseen circumstances. These are the province of the support officers conducting the surveillance.

Second, it should be remembered that there are several basic functions of the surveillance officer while assisting the undercover officer. All of these functions are important and should be remembered at all times. These include the following:

To protect the UC officer by monitoring his contacts with suspects

To locate any possible countersurveillance suspects in the area

To accurately log any activity associated with the UC contact, for example: people coming and going, vehicle descriptions, etc.

In addition, the observation of a UC officer may pose other surveillance problems:

Neon signs and large buildings tend to reduce the transmitting range of the body transmitter (RF transmitter)

Officers conducting surveillance in parking lots where transactions are scheduled may be observed by employees of stores or businesses in the area. The local police may be called in this circumstance because of the employee's belief that the officers are would-be burglars or armed robbers.

Stationary Surveillance

Stationary (fixed) surveillance is used when the suspect is expected to come and go from a particular location. This method (a stake-out) is considerably easier: many of the factors contributing to confusion and lack of safety in a moving surveillance are minimized. Sometimes stationary surveillance can be conducted from a specially out-fitted house or apartment. This is also called a "base," and it should be located to afford maximum observation of the target location's entrances and exits.

It is more common, however, for stationary surveillance to be conducted from a vehicle; in some cases, the vehicle may be an undercover vehicle or a special "decoy" vehicle (possibly disguised as a telephone or utility truck). In stationary surveillance conducted from a vehicle, certain factors should be considered:

1. The type of vehicle used must fit in with the area.
2. When conducting surveillance in a residential neighborhood, the vehicle's license tags should be local rather than out-of-state in order to avoid looking suspicious.
3. Policy should be established for explaining the surveillants' presence in the neighborhood if they are questioned by the police or curious neighbors.
4. In cold weather, an idling vehicle will emit exhaust fumes, which can easily be seen by neighbors. Moreover, exhaust fumes may make the surveillants drowsy and inattentive.
5. If more than one vehicle is used, one should have the point while the others are nearby for relief or for use in case the surveillance becomes mobile.
6. To safeguard against suspects monitoring police radio frequencies, surveillants should use a radio "scrambler," a device that garbles radio traffic and is affixed to each officer's radio (see Chapter 2).

Although vans have traditionally been used in surveillance, suspects are now alert to such parked vans, thus requiring drug enforcement personnel to consider other types of vehicles. One possible alternative is a "drone." Basically, a drone is an unmanned, nondescript type vehicle (such as an older Ford Pinto or Chevrolet Vega) that contains surveillance equipment. Most of the monitoring equipment is placed in the trunk, and a pin-hole lens camera is mounted in the headrest and focused on the target. Because the vehicle is an older car and because no equipment is visible, the drone can sit unobtrusively while surveillance equipment is left running. To help safeguard equipment stored in the trunk, a motion-sensor auto alarm may be installed to prevent tampering.

Another application for vehicles of this type is to remove the rear seat and darken the window glass of the vehicle. As the vehicle appears to be unoccupied, surveillance officers can occupy the vehicle for short periods to observe suspects or locations. Occasionally surveillance vehicles may be used in conjunction with the base for optimum coverage.

Whether conducted from a base or a vehicle, officers engaged in stationary surveillance must maintain a chronological log of all activity associated with the location: descriptions and times of individuals and vehicles coming and going, and any items brought to or taken from the location. The log may allow officers to trace evidence of other crimes such as illicit laboratory activity or fencing of stolen property. As previously mentioned, all of the basic equipment — cameras, binoculars, tripod, video camera, paper, and pencils — should be on hand.

Electronic Surveillance

Electronic surveillance is the documentation of persons, vehicles, or locations by electronic means; electronic devices are frequently used in conjunction with foot or vehicle surveillance. In order to secure a conviction in a drug case, most prosecutors now require not only the testimony of officers and police chemists, but also supportive evidence such as photographs of the defendant, a recorded tape of the defendant's voice, or a videotape showing the defendant's criminal involvement.

Many devices are available, and their quality and expense will vary from manufacturer to manufacturer. Basically, electronic surveillance devices fall into two categories: audio and visual.

Audio Surveillance

The ability to record the suspect's voice before, during, and after a criminal transaction is an asset to any case. Even during the initial negotiations — long before any transactions have taken place — recorded conversations can provide valuable evidence of suspect's "criminal intent."

Typically, a concealed transmitter, or so-called body-mike, is worn by undercover operatives when personal contacts are made. Officers should always test the unit before it is used because a body transmitter may occasionally transmit over cable TV channels inside a suspect's residence. Body transmitters are also usually expensive; a small tape recorder may serve as a substitute.

Another way to record conversations with a suspect is to have an undercover agent or informant phone the suspect and record the call with "induction coil pick-up." An induction coil pick-up is relatively inexpensive, and is readily available at most electronics stores. It is also easy to use: simply attach the pick-up to a telephone receiver and insert the plug into a standard tape recorder microphone jack. This procedure is not considered an illegal wire tap because one party of the conversation (the undercover officer) has given permission for the recording.

6-2   A "RF" (radio frequency) surveillance set-up where an adjacent motel room is "wired," permitting agents to monitor conversations between the undercover agent and the suspects.

Still another method of recording criminal conversations is the use of the "spike-mike." When a suspect is located in a particular location (e.g., an apartment or motel room), the spike-mike can be placed against an adjacent wall and conversations can be monitored (Figs. 6-2, 6-3). Here, however, the suspect's constitutional rights must be protected. If no agency personnel is participating in the conversation, use of a spike-mike must first be authorized by the local prosecuting attorney (see Wiretaps, below).

Bumper Beepers

For a moving surveillance, a vehicle tracking device (or so-called bumper beeper) might be considered. A bumper beeper is an electronic transmitting device, usually attached to the underside of the suspect's vehicle, which emits a signal that is picked up by special receiver. The receiver indicates which direction the suspect is traveling by emitting a series of "beeps"; the beeps are rapid when the suspect is close, and spaced out when the suspect is farther away. A bumper beeper makes it easier to maintain a "loose tail" of suspect. Bumper beepers, however, can be installed on vehicles only pursuant to a lawful court order.

Bumper beepers are also somewhat problematic. Ideally, they are

6–3 (A&B) A seemingly innocent looking wall outlet (A) but actually a highly concealed microphone (B) for recording conversations in a room.

connected to the car's battery (12 volt), but the hook-up could be discovered by the suspect. Failing this, one can rely on the beeper's internal 9 volt batteries. However, these are only good for short periods of time, thus making it necessary to retrieve the unit periodically and to replace the batteries. Finally, the suspect may discover the beeper, thus jeopardizing the investigation, losing the unit (usually), incurring a financial loss, and perhaps embarrassing the department.

Wiretaps

The wiretap is the most commonly discussed form of electronic surveillance. The wiretap is considered to be a sensitive and technical method of electronic surveillance. Although it may be legally authorized under federal law (and most state laws), a few states still have legislation that forbids wiretapping or eavesdropping.

Even in states where a wiretap may be legally used, it still must be the last resort in the investigative process: officers must show that all other avenues of investigation have been tried and have failed, or they must show those not tried are too dangerous to attempt. Furthermore, all details of the previous investigative attempts (and the reasons why other techniques should not be tried) must be specifically documented in the application (affidavit) for the court order authorizing the wiretap. Moreover, the courts have ruled that to conduct electronic eavesdropping lawfully, officers must do everything reasonably possible to respect the suspects' right to privacy. This means that should a wiretap be authorized, officers can only listen to criminal conversations and therefore must "minimize" intrusions into conversations not relating to criminal conduct.

In addition to being legally complicated, wiretap investigations are also expensive and time-consuming. In addition to carefully planning a wiretap investigation, it should be remembered that a wiretap merely facilitates a conspiracy investigation (see Chapter 2). It is a means of documenting an agreement between two suspects to commit a particular criminal act. Because an overt act is necessary to prove a conspiracy, surveillance officers must then be on 24-hour standby to properly observe and document the subsequent overt act. This represents a considerable commitment of time and manpower; it often cannot be justified by many departments.

If a wiretap is employed, however, it will prove to be a good investigative tool. It permits law enforcement officers to record criminal conversations, and the recordings provide excellent evidence for the prosecution of conspirators.

The Legality of Audio Recording

As mentioned above, in order to monitor and/or record a private conversation between two suspects lawfully (third-party interception), officers must first obtain a court order. The U.S. Supreme Court has held that people have a "reasonable expectation of privacy" when conversing under certain private circumstances. Such circumstances include a meeting between two suspects at a private room or when conducting a private telephone conversation (when no party line is involved).

Recording Telephone Conversations

If an undercover officer is a party to the conversation, however, he or she is not violating the suspect's reasonable expectation of privacy; therefore the recording of the conversation is lawful. This enables officers and informants to record (and thus document) valuable and incriminating conversations in the course of drug investigations.

A second area of misunderstanding involves recording suspect phone calls by officers in an undercover apartment. Caution should be observed because even though the officers may be renting both the apartment and telephone, a suspect still has a reasonable expectation of privacy when using the telephone outside the presence of informants or undercover officers.

Use of Concealed Transmitters (Body-Mikes)

Drug enforcement agents frequently use concealed transmitters when meeting suspects to allow support officers to monitor and record conversations. Monitoring is desirable for two reasons: (a) to determine if the undercover officer is in any danger during the transaction, and (b) to record the conversation for later use as evidence for the prosecution of the suspect. Concealed microphones are also commonly used in a suspect's residence or in other locations where criminal conversations are anticipated.

As with recording telephone calls, the circumstances surrounding the appropriate use of a concealed transmitter must always be considered by investigators. There are times when recordings may be made lawfully and times when they are unlawful.

If officers wish to listen to a suspect's conversation and there is no police agent (either an officer or an informer) in the room with the suspect, a court order is required. Any time a police agent is not part of the conversation, it is considered eavesdropping. Eavesdropping is a violation of the suspect's civil rights and an intrusion of his or her reasonable expectation of privacy (*Katz v. United States* [1967]).

If, however, a police agent is present, officers may lawfully monitor the conversation. The suspect's reasonable expectation of privacy is not violated provided the police agent is participating in the conversation or is present while the conversation is taking place; therefore, a court order is not required. If, however, the police agent leaves the room where the suspect is located, surveillants may not continue to monitor a suspect's conversations in the officer's absence. This reverts back to the rules governing third-party intercepts (specifically the rule of minimizing), and absent a court order it is unlawful.

The exclusionary rule requires that any evidence obtained against a suspect be accomplished according to the requirements of the Fourth Amendment. Electronic surveillance, under certain circumstances, is considered a form of search. Any third-party interception (such as a wiretap or concealed microphone) must be based on probable cause and authorized by a magistrate.

Finally, in the event officers use an informant to contact a suspect, the case officer should obtain written authorization to record the conversation between the informant and the suspect. This protects the officer in the event the informant later claims that no such permission was given (see Chapters 3 and 5).

Passive Monitoring

Passive monitoring (that is, without electronic equipment) of suspect conversations is permitted under certain circumstances. The same considerations with regard to the suspect's reasonable expectation of privacy, however, still pertain.

An example of permissible passive monitoring would be when two suspects are discussing a drug deal while standing at a pool table in a public tavern. If an undercover agent were legally present in the tavern (posing as a customer) and close enough to overhear the conversation, the suspect's reasonable expectation of privacy would not have been violated. Any conversation overheard regarding criminal activity could then be used against the suspect in court.

Video and Photo Surveillance

Whenever possible, visual surveillance equipment should be used to corroborate audio tape recordings or testimony of prosecution witnesses. The most typical (and underrated) means of visual recording is the camera. Whether it is a 35-mm or even a small 110 camera, it can provide a reproduction of all or parts of the crime for prosecution. If budgets are not too restricted, a 35-mm camera with a full array of attachments (such as infrared filters, telephoto and fiberoptic lenses) will give officers clear and detailed photographs. Many cameras are equipped with a device that automatically dates each print at the time it was taken.

The use of video cameras is also generally accepted in sophisticated criminal surveillance operations. Generally, videotaped evidence provides a more comprehensive reproduction of a crime than a still photograph (even though some argue that still photographs afford greater detail and clarity). Unit managers, especially, should be aware that video technology is constantly changing, and they should try to stay current with what is available. The newer smaller cameras, for example, are more easily concealed and may be worth an additional expenditure.

Because many covert operations involve nighttime maneuvers, methods should be developed to use cameras and video equipment at night. The starlight scope, for example, will illuminate an otherwise almost totally dark area, and may be used with or without a camera (Figs. 6–4, 6–5). The starlight scope produces a greenish, somewhat grainy image, but it permits acceptable-quality photos of nighttime meetings between suspects and police agents. In the case of total darkness, the starlight scope will, however, require some light source to provide an image. The source cannot be too great, such as a nearby street light, but a mild source of light (starlight, mild moonlight) will create sufficient illumination to an otherwise dark area, permitting suspect identification, the reading of automobile license tags, and tracking of undercover agents.

6-4 (A&B) At first glance these photos would appear to be of poor quality, but considering that the picture was taken in total darkness with the use of a starlight scope, it provides a useable and identifiable surveillance photo.

6-5   A starlight scope enables investigators to see objects in the night with a passive light source such as moon or stars.

Another solution to the problem of nighttime surveillance is the use of a 35-mm camera with an infrared lens. An infrared lens allows excellent quality photos under minimal lighting conditions. One source, which provides more than sufficient lighting, is a Cyalume infrared lightstick (Fig. 6-6). The Cyalume lightstick is an inexpensive light source that, when broken in half, emits ample light for infrared photography while the light source itself remains literally

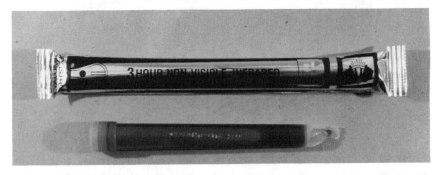

6-6   Infrared Cyalume lightsticks emit an invisible light source which will adequately illuminate subjects for use with a camera equipped with an infrared lens.

invisible to the naked eye. Suspects will be unable to detect anything unusual unless they, too, are using infrared equipment for countersurveillance.

Infrared lightsticks have still other benefits. An infrared lightstick can be placed in an undercover agent's jacket pocket, thus allowing surveillants using infrared equipment to more easily distinguish the agent from suspects during a nighttime contact. In office buildings, when it is not feasible to turn on the indoor office lights, lightsticks placed in a ceiling vent will emit enough light for infrared photography or visual surveillance. Even in a room that appears to be totally dark to the naked eye, infrared lighting will illuminate the room so that a positive identification of suspects is possible through an infrared camera system.

Undercover Apartments

A highly recommended surveillance tactic is the use of a specially equipped undercover apartment as a meeting place between undercover officers and suspects. The apartment should be selected for its strategic location and for ease in incorporating surveillance equipment. Ideally, the undercover apartment should be a two-bedroom dwelling in which a bedroom and the living room share a common wall; such a layout enables support officers to more closely monitor meetings between undercover officers and suspects. When locating an appropriate apartment, however, a background check of all neighbors should be performed to ensure that known felons are not living nearby.

In the undercover apartment there should be a specific seat — such as a sofa or chair — in the main surveillance room upon which video cameras, microphones, and special lighting will be targeted. This is where the undercover officer tries to have the suspect to sit so that the suspect's image and words can be clearly recorded. The officer should be trained to be able to lead the conversation to what the officer wants to discuss (see Chapter 11).

The undercover officer must have the ability to read the suspect's body language in order to detect nervousness. Moreover, the undercover officer must also feel comfortable in front of a camera. It is important that he or she does not talk too much, act nervous, or otherwise fail to think clearly during the undercover contact. To prepare officers for the videotaped encounter, in some cases it might be advisable for officers *not* to tape the first transaction in an investigation. When subsequent transactions are made, the officer should be more comfortable with both the camera and the suspect. If the subsequent videotaped drug buys go smoothly, the officer may choose not to file charges on the unrecorded initial purchase.

The proper placement of low-light video cameras is crucial to the proper documentation of meetings between undercover officers and suspected drug violators. The cameras may be placed in almost any location within the room where both the officer and suspect can be filmed, but to avoid detection they should never be placed at the suspect's eye level. People have a tendency to look around at eye level much more often than they do above or below it. Good locations for camera placement include ventilation vents, stereo speakers, flower pots, and behind posters and pictures (see Fig. 6 – 7).

Two-way mirrors, although still used, are no longer recommended. Their use is somewhat dated, and suspects may expect that cameras are concealed behind them. If mirrors are used, however, a black cloth should be positioned behind the mirror so that surveillance cameras cannot be detected. In addition, if concealed cameras are employed, steps must be taken both to shield the cameras from view and to position the cameras so that light reflections from the lenses do not give away its hiding place.

6–7 A video camera located behind a wall and focused through a heating vent in an undercover apartment.

When placing a video camera in an undercover apartment, officers must take care to position it where images can clearly be recorded. Preferably, a 17-mm to 25-mm wide-angle lens should be used, as the field of view will most likely take in the entire room. When placing the camera, a rule of thumb is to manipulate the suspect to an area of the room where the image of his head appears on the video monitor just slightly larger than a thumb when placed on the monitor screen over the image. If a clear image is unobtainable on the video tape (Fig. 6–8), subsequent identification of the suspect may be difficult in court proceedings, thereby jeopardizing the case.

Other technical modifications can be made to not only conceal surveillance cameras but to more easily cloak the surveillance process. Such modifications include the installment of silent plastic gears in camera auto-winders, appropriate interior lighting in undercover apartments, and the placement of specially designed concealed power microphones, which can clearly transmit voices within a particular room (see Chapter 2).

6–8   A video editing system, which is necessary for making tape duplications and photos from video tapes.

Summary

The effective use of covert surveillance in the drug investigation cannot be overemphasized. It is through this process that much is learned about the activities of suspected traffickers. Employment of surveillance agents to monitor contacts with traffickers is necessary in drug enforcement, as this protects the undercover officers and successfully documents actions, conversations, and other evidence that will later benefit the prosecution of the case.

Techniques for a proper surveillance include vehicle, foot, and electronics methods, and all are designed to permit the officer to observe without being observed himself. In accordance with this, investigative personnel must be cognizant of the suspect's right to privacy and the need to gain the proper authority to observe the suspect in various circumstances.

In addition to the techniques of observation in surveillance, it is often necessary for the officer to be trained in the use of sophisticated electronic devices which enhance the officer's ability to conduct his surveillance duties. The use of these devices will enhance images of suspects so identification can be made in court proceedings. Such devices will also increase the degree of safety afforded the undercover officer during his contacts with suspects.

Suggested Readings

Bennett, Wayne W., Hess, Karen M., *Criminal Investigation*, 2nd ed. St. Paul, MN, West Publishing, 1987.

Pollock, David A., *Methods of Electronic and Audio Surveillance*, 2nd ed. Springfield, IL, 1979.

Sijiander, Raymond P., *Applied Surveillance Photography*. Springfield, IL, Charles C. Thomas, 1975.

Swanson, Charles R., Jr., *Criminal Investigation*, 3rd ed. New York, NY, Random House, 1984.

Vehicle Tracking Devices, U.S. Department of Justice, National Institute of Justice, NIJ Standard-0223.00, May, 1986

Ware, Mitchell, *Operational Handbook for Narcotic Law Enforcement Officers*. Springfield, IL, Charles C. Thomas, 1975.

Special Enforcement Problems 7

Because of the pervasiveness of drug trafficking, law enforcement agencies will commonly involve themselves in both street and high level investigations. It is therefore essential that officers be adequately trained in both technical and tactical methods of investigation. These investigations will frequently focus on cultivated marijuana fields, illicit laboratories, smuggling operations, and pharmaceutical diversion investigations. Each represents a significant contribution to the country's illicit drug supply, which is why investigations into these areas should be undertaken regularly.

This chapter will examine each of these areas of criminal investigation and identify problems and investigative methods used in each.

Marijuana Cultivation

Marijuana (*cannabis sativa*) is considered the most widely abused drug in the country, and its domestic cultivation is one of the main sources of illicit drugs in the United States. According to a 1988 National Institute of Drug Abuse Survey, 50–60 million Americans (20%–25% of the population) have tried it. (The effects of marijuana are discussed in Chapter 4; this chapter focuses only on methods of production and trafficking.) Many unrelated cultivation and trafficking groups exist throughout the country. Generally, marijuana is grown in plots of 100 plants or less; it is usually planted between April and May and harvested between August and October (or by the time of the first frost). Marijuana plots have been discovered on rental property, privately owned property, and, frequently, along creek and river banks. In addition, there is a growing number of cultivation operations that secretly make use of the thousands of acres of land owned by the National Forest Service.

Because of easy market entry into the marijuana trafficking business, those involved in marijuana cultivation and distribution range from seasoned criminals to novice entrepreneurs, and from farmers in financial straights to "well-to-do businessmen," who act as financiers of local cultivation operations. Many finance their operations by revenues acquired from previous drug sales, from funding by financiers, or from money borrowed from other traffickers. Other individuals finance operations by supplying equipment such as grow-lights and fertilizer.

Growing Marijuana

As briefly discussed in Chapter 4, there are three types of marijuana commonly found in the United States: Indian hemp, commercial grade, and sinsemilla. The two cultivated grades are commercial and sinsemila, which have significant growing differences.

Commercial Grade

Commercial grade marijuana is produced from *cannabis* plants that have been cultivated in plots in which the male and female plants have been allowed to grow together and the female plants have been fertilized. The whole plant is harvested, stripped of its stems, and marketed. At maturity the plant will range from 7 to 15 feet high. Most of the leaves have 7 to 11 leaflets (almost always an odd number), with the center leaflet the longest.

Sinsemilla

Sinsemilla reflects a growing trend to develop higher potency marijuana plants, which result in greater profits. Many of these growers are horticultural specialists in their own right, and they will crossbreed different strains of marijuana to produce the highest potency plants possible. Some growers select high potency seeds from areas such as Mexico, Afghanistan, and Thailand; others attempt to produce their own high-quality seeds. In the latter case, a grower selects the largest female plant, impregnates a Q-Tip with pollen, and places it on the largest bud of the plant. The Q-Tip and bud are then covered with a plastic bag to protect the rest of the buds from pollen. These fertilized buds will then produce seeds for the next growing season.

In 1986, the U.S. government estimated that 37% of the domestic marijuana crop was sinsemilla. Sinsemilla is produced from the unfertilized female plant, which is grown in plots from which all male *Cannabis* plants have been removed prior to pollination. When grown in this fashion, the female plants flower more readily and produce more resin in an attempt to attract male pollen. The resin contains THC (Δ9-tetrahydracannabinol), which is the active agent in marijuana. The THC content in sinsemilla plants may be twice that of the commercial grade plants.

On average, a cultivated marijuana plant will produce one pound of marketable product. A plant that has had its flower tops removed, however, (topped-off) may be harvested two to three times in a growing season, thereby producing from two to three pounds of marketable product. Prices of cultivated marijuana vary greatly from region to region, but range from $800 to $2,000 per pound, and up to $200 per ounce for the higher grades.

Most cultivated marijuana plots are discovered as a result of so-called search and destroy missions by police officers. Such activities have proven fruitful, but they frequently require four-wheel drive vehicles, spotter aircraft, and substantial training in guerilla warfare type tactics in order to combat the snipers, guard dogs, and booby traps commonly associated with these operations.

Indoor Growing Operations

In addition to outdoor marijuana plots, many criminals are resorting to indoor growing methods, which (a) make police detection more difficult, and (b) enable growers to produce marijuana year-round. Growing structures such as greenhouses, converted residences, barns, basements, and chicken houses have been encountered by drug enforcement officials. According to the Drug Enforcement Administration, two methods are commonly used for indoor cultivation:

Cloning: Cloning originated on the West Coast and has resulted in a system where hybrid marijuana is cultivated and superior plants are selected for new cultivation. A cutting from a plant is performed underwater, which prevents air from affecting the exposed ends. The cutting is then wrapped in a paper towel that has been soaked in a root-stimulant and then placed in a pot to grow. The cutting will now develop roots. Growth is sometimes accelerated by the use of halide lights. Cloning permits a grower to produce hundreds of plants from a select few, and avoids the time-consuming process of waiting for the seeds to germinate.

Hydroponics: This is a popular cultivation process, which was originally perfected for plants such as tomatoes and cucumbers.

In hydroponic, plants are grown in a soil-free, mineral-rich solution. Marijuana seedlings are taken to the hydroponic greenhouse and placed in 4-inch pipes, which contain the solution. In this environment, a sinsemilla plant measuring 8 to 10 feet high can be grown in 4 to 6 weeks. Cultivated marijuana plants grown hydroponically will contain up to twice the THC content found in even the highest commercial grades. One benefit of producing plants in this fashion is that greenhouses may be as small as 400 square feet: only one square foot is required to grow a mature plant. Such operations may operate year round and could possibly produce up to $5 million worth of marijuana annually. One way to investigate a possible greenhouse operation is to compare the suspect's utility bills with those of neighboring residences to check for excessive use of electricity and water (see Chapter 1).

Evidence of Marijuana Cultivation

Once manicured, the packaged marijuana is transported by various means: pick-up trucks with camper shells, vans, rental trailers, passenger vehicles, and (in some cases) general aviation aircraft. Commercial airlines are being used more frequently to transport smaller quantities of drugs to various destinations within the United States. In addition, common carriers — even the U.S. Postal Service — have been discretely used by traffickers to ship small quantities of marijuana. Because cultivation is mostly a rural operation, a lot can take place undetected by police or inquisitive neighbors. There are certain types of behavior, however, that might indicate the existence of a cultivation operation:

1. Individuals purchasing wooded lands, erecting high fences with heavy chains and locked on gates, and displaying "KEEP OUT" signs.
2. Individuals buying land that could be used for farming or ranching, but not using it for those purposes.
3. Individuals from out-of-state who make large cash payments for tracts of land, or who pay for land in cash outright.
4. Buyers who purchase property through third parties and do not want to leave their telephone number or address with the seller.
5. Persons with no experience or knowledge of ranching or farming who buy farm or ranch lands, and then show no visible means of support.
6. An unusual amount of vehicular traffic, either during the day or at night, in which unknown individuals are transported on and

off the property and the entrance gates are always locked after each entry or exit.

7. The erection of large greenhouses or tin buildings on property where these structures would not normally be utilized (for example, on very heavily wooded land where there are no animals to feed).

8. The use of guard dogs, alarms, and surveillance systems on property in the country (for example, dogs around a tin barn in an isolated area of the property).

9. A house out in the country where men are constantly coming and going, but women and children are seldom seen.

10. Large purchases by individuals of fertilizer, garden hose, plastic PVC pipe, chicken wire, long 2 × 2″ lumber, different sizes of pots, machetes, camouflage netting, camouflage clothing, or many sizes of step ladders (usually painted green and brown).

11. The erection of tents or the use of camper trailers or other recreational vehicles on wooded property with no evidence of recreational activities.

12. An unusual pattern of vehicular traffic or a particular vehicle regularly seen in the same isolated area.

13. Large purchases of green plastic sheet material, green spray paint, large trash bags, lanterns, portable heaters (e.g., large kerosene heaters), extension cords, heat lamps, and fans.

14. New owners of property who refuse to talk to neighboring property owners about how they use their property.

15. The purchase of large amounts of heavy plastic materials with the buyer being evasive about their use.

16. Unexplained and unreasonably high utility bills.

17. The purchase of property formerly used as chicken or turkey farms by buyers whose use of the property would be suspicious.

Domestic Eradication

Domestically cultivated marijuana constituted approximately 19% of the total U.S. supply in 1985 and 18% in 1986. It is thought that these figures, which have increased since 1984, are a result of not only domestic interdiction programs but also eradication efforts in foreign source countries. In 1987, the Drug Enforcement Administration reported that more than one-third of the cultivated *Cannabis* plants eradicated in 1985 and 1986 were sinsemilla, which is preferred over the commercial grade for its high THC content.

Marijuana eradication involves locating and seizing both cultivated plots and wild-growing patches. This is a difficult and expensive undertaking for law enforcement agencies and usually requires a joint effort on the part of several agencies. The U.S. Drug Enforcement Administration first provided financial aid for marijuana eradication in Hawaii in 1979. Since then, this federal program, which offers funding and investigative and aircraft resources, has been expanded to all 50 states. The program is considered to have been successful: in 1984, for example, an estimated 3.8 million marijuana plants were eradicated in 48 states. In most states, the National Guard now assists local drug enforcement officers in eradication maneuvers. This means that equipment such as trucks, helicopters, and additional manpower can be placed at the disposal of local law enforcement agencies, thereby making such operations easier to complete.

Even with federal assistance, however, marijuana eradication is one of the most tedious and exhausting tasks in drug enforcement. Officers must be prepared to encounter cultivators who have military experience, police criminal records, and weapons. In addition, officers must also face long, hot days, with the risks of heat exhaustion, hornet and wasp stings, snake bites, poison ivy, sun stroke, and spider bites.

Each eradication effort should be properly documented by the unit. All pertinent information should be cataloged and indexed: the type of field (cultivated or wild growing); the names and identifiers of suspects; the items seized (weapons, vehicles, cultivation equipment, etc.); and other information (booby traps, type of marijuana, number of plants, etc.).

Such documentation may be required under local or state law. In many cases, a state investigative police agency may collect the data from local law enforcement agencies throughout the state and maintain a master file of all plots and violators.

Smuggling Investigations

Typically, smuggling calls to mind national and international organizations, with far-reaching implications. After all, we are aware that heroin, for example, originates in Mexico and Southeast and Southwest Asia. Cocaine, for the most part, originates in South American countries such as Colombia, Peru, and Bolivia. And marijuana, aside from its domestic sources, is brought in from Mexico, Colombia, Panama, and Jamaica.

Given the above premise, however, it should be obvious that once drugs arrive in the United States, there must be a domestic smuggling network, which then transports the drugs to their respective places of distribution within the country. This is where local law enforcement must have sufficient expertise to deal with the problem of interstate and intrastate smuggling. This text will not address the

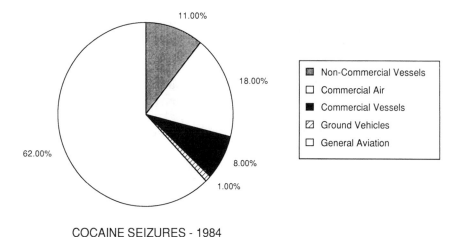

COCAINE SEIZURES - 1984

7 – 1   Chart showing types of conveyances used in cocaine smuggling operations. (*Source:* U.S. Drug Enforcement Administration.)

task of international drug interdiction, but will focus on the role of domestic law enforcement in detection and investigation of the various modes of domestic smuggling (Fig. 7 – 1).

Air Smuggling

Traditionally, the investigation of air smuggling has been the province of the federal government. During the last ten years or so, however, it has become more and more common for state and local law enforcement agencies to conduct full-scale investigations into drug trafficking by air. Moreover, the recent federal task force concentrations in coastal cities and traditional ports of entry have caused many smugglers to transport their payloads further inland to areas considered safer by traffickers.

The U.S. Customs Service estimates that there are between 3 and 10 successful smuggling flights each day in the United States. Evidence of this is found in the number of aircraft (large and small) being seized by authorities during the off-loading process. Moreover, some planes are occasionally discovered abandoned — full of drugs and out of fuel.

The Federal Aviation Administration (FAA) requires all flights by private aircraft originating in other countries to file a flight plan 24 hours in advance and to land at the airport nearest to its point of entry that has a customs officer. By coordinating flight plan information with radar surveillance, any aircraft crossing a U.S. southern border without a flight plan can be identified as suspicious. Unfortunately, many areas of the U.S. southern border do not have low-altitude radar coverage, allowing many small aircraft to go undetected.

Air smuggling investigations are tedious and difficult to conduct as pilots often change their destinations, making detection difficult. To help combat this problem, law enforcement officers may "wire" a suspected aircraft to help them track it. A law enforcement transponder is placed in the suspect aircraft, which emits a signal (or "beep") that can be received by FAA control towers. These transponders look exactly like a standard aircraft transponder, thus leaving little clues as to its true function. These devices must be surreptitiously installed by investigators, and pursuant to a lawful court order. In investigations requiring the installation of a transponder, the U.S. Customs Service is usually contacted — which usually gives assistance in preparing the court order and technical assistance in installing the transponder.

Another way of detecting air smuggling is by locating and surveilling a suspected "ground crew." The ground crew consists of individuals employed by smugglers to meet the aircraft at a designated time and location, and to off-load the drugs for transport to various distribution points. These players may be hired to conduct only this particular task, or they might be involved in the overall planning of the operation. The ground crew usually employs two kinds of vehicles: vans, or pick-up trucks with camper shells (which are sometimes vented for the operation). The ground crew will usually be equipped with two-way ground-to-air radios to communicate with the pilot as he or she approaches the landing site. The specific landing site will vary in each air smuggling operation; typical sites include small, out-of-the-way airports, or even sections of highways that are seldom traveled.

The actual capture of a smuggling aircraft should be accomplished with caution: pilots and ground crew are often heavily armed to prevent possible ambushes by poachers. In addition, state and local agencies should always contact the U.S. Customs Air Branch, which will offer support and expertise in the pursuit and capture of suspect aircraft. The Customs Service currently has planes equipped with forward-looking infrared sensors for tracking smugglers at night without making visual contact. Dealing with such an operation can be complicated and lengthy, which further requires interagency cooperation (see Chapter 9).

Smuggling Aircraft

To properly investigate a suspected air smuggling operation, officers should have a basic knowledge of the various types of aircraft smugglers use, and which planes are best suited for different smuggling operations. Marijuana is usually brought in by bails (50 or 100 pounds each), and marijuana smuggling normally requires larger aircraft, such as a C-123 or DC-3. Many other types of aircraft are commonly used, but regardless of type, most traffickers prefer older aircraft that can be abandoned (ditched) if necessary; older aircraft represent less of a potential financial loss than newer, more expensive planes.

Cocaine, however, is usually brought in on smaller planes (see Fig. 7-2). The payload is smaller, and smaller aircraft normally fly much faster than larger planes. Popular planes for cocaine smuggling are single- and twin-engine aircraft such as the Cessna 400 series; other preferred models are the Aerocommander 680 and 690, Piper Aztec, and Piper Navajo twin-engine models. These planes can generally transport about a ton of cocaine over a range of about 1800 miles, and can stay airborne for about 11 hours with a standard fuel system —and even longer with a bladder tank.

To maximize range and capability, smuggling aircraft are frequently "plummed" or outfitted with auxiliary fuel systems. These systems, called "bladder tanks," are sometimes installed on the outside of the aircraft or on the wing. Some smugglers prefer to conceal the bladders by using a collapsible tank inside the aircraft; this may consist of nothing more than a water bed, which is used for a one-

7-2 Photo of small general aviation aircraft seized in rural Oklahoma containing a payload of illicit drugs, which ran out of fuel and was forced to make an emergency landing. (Photo courtesy of the Oklahoma Bureau of Narcotics and Dangerous Drugs Control.)

way trip and thrown away after the flight. In this way, the space occupied by the bladder can be used for storing cocaine on the return journey.

Air smuggling via general aviation aircraft is the most common method of importing cocaine from South America. Nearly two-thirds of the cocaine smuggled into the U.S. is transported in this fashion, though use of commercial aircraft is also fairly common. (An estimated 64% of the marijuana consumed by American drug users is smuggled in from foreign sources.) Planes that do not contain bladder tanks must refuel at predetermined "transshipment" points between the country of origin and the U.S. These points are critical in the smuggling phase and can be found throughout South America, Cuba, the Bahamas and Puerto Rico. Transshipment stations may simply be refueling stops, or they may be areas where the drugs are off-loaded and repackaged.

Smugglers land at airports of every size and in cities both large and small throughout the country. Although the planes may appear to be entirely "normal," there are tell-tale signs when profiling aircraft used in smuggling. These signs might not only be an indicator of smuggling activity, but they could give investigators other leads to follow up and verify. Some physical characteristics of smuggling aircraft are:

1. Passenger seats missing from the aircraft.
2. Strong, unusual odors, such as perfume (used to cover the scent of marijuana).
3. Numerous cardboard boxes, duffel bags, plastic bags, or other containers inside the aircraft.
4. Aircraft registration numbers that are altered or otherwise falsified.
5. Landings wherein aircraft meet ground vehicles and depart after only a brief period on the ground.
6. Aircraft flying or landing after dark without lights.
7. Trucks, campers, or vans waiting at or near areas suitable for aircraft landings; these are often equipped with radios for use in communications with aircraft.
8. Pilots or passengers displaying large amounts of cash, and making cash payments for fuel and services.
9. Windows of aircraft covered by curtains or temporarily taped over.
10. Pilots or passengers reluctant to leave the aircraft unattended during ground servicing.
11. Aircraft parked a long distance from the line shack, or at the far end of a ramp.

Aircraft Data Plates

When investigating suspect aircraft, it is often necessary to check the data plate of the aircraft to verify the authenticity of its externally displayed registration and to determine true ownership. Occasionally, the plane's external registration will also show signs of being altered, or the aircraft may be devoid of any registration markings at all. The latter is usually true when a plane crashes and burns out. The most common smuggling aircraft are listed in Table 7 – 1 below along with their data plate locations.

Search of a Typical Light Plane

In the event a suspected smuggler aircraft can be documented entering the country, U.S. customs officers may search the aircraft without a warrant (a customs search). If this cannot be shown, however, and absent any extigent circumstances, a search warrant or consent to search must be obtained (see Chapter 3).

Searching an airplane is quite different from searching an automobile or marine vessel. Certain tools should be kept on hand for the task: flashlight, an aircraft reference book, an inspection mirror, and a screwdriver (used as a probe). In addition, it will most likely be necessary for officers to seek the assistance of a certified mechanic in order to ensure the future airworthiness of the aircraft. Listed below are the main areas to search when concealed contraband is suspected (see Fig. 7 – 3):

1. *Engine Compartment:* Have the pilot open the engine cowling on both sides. With the aid of a flashlight and inspection mirror, check for small packages, which might be attached to the engine mount structure and other parts of the powerplant.
2. *Wheel Wells:* With the aid of a floor creeper, inspection mirror, and flashlight, check the surrounding structure for small concealed packages. In most light planes, a large area of the internal wing structure may be viewed from the main landing gear wheel wells because of access holes.
3. *Cabin Area:* With the aid of an inspection mirror and flashlight, check under and behind the instrument panel; in the glove compartment; under seat cushions; in seat pockets; in the headliner if it has a zipper for inspection access; in ashtrays; in any open compartments; under the floor and above ceiling panels; in ventilation ducts; in baggage, map cases, and flight kits.
4. *The Baggage Compartment Behind the Rear Bulkhead Cover:* In most light planes the rear bulkhead cover is either canvas or a plastic sheet that is easily removed (it is usually held in place by snap fasteners, thumb disconnects or Velcro fastener tape). With

Table 7-1 Aircraft Data

Make	Common Name	Model	Data Plate Location
Smith	Aerostar	600, 601p	Left side of fuselage under horizontal stabilizer
Beech	Baron	55, C55, 56TC, 58, 58TC	Left side of fuselage under horizontal stabilizer
	Bonanza	33, 36	Left side of fuselage under horizontal stabilizer
		35	Underside of fuselage at tail, or left side of fuselage under horizontal stabilizer, or right side of fuselage inboard of wing flap
	Duke	60	Left side of fuselage under horizontal stabilizer
	King Air	90, 100	Aft frame cabin door, or left side of fuselage under horizontal stabilizer
	Queen Air	65, 70, 80, 88	Aft frame cabin door, or left side of fuselage under horizontal stabilizer
	Twin Bonanza	50	Left side of fuselage under horizontal stabilizer
	Twin Beech	18 (C-45)	Aft edge of cabin door, or left side of fuselage under horizontal stabilizer
Cessna	Cardinal	177	Inside left-hand door post, at eye level
	Golden Eagle	421	On forward or aft door post
	Sky Hawk	172	On floor inside copilot's door
	Sky Lane	182	Forward left-hand door post
	Super Sky Lane	206, 207, 210,	Forward left-hand door post
	Sky Lark	175	On floor inside copilot's door
	Sky Master	336	Left side of fuselage under horizontal stabilizer
	Sky Master	337	On floor inside main entrance door
	Sky Night	310, 320	On aft door post
	Sky Wagon	140, 170, 180, 185	Inside surface of left-hand door post
	Super Sky Wagon	195	Inside on rear door post
		401, 402, 404, 411, 414	Forward or aft of entrance door post
Convair		240, 440	On bulkhead post at entrance to flight deck, on right side

Manufacturer	Model	Designation	Location
Dehavilland	Beaver	DHC-2	On control pedestal in cockpit, or on battery box or radio rack in baggage compartment
Grumman	Cheetah	AA5A	Left side of fuselage under horizontal stabilizer
	Gulfstream	G-159	Left side of aircraft interior, inside hydraulic compartment door between forward cabin and flight deck
Gates	Lear Jet	23, 24	Nose wheel well, or on lower entrance door frame
Mitsubishi		MU-2	Left side of fuselage under horizontal stabilizer
Piper	Apache	PA-23	Aft fuselage, center line under rudder (move rudder)
	Aztec	PA-23	Tailcone left side under horizontal stabilizer (older models); under floor mat at right front seat position (newer models)
	Cherokee	PA-28, PA-32	Left side of fuselage under horizontal stabilizer
	Commanche	PA-24	Inside baggage compartment on fuselage frame
	Navajo	PA-31	Left side of outside fuselage under passenger door
	Seneca	PA-34	Left side of fuselage under horizontal stabilizer
	Twin Commanche	PA-30	Inside baggage compartment on fuselage frame
Rockwell	Aerocommander	112, 114	Left side of fuselage under horizontal stabilizer. Possibly on the inside entrance to the cabin door or frame
	Shrike	500	
	Commander	520, 560	
	Grand Commander	680	
Curtiss–Wright		C-46	On control pedestal on flight deck, or on aft fuselage under horizontal stabilizer
Martin		202, 404	Aft fuselage under horizontal stabilizer
Pembroke		MK-51	Behind copilot's seat on bulkhead at head level
Martin	Marauder	B-26	Aft side of forward bomb-bay bulkhead, on right side
Douglas		DC-3, DC-4, DC-6, DC-7	Forward side of bulkhead on flight deck behind co-pilot's seat, head high; or, on forward bulkhead entrance to flight deck, right side facing inboard, head high

Source: U.S. Customs Service.

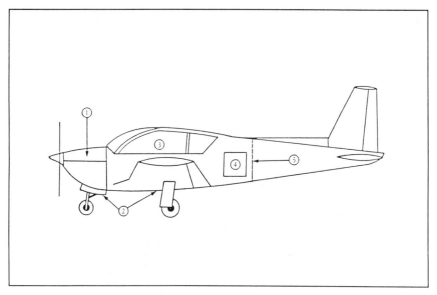

7-3   Areas searched in light aircraft.

the aid of an inspection mirror and flashlight, examine the aft
portion of the fuselage.
5. *The Baggage Compartment:* Examine all baggage and the interior
   of compartment. Do not place baggage on top of wing. The wing
   skin is light and may be easily damaged. Most light twin-engine
   aircraft also have a baggage compartment in the nose of the plane.
6. *The Exterior of the Plane:* Examine the following areas for improper condition or operation, which may indicate the concealment of contraband: the nose cone; the prop spinner; light assemblies and bulbs; exhaust pipes; recessed areas in the landing gear;
   fuel cells; wing flaps; the aeileron tab; elevators; wheels and hubs;
   luggage compartments; wing-tip fuel tanks and filler caps.

The Search of a Commercial Aircraft

Commercial aircraft are frequently used to hide and transport drugs.
A search of a commercial aircraft should include the baggage and
storage compartments; the restrooms; life raft compartments; trash
containers; wheel wells; liquor locker; under floor of cockpit.

The Pilots

It is somewhat difficult to profile a smuggler pilot: no stereotypes
seem to obtain. Pilots may be of any nationality, age, or either sex. In

7-4 Photo of a twin engine aircraft and bulldozer seized on a makeshift clandestine airstrip in South America. (Photo courtesy of the U.S. Drug Enforcement Administration.)

addition, they may be licensed commercial pilots, unlicensed pilots, or even former military flight personnel. Because the drug business is so lucrative, most smuggler pilots usually operate with some extremely sophisticated equipment (Fig. 7-4). In many instances, this equipment is more sophisticated than that used by police agencies:

1. Sophisticated electronic equipment to maintain communications within their organization: air-to-air radios, ground-to-air radios, and advanced radar.
2. Equipment to monitor law enforcement radio transmissions.
3. State-of-the-art communication scramblers; these are used to "garble" ordinary radio transmissions to anyone listening without a receiver having a scrambler with the same code.
4. Pocket pagers.
5. Digital inscription devices; these are used to send messages in code, and they can be accessed only after a security code is entered directly into the device.
6. Radar altimeters.
7. Beacon-interrogating digital radar.
8. Position-tracking equipment.

9. Long-range navigational instruments.
10. Night-vision goggles; these are used to intensify any available light by a factor of 50,000 thereby reducing the smuggler's risk of detection by being able to fly "dark," or without lights.

Ground Smuggling

Authorities are discovering an upsurge in ground smuggling operations. Vehicles are used both to transport drugs from aircraft and vessels to destinations within the U.S., and to transport drugs directly across the borders of the U.S. At the border, the Border Patrol now uses a variety of sophisticated equipment to detect illegal intrusions: buried ground sensors, infrared heat sensors, night-vision goggles, and pocket-sized starlight scopes.

Search of a Typical Automobile

The legality for searching an automobile is discussed in Chapter 3, and should be considered before any search is conducted. Given legal grounds for a search, it should be determined whether or not the case involves smuggling or if the vehicle is just being used as a temporary hiding place for drugs. Normally, a smuggling operation will reveal a more extensive effort on the part of the driver to conceal drugs; they will, therefore, be more difficult to locate.

In either case, the search must be conducted thoroughly, with officers knowing specifically what areas to search. Officers should begin at one end of the vehicle and slowly work toward the other. It is a good idea for more than one officer to be present for the search; both officers should search the vehicle, so that evidence will not be overlooked. In most cases, drugs will usually be concealed in a few standard areas (see Fig. 7–5):

1. *Radiator, grill, and bumpers:* Drug packages may be attached with duct tape to the rear of licence plates or inside a locking gas cap.
2. *Fenders and front wheels:* Look inside hubcaps and behind headlights.
3. *The powerplant area:* Search inside the air filter, and look for packages affixed to electrical wiring, hoses, or under the hood.
4. *Dashboard area:* Removable panels could be installed by the driver, and these should be checked for by operating any knobs. Search for packages affixed behind the foot pedals or in ventilation ducts.
5. *Header area:* It is common to discover concealed drugs within the cloth area of the headboard lining or within the sun visors.
6. *Front and back seat areas:* Drugs may be concealed between seats,

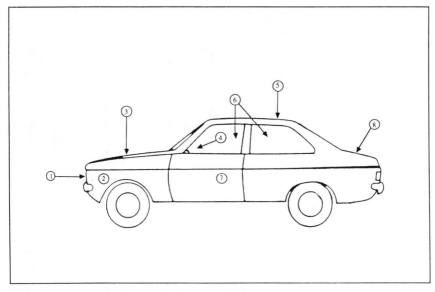

7-5   Areas searched in typical automobile.

within the seats and spring assemblies, or within hidden compartments in the seat.

7. *Door panels:* Door panels are removable and offer the smuggler areas to hide drugs, which might go undetected by unobservant police officers.

8. *The trunk area:* Look within the trunk lid frame and beneath any insulation. Drugs are also commonly hidden within hollow tools, inside the spare tire assembly, under carpeting, or within any clothing contained within the trunk.

Water-Borne Vessels

Jurisdictions bordering ocean coasts, lakes, or rivers experience unique problems with regard to drug smuggling. Bodies of water are often excellent conduits between points of entry and destinations for drugs. Smuggling through these arteries may be difficult to detect. The vessel used in each instance will vary with the size and type of the body of water, and according to the financial resources of the trafficker. International deliveries by vessel are initially transported by a "mother ship," which is normally a large vessel traveling inbound from its source country. These ships will usually remain in international waters (12 miles or more off the coast of the U.S.), and commission smaller and faster ("go-fast") boats to transport small

7-6 Photo of a small speed boat that was used by smugglers to transport quantities of cocaine and marijuana from the mother ship to a coastal region of Florida. (Photo courtesy of the Florida Department of Law Enforcement.)

amounts of its cargo to shore (Fig. 7–6). Once inland, the drugs are off-loaded and placed in aircraft or ground vehicles for transportation to their ultimate destinations.

Search of a Vessel

Once captured, the vessel must be properly searched. Officers should be aware of prescribed searching methods because concealment aboard vessels can be quite tricky. Officers must assume the drugs might be located virtually anywhere within the vessel: between the deck and the hull; within hollowed-out guard rails; under floor joints; inside fuel and oxygen tanks (and all other containers). Weighted objects at the bottom of tanks and articles floating inside tanks should be inspected. Searchers should be suspicious if the crew claims to have been at sea for a long time and the fuel tanks are full. False decks, removable paneling, or blanked-off spaces in the bow should also be anticipated. In the case of larger boats, once below the deck, searchers should locate and inspect heads, sinks, and basins as soon as possible in case smugglers attempt to flush the drugs. If flushing is suspected, the water surrounding the vessel should be inspected for evidence of contraband. The investigator's imagination is his or her only limitation when searching vessels, and a thorough job will most likely prove productive (Fig. 7–7).

7-7 Photo of a small vessel transporting cocaine, which is being approached by a U.S. Coast Guard interdiction ship for arrest. (Photo courtesy of the Florida Department of Law Enforcement.)

Smuggling and Prisons

Another growing area of concern is the problem of illicit drug smuggling into prisons. Prison smuggling takes place in federal, state, and county institutions, and it poses a tremendous challenge for law enforcement officials.

Generally, inmates may possess only items issued to them by the institution; any other items are considered contraband: drugs, weapons, money, cigarettes, etc. Drugs are among the most sought-after form of contraband because of its recreational and profit potential within the prison. The methods of smuggling vary from case to case but may include being thrown over the walls by associates; being transported into the institution via service trucks and other civilian personnel; being carried into the institution in the body cavities of inmates (see Chapter 3); being brought in by visitors; being shipped through the postal service; or being carried in institutions by corrupt employees.

In many cases, penal drug smuggling is conducted by an organized gang that operates within the institution. These gangs are widespread and exert great influence over their members. Many gangs have chapters operating in several institutions at the same time, and they frequently operate in the free society as well. Among the gangs are, the Aryan Brotherhood (ABs), the Texas Syndicate, the Mexican Mafia (EME), Black Guerrilla Family (BGF), Neustra Famigla (NF).

Many of these groups seek to monopolize drug trafficking in their particular institution. Moreover, because of conflicting goals and philosophies, many of these gangs are constantly at war with each other, which poses additional enforcement problems for officials.

Drug Detection Dogs

The use of drug detection dogs has increased during the last decade, for obvious reasons. The dog is trained to locate or "alert" on the scent of certain drugs such as heroin, cocaine, marijuana, methaqualone, and methamphetamine. Traffickers who attempt to conceal drugs may feel that officers may have a difficult time locating them, but a dog's sense of smell is difficult to fool (Fig. 7 – 8).

Training is a lengthy process, which requires detailed documentation of the dog's successes in locating drugs. Once certified, a certificate is issued to the dog handler who will use it as evidence of training and competency if the "alert" is later questioned by defense attorneys. If the dog "false-alerts," then this also needs to be documented. This detracts from the dog's credibility, and in many cases a false alert will require a dog to be recertified for continued service.

Drug detection dogs may be effective in searching storage lockers, vehicles, schools, correctional facilities, and airports. The use of drug

7 – 8   Photo of a state drug detection dog commonly used for searching prisons and self-storage lockers for illicit drugs. (Photo courtesy of the Oklahoma Bureau of Narcotics and Dangerous Drugs Control.)

detection dogs also make search warrants easy to acquire because the alert (along with the dog's certification) is usually considered probable cause for the warrant (see Chapter 3).

Pharmaceutical Diversion

The problem of the diversion of pharmaceutical drugs is considered an expanding one within the drug enforcement community. More and more criminal investigations are revealing the widespread involvement of health care professionals (physicians, pharmacists, and nurses) in the diversion of controlled substances from hospitals, clinics, pharmacies, and doctors' offices. Additionally, the involvement of street criminals (or "professional patients") in this lucrative business is also on the increase, and will be discussed later in this section.

It is estimated that the diversion of pharmaceutical drugs accounts for an estimated 32% of the illegitimately consumed drugs in the country. In 1983, the Drug Enforcement Administration estimated that 2% (or 13,000) of practicing physicians and pharmacists were involved in some form of illegal diversion activities, which account for a significant amount of diversion of controlled substances.

The Law

Under the Controlled Substances Act of 1970, "any person who handles or intends to handle controlled substances must obtain a registration issued by the Drug Enforcement Administration." In addition to federal law requiring registration of those who handle controlled substances, many states (approximately 25 of them) also require that a firm or individual obtain a state controlled-substances registration. In some states, a state registration is necessary as a prerequisite "before" one is eligible for federal DEA registration.

Because of the differences in regulation of registrants, police officers should be familiar with their own state law regarding registration of controlled substance handlers. They should also know which state agency is responsible for registration so that they are able to verify quickly whether or not a particular person or firm involved in dispensing drugs is lawfully registered.

The registration itself consists of a unique number, which is assigned to each legitimate handler of controlled drugs: importers, exporters, manufacturers, wholesalers, hospitals, pharmacies, physicians, and researchers. The number must be made available to the supplier by the customer prior to any purchases of controlled substances, thus reducing the opportunity for unauthorized transactions.

Combating the problem of pharmaceutical diversion is a difficult task. Many law enforcement officers and prosecutors are unfamiliar with the problem or how to deal with it. The violator in a drug diversion case may be a properly licensed registrant who is abusing his or her authority, or a street criminal who might be running numerous scams aimed at deceiving unsuspecting physicians. We will now examine those who most commonly divert controlled substances and their preferred methods.

Medical Practitioners as Suspects

An unfortunate but necessary task of drug enforcement officials is the investigation of those registered legal handlers of drugs such as physicians, pharmacists, and nurses. Diversion investigations have revealed four general types of physicians who are commonly involved in diversion of controlled substances.

Doctors in Diversion

Generally, there are four types of doctors who are involved in the diversion of pharmaceutical drugs.

1. *Dishonest:* This is the doctor who actually makes a profit from the illegal sale of pharmaceutical drugs, or who may be involved in cases where prescriptions are given to suspects for the purpose of unlawfully distributing illicit drugs.
2. *Impaired:* It is unfortunate, but many physicians use drugs themselves, both on and off the job. Drug dependency may develop in the physician for a number of reasons: marital problems, stress on the job, and recreational use. The recidivism rate, however, is generally low for those who are treated properly and on a timely basis.
3. *Dated:* This is the doctor who has been in practice for a number of years and has grown to be somewhat of a pillar in his own community. He or she is willing to indiscriminately hand out drugs to anyone who has an apparent legitimate need for medication. Doctors who fall into this category are not necessarily criminals, but more likely are set in their ways and unwilling to conform to new rules and regulations.
4. *Gullible:* This physician is not cautious enough to recognize a scam when he or she sees one. Although possibly an otherwise competent doctor, he or she will easily fall victim to the scams of "professional patients."

Listed below are some of the specific methods physicians have commonly used:

1. A physician writes a prescription in a patient's name, picks up the drugs personally, and tells the pharmacist he or she is going to take it to the patient.
2. A physician sends a patient to a pharmacy to have a prescription filled, but requires the patient to bring the drugs back to the doctor's office. Only part of the drug is administered and the physician keeps the rest.
3. A physician writes a prescription in the name of a family member, but picks up and uses the drugs himself or herself.
4. A physician writes a prescription in his or her own name at various pharmacies at the same time.
5. A physician (or nurse) self-administering injectable drugs taken from nurses stations, hospital emergency rooms, or hospital pharmacies.
6. A physician orders drugs from several pharmacies at the same time, using DEA official order forms, while at the same time he or she orders the same drugs from a mail order drug company.
7. A physician obtains drug samples and self-administers them.

Although medical care institutions bear legal and moral obligations to their employees, many shun their obligation to report a suspected diversion problem, or simply look the other way rather than acknowledging the situation. Hospitals, through their board of directors, should adequately regulate personnel and establish formal policy regarding impairment (with strict enforcement provisions). In the case of addicted registrants, many state hospital boards have a system whereby a physician or nurse can voluntarily submit to treatment (employee assistance program) and remedy the problem before it results in criminal prosecution.

Nurses in Diversion

In addition to diversion problems experienced with physicians, there are similar problems involving nurses. A distinction needs to be made here between diversion of drugs for resale and diversion because of personal addiction. Both present unique problems, and each may require a different solution. Studies have shown that of those nurses who are diverting drugs, more are physically addicted than are actually selling drugs for profit. This distinction may affect the manner in which an investigation is approached and how the suspect is dealt with after being caught.

Drug Theft

Most health care institutions experience some degree of diversion, and it is generally the employees who are the culprits. As indicated, those employees most likely involved with drugs are those who have access to drugs — physicians, nurses, pharmacists and other employees. The most commonly diverted drugs are Valium, morphine, Demerol, Tylenol III with Codeine, Percadan, Percaset, and Ritalin. The type of drug user and available opportunities will have a bearing on whether tablets, capsules, or injectable substances are preferred. Diversion may occur in many different areas of the health care facility, but it will most commonly take place at the hospital pharmacy, the nursing station, or the recovery floor.

Substituting Drugs

If an outright theft is not considered safe by the violator, he or she may substitute a noncontrolled drug for a controlled drug. Drug substitution may be accomplished, for instance, by appearing to inject a patient with a prescribed medication while in fact a worthless substance may be used in its place. This may cause the patient to suffer, believing the prescribed medication is not effective, and could result in additional medical setbacks for the patient.

Substitutions are commonly carried out through "charting" (backdating patient charts to show that drugs were administered, which were in fact stolen), or forging other nurses' names. To avoid the possibility of substitution, two nurses should be required to obtain drugs when they are needed on the floor. This would add a check-and-balance to safeguard against one of them diverting the drugs.

Diversion and Punishment

The problem of diversion is growing not only because many facilities fail to address the problem, but also because the violators themselves have methods of avoiding punishment.

Suspected users often quit and join other hospitals. In this circumstance an on-the-job user might be suspected by other employees, and to avoid being confronted with a diversion charge, he or she simply changes jobs. When the new hospital calls for a reference, information is not shared regarding any possible involvement in drug use or diversion. The user is therefore allowed to carry on with his or her unlawful activities.

Employees who have been caught are often simply transferred. It has become evident in many investigations that some hospitals are more willing merely to transfer employees caught in diversion activity to different units within the hospital rather than terminate their employment or seek prosecution. This situation becomes evident when one realizes that medical care professionals are somewhat clannish and reluctant to "snitch" on fellow workers. By transferring suspected employees, the problems of stigmatization by co-workers and embarrassing publicity for the institution are eliminated. Unfortunately, this offers no incentive for violators to discontinue their involvement in diversion activity.

Finally, there is the problem of outright denial. One mistake investigators frequently make is to approach a suspect before any concrete evidence of the diversion has been documented. When this occurs and the suspect denies his or her involvement in the diversion, the investigator's bluff is called and there is no immediate recourse. Having a sound case prepared when approaching a suspected violator also maximizes the deterrent effects of diversion investigations within the medical facility.

The Professional Patient (The Scammer)

To understand the problem of drug diversion, investigators should also look at the various scams used by street criminals to obtain pharmaceutical drugs. The word "scam" is defined by Webster as "to cheat or swindle, as in a confidence game." This is precisely what is happening within the medical care community. Street criminals are acquiring drugs through deceit and selling those drugs on the street for profit.

Of all of the scammers' targets, the most likely one is the physician. Once the scammer is successful in conning a prescription out of a physician, he or she will usually experience little trouble in having it filled by a pharmacist.

Pharmacists are the second-most likely target of the scammer, especially in trying to pass forged or altered prescriptions. In addition to forgery and alterations of prescriptions, a pharmacist can be an unwitting partner in a scam when he or she (a) fills prescriptions for the same drugs for the same patient from "different physicians"; (b) fills prescriptions for the same patient too frequently; or (c) accepts refill orders for prescriptions when the scammer calls in the prescription pretending to be a physician.

Hundreds of diversion schemes have been uncovered by investigators over the years, and it would be too lengthy to attempt to list them all here. Some of the more common scams experienced by many different jurisdictions, however, are offered in brief* below.

Source: "Scam of the Month" publication, Missouri Task Force on the Abuse, Misuse and Diversion of Prescription Drugs, November 1986.

The Fat Lady Scam

This is a common deception, usually perpetrated by several women who are severely overweight. The women move into a new community and develop a schedule in which each member visits a maximum number of physicians each day for a week or so. As the scam unfolds, each woman tells each physician she visits that she is chronically unhappy with her life because of being overweight. Additionally, her husband is going to leave her and fight for custody of the children and she is considering having her stomach stapled, etc.

At this point the "patient" begins hinting about a particular drug (e.g., Preludin, amphetamines, or another Schedule II drug). The physician will usually refuse to prescribe Schedule II drugs for weight reduction, but might be willing to prescribe Didrex. After the patient is issued a prescription for Didrex, she might then request a prescription for Valium to keep from "getting too edgy."

The Breast Cancer Scam

It is unfortunate, but drug diversion scams like this actually exist; the scam involves individuals who are actually experiencing a legitimate medical problem. This scam was documented in the St. Louis area, and it involved a woman who actually had a form of breast cancer. She would simply show up at a physician's office and present her case for treatment. In this case, Dilaudid was the only drug that gave her relief, and the physicians would usually see fit to give her a prescription. As it turned out, the woman was seeing seven doctors on a regular basis in different surrounding towns. Physicians should be cautious about treating patients who are unknown to them, who have insufficient identification, or who otherwise behave suspiciously.

The Toothache Scam

This scam is popular among narcotics addicts who are also experiencing a tooth-decay problem. The addicts will try to obtain Schedule II narcotics from dentists and physicians at the same time. It has happened where addicts have attempted to obtain telephone prescriptions for the desired drug without even seeing the dentist. If the addict actually chooses to see the dentist, he or she will present a legitimate "reason" for having to be somewhere else so that the dentist will issue a prescription for a drug such as Demerol or Dilaudid. Dentists, in a case like this, should be suspicious of numerous patients he or she has never seen before, showing up all in a brief period of time. This might indicate the existence of an organized diversion ring operating in the area.

The Altered Scrip Scam

Those prescribers who short-cut proper prescription writing practices — especially those who use arabic numerals for dose amounts and do not write out the number — are easy targets for professional patients. By simply matching the ink color of the pre-scribers' pen, a 10 can be altered to 40, 5 can become 25, and so on. A prudent prescription becomes excessive, and proportionally more profitable to the professional patient.

The Phantom Refill Scam

Investigations are revealing an increasing number of prescriptions with refill numbers that have been altered by the patient and without the knowledge of the physician or dentist. Professional patients — especially those who are addicted to or selling codeine-containing drugs, Schedule III drugs, Schedule IV tranquilizers, or sleep medications — are commonly adding refills to prescriptions, which are not properly completed by the physician or dentist.

Physicians and dentists are reminded to mark refill information so that alterations cannot easily be made, or to place an "0" in the refill column. Pharmacists are also reminded of this scam, and they are advised to verify refills with the patient's physician or dentist.

Drugs obtained in this fashion provide the violator with a consid-erable profit margin, which in turn acts as an incentive for the commission of the act. For example, one Dilaudid tablet may bring as much as $50 to $60 on the street. A 10-mg Valium tablet (diazepam) may sell for from $5 to $20. Some of the most popular drugs ob-tained by these scams are: Dilaudid, Dolophine, Ritalin, Tuinal, Talwin, Preludin, Percodan, Valium, Seconal, Tylenol III and IV, and amphetamines. Officials in many cities are also now reporting an increased demand for Ritalin and Talwin tablets, which are usually ground up, dissolved in water, and injected by the user. This creates a "speedball effect" which is sought after by many users. The Ritalin–Talwin combination is cheaper than the traditional speedball, which is a combination of heroin and methamphetamine (or cocaine) powder.

Many other scams exist, which are facilitated by con artists who are elderly, handicapped, or simply clever or brazen enough to at-tempt such a fraud. All professionals within the medical community are duty bound to report any such attempts by criminals as soon as they are detected.

The Drug Audit

In addition to the nine control mechanisms contained within the 1970 Controlled Substances Act (see Appendix), all registrants must keep full records of all controlled substances they may manufacture, purchase, sell, or keep in inventory, regardless of which schedule the drugs fall under. (Limited exceptions to this requirement are only available to researchers and physicians.) It is from these records that audits can be performed to trace the flow of any drug from the time of manufacture, through the wholesale level, on to its destination at a pharmacy, hospital, or physician's office, and then on to the patient. The mere existence of this requirement is often enough to discourage many types of diversion.

Under the recordkeeping requirements, one distinction is made. All records for all Schedule I and II drugs must be maintained separately from all other records of the registrant. The purpose for this requirement is to allow investigators the ability to audit the more abuseable drugs more expeditiously.

Clandestine Laboratories

Many sources contribute to the availability of illicit drugs to users and consumers. Other than foreign source countries (such as Southeast and Southwest Asia, Mexico, and South and Central America), many significant sources exist within the United States. As mentioned, the cultivation of marijuana and numerous illicit diversion scams contribute greatly to the problem. Yet another major domestic source of illicit drugs are clandestine laboratories.

Drugs such as LSD, Psilocybin (magic mushrooms), mescaline (peyote cactus), and others have been produced clandestinely for decades. But in the last ten years or so laboratory technology has become so generally available among the criminal element that these laboratories now are somewhat commonplace.

Success in federal interdiction efforts has caused many international traffickers to reduce their efforts in smuggling illicit drugs to the United States. In some cases, this has caused a reduction in the availability of certain drugs, thereby causing their street prices to rise. Against this background, domestic traffickers have found new sources of revenue in clandestine laboratories.

Although many labs are located in urban areas, the clandestine laboratory is generally a rural law enforcement problem, and usually involves PCP and methamphetamine. (Although LSD is a significant clandestine laboratory drug, it has not seen the popularity of PCP and "meth" in recent years.) Many traffickers prefer rural settings because the odors from a PCP or methamphetamine lab are so pronounced, they would be easily detected by neighbors or passers-by in more populated areas. (Exceptions to this, however, have been documented by investigators in larger cities where abandoned warehouses and other isolated structures have been used.) In addition, remote laboratory sites enable traffickers to spot surveillance officers or incoming police for raids.

The operators of these laboratories may be highly educated chemists or low-level street criminals. In many cases, when suspects without a knowledge of chemistry decide to set up a clandestine laboratory, qualified and experienced chemists ("cookers") from outside the area are hired to set up the lab for a fee or a percentage of the anticipated profits. Once paid, the chemists return to their originating areas.

Types of Labs

Although there are many different types of drugs produced by clandestine laboratories, there are three basic types of operating types of labs:

1. *Extraction Labs.* This type of lab is used to produce illicit substances by removing certain elements from one substance and creating another. Examples are:
   a. Hashish. This is an extraction of the marijuana plant made from boiling marijuana in a solvent and alcohol solution. The precipitate is then filtered through a strainer and the resulting material is allowed to dry.
   b. Methamphetamine. One somewhat primitive method of making a crude brand of methamphetamine is by collecting a large amount of benezedrine inhalers and removing the cotton parts of the inhaler. This material is then placed in a vat filled with muriatic acid and heated until a film forms on the top of the solution.
2. *Conversion Labs.* This is a lab used to convert existing controlled substances into different forms for street sales. A typical example:
   a. Crack. This freebase form of cocaine is made by mixing powdered cocaine with baking soda, ammonia, and water and heating the solution until a residue is formed and dried.
3. *Synthesis Labs.* A synthesis lab is used in converting one chemical to another. PCP and methamphetamine laboratories are typical examples. Such labs use controlled chemicals such as "P2P" to create yet a different product.

PCP

In the late 1970s, PCP was most commonly found in powder form and was called "angel dust" on the street. The powder was usually sprinkled on marijuana cigarettes by users, and smoked to achieve the desired high. The popularity of the powdered form of the drug,

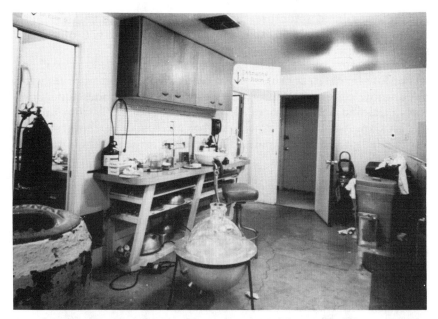

7–9 Photo of a seized illicit methamphetamine laboratory. (Photo courtesy of the U.S. Drug Enforcement Administration.)

however, has gradually faded and is being replaced by the current liquid form of the drug. Moreover, liquid PCP is relatively easy to manufacture once the necessary materials have been acquired (the synthesis process is not nearly as long as the powdered form, and profit margin is still high). Because of its relative ease in setting up, the PCP lab can also be taken apart and moved with little effort, which presents investigative problems for law enforcement (see Chapter 4).

Methamphetamine

As discussed in Chapter 4, methamphetamine is also a popular illicit drug. A tremendous market exists for this drug because of its effects, which are similar to those of cocaine, thereby creating a significant profit margin for traffickers (see Fig. 7–9).

Investigation Techniques

Again, the strongest weapon in fighting illicit laboratories is sound criminal intelligence. This can be acquired from other law enforcement agencies, informants, or surveillance activities. Before moving against a laboratory, investigating officers should learn:

1. Number of inhabitants of the lab
2. Identity of inhabitants
   A. Names and other personal identifiers
   B. Criminal histories
3. Any weapons located in the residence
4. Information on guard dogs, booby traps, and any exterior fortification
5. The progression of the cooking process (is there any finished product available for seizure?)

Additional intelligence can sometimes be acquired through a close working relationship with chemical and laboratory equipment suppliers. Although it is likely that some of these manufacturers may be involved with the criminals themselves, those who are not can be a valuable source of intelligence. Employees of these companies should watch for customers who

1. Use names of unknown companies for orders
2. Pay cash for items purchased
3. Order unusually large amounts of chemicals that are commonly used in laboratory operations
4. Request shipments of chemicals or equipment sent to residences or post office box numbers
5. Phone in orders representing themselves as employees of companies

In some cases, law enforcement agencies have attempted to establish chemical "store-fronts," which are "sting" type operations consisting of undercover agents operating a contrived chemical distribution company. In this case, officers provide needed chemicals to suspected lab operators and follow the suspects to their destination. Subsequent surveillance results in acquiring search warrants and raiding the location of the suspected lab. Although generally considered a successful strategy, problems are created when officers fail to maintain surveillance of suspects and thereby lose track of the perpetrators, who have possession of valuable chemicals.

The presence of illicit laboratories may be detected by the abundance of methamphetamine or PCP in the area at an unusually low price, indicating a fresh "cook-off." If a laboratory is suspected in an area, the following points should be considered:

1. A check with local utility companies may show an excessive use of electricity or water.
2. Postal officials may render information regarding residents' receiving mail at the suspected address, including any large deliveries.

3. Once identified, all of the residents' criminal backgrounds must be checked to determine previous involvement in drug violations. This could be used later in establishing probable cause for a search warrant.
4. When surveilling the suspected residence, officers should look for ventilation systems such as a window fan.
5. Investigators should be aware of any unusual odors in the area that might indicate the presence of an operating laboratory.
6. A trashing of the suspects' residence should be considered if the location provides such an opportunity (See Chapter 1).
7. A list of the suspects' long-distance telephone tolls (a subpoena will be required) will provide a readout of all direct-dial long-distance calls made from the residence, thereby identifying possible associates, or chemical supply companies used.

Chemicals Found in Laboratories

Officers need to be aware of three distinct categories of chemicals, which are found in illicit laboratories: precursors, reagents, and solvents (see Table 7–2).

Precursors

Precursors are raw materials used for manufacturing a controlled substance, and which later become part of the finished product. The law requires that these chemicals be reported when anyone sells, transfers, or furnishes these substances.

Reagents

Reagents are substances that chemically react with one or more precursors, but are not part of the finished product.

Solvents

A solvent does not react chemically with a precursor or reagent, but it does become part of the finished product. These are used to dissolve solid precursors or reagents and to purify other chemicals. Solvents are explosive and should be considered extremely volatile and dangerous.

Hazardous Chemicals

Most laboratories will contain chemicals that are extremely volatile. In the interests of their own safety, officers should become familiar with the more hazardous compounds:

Table 7-2 Illicit Laboratory Chemicals and Precursors

Drug	Chemicals/Precursors
Amphetamine, Methamphetamine, and P₂P	
	Phenylacetic acid
	1-Phenyl-2-propanol
	Benzyl chloride
	Benzaldehyde
	Phenylacetonitrile
	1-Phenyl-1,2-propanedione-2-oxime
	Propenylbenzene
	Ephedrine or pseudoephedrine
	Phenylalanine
	Chloroacetone
	Phenylacetyl chloride
	Methylamine
	Acetaldehyde
	Nitroethane
	Thallium III nitrate
	α-Methyl styrene
	Formamide
	Formic acid
	Mercuric chloride
	Sodium
	Acetic anhydride
PCP and PCP Analogs	
	Cyclohexanone
	Phenylmagnesium chloride or bromide
	Bromobenzene 4-piperidine
	Pyridine
	Pyrrolidine
	Ethylamine
	2-Bromothiophene
	Magnesium metal turnings
	p-toluene sulfonic acid
	Ethyl ether
	Sodium cyanide
Cocaine	
	2,5-Dietnoxy-tetrahydrofuran
	2,5-Dimethoxy-tetrahydrofuran
	Acetonedicarboxylic acid or esters
	Citric acid
	Troponone
Methaqualone	
	Anthranilic acid
	O-Toluidine
	N-acetylanthranilic acid
Tryptamines	
	Indole (2,30 benzopyrrole)
	Oxalyl chloride
	Diethylamine
	Dimeithylamine

Ether

Ether is a common ingredient used by lab operators. It is an extremely flammable liquid, which tends to form explosive peroxides when evaporated to dryness. Empty or near-empty cans of ether should be handled with extreme care.

Mercuric Chloride (Bromide)

These are extremely violent poisons. Officers should avoid breathing the dust from these chemicals.

Lithium Aluminum Hydride

Lithium aluminum hydride (LAH) is commonly used in the manufacture of methamphetamine and amphetamine. It is a highly unstable compound that reacts violently to moisture or heat. *Keep moisture away from this reagent!* A chemical called Vitride has, in some instances, replaced LAH, but it should be handled with the same precautions.

Sodium or Potassium Cyanide

Sodium or potassium cyanide is used in processing PCP and phenylacetic acid. When cyanides come in contact with acid, they form hydrogen cyanide gas (the same gas used in gas chambers). Hydrogen cyanide has the odor of almonds. Always make sure the area is well ventilated.

Sodium

Sodium is a soft, shiny metal, which becomes a dull grey color when exposed to air. Sodium also reacts explosively with water. It should be stored in liquids containing no oxygen, such as kerosene.

The Laboratory Raid

Laboratory raids usually require a search warrant; probable cause will be established through surveillance, informant information, or other information accumulated during the investigation. Because large quantities of ether and other volatile and corrosive chemicals are normally used in laboratory set-ups, standard raid procedures must be followed to minimize casualties, and should be coordinated with both the prosecutor and a police chemist experienced in dealing with clandestine laboratories.

Caution should always be practiced in lab raids. Carelessness during the raid and search could result in a fire or explosion, resulting in personal injury, death, and/or destruction of evidence. During the search, the equipment and chemicals (primary and secondary precursors) to be seized should be pointed out to officers by the police chemist for seizure. In addition, officers should search for finished product (e.g., methamphetamine powder or PCP liquid). These items, along with formulas and any in-process material, will be used as evidence. At the conclusion of the raid, all items seized must be inventoried to eliminate confusion.

Precautions for the Raid

The following precautions are recommended during laboratory raids:

1. The fire department should be placed on stand-by alert.
2. A chemist should accompany officers during the raid.
3. There must be no smoking in or near the laboratory site.
4. No combustible items, such as flashbulbs, should be used on the lab site.
5. Neighborhood or area evacuation plans should be prearranged if needed.
6. Gas masks should be available to assault and search team officers.

All officers, chemists, or other personnel working in the laboratory should wear safety glasses and protective clothing in case of any accidents. When spills do occur, a convenient, commercially available method of clean-up is chemical absorbant pillows. Another method is to throw sand or baking soda on the spill, creating a mixture that can then be scooped into a bucket for disposal.

Other dangerous chemicals found in the lab are concentrated inorganic acids such as hydrochloric, sulfuric, and nitric acids. Any skin contact with these chemicals will result in burns, inhalation of their toxic vapors will cause irritations of the mucus membranes and respiratory tract. The chemicals are, however, water soluble and can be washed away with large amounts of water, followed by the application of baking soda to the burned area to neutralize the action of the acid.

Packaging Evidence of the Laboratory

If an informer is not available to furnish information about the progress of production in the laboratory, officers may have difficulty determining whether or not any finished product is present to be seized as evidence. In this case, the investigators should consider filing conspiracy charges against suspects involved in the laboratory (see Chapter 2).

Much thought must be given to the packaging and transportation of materials, mixtures, and chemicals seized during the lab raid. Reaction mixtures should be placed in sturdy, leak-proof containers. Highly volatile chemicals should be placed in nonglass containers, because the pressure build-up in glass containers could create a safety problem. Strong acids, such as sulfuric acid and hydrochloric acid, should never be placed in the same containers as strong bases such as sodium hydroxide (lye) methylamine.

The Crack House Problem

With the crack cocaine boom of the late 1980s comes the popularity of "crack house" operations, a renewal of a traditional police problem with fortified structures. The crack house is a residence where crack dealings take place in volume, and because of the way in which it is managed, many unique investigative and tactical problems arise.

The crack house is a retail outlet for rock cocaine sales. There is usually only a small amount of drugs present at the location and they can easily be destroyed in the event of a raid by police. The amount of drugs on hand is usually limited to 50 – 100 rocks, selling from

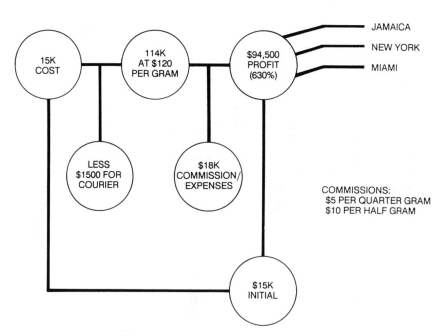

7 – 10   Crack profit margin.

$10 to $50 each. As the on-hand stock is depleted by buyers, however, it is rapidly replenished (Fig. 7–10). The house itself is commonly fortified with steel bars on the windows, steel doors and door jams, 3–4 foot iron posts around the front door to stop ramming vehicles, and in many cases there is an entry "buffer" to delay entry by police officers who attempt to serve search warrants. As mentioned, this is done so that the dealers have time to dispose of the drug evidence by flushing or hiding it before police have a chance to seize it as evidence.

In many cases the crack house is a residential house or apartment, but in some cases private clubs are used as a front for crack distribution. In recent cases, otherwise law-abiding citizens have been approached by crack dealers offering a percentage of drug profits in exchange for letting their house be used as a base for drug deals. In other cases vacant houses are commandeered by enterprising dealers looking for a low-cost retail outlet for their drugs. In most cases, however, there are usually three to four persons present at the location to distribute the drugs, to maintain records of drug sales, and to safeguard money (see Fig. 7–11).

It should be understood that even though they are a relatively easy

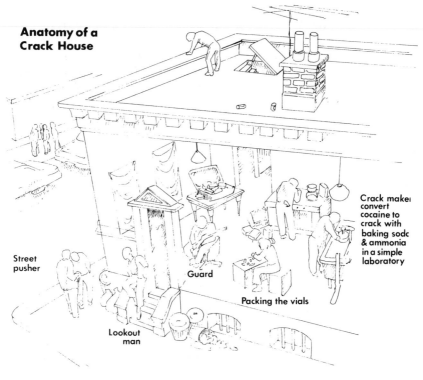

Anatomy of a Crack House

Crack maker convert cocaine to crack with baking soda & ammonia in a simple laboratory

Street pusher

Guard

Packing the vials

Lookout man

7–11

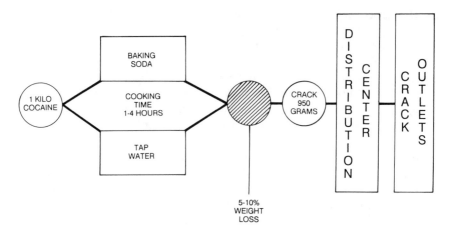

7 – 12 Crack production process.

target, it is probably fruitless to target only crack "street dealers," because crack dealers are many in number and generally are replaced quickly after being arrested or removed from the operation. It is therefore essential for law enforcement officers to target those who are responsible for establishing and financing the crack house itself.

It is also common for a crack house operator to control several other houses at once and keep couriers busy by dropping off crack and picking up money during the day. Operations such as this create large distribution networks with many members (called "cells") and due to the volume of sales at crack houses, profits are great and may easily range from $10,000 to $20,000 per house daily (Fig. 7 – 12).

Although law enforcement agencies use many methods with which to deal with this problem, it is typical for the crack house, once raided, to be back in business in a short time. Because arresting crack house operators usually is not in itself a sufficient tactic, additional incentives are offered crack dealers to leave the area. This is where useful forfeiture sanctions under state and federal laws are beneficial (see Chapter 2).

Enforcement initiatives include the use of undercover drug buyers to verify the presence of drugs at the house, and the subsequent use of search warrants for raiding the location. As mentioned, forced entry into the residence is a common tactical problem for police. Typical devices used in forced entry include battering rams, sledge hammers or other similar devices for entry through doors and windows, as well as armored vehicles or even tractors to enter through doors or even through walls.

Short of initiating a full-scale investigation, the local police depart-- ment can implement several preventive policing strategies which may prove effective in deterring crack dealers in a given neighborhood. For instance, the patrol division can consider using the following initiatives:

1. A higher visibility patrol policy in the affected neighborhood.
2. Individuals suspected of criminal activity in the vicinity of the crack house should be stopped and questioned (using field interview techniques) by patrol officers.
3. If the crack house is rental property, the lawful owner should be contacted by investigators and advised that continued criminal activity will result in the property being seized by police (see Chapter 2 on asset forfeiture).
4. If the crack house is located in an abandoned house, the local Public Works Department and/or the Fire Marshals Office can cite the lawful owner for code violations which could include abandoned, unoccupied, structurally unsound, or dangerous premises. Such violations could result in fines as high as $1,200 in some cases.
5. If the crack house is located in a restaurant or liquor-serving establishment, the Health Department can conduct code inspections 24 hours a day (in most jurisdictions).

The methods of control discussed above are nontraditional ways to attack the crack house problem. Such methods are only minimally effective with large crack operations, in which the loss of one or two houses is considered only a temporary inconvenience for the dealers. Again, this illustrates the necessity for attacking the operators of the crack house rather than just the street dealers.

Controlling the crack house requires cooperative law enforcement effort among several divisions within the police department, including the drug enforcement unit, the patrol division, the street gang unit (if applicable), and the tactical division. Additionally, as with most other areas of drug enforcement, police agencies should properly communicate with one another by sharing intelligence information on crack house locations and their operators.

Booby Traps

Complicating enforcement efforts in marijuana eradication operations, raids on clandestine laboratories, and numerous other drug enforcement operations is the risk of encountering deadly booby traps. Indeed, booby traps are becoming an ever-increasing hazard for drug agents. Like the spreading technology in drug manufacturing, knowledge of how to manufacture new and ingenious traps is also spreading among traffickers. Much of this knowledge was originally acquired in Vietnam, where traps of this nature were somewhat commonplace.

Traffickers plant booby traps in and around their operations because (a) the parts for the traps cost virtually nothing, and (b) the effectiveness of the devices are substantial. Traffickers use booby traps for three basic reasons:

1. To warn suspects of intruders (by the sound of explosions or by floodlights).
2. To deny intruders (police) access to the inhabited area by injuring or killing him or her.
3. To slow down police pursuit during a raid by injuring or killing officers.

When considering a laboratory raid, officers must realize that in the event even one officer is injured, a minimum of one additional officer will most likely be needed to render assistance. If there is already a shortage of officers in the assault, the raid team will be even more undermanned and that much more vulnerable to attack. Therefore, just as a police chemist is recommended for the raid of a clandestine laboratory, officers who suspect booby traps should be accompanied by a qualified emergency ordinence disposal (EOD) specialist to help identify traps or bombs and otherwise assist the officers in the drug raid. In the absence of an EOD expert, however, officers should be aware of the clues that might indicate booby traps have been used:

Handbooks in the residence that give instructions on how to assemble traps: *The Anarchist Cookbook* by William Powell; *The Poor Man's James Bond* by Kurt Saxon; *The OSS Special Weapons Devices and Equipment*, published by Paladin Press. These publications are manuals for bomb and booby trap assembly; if the books are present, officers should assume that booby traps will also be present.

If the profile of any suspect includes either a criminal history involving prosecution for weapons offenses, or past military services in Vietnam, booby traps should be expected.

With few exceptions, most booby traps fall into two categories: explosive and impaling. They can be activated by remote control, manual control, or by the victim (usually via a trip wire). They may be located either outside or inside a structure. Traps may be used either to scare the intruder, or to injure or kill. In all cases, however, they are to be considered extremely hazardous to investigating officers.

Officers who are not trained in dismantling or disarming bombs or booby traps should *not* attempt to disarm the device. They should, however, be capable of identifying them. Normally, the trap will be located along an entrance to a location (a doorway, entry path, or stairway). It would therefore be advisable for officers to approach the target area off the main path, with a lead scout-man looking for hard-to-spot signs of traps (such as trip wires) by using a probing rod, or even a belt or strip of cloth dangling from a stick.

Locating Exterior Booby Traps

Regardless of the specific rank or assigned duties of each officer on the raid team, all officers should be aware of the obvious or telltale signs of booby traps in the area and realize that they could be installed anywhere. This is a difficult task as traffickers will usually succeed in hiding most traps. Investigators should be alert for seemingly insignificant signs that might indicate the existence of a trap.

Officers should look for booby traps in the following areas:

1. Any cleared trail or pathway.
2. Near any object that arouses curiosity (e.g., a dead animal used as a decoy for intruder observation).
3. Along escape routes.
4. Affixed to any innocent looking, movable object, such as doors, windows, or gates.

The following signs may indicate the presence of traps:

1. Any disturbance in the terrain that looks unusual (like a cover-up).
2. Dead leaves in one area, surrounded by green leaves or any vegetation in a pile, which does not fit the area (possibly a punji-pit cover).
3. Any depressions in the soil caused by settling of the earth (possibly covering up a pit).
4. Any wires strung across walkways (possibly linked to explosive devices).
5. Items such as ropes, nails, or other fasteners that serve no obvious purpose (possibly used to activate explosive devices or anchor trip-wires).

When encountered, officers should immediately notify fellow officers either vocally or via radio, and then identify it with a noticeable marker (e.g., an orange ribbon) to alert other officers entering or leaving the area. Again, nonspecialist officers should refrain from attempting to disarm booby traps and simply bypass the area.

Safety Precautions

As mentioned, an explosive expert is recommended for each raid where traps are anticipated, and certain precautions should be practiced:

1. Only one officer should approach a trap. Other officers should be in nearby covered positions.
2. When a trip-wire is located, *both* ends of the wire should be checked.
3. All devices should be checked for more than one trip wire.
4. Trip wires should be cut only after any safeties are replaced.
5. Electric-looking wires should *not* be cut.
6. If twisted-type wires are present, only one wire at a time should be cut.
7. A mercury fuse may also be present in a device that has an obvious means of detonation (e.g., conspicuous fuse).
8. Before wires are traced, all suspect devices should be checked for a human operator, who might attempt to detonate the device from a hand-held controller.
9. If a suspect is apprehended in a raid, he or she should then be required to lead the search team through the site.
10. All officers in the raid team should move in pairs. In addition to having two sets of eyes on the alert, it also enables each officer to have first aid nearby in case of a casualty.
11. If one team member is injured as a result of a trap, remaining officers must approach the injured officer with caution so that no additional injuries result.

Locating Interior Booby Traps

As mentioned, booby traps can be located both outside and inside a residence. Once the outer perimeter has been cleared, the danger of encountering a trap is not yet over. Interior traps may be even more dangerous because they are usually contained in or wired to an object that appears to be perfectly normal; a lamp, a book, a door. Caution must be practiced by all raid team members at all times.

Indoor traps can be activated by trip-wires, electrical switches, or remote control. Typical indoor locations for traps are doors and windows; stairs and floorboards (pressure-type devices); gates; books or x-rated magazines (spring-release devices); the refrigerator; drawers; packages; or furniture (pressure-type devices).

Officer Safety Precautions

As with outdoor types, an explosives expert should be present. Other officers should observe the following precautions:

1. Do not attempt to open books or magazines.
2. No containers should be opened without a thorough examination.
3. Furniture should be closely examined before use.
4. Electrical switches should not be used if possible.
5. Officers should not consume food or beverages while at the raid site.
6. Anything that appears unusual should be regarded as suspect, and treated as such.
7. Booby traps that are located should be treated the same as outdoor traps: marked and avoided.

No single strategy can completely safeguard law enforcement officers in all raids in which booby traps are in place. Each raid is different and should be evaluated on an individual basis, with consideration given to the type of case, the number of possible suspects (and their backgrounds), and the location of the raid.

Types of Traps

The types of traps officers may encounter will depend on only the perpetrators' imagination and cunning. Officers should always remember the cardinal rule, "Notice the inobvious and expect the unexpected."

Exterior Traps

The Punji Pit. A standard in guerilla warfare, the punji pit (Fig. 7–13) was widely used in World War II and Vietnam. The punji pit is a large, deep hole in the ground containing many bamboo spikes or rusty nails, which are coated commonly with feces, urine, antifreeze, or other substances designed to promote infection and cause discomfort for the victim. The punji pit is difficult to spot because it is covered with leaves and small tree branches. The intruder steps on the covering and his or her body weight breaks the branches, dumping the victim into the pit. Investigators should look for leaves and branches that are dead and obviously not part of the surrounding greenery, or for anything in the road that does not seem to fit in the environment. Sometimes dead animals are nailed to or hung from trees to distract the attention of the intruder, or to lure him or her to the trap.

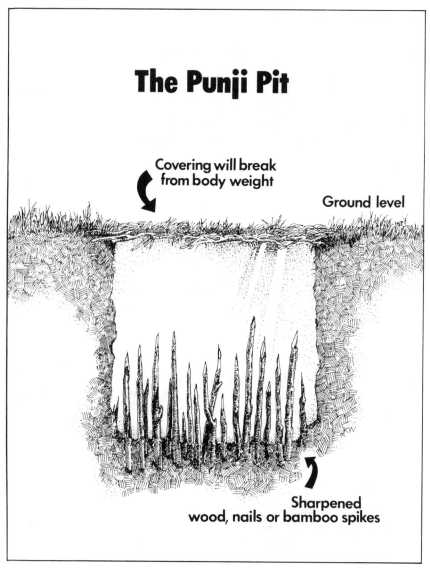

The Punji Pit

Covering will break
from body weight

Ground level

Sharpened
wood, nails or bamboo spikes

7–13

The Foot Breaker. This device can be manufactured by the perpetrator or purchased through some mail order survivalist-type magazines. It consists of a metal pipe, which is used to house a .22 or .25 caliber bullet. The bullet is placed inside with a spring-loaded firing pin at the base of the pipe. The pipe is then anchored in the ground (Fig. 7 – 14). When it is stepped on, the weight of the victim activates

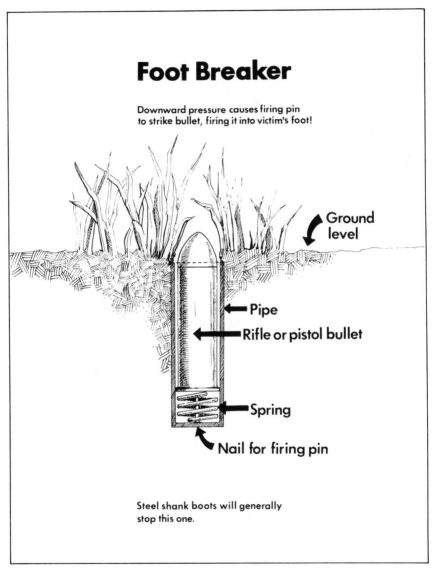

Foot Breaker

Downward pressure causes firing pin
to strike bullet, firing it into victim's foot!

Ground
level

Pipe

Rifle or pistol bullet

Spring

Nail for firing pin

Steel shank boots will generally
stop this one.

7-14

the firing pin and shoots the bullet into the victim's foot. Although
this device is not designed to kill the intruder, it will wound suffi-
ciently to remove the officer from the assault team. Officers who
wear boots with steel-shank soles may find these are sufficient to
stop the bullet. This trap is difficult to detect, and it will most likely
be located on the entry path to the target area.

7-15

The Trotline. This trap is inexpensive, easy to manufacture, and extremely effective. The trap consists of a monofilament fishing line strung between two trees at eye level. Anchored on the line are numerous fishing hooks, which injure the intruder. This trap is almost impossible to see, even under the best of lighting conditions.

Venus Fly Trap

This device can be made from an old flower pot planter
or a steel pot. Barbs can be sharpened steel spikes or
even fishhooks that are bent straight. The pot is buried
and then covered in order to appear natural. It may be
anchored in concrete.

Ground level

To escape from this trap — either break spikes or bend
them downward Never attempt to pull foot out! Seek
medical help immediately.

7 – 16

As with many of the other types of traps, it is not designed to kill,
only to maim (Figs. 7 – 15, 7 – 16).

The Mouse Trap. The mouse trap is designed to kill and maim. It
consists of a standard mouse trap, which is used as a firing pin for a

shotgun shell that is attached to the trap. A trip wire activates the catch on the mouse trap, thereby detonating the shotgun shell. These traps are commonly attached to trees at both knee and head level. Although the trap is usually fatal, sometimes they are used merely to warn suspects of intruders.

Interior Traps

Magazine Bomb. This device is a magazine that has had a portion of the inner pages removed so a mouse trap will fit inside unobtrusively. The mouse trap is affixed to a blasting cap, which will detonate when the magazine is opened. X-rated magazines are normally used to lure the victim. Magazine bombs can cause injury to the face, loss of fingers, or even death.

Hot Light. This is an incendiary device consisting of a standard light bulb that has been filled with a combustible liquid such as ether, kerosene, or gasoline. When the light switch is turned on, the device detonates, creating an explosion, and possibly igniting the victim's clothing. Variations of this trap include hand grenades that have been affixed to light sockets in place of light bulbs.

Armstrong's Mixture. Armstrong's mixture is a fairly new device, usually found in methamphetamine laboratories operated by outlaw motorcycle gangs. The device is made from a mixture of red phosphorous and potassium chlorate. After the explosives are made, they are then rolled up in an aluminum foil ball. Once the chemicals are mixed together and put in the foil, they are immersed in alcohol to render the material harmless. When the alcohol dries, the chemicals become volatile.

The devices are designed to look like packages of drugs wrapped in foil. When an officer attempts to open the package to check its contents, the tin foil activates the chemicals by rubbing against them, thereby triggering an explosion. The balls usually come in three sizes, and the extent of injury will depend on the size of the ball: (a) marble sized: loss of fingers or eyesight, and facial damage; (b) egg sized: loss of hand or part of an arm, loss of eyesight, facial damage, possible fatality; (c) baseball sized: always fatal (Figs. 7–17, 7–18).

Other Weapons

Whether engaged in the search of a car or a residence, the investigator should be aware of weapons other than traditional firearms

**Flash
Fire Bomb**

2-liter bottle contains
concentrated
sulfuric acid and
gasoline

Tea bag contains
potassium chlorate
and sugar

7–17

(handguns, shotguns, rifles) that are commonly used by drug traffickers and may be cleverly hidden or otherwise unnoticed. One such
weapon is the "bolt gun." This device appears to be an ordinary bolt
and might even be used as an ordinary bolt in a motorcycle, car, or
truck. The weapon is made from a standard 5/8" diameter (4½" long)
machine bolt that is hollowed out to fire a .22 caliber long rifle or
standard cartridge. To discharge the weapon, the hexagonal head is

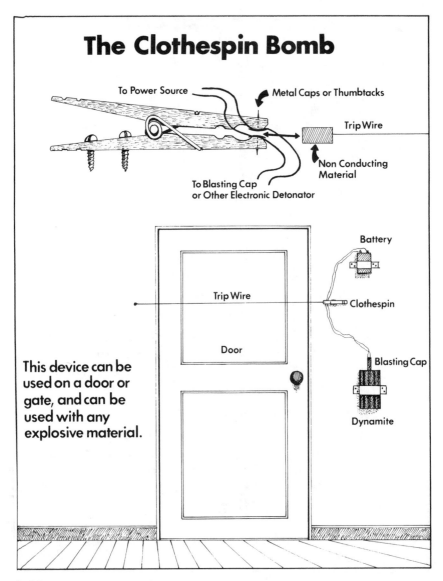

The Clothespin Bomb

To Power Source

Metal Caps or Thumbtacks

Trip Wire

Non Conducting Material

To Blasting Cap or Other Electronic Detonator

Battery

Trip Wire

Clothespin

Door

Blasting Cap

This device can be used on a door or gate, and can be used with any explosive material.

Dynamite

7-18

pulled back, and a spring-loaded firing pin comes into contact with the cartridge (Fig. 7-19).

Knives can also be concealed from the unobservant in belts, gas tank caps, ink pens, and rulers. All in all, the officer should remain cognizant of such devices when approaching suspects or their residences.

7–19 Photo of a bolt made into a gun which shoots a single small caliber bullet and is difficult to detect. (Photo courtesy of United States Marshals Service.)

Drug Raid Procedures

Raids are one of the most life-threatening situations encountered by law enforcement officers. Because they are used so frequently in drug enforcement, it is essential that all drug enforcement personnel be aware of the procedures for planning and conducting a raid in order to minimize casualties and confusion. It is impossible to discuss every possible raid situation and how properly to plan for all unexpected predicaments. All raids hold surprises. But to best avoid unforeseen dangers, the drug agents' best weapon is quality intelligence (see Chapter 1 and Chapter 9). Good intelligence can reveal much-needed information about the circumstances officers will encounter: weapons or booby traps inside the residence; associates who might be present at the time of the raid; booby traps in or fortification of the residence; if stolen goods are expected to be at the raid location. Raid planners must always prepare for the worst. When considering a drug raid, "Murphy's Law" should be remembered: "if anything can go wrong, it will!"

It is also important to know the type and amount of drug being sought in a raid. This could make a difference in how the house is entered. If there is a suspected 100 pounds of marijuana in the residence, it is unlikely that suspects will be able to dispose of it prior to entry by officers. If, however, there is one pound of cocaine suspected in the residence, then it is likely that it could be flushed or otherwise destroyed prior to entry; in this case, a "no-knock" warrant should be obtained (see Chapter 3).

In addition to the risk of encountering armed suspects during a raid, there is also the danger that officers may accidently shoot each other in a cross-fire situation, or through mistaken identity. This has happened on numerous occasions, and the possibility increases when all members of the raid team are not thoroughly acquainted with each other and the raid plan. When casualties occur in raids, it is usually not as a result of poor planning but *over*planning. Raid plans should not be so complex as to create confusion and misunderstanding among officers. As most experienced officers will attest, there are enough unforeseen surprises in each raid without having an overly complex plan to further confuse the officers and otherwise complicate the situation. The key to success with raids is simplicity.

Checklist for Raid Preparation

Although there are many considerations for the planning of a raid, basic planning should include the following:

1. Collect all intelligence regarding the suspects, associates, the structure to be raided, and the neighborhood (area) to be raided.
2. A thorough reconnaissance of the area should be conducted to identify all entrance and exit routes as well as any one-way or dead-end streets.
3. A sketch, drawing, or map should be available to actually show team members where they are expected to be.
4. Organization of the raid team should be evaluated where the number of personnel and the type of equipment needed are to be considered.
5. Communications are essential during a raid, in particular when multiple agencies are participating. Because most law enforcement agencies use different frequencies, a team leader from the host agency should be assigned to each team with reliable communications for unit to unit and unit to base.
6. Arrangements must be made for emergency response personnel, including SWAT officers, fire, and ambulance personnel.
7. If needed, a police chemist should be available to assist in the search and dismantling of any chemical laboratories.
8. The time of raid execution must be established. In addition a briefing time should be established at least one hour prior to the designated time of the raid.
9. A chain of command must be established and understood by all members.

The Raid Leader

The team leader is responsible for coordinating all aspects of the raid and should have sufficient authority within the unit to make field command decisions when necessary. Initially, all plans for manpower, equipment, and communications must be understood: the time to recognize deficiencies in planning is before the raid, not during it. Additional considerations such as food, water and first aid must also be accounted for in the event of an extended operation, as should plans for the proper evacuation of neighbors in the area in the event of a possible shooting situation or explosive laboratory. The team leader has the responsibility of selecting team members for various tasks during the raid. These members must possess the necessary physical abilities, skills and knowledge to conduct such an operation and all team members must be properly outfitted with equipment (raid jackets, body armour, radios, shotguns/rifles, etc.) and have sufficient knowledge of the investigation including information on suspects, weapons, vehicles, etc.

As mentioned, it is common for multiple law enforcement agencies to participate in drug raids, so the team leader must be sure every officer is familiar with the other officers involved in the raid (especially when undercover people are used). This is usually accomplished during the briefing where all parties are present. Secondly, raid/search teams must be established if there is more than one residence to raid. The teams will usually consist of five to seven officers. Again, the team leader for each team should be a member of the host agency for the raid and should possess communications between other team members.

To properly prepare a raid team for the raid, the following checklist should be considered:

1. Communications
   A. Electronic: radios (encoded), battery powered headsets, flashlights
   B. Other: flares, whistles, vocal or hand signals
2. Equipment for the raid
   A. Weapons
   B. Uniforms (i.e., raid jackets)
   C. Camouflage
   D. Specialized equipment: night vision devices, bolt cutters, etc.
   E. Food and water
   F. Contingency plan for a shooting situation
   G. Prisoner transportation plan
   H. Transportation of team members
3. Investigative considerations
   A. Searching techniques (see Chapter 3)
   B. Search warrant execution (see Chapter 3)
   C. Arrangements for prisoner interviews
   D. Processing crime scene and prisoners: sketches and photographs (see Chapter 3)
   E. Arrangements for proper press release (see Chapter 10)
4. The Search Team Members (see Chapter 3)
   A. Recording officer (the search unit)

B. Evidence seizing officer (the search unit)
C. Prisoner control officer (optional)

Tactical Considerations

Because many raid situations do not offer the luxury of a trained SWAT (Special Weapons And Tactics) team, raid team members must be knowledgeable about basic assault tactics. The tactics discussed in this portion of the text are general and should be considered for each raid situation on an individual basis.

Raids will be conducted in both urban and rural environments, so the individual raid plan will vary in each case. For example, a raid in a rural area, such as a cultivated marijuana patch or illegal laboratory, may present different dangers than if it were conducted in the city. This is true because of the lack of sufficient cover for officers involved in the initial assault, as well as the possibility for hidden booby traps and snipers located in wooded areas of the property. For this reason, a raid conducted on a structure suspected of containing booby traps, should be conducted in three phases: (a) the securing of suspects, (b) a sweep by a EOD expert for hidden booby traps to remove the hazard, and (c) the search of the residence for contraband (if authorized by a search warrant).

As indicated, all suspects must be controlled immediately upon the assault of the structure. Once under control, all suspects (whether under arrest or not) should initially be detained and turned over to the prisoner control officer for monitoring. It can later be determined who should be placed under arrest after the search of the residence is conducted and evidence is located. In this phase, the team leader must also maintain control of his or her own team members. Prior intelligence of the structure and area should assist officers in knowing which strategy of entry to use.

The initial assault of the raid location usually requires four unit functions:

1. *Perimeter unit:* This unit is one that seals off the raid site from intruders (curious bystanders) and may aid in apprehending persons attempting escape from the structure. The perimeter unit might also be used in the event neighbors need to be evacuated from the raid site prior to the assault of the premises.
2. *Assault unit:* This is the initial entry unit whose primary responsibility is to control all suspects within the structure, thereby making it possible to safely conduct a search.
3. *Cover unit:* This unit supports the assault unit in case of an

altercation or confrontation by suspects, and it usually enters the structure immediately after the assault unit.

4. *Search unit:* This unit is assigned to conduct thorough search of the structure once the suspects are accounted for and secured (see Chapter 3).

There are several assault and control maneuvers that should be considered and discussed with team members during the raid briefing. These tactics cover both the approach to a structure as well as entry methods and should remain somewhat flexible to adapt to any raid situation.

External Control Methods

The tactical plan is only a tool or guide to be used in the planning process. It should not become a biblical or administrative panacea for the "paper tiger" type commanders who are neither "street wise" nor adaptable to split-second change and are usually more concerned with "form" and "control" of personnel than with the specific objectives of the investigation. This type of supervisor has been known to use such forms as "cover" in the event that something goes wrong during the investigation, and should not be assigned to "operational-type" commands.

A more realistic approach should be to appreciate the different variables available to the supervisor, choose among alternative actions, develop a "game plan," and then remember: "the only thing that you can be sure of in a narcotics buy is that you cannot be sure about anything." (From Vernon J. Geberth's "Narcotic Buy Operations," *Law and Order Magazine*, 1979.)

If the suspect inhabiting a raid structure detects approaching officers, he or she will then be forewarned to either destroy any evidence, acquire weapons with which to attack officers, or escape. Organized methods of approach are essential in ensuring the officers greatest assistance in any raids: the element of SURPRISE.

Immediate Reaction Maneuver

This is an assault maneuver conducted primarily in rural areas while approaching marijuana patches or clandestine laboratories. A point man must lead the raid team and act as an initial scout for suspects, guard dogs, or booby traps. If the suspect is sighted, the point man should quietly but immediately move off of the path toward the area with the most cover. The rest of the team moves off the path in the same direction thus eliminating a crossfire situation (Fig. 7–20).

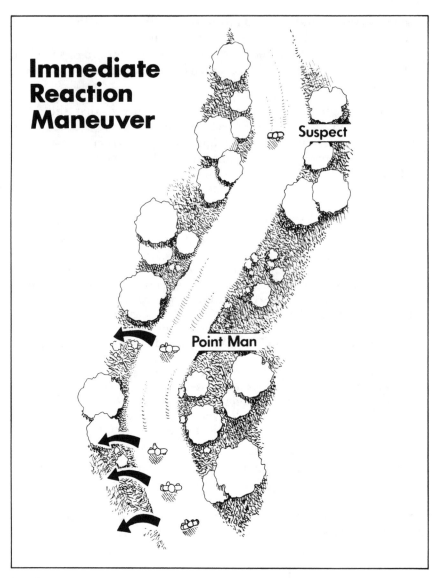

Immediate Reaction Maneuver

Suspect

Point Man

7-20

L-Shaped Clearance Maneuver

In the event there are several structures on the property of a raid site, the use of the L-shaped clearance maneuver should be considered. This will help to prevent a possible crossfire situation and to most effectively contain any suspects. In this scenario, team "B" must be in place before team "A" arrives on the scene. This plan also allows

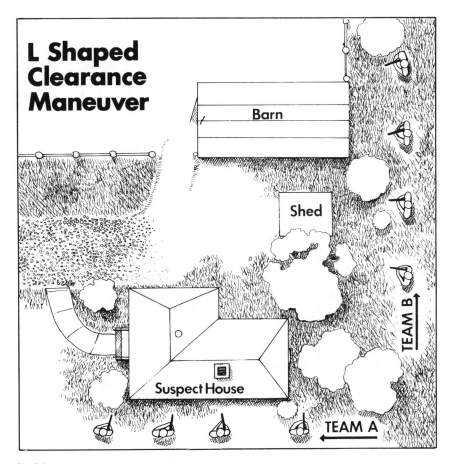

L Shaped Clearance Maneuver

Barn

Shed

Suspect House

TEAM B

TEAM A

7-21

team "B" to converge on the out-buildings prior to moving in on the suspects' residence (Fig. 7-21).

L-Shaped Sweep Maneuver

Again, a maneuver most appropriate for marijuana operations, as it automatically flanks any opposing targets that are encountered and concurrently eliminates the possibility for escape. In this sequence, the team leader is positioned at the corner of the L formation so he or she can better direct all team members. In the event the suspect confronts either flank with gunfire, the flank fired upon immediately halts and lays down the first base of fire. The remaining team then changes position and returns fire. Containment and control are the ultimate results of this paramilitary maneuver (Fig. 7-22).

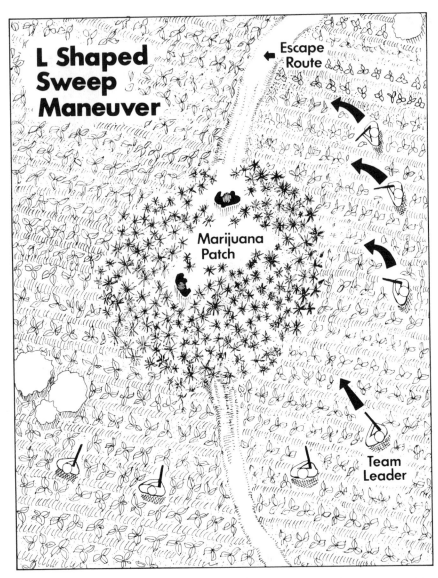

L Shaped Sweep Maneuver

Escape Route

Marijuana Patch

Team Leader

7 – 22

It should be noted that in many cases, the use of hand-held radios may give away the location of agents seeking cover; the raid team should develop hand signals (in advance) to use when radios must be turned off and silence is necessary for either a discrete approach or officer safety.

Internal Control Methods

One of the most dangerous duties in drug enforcement is when officers enter the residence of a suspect during a raid. Most of the officers injured or killed make the same mistakes, usually while passing through the doorway into the residence. The most common mistake is that when the door is first opened, the first officer through the door will, more often than not, stand in the doorway and scout the layout of the room. The danger is that no matter where the suspects are located in the room, their chances of hitting a target standing in the doorway (the "fatal funnel") is almost 100%.

Given that there are only so many ways to enter a doorway in a raid situation, officers should practice accepted entry methods and remain in the doorway only long enough to enter the room: never linger in a doorway! There are three methods of entry during a raid, which might eliminate complications and maximize the control of suspects.

The Wrap-Around Entry Method

Although dangers may exist within the residence, officers are at much less risk using this approach. Two officers should be used when possible, thus enabling each officer to survey one-half the room for possible suspects. As these officers maintain their posts, other officers enter the structure and practice the same method for each additional room encountered (see Fig. 7 – 23).

The Criss-Cross Entry Method

This method of internal structure control is generally considered effective because it allows two officers to enter the structure and immediately position themselves inside the structure, which provides mutual coverage of the control area. Once in position, the entry officers can maintain control of the room and permit support officers to enter and perform the same maneuver for each room within the structure until all occupants are accounted for and controlled (see Fig. 7 – 24).

The High-Risk Entry Method

When entry must be made into a structure where risk factors are usually high, the high-risk entry method should be considered (see Fig. 7 – 25).

Wrap-Around Entry

7-23

The Final Raid Report

At the conclusion of each raid, the case agent should prepare a report summarizing all significant aspects of the raid. It is advisable for the case agent to prepare this report as he or she will be most familiar with the suspects, addresses, and other aspects of the case. The final raid report may be prepared back at the office, but notes for the report should be taken at the scene of the raid to ensure accuracy of times, locations, suspect names, officers present, and other details.

When structuring the report, certain fundamentals must be included:

1. Information on the raid team.
   A. The size of the team.

7-24

    B. Names of each team member (plus each jurisdiction, if applicable).
    C. The specific task of the team.
    D. Times of the arrival and departure.
2. Information on the raided structure.
    A. Entry and exit routes.
    B. Environmental information (rain, snow, night, dawn, etc.).
    C. Terrain information, including sketches, photographs, and/or diagrams to depict the approach methods and the location of any important pieces of evidence.
    D. Other locations of evidence inside structure.
    E. Locations of weapons.
3. Information on suspects.

High-Risk Entry

Prone

7-25

    A. Suspect information.
    B. Confrontations with suspects.
4. Other information.
    A. Officer injuries.
    B. Any other information that may later be important.

Summary

Much is to be considered when addressing the many different situations encountered in drug enforcement. A technique that is effective in one investigation may not be successful in another. The investigator must be flexible in his or her approach in dealing with all types of investigations.

The marijuana cultivation operation is a drug enforcement problem that poses many unique hazards and investigative challenges. The actual recognition of such an operation is the first step in the investigation, which can be best accomplished by the receipt of credible informant information; in some cases, this may be difficult to obtain. Locating cultivators may also require investigators to profile the violators themselves by observing their actions, growing equipment or supplies, and the type of land most commonly chosen for such an endeavor.

Another significant source of drugs is drugs obtained through diversion scams practiced by drug registrants, medical care facility employees, and street criminals. This source of drugs is perpetuated by registrants through substitution scams, false-charting, and outright theft. Careful observation of employees' actions and quality of work may indicate diversion. When investigating this type of violation, it should be remembered that violators divert drugs both for profit motives and for reasons of personal addiction.

Investigators must also be cognizant of the street criminal who will try to scam physicians by claiming false ailments or by attempting other inventive scams. When investigating these violations a paper trail must be established to determine the origin of stolen or forged prescriptions. The problem of drug smuggling creates other unique challenges for the investigator. There are several types of smuggling operations: air, ground, marine vessel, and body packing. Each requires a degree of surveillance and the ability to search persons, places, and things effectively.

Like the marijuana cultivation operation, the clandestine laboratory operation is also largely a rural phenomenon, which makes detection both tedious and difficult. The operator will set up his or her laboratory after first accumulating chemicals and hardware from numerous sources. Investigators who identify such a violator should conduct extensive surveillance to determine the sources of supply for necessary equipment and precursors. Observing the suspect in possession of special equipment and chemicals may be sufficient probable cause for acquiring a search warrant for those locations associated with the suspect. Lab operators commonly choose the rural environment for their laboratory because of the distinctive odor emitted from the lab while it is in operation. This odor would easily be noticed by passers-by if it were in a more populated environment. Again, the odor alone may be sufficient probable cause for a search warrant if detected and properly documented.

Compounding problems in cultivation and laboratory operations are deadly booby traps, which are commonly associated with these operations. When approaching a location suspected of being booby trapped, a qualified EOD expert should be present to help identify possible traps. If an EOD expert is not available, officers should be knowledgeable in how to recognize a trap. When raids are considered, precautions should be taken in the handling of prisoners, collection of evidence, and coordinating the raid while multiple jurisdictions are present. If the raid plan is kept simple, confusion and casualties will be minimized.

Suggested Readings

Davis, James Martin, *Raids.* Springfield, IL: Charles C. Thomas, 1982.

Lyman, Michael D., *Narcotics and Crime Control,* Springfield, IL, Charles Thomas, 1987.

Lyman, Michael D., *Gangland: Drug Trafficking by Organized Criminals,* Springfield, IL: Charles C. Thomas, 1989.

Macdonald, John M., *Criminal Investigation of Drug Offenses, The Narcs Manual.* Springfield, IL: Charles C. Thomas, 1983.

Report to the President and the Attorney General, President's Commission on Organized Crime, America's Habit, U.S. Government Printing Office, March 1986.

Schultz, Donald O., *Police Operational Intelligence,* 3rd ed. Springfield, IL: Charles C. Thomas, 1986.

II

The Administration of the Drug Enforcement Unit

Drug enforcement is a complex law enforcement endeavor which must maintain a critical balance between managing personnel and conducting administrative functions within the agency, such as the handling of funds, equipment and other resources. Managers must strive to minimize growing attrition rates among agent personnel by affording the employees knowledge and information about the interworkings of the agency and the reasons why certain administrative and operational decisions are made.

Theories of Management   8

In this chapter we will "shift gears" somewhat and turn our focus from drug enforcement techniques to traditional and contemporary theories of managing drug enforcement units. A lot has been written about management theory, but in this chapter we will attempt to identify those theories that are most closely associated with and/or applicable to management of a drug unit. Careful consideration of these theories is essential for managers concerned with the needs of both the law enforcement agency and the individual worker.

Law enforcement administrators are faced with many supervisory challenges: the inherent responsibilities of police management, changing legal and social conditions, advances in police training, new procedures, increased expectations of police professionalism, rising public demands for a reduction in drug-related crime, personnel management, agency management, and the deep-rooted politics, which traditionally accompany the job. Early pioneers in police administration, such as Sir Robert Peel and August Vollmer, made great strides in professionalizing police work through better agency organization, improved public image, and utilizing new technologies in order to help suppress and control crime. Such goals epitomize the administrator's need for a defined hierarchy of authority and maximum control within the agency. Other innovators followed, offering both theoretical and practical contributions that promoted better organization and management of police functions.

Over the years, many business management philosophies have been adapted to law enforcement administration. Some have proven more beneficial than others, but most offer valuable points for police managers to consider. The complexity and diversity of management theories, however, may create questions of which theory (or combination of theories) may be best suited for a particular function within a law enforcement agency.

In managing a drug enforcement unit, there are two fundamental tasks that must be subsumed under successful administration: employee control and employee motivation. Before considering management theories the unit's specific goals and objectives must first be established. These are long-range aims of the organization, which in many cases are interrelated.

The goals of a drug enforcement unit should reflect and support those of the agency within which the unit operates. Such goals may include specific priorities unique to the unit, including the basic premises underlying the unit itself. For example, it is not plausible for a small city police department to target international drug trafficking as their primary mission because of lack of jurisdiction, manpower, intelligence-gathering capabilities, and other resources. Such a goal is more realistic, however, for a national law enforcement agency such as the U.S. Customs Service or Drug Enforcement Administration.

Although the existence of a drug enforcement unit may look good on paper, it must possess an actual ability to produce cases consonant with the ideals and expectations of the public it serves. Conversely, the objectives of the drug unit may be more specific and short-term. For instance, objectives in a drug enforcement might include a reduction in local cocaine and crack distribution, or an emphasis on arresting larger scale dealers rather than street level violators (dealers and users). Both objectives are specific and do not necessarily require long-term commitments by the unit. Having established goals will help lend direction to the operations of the unit with regards to staff requirements, specialization, daily operations, and overall productivity.

Management Concepts

The term *theory* is defined by Webster as, "a belief, policy or procedure proposed or followed as the basis of action." It could also be stated that a theory is an idea of how to attain a specific goal. Goals in police work are varied and require the implementation of many different ideas and strategies, sometimes simultaneously.

There are three general schools of thought regarding police management theories. These include:

1. The Traditional Organizational Theories
2. The Open Systems Theory (Human Resources & Behavioral Systems)
3. Bridging Theories

Each represents a management viewpoint, which leans either toward rigid control of the employee or a more flexible working environment. As mentioned, many theories have evolved from each of these schools of thought over the years and some of these are discussed below.

Traditional Organizational Theories of Management (Closed System Theories)

It is clear that with regard to personnel and business management, some agencies seem to operate more smoothly than others, and the degree of efficiency and harmony in those organizations that succeed is directly associated with the management philosophy practiced by the agency. As in the open system theory of management (discussed below), many different theories exist.

The traditional theories of management are those which are rigid and unresponsive to the personal needs of the employee, focusing instead on the success and efficiency of the organization. Although actual police work requires officers to be flexible in their duties on the street, the management of the police function is generally considered rigid, as one might guess from the paramilitary structure of most police agencies. A couple of the traditional philosophies supporting a strict management policy are discussed below, and are commonly associated with police management. Additionally, these will address questions of how to best keep an organization together, and how to best maintain the effectiveness of management.

Fredrick Taylor's Theory of Scientific Management (The One-Best-Way Method)

This American management philosophy originated in the early 1900s by an American machinist named Fredrick Taylor. Basically, Taylor held the philosophy that all workers must give their all for the company, and that the efficiency of the organization must surpass any personal needs of the employee. In Taylor's theory, only first-class workers were to be employed, which were defined as those who performed their jobs in the most efficient way possible.

The definition of "scientific management," according to Taylor's book *Principles of Scientific Management*, is a system of administration based on the supremacy of science and the quest for efficiency. Each work task should be broken down into specific detail so each position can be standardized and measured scientifically. This system is arbitrary, leaving no room for personal improvements based on experience with the given task. To formulate this theory, Taylor worked with factory and postal employees who had specific tasks within their organizations. This substantially differs from police work in that even though officers have specific goals to attain, there may be many different ways to achieve those goals.

Some of the distinctive features of Taylor's theory are:

1. *Scientific analysis*: All phases of each task are scrutinized minutely.
2. *Time and motion studies*: All tasks are timed and scrutinized to minimize wasted time and effort.
3. *The "best-way" theory*: The scientific way to perform a task is the best and only way.
4. *Training*: Employees should be trained to complete all tasks quickly and efficiently.
5. *"First-class" workers*: Only those workers who work according to the best-way concept will be permitted to continue their employment with the organization.
6. *Piece-rate wages*: Those workers who produce the most will be paid accordingly, as will those who fail to produce. This serves as an incentive to work harder.
7. *Planning and supervision*: Planning must be done by those most competent to do so, and supervision must be geared toward production rather than rank.
8. *Prosperity*: If the work is done efficiently, then the costs of production will be minimized.

As one can see, the Taylor theory of management has many potential pitfalls. If applied to the already existing paramilitary structure of the police organization, the additional regimentation could result in increased personnel attrition, which would be unacceptable. In addition, police administration may best be served with the expansion of training, enabling officers to learn not just one task, but instead becoming proficient in several (cross-training).

Max Weber's Theory of Bureaucratic Organization

Weber was a German social philosopher with many interests, including sociology, economics, and political science. He is credited for formulating the basic theory of bureaucracy, which meant "power of the office." The nucleus of bureaucratic theory is that the establishment of a governmental bureaucracy helps to ensure efficiency through hierarchy, authority, and standards of regulation and procedure. The bureaucratic model rests on the idea that jobs should be broken down into specifically defined tasks, and these tasks should then be assigned to individuals having a particular degree of related experience.

Clearly, this is the case in police agencies where specialization has become commonplace. Many police agencies recruit new drug enforcement personnel from those officers already employed by the agency but who have had previous or related experience in the drug enforcement field, rather than hiring a civilian who would require considerable training and indoctrination.

As in any bureaucracy, there is a hierarchy of authority. This consists of positions within the organization that are held accountable for the success of the organization's mission. The hierarchy extends from the highest position of authority to the lowest position of obedience within the agency. As with most bureaucratic structures, business is conducted in a formalized, impersonal manner with strict adherence to intra-agency communication through an established chain of command. Job appointments are arbitrary and career oriented, with strict observation of a candidate's qualifications. In addition, most bureaucratic appointments are contingent upon a period of probation in which the new employee must prove his or her worth for continued employment.

The theory of bureaucratic organization has another interesting component, which places it parallel to traditional police structures: there are several general groups of personnel who occupy levels below that of chief executive.

1. *Upper management*: In a law enforcement agency, there are positions of executive management immediately under the chief administrator (e.g., Assistant Chief or Under-Sheriff). These individuals support the executive officer, and each assumes responsibility for a particular area of administration within the organization.
2. *Middle management*: Middle managers operate at the pleasure of those in upper management, and usually command specific units within the agency such as intelligence division, pharmaceutical drug diversion division, or special services division.
3. *Lower management (line supervisors)*: This the lowest level of managerial personnel. These individuals supervise officers in the field and make any necessary low-level managerial office and field decisions.
4. *Line personnel*: Workers without management authority make up the majority of any bureaucratic institution, and they must answer to any and all superiors, from lower management to the chief executive.

Weber considered this theory of management far superior to any other because of the rigidity of the structure and the minimal opportunity for mistakes. As mentioned, most police agencies in fact adhere strictly to this philosophy because public service work is so closely scrutinized by the public. The bureaucratic method reduces the chance for error.

Critics of the bureaucratic theory of management claim that it is an unrealistic way to achieve agency goals effectively while treating employees' needs individually. In addition, employees who work in this repressive atmosphere may constantly experience work-related stress and constant pressure from supervisors to perform (see Chapter 9).

The Open Systems Theory of Management

In contrast to traditional theory, the open systems theory generally considers the personal needs of the employee first. In open systems theories, it is generally held that a satisfied employee is also a productive employee; therefore the needs of the subordinate should be identified and addressed in to help further the goals and objectives of the organization. The two theories that evolved out of the open systems concept are (a) the human relations theory, and (b) the behavioral system theory.

The Human Relations Theory

There are many theories about human relations in management. Generally, human relations theory is the "people oriented" or "open systems" study of groups of human beings in a work environment, which focuses on their common values, aspirations, and problems. The human relations school actually developed out of the traditional organizational theory (previously discussed), and it has developed an informal study of personal relations, work conditions, and organizational cohesiveness.

There are three studies in human relations management which apply to the administration of police organizations and might work well in the organization and management of drug enforcement units.

The Hawthorne Studies (Elton Mayo)

When striving for a positive and productive working relationship between managers and subordinates, the Hawthorne studies of 1927 should be considered. The Hawthorne studies illustrate the significance of close manager–subordinate interaction, and they further show that work environments are, in fact, social systems. The Hawthorne studies were undertaken at the Western Electric-Hawthorne Plant in Chicago over a period of five years.

Basically, the experiment consisted of two separate studies. The first study involved placing five female employees in a special room to perform the task of assembling telephone relays. The physical conditions in the room varied throughout the experiment to provide both pleasant and unpleasant environments for the women. Despite the changing working conditions, productivity increased. It was determined at the end of the study that regardless of the adverse *physical* conditions in the environment, the employees found the structure of the environment to be less formal, creating conditions in which the group became a close-knit unit. Additionally, they had been receiving constant attention from the experimenters, thereby creating the "Hawthorne effect," which ultimately resulted in a higher productivity.

The second study, however, was somewhat different. Fourteen men who wired switchboards were placed on a "piece rate basis," which allowed them to earn more money if they worked harder and produced more finished switchboards. Theoretically, it was to their own best financial interest to become more productive; this group was also placed in a special room. Their productivity, however, did *not* increase. It was determined that because the group had determined that financial betterment was not as desirable as the "informal" values within the group: to not produce too much, not to be a "rate-buster," and not to be too subservient to supervisors.

In conclusion, the Hawthorne studies determined that:

1. Financial incentives offered by management are somewhat limited or offset by the informal values established by the work group.
2. Some workers may not work well alone but may be productive when working as part of a group.
3. The work output level is determined not by the physical setting in a work environment but by social norms established by the workers themselves.

It is a well-known fact that police work creates a powerful social system of its own and tends to bond those officers who work closely together. Perhaps the Hawthorne studies can benefit the police manager in illustrating that positive psychological work incentives are essential in properly motivating subordinates. Regardless of adverse working conditions (long periods of stationary surveillance, working outdoors in adverse weather) the police manager may be more successful in applying the "carrot on the stick" motivational philosophy rather than the traditional "kick in the pants" philosophy.

Maslow's Self-Actualization Theory

Considered a significant breakthrough in the study of human motivation, Abraham Maslow's self-actualization theory has helped police managers realize the needs of subordinates. Basically, Maslow (1908–1970) believed that people have basic needs that must be addressed before they become useful and productive employees. Maslow's theory is based on five fundamental needs of the employee, and is diagrammed in Figure 8–1 below.

These needs, listed in order of necessity could be described as follows:

1. *Physical needs*: Food, shelter, and sex.
2. *Security*: Job security, physical safety.
3. *Love*: A person's need to belong or be accepted by friends, family, and peers.
4. *Self-esteem*: A feeling of self-worth, status, and admiration by others.
5. *Self-actualization*: One's ability to fulfill one's potential.

In summary, Maslow's theory holds that the first two (bottom) levels of the structure are the most difficult to attain. Moreover, an individual will not strive to achieve the next level until he or she has first conquered the lower levels. Problems in managing employees occur

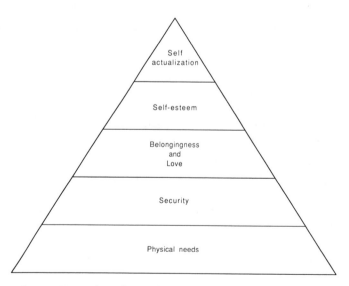

8–1   Maslow's Hierarchy of Needs

when the different levels cannot be mastered, creating problem behavior in subordinates. The ultimate goal of the worker is to achieve self-actualization, thereby fulfilling all basic needs and becoming a confident, mature, and responsible employee.

Williams' "Clash of Pyramids" Theory

The "clash of pyramids" theory was developed by J.D. Williams, and it attempts to consider the problems of fitting social beings into bureaucratic systems such as police work. In this theory there exist two pyramids: the organizational pyramid and the social pyramid. Each has special and unique features.

The Organizational Pyramid

Williams first contends that most bureaucratic organizations have a pyramidal shape, with authority and command at the top and loyalty and obedience at the line level (Fig. 8–2). Positioned in between are the functions and goals of the organization. Agency objectives are regulated by authority and discipline.

The Social Pyramid

In this concept, Williams suggests that because the people who make up an agency are social beings, then the agency must consequently become a social agency. The personal needs of those within the agency create a second pyramid (Fig. 8–3). This second pyramid has many of the same levels of needs as those in Maslow's theory (above), and it is one that strives toward personal self-actualization. In other

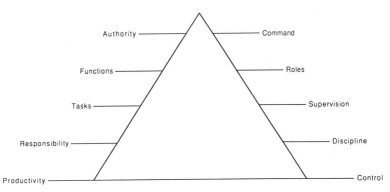

8–2 Williams' Organizational Pyramid of Public Agencies

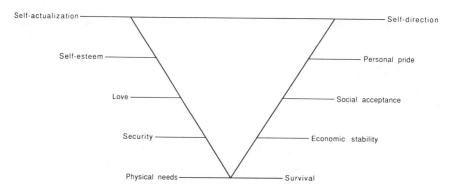

8-3 Williams' Social Pyramid of Organization Workers

words, the goal of this pyramid is the attainment of personal satisfaction rather than the needs of the organization.

The "Clash of Pyramids"

This is the marriage of the two philosophies discussed above. The "clash" occurs when the different goals and objectives of each pyramid work against each other (Fig. 8-4). For instance, the objectives of the agency might inhibit the attainment of certain personal goals. Williams gives five reasons for the pyramid clash.

1. *Coercion versus liberation*: The organizational method relies on coercing workers through discipline (thereby restricting their personal achievements), while the social method liberates employees resulting in higher quality work.
2. *Organizational goals versus personal goals*: Each pyramid has its own goals, which are in direct conflict with one another.
3. *Suppression versus growth*: In controlling workers the organizational pyramid tends to suppress personal growth and allow for growth only in work-related areas, while the social pyramid frees workers and allows for personal growth.
4. *Stationary versus flexible structures*: The general structure of each also varies greatly. The organizational pyramid is much more permanent than the social pyramid.
5. *Regulation versus sociability*: The organizational pyramid is composed of rules and regulations where the social pyramid is made of compassion, emotion, friendship, and unity.

In conclusion, Williams' theory shows that it is not likely that this conflict can be avoided in administration. Employers and subordinates must instead strive to minimize the clash whenever possible in

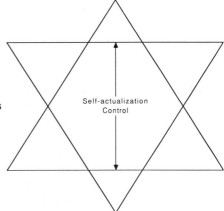

8-4 Williams' Clash of Pyramids

order to ensure the effectiveness of the agency. In addition, it should be noted that a total yielding to either pyramid would result in a nonproductive environment for both groups.

The business of drug enforcement reflects many of these "pyramidal" conflicts. A good example is the problem of employee overtime, which is a common occurrence in drug enforcement. In this scenario, the unit requires employees to work overtime because of numerous backlogged cases. The job, thereby, requires the removal of the employee from his or her personal life to serve the needs of the organization. When practiced in excess, there is the possibility of erosion of employee morale and dissension within the unit. If not properly managed, this could ultimately result in a rising attrition rate, which creates additional expenses for the agency (hiring and training new personnel), which works against the needs of the organizational pyramid.

The Behavioral Systems Theory

Behavioral systems theory was developed around 1960, and is a spin-off of human relations theory. Behavioral systems theory looks at organizations as being composed of interrelated behaviors, and generally embraces the concept of a more democratic work environment.

McGregor's "Y" Theory

In 1960, Douglas McGregor (1904–1964), a one-time student of the Maslow theory, identified two different assumptions that managers make about people, known as the X and Y theories. Theory X (organization oriented) holds that people are basically unmotivated and require coercion to become effective in their jobs. In addition, this theory states that most people dislike work and that they will avoid it whenever possible, thus requiring strict and close supervision. Theory Y (employee oriented) holds that most people desire responsibility and that they will show much more promise and potential when committed to a particular task or organization goal. In particular, the theory holds the premise that people will perform better and will be more confident when they are performing meaningful jobs.

McGregor theorized that an individual's needs must be met before the needs of an organization can be satisfied. In addition, a worker can be motivated by financial gain if such a reward has not already been achieved. If, however, an employee has achieved a certain degree of financial success, then psychological needs must be fulfilled to successfully motivate the employee.

Law enforcement agencies have traditionally functioned under the X theory of management, which focuses on control and dominance of the employee. Conversely, use of the Y theory in police work advocates a marriage of the needs of the organization with the needs of the employee.

Quality Circles

The use of quality circles is a kind of spin-off of the McGregor theory Y, and is beginning to be more widely used in police departments. What are quality circles? The term quality circles refers to a employee participatory approach to problem-solving. Under this theory small groups of employees from the same unit, primarily nonmanagement personnel, should be allowed to work together in meetings to identify problems and recommend solutions.

The quality circles concept has gained currency in recent years in the United States, but it has its roots in Japan where its principles have been applied to the workplace. In the late 1970s many U.S. industrial companies such as 3M, Chrysler, and Lockeed, began applying the quality circle concept of management. As of 1978, many government agencies have adopted this theory of management discipline. Generally speaking, quality circles involve small groups of workers from the same unit (usually between 6 and 12 individuals), who voluntarily meet at designated times to discuss problems and their solutions. This concept differs from "management by objectives" (discussed next), as it is typically composed of nonsupervisory personnel. A group leader or "facilitator" is chosen from outside the unit and guides the group in focusing on the problems at hand and their solutions. The circle, however, may choose its own problems to study.

Although the problems studied include many different areas, typically, the circle will focus on the improvement of working conditions of the unit rather than the quality or effectiveness of services provided by the unit. These conditions would include the overall working environment, worker morale, and individual development of circle members. A circle will usually work in the following manner:

1. Members are usually given training in group interaction and problem-solving techniques.
2. The group meets weekly to select problems with which to work on. Meetings usually last an hour and are held during work hours.
3. Once problems are identified, the group analyzes them and searches for a solution (provided it is within the group's expertise). Meeting minutes are recorded for later review.
4. The result is a formal written recommendation to management. All team members participate in the presentation to upper management and explain both the reasoning involved and the projected costs of the changes.
5. Once the particular solution to the problem is approved, they may help in implementing the idea and then go on to address another problem.

This concept has been used successfully by police departments around the country: the Orlando, Florida Police Department; Dallas, Texas Police Department; Mesa, Arizona Police Department; Los Angeles, California Police Department; and the Fort Collins, Colorado Police Department. Most of this experience with quality circles and police personnel is fairly new. The primary issues police departments must consider in the adoption of the quality circle plan are: What types of problems should be addressed? How can attendance be maintained? What tracking of the circles should be done? How long should circles last and what are the effects of quality circles?

Answers to these questions may be obtained through a process of trial and error, but much has to deal with the individual workings of each department. For instance, problems addressed by quality circles in police work have been alterations in shift staffing and manpower allocation; better prioritization of service calls; and designing procedures to provide better service to citizens using the customer service desk.

Certainly there are many areas of law enforcement that could be improved. Moreover, there are the unique problems in drug enforcement which quality circles could address: new policies to cut down on excessive employee overtime; new procedures to integrate more closely the services of outside law enforcement agencies; new policies on providing undercover officers a clothing allowance; improved or expanded cross-training, so that officers with varying responsibilities may be used in different investigations.

Bridging Theories

Just as Fredrick Taylor's philosophy is the "one-best-way" method, the contingency theory within the bridging theory school holds that "there is no one best way." In other words, depending on the individual circumstances of each organization and situation, managers can adapt portions of many philosophies in structuring a management ideal for their own organizations.

Performance Management

Having discussed both human relations and behavioral systems theory in management, let's now look at how performance management theories have been used by managers in the administration of justice.

Management By Objectives

Although management by objectives (MBO) is generally considered to be a successful motivational management tool in the private business sector, its lack of flexibility for use in law enforcement management has tended to stifle its growth in this area. It is necessary, however, to examine MBO because it is becoming more rapidly accepted by progressive police agency managers.

As with many management theories, the ultimate goal of MBO is to improve agency productivity and performance. In police work, many issues concerning leadership practices and personnel management are regulated by a system of disincentives (such as personal disciplinary action), as opposed to positive reinforcements.

Management by objective is a 30-year-old concept, which has been adapted to police management only since the 1970s. It is basically a process whereby individual managers identify specific objectives for the coming performance period (e.g., a quarter or year), and then periodically review the extent to which the objectives have been met. MBO focuses on the manager rather than the worker, but it is geared to improve worker performance. Additionally, it focuses on the result of a task rather than the process required to achieve it. An objective can be defined as a precisely stated condition or as an end product to be achieved. In MBO, however, objectives should be clearly defined as how to achieve their successful completion. More and more police agencies have adopted this system, and it is now recognized by the Commission on Accreditation for Law Enforcement Agencies.

An MBO system may require certain unit or departmental commitments in order to achieve the desired goal. This includes the preparation of paperwork and filing and access to informational systems to determine progress toward the goal. Under MBO, all units within a department participate, including sworn as well as civilian personnel. In drug enforcement, this requirement is essential anyway because of investigations which require input from so many different sources within the agency. The success of MBO depends greatly on input from not only top and middle managers, but line supervisors alike (senior officers and sergeants). All of these can help identify individual performance targets.

The problem with MBO's emphasis on the establishment of objectives is that they are often too general and their achievement is difficult or impossible to document. For example, "Begin to reduce the amount of crack being sold in the city." Well, how does the department "begin?" Through bar checks? Undercover operations? Search warrants? Vehicle roadblocks? Additionally, how is the word "amount" defined? Small quantities of crack possessed by street dealers or the large amount of crack produced in crack manufacturing houses? This objective is not specific enough and its success may not be measurable.

For the MBO approach to work at all, police units must decide whether their managers should focus on one of three types of objectives: process objectives, outcome objectives, efficiency objectives, or a combination of these.

1. *Process objectives*: A process objective focuses on a particular end or activity to be undertaken rather than a outcome to be achieved. For example, an objective may be this workload to be completed: "Conduct narcotics investigations in at least 10 of the 33 taverns within the city limits." Process objectives may involve a continuation of previous objectives, or the implementation of new ones.
2. *Outcome objectives*: Outcome objectives focus on the results of an activity rather than the means used to achieve it; for example, "increase cocaine arrests by 4% over last quarter," or "increase the number of marijuana plants seized or eradicated over the previous year by 10%."
3. *Efficiency objectives*: Efficiency objectives focus on containing or reducing department expenditures. These may be specific expend-

iture reductions or reductions in certain activities that affect costs. As examples of police departments using this method:

The police department in Lakewood, Colorado, addressed efficiency objectives such as cost per patrol hour and cost per traffic accident response.

The police department in Compton, California, set several objectives, including reduce the previous year's fuel consumption by 10%, reduce sick and injury time by 20%, and maintain minimum of downtime on department fleet vehicles.

An example of a drug enforcement unit efficiency objective might be to compare the costs and results of a 60-day undercover street operation to a series of pharmacy drug audits lasting the same period of time (staff hours, expenses, and number of arrests).

MBO has distinct benefits for the worker and the agency alike, and it should be considered by agency administrators and managers for a more efficient and accountable work performance. For a successful program, however, administrators must realize that MBO takes time to establish (possibly up to 90 days), and to be considered a success, employee participation is a must.

Blake and Mouton's Managerial Grid

In 1962, a managerial grid theory was developed by Robert Blake and Jane Mouton, which would allow for supervisory flexibility in police work. Basically, the grid (Fig. 8–5) has two components: concern for production and concern for employees. The different dimensions of the grid are rated from 1 (lowest concern) to 9 (highest concern), and leadership style of managers is thus identified by how each of these areas are combined. According to Blake and Mouton, the degree of interaction of both components of the grid creates five different management styles:

1. *Authority–Obedience (9,1):* An authoritarian approach where efficiency in operations results from arranging conditions of work in such a way that human elements interfere to a minimum degree.
2. *Impoverished Management (1,1):* A laissez-faire approach in which minimum efforts are exerted to accomplish required work and to sustain organizational membership.
3. *Organization Man Management (5,5):* A democratic approach in which adequate organization performance is made possible by

balancing work output with the maintenance of satisfactory employee morale.

4. *Country Club Management (1,9)*: Thoughtful attention to the needs of people for satisfying relationships, which leads to a positive, friendly working atmosphere.

5. *Team Management (9,9)*: Work accomplishment is achieved through committed employees; interdependence through a common stake in organizational purpose creates a working atmosphere of trust and respect.

As indicated, each style is characterized by a numerical assignment indicating emphasis on production or employee concerns throughout the management process. According to the grid theory, the best style of management begins in the 9,9 area, and effectiveness decreases through 5,5 and ultimately to 1,1, which is considered the least effective and productive area.

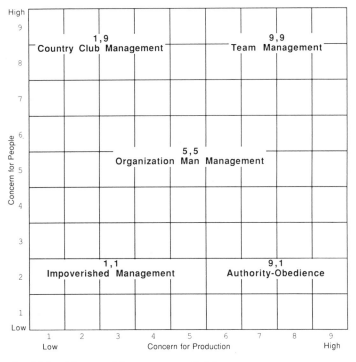

8–5 The Blake-Mouton Management Grid

Summary

There are many different management theories. Before adopting or adapting any of them, however, managers must closely evaluate conditions within their own agencies with regard to goals, resources, and/or special problems. After careful consideration of agency conditions, a particular management philosophy may be successfully adopted, maximizing unit productivity and positive officer morale. Agency managers should also actively communicate with other agencies and managers who work in a similar environment, to compare supervisory strategies.

To best determine an appropriate direction for management, much consideration should be given to the balancing of organizational productivity and the needs of the employee. As early management philosophies indicate, the method of administration may focus on the goals of the organization with little consideration given to the needs of the individual employee. Conversely, some management theories are geared to the needs of the employee, with the belief that agency productivity will be enhanced by keeping those personal needs satisfied.

Suggested Readings

Gerth, H. H., and Wright, Mills C., *From Max Weber: Essays in Sociology.* New York, Oxford University Press, 1946.

Goodsell, Charles T., *The Case for Bureaucracy*, 2nd ed. New Jersey, Chatham House Publishers, 1985.

Hatry, Harry P., and Greiner, John M., *Improving the Use of Quality Circles in Police Departments.* The U.S. Department of Justice, National Institute of Justice, 1986.

Hatry, Harry P., and Greiner, John M., *Improving the Use of Management by Objectives.* The U.S. Department of Justice, National Institute of Justice, 1986.

Kast, Freemont E., and Rozenzweig, James E., *Contemporary Views of Organization and Management.* Chicago, Science Research Associates, 1973.

Knapp, Whittman (Chairman), *Commission to Investigate Allegations of Police Corruption and the Cities Anti-Corruption Procedures.* Commission Report, New York, 1972.

Maslow, A. H., *Motivation and Personality.* New York, Harper & Row, 1954.

McGregor, Douglas, *The Human Side of Enterprise.* New York, McGraw-Hill, 1960.

Swanson, Charles R., *Police Administration*, 2nd ed. New York, Macmillan, 1988.

Agency Organization and Structure

9

This chapter will examine the general structure of the drug enforcement agency or unit and attempt to explain the necessary functions of each division within the unit. Additionally, to help illustrate the text, some reports and forms commonly required to run the unit are also discussed. It should be noted that because drug units operate as part of governmental bureaucracies, only certain forms are featured; it would be too lengthy a process to itemize every form required for the successful operation of the drug unit.

Agency Organization

As discussed in the preceding chapter, one of the basic functions of organizational management is the division of labor or specialization of services. It is generally held by police administrators that to best meet the functional responsibilities of law enforcement agencies, specialization of services is usually required — in particular, the allocation of specific jobs to individuals within the department who are especially qualified to perform those jobs. From a supervisory standpoint, however, this philosophy may create problems in coordinating the efforts of both staff and sworn personnel within each specialized division with the organization.

Specialization may create additional problems resulting from jobs within the division that are somewhat narrow in scope, thereby increasing the likelihood of complacency and poor performance. The same problems may apply to agents working within the unit. If an officer within the unit is uncomfortable working undercover, it is possible that he or she might have a talent that could benefit the unit in a different capacity (document examiner, evidence technician, or photography specialist). With these points in mind, we can now more closely examine the specific functions of the drug enforcement unit and its overall administration.

From a traditional standpoint, most drug enforcement units operate within municipal police departments; many have grown out of already existing vice units dealing with prostitution, gambling, and, in some cases, liquor control. Because drug enforcement units are specialized and usually employ undercover police personnel, they will frequently operate separately from the rest of the department. This helps to insure that officers' covers can be maintained by not being associated with uniformed officers and by not being seen entering or leaving the police department facility.

Another primary reason covert units operate separately from the rest of the department is because of the sensitive information handled by undercover officers and their informants. If not handled properly, the credibility of the investigation and the reputation and liability of the department could be at risk. As a consequence, the covert unit will sometimes be required to avoid the normal chain of command and report directly to the agency administrator. The agency head may act as commander; in some cases he or she may directly supervise the unit and act to restrict other divisions within the department from gaining knowledge of the unit's covert activities.

In most instances, however, agency administrators may not have the time (or expertise) to command such a unit effectively, and the department may choose to place the unit under the criminal investigation division, thereby placing it within the established chain of command within that division. This can be advantageous to the narcotics personnel as well as the general investigative personnel: both deal with suspects in all aspects of criminality, and information and sources can be easily exchanged.

In smaller departments, drug enforcement responsibilities may lie with one or two detectives who may or may not operate in an undercover capacity. In this case, the narcotics duties are usually considered to be a part-time activity while the investigator handles other types of investigations (Fig. 9–1).

Additionally, investigators in smaller departments would probably use informants in lieu of using department officers for undercover work. Most often informants would be used to establish probable cause for a search rather than for making drug purchases for prosecution (see Chapter 5).

In the case of a state agency or larger jurisdictional agency (such as a metropolitan police department), the decentralized use of substations or district offices is common. This enables enforcement officers to more adequately cover their assigned area and reduce the possibility of duplication of efforts and "burns" of undercover personnel. Although decentralization is somewhat debatable, there are several specific advantages (Figs. 9–2, 9–3, 9–4).

1. An individualized district office may have more flexibility when managing cases and planning arrests and raids.
2. Agents will usually be working with local informants, and they will be generally more familiar with the community and different drug dealers operating in the area.
3. A local supervisor might be in a better position to control personnel than a central manager working out of headquarters.
4. There is closer supervision of personnel and more frequent contact between agents, dealers, and users in districts, thus increasing the incidence of arrests.
5. Drug enforcement in district patrol divisions is more successful because agents have closer contact with uniformed officers and can be advised of high activity drug areas.

From an administrative standpoint, however, decentralization of drug enforcement units may have more disadvantages than advantages. One such disadvantage is that the overall mission of the unit may become confused when the unit is split up and commanded by several supervisors rather than a single manager. Other problems are that agency-wide directives may not be disseminated properly, investigative procedures may vary from one station to another, and overall communication may suffer greatly — all resulting in low productivity of the unit. It is also generally thought that a central command structure may better administer police procedures, budgeting, and general planning activities.

Other disadvantages of decentralization are:

1. Drug enforcement priorities may vary in a decentralized structure (an emphasis on street dealers in one unit, an emphasis on larger scale suppliers in another).
2. Drug enforcement personnel in district offices may be used for other nonnarcotics assignments such as prostitution or gambling.
3. Unproductive competition may develop between districts which may result in lack of communication and failure to share and exchange resources.

Investigative Functions

Whether a drug enforcement unit operates as a division of a law enforcement agency or as a separate enforcement entity (such as a

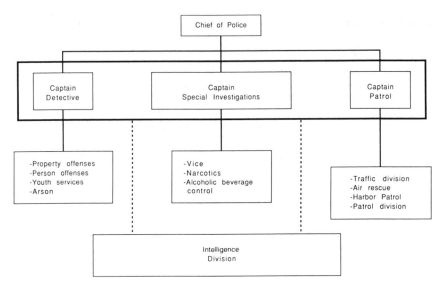

9 – 1 Functional structure of a police department

state investigative bureau), enforcement goals and priorities must be established. To best carry out these priorities, specialized divisions within the unit or agency should be established. The various investigative sections may include narcotics intelligence, street-level enforcement, drug diversion investigations, or specialized services (air smuggling, organizational charting, electronic surveillance and organized crime).

The ability of an agency to support a specialized unit largely depends on its manpower and financial resources. When considering the best scenario, the following drug unit divisions should be considered:

The Narcotics Intelligence Section

A sound intelligence base is essential for the successful operation of any criminal investigation unit, and drug enforcement is no exception. Because illicit drugs are so widespread, individuals from any level of society may either be involved or associated with those who traffic in drugs. Careful documentation of criminal information regarding who is doing what and where is critical.

The intelligence section as a central depository for information, and it may operate in a number of ways. The ideal role of an intelligence section is to deploy undercover officers to infiltrate areas within the community that are considered high-crime or known drug

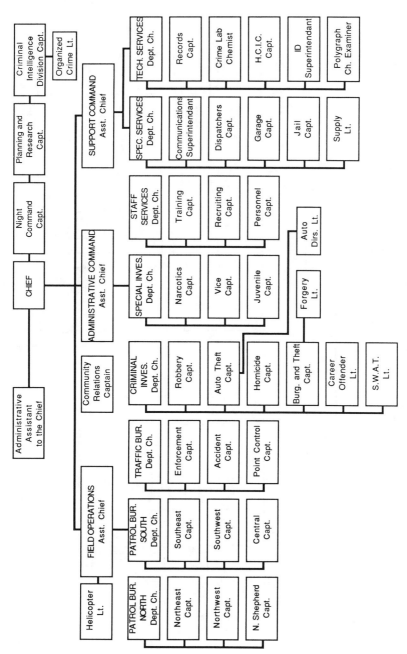

9-2 Organizational structure of a metropolitan police department

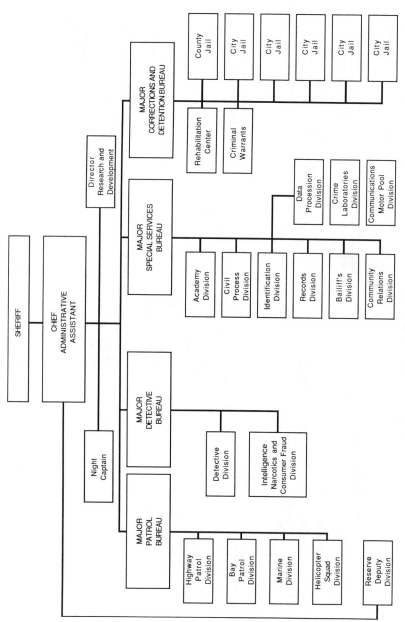

9-3 Organizational structure of a sheriff's department

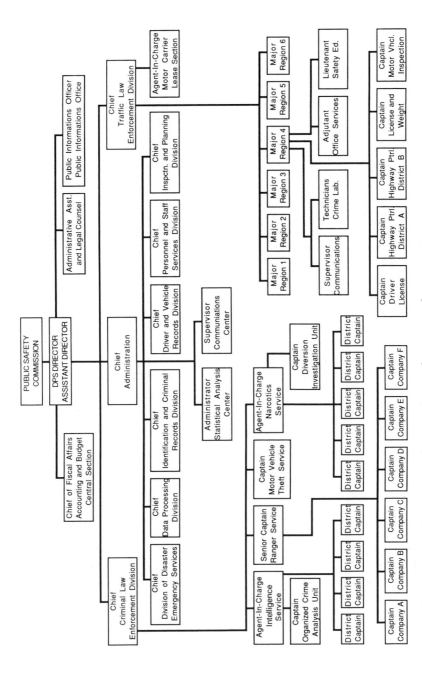

9-4 Organizational structure of a state law enforcement department

trafficking areas. Informants may be used for this function but information reliability may be impaired (see below).

Timely and accurate reporting procedures must be maintained, where information is constantly relayed back to the command unit for possible case initiation. Ideally, undercover intelligence officers should not become involved in arrests or any other high-visibility situation where their covers could be jeopardized. The job of undercover officers is to *remain* undercover and penetrate as far into the criminal element as possible while reporting information back to the unit. In the event drug buys are set up or a particular crime is planned requiring enforcement intervention, the intelligence officer should turn the case over to an undercover enforcement officer to investigate further.

Intelligence units are occasionally structured where an analyst is assigned to the unit and any intelligence reports gathered from personnel and their informants are subsequently catalogued and rated according to the reliability of the source. The analyst should be able to cross-reference and chart information on criminal suspects in a way that is beneficial in investigations involving multiple suspects and large criminal organizations.

Strict guidelines must be established regarding the type of information collected as well as the storage, retrieval, updating, and purging of documented information. In addition, security measures must be established to protect sensitive information from unauthorized dissemination (see section on intelligence gathering discussed later in this chapter).

The Street Level Enforcement Section

Generally, this is the core of the drug enforcement unit, which undertakes investigations covering a broad range of drug violations. (Undercover investigations should only be attempted when a traditional criminal investigation is considered ineffective, due to the potential danger involved in undercover contacts.) The street enforcement unit is a general assignment unit with the most manpower, confidential funds, and working informants. Violators at the user, dealer/user, and dealer level are most commonly investigated by this unit. Much street level enforcement activity involves working in taverns, with prostitutes or pimps, and with opportunist criminals who may be involved in other criminal activities (burglary, robbery, etc.). The street enforcement unit is also used to (a) obtain information on suspects and organizations; (b) obtain evidence for prosecution; (c) identify individuals suspected of criminal activity; (d) document association between suspects to prove conspiracies; and (e) verify the reliability of informers (see Chapter 5).

The street level enforcement unit must have adequate manpower at its disposal. Drug deals involving dangerous, armed, and unpredictable criminals mandate that a surveillance team be available to ensure officer safety as well as to help document the violation itself. It is recommended that a minimum of three surveillance officers be available for each undercover contact (more will be needed for an arrest). In the event that suspects are discovered conducting counter-surveillance during the deal, or in case the dealer or associates travel from one location to another during the course of the transaction, additional officers should be available to observe.

The use of undercover agents is a longstanding practice in drug enforcement. It should be noted, however, that in most investigations undercover agents remain on the same level of distribution on which they enter: Suspects higher up the trafficking ladder are usually less willing to conduct business with customers who are unknown to them. Because of this, officers specializing in electronic surveillance (special operations section) should be considered for continuing investigations.

The Diversion Section

A large percentage of the dangerous drugs consumed in the United States are pharmaceutical drugs diverted from legitimate channels of distribution. The diversion section investigates this type of activity by means of undercover work and investigative audits of registrants (hospitals, pharmacies, and physicians). The crime of diversion may involve street level criminals as well as those who are classified as registrants; the diversion unit must therefore be prepared to undertake both undercover and traditional criminal investigations alike (see Chapter 7).

The Special Operations Section

Drug investigations requiring a particular expertise should be conducted by a special services section. For example, an air smuggling investigation would employ officers knowledgeable about the aviation industry: the ability to identify the various aircraft commonly used in smuggling (profiling), how airports are managed, and close working relationships with the U.S. Customs Service (see Chapter 7).

The specialized services section may also concentrate on larger scale dealers in the community rather than street level dealers. In this case, extensive experience in conspiracy investigations, covert surveillance, and the operations of specific organized crime groups (La Cosa Nostra, Latin and Carribean OC groups, and outlaw motorcycle gangs) would be required. Still other examples of the special services section's responsibilities would be canine handlers, the installment and operation of pen registers and wire-tap equipment, the installment of audiovisual surveillance equipment in undercover apartments and houses. (This last function, however, might also be performed by the intelligence section.)

The RISS Projects

When considering the collection and dissemination of criminal intelligence, a valuable investigative resource is the federally funded RISS project. The Regional Information Sharing Systems (RISS) projects, directed by the Bureau of Justice Assistance, are multistate agencies designed by the U.S. Department of Justice to support state and local law enforcement efforts in tracking the traveling criminal or major criminal conspiracies. This RISS concept, as the name implies, is a regional intelligence gathering function which, for member agencies, offers an exchange of intelligence information for more than 1600 criminal justice agencies across the country. Specifically, RISS programs offer member agencies loans of investigative equipment, confidential funds, criminal information bulletins, training, technical assistance, referrals, access to telecommunication systems.

As of 1984, RISS projects had seized or recovered over $2 billion in illicit drugs and stolen property, and could boast of more than 10,650 arrests directly attributable to the assistance given to law enforcement agencies by the program. There are six RISS programs, which are located in the following geographical areas:

Mid-States Organized Crime Information Center: Kansas, Nebraska, Illinois, South Dakota, Minnesota, Missouri, Iowa, Wisconsin, and North Dakota.

New England State Police Information Network: Massachusetts, Vermont, Connecticut, New Hampshire, Maine, and Rhode Island.

Middle Atlantic–Great Lakes Organized Crime Law Enforcement Network: Michigan, Ohio, New York, New Jersey, Indiana, Pennsylvania, Maryland, and Delaware.

Regional Organized Crime Information Center: Texas, Arkansas, Mississippi, Alabama, Georgia, North Carolina, Virginia, Oklahoma, Louisiana, Tennessee, Kentucky, West Virginia, South Carolina, and Florida.

Rocky Mountain Information Network: Montana, Wyoming, Colorado, New Mexico, Idaho, Nevada, Utah, and Arizona.

Western States Information Network: Alaska, Oregon, Hawaii, Washington, and California.

Records Management

Due to the considerable bulk of paperwork generated by the drug enforcement unit, a system of evaluation, cataloging, and retrieval of information must be maintained. Regardless of what type of report is produced, it should be reviewed by a designated manager before it is filed; it is usually a good practice for paperwork to be also read by a member of the administrative staff. This procedure will ensure that reports on file will be accurate, complete, clearly written, and generally acceptable in a criminal court proceeding. The review process also gives managers an opportunity to identify and purge sensitive, unfounded, or irrelevant material prior to filing and storage.

Illicit drug use frequently involves people in all levels of society; in many instances this may include friends and relatives of police department personnel and associates of other highly visible individuals within the community. Because of this, drug enforcement personnel must be cautious with how they catalog, index, and disseminate activity reports — including investigation and intelligence reports.

With regards to on-going investigations, drug enforcement personnel should have exclusive access to these files. Drug investigations must be kept discrete so as not to jeopardize the investigations or to compromise the safety of undercover officers and their informants. Problems arise, however, in deciding who in the department has a right-to-know, and who has a need-to-know. Unfortunately, at times high-ranking officials within the agency may, out of curiosity, inquire about on-going investigations and want to know the names of those being investigated (this is a particular problem with regard to intelligence files). Strict policy should be established regulating those who claim to have a right-to-know (because of rank). Access should be permitted only to those who have a legitimate need-to-know (because of their assigned function within the agency).

In most cases, this would require the drug enforcement unit to maintain its own files apart from the rest of the agency. Problems in case management and accountability can be minimized by the unit requiring a case number for a particular investigation without releasing details of the subject of the investigation. The main records division can then place an indicator card in the file to show that the particular case number has been assigned to a certain officer in the drug enforcement unit. After arrests have been made, the drug unit can forward all necessary paperwork to the proper file; in this way, strict secrecy can be maintained during the course of the investigation. Proper case documentation requires the drug enforcement maintain several files for its primary files: a master index file, general case file, an intelligence file, an information dissemination log, and special information files.

The Master Index File

This file consists of the names of individuals who have come into contact with the drug enforcement unit or who have been mentioned in case reports. Only a few years ago such files were maintained on 3 × 5 cards, which were periodically updated; many departments are now computerized, and the information is easily stored and quickly retrieved. Other specific information commonly kept in these files (besides proper names) are: nicknames, dates of birth, places of birth, physical descriptions (including any identifying characteristics such as tattoos or scars), or Social Security numbers. Reports indexed in this file include: complaints, reports of investigation, and supplemental reports (not intelligence files).

The General Case File

All police agencies should maintain a general case file. The general case file contains not only the case files on drug violations recorded by the unit, but also drug cases investigated by other units within the department; for example, a case in which the general vice unit had charged individuals with drug violations as well as prostitution charges. In this case, both types of violations would be cross-referenced to both the vice and the narcotics units. Another example of a cross-referenced drug violation would be drug seizures by the patrol division, which resulted in an arrest.

Regardless of who generates the report, each is assigned an individual case number, which is usually issued at the time a case is initiated. Most case numbers will usually begin with the two digits of the current year followed by a chronological sequence number indicating the order of issuance. Other digits in the case number may indicate the district or division in which the case was generated (patrol or burglary division). Other identifying characters might be considered in cases where violations other than narcotics have been documented; for example, 89-137-SS (year case was opened, sequential number of case, unit generating the case).

The Complaint Report

Once the basis for a open criminal case has been established, the basic criteria for the case is documented first on the "complaint report." The complaint is the first official paperwork to be filed on a case, and it should only contain one or two paragraphs of data summarizing the basic details of the case; it is filed in the general case file. This "front sheet" is an at-a-glance record of the circumstances surrounding the opening of the case, including suspect's name, address, identifiers (date of birth, place of birth, social security number), and a brief narrative of the violation (see Fig. 9 – 5).

The report of investigation is also prepared with the complaint and should contain details of the same incident outlined in the complaint. As mentioned, the complaint is an at-a-glance report of the initial violation, whereas the report of investigation is the first de-

COMPLAINT FORM

Note: Hand print names legibly: handwriting satisfactory for remainder.

Subject's name and aliases			Address of subject			Character of case
Complainant			Complainant's address and telephone number			Complaint received ☐ Personal ☐ Telephonic Date _____ Time _____
	Race	Sex ☐ Male	Height	Hair	Build	Birth date and Birthplace
	Age	☐ Female	Weight	Eyes	Complexion	
	Scars, marks or other data					

Facts of complaint

Action Recommended

_____
(Agent)

9–5

tailed report to be entered in the general case file, showing all pertinent information of the violation (Fig. 9 – 7).

The Supplemental Report

Also contained in the general case file are any subsequent reports
documenting the progression of the case. This is called the supplemental report, and it is normally a report that is much longer and

CITY POLICE DEPARTMENT	CASE NUMBER	PAGE 1 OF
SUPPLEMENTAL REPORT	TYPED BY	DATE
FILE TITLE	ADDITIONAL VIOLATION ☐ SURVEILLANCE ☐ ARREST ☐	
	OTHER☐	
	STATUS CLOSED ☐ PENDING ☐ INITIAL ☐	
	REPORTED BY	DATE REPORTED

DISSEMINATION RECORD	SIGNATURE (Agent)	
	APPROVED (Name & Title)	DATE

OFFICIAL USE ONLY

9–6 Report of Investigation form

more detailed than the complaint, but it will use the same case number as the original complaint for filing purposes (Fig. 9–6). The supplemental case report fully documents any progressive actions taken by the case officer in the course of the investigation, such as subsequent drug purchases, surveillance activities or undercover contacts between the suspect and officers/informants. Before a case is opened such information should also be documented in an intelligence report.

CITY POLICE DEPARTMENT	CASE NUMBER	PAGE 1 OF
REPORT OF INVESTIGATION	TYPED BY	DATE
FILE TITLE	VIOLATIONS	
	STATUS CLOSED □ PENDING □ INITIAL □	
	REPORTED BY	DATE REPORTED

DISSEMINATION RECORD	SIGNATURE (Agent)	
	APPROVED (Name & Title)	DATE
OFFICIAL USE ONLY		

9–7 Supplemental Report form

The Intelligence Function

An essential function of any covert police unit is the collection and storage of criminal intelligence information. Police agencies collect intelligence information for the purpose of better understanding a particular problem within a community, and once a problem has been identified and understood it is then more likely that a solution can be found. Intelligence may be collected in a number of ways: newspaper articles, covert surveillance, business or personal records, computer networks (such as NCIC), general case files, statements from citizens or suspects, testimony and court records. Intelligence may be collected overtly or covertly, depending on the suspected nature and sensitivity of the case.

To best understand the intelligence function in a law enforcement agency, let us first define the term *intelligence*:

> The knowledge of past, present and future criminal activity which results from the planned collection of information which, when evaluated, combined with other relevant information and analyzed, provides the user with a basis for rational decision making.

Types of Intelligence

Because of the many varied sources of data, it may at times be difficult to differentiate between the types of information collected. A single piece of information, for instance, may be considered either strategic or tactical (or both), depending on the goals and objectives of the unit. To better understand how to categorize information, the types of intelligence must first be defined.

Strategic

Strategic intelligence is useful in formulating *long-range* planning and policy management. It provides information regarding the capabilities, vulnerabilities, and intentions of intelligence subjects. In particular, strategic intelligence is useful in targeting areas of criminal activity over long periods of time. If, for example, a crack-house is discovered in a particular area, strategic intelligence would include the number of individuals (sellers and buyers) involved in the operation, the names and identifiers of those associated with the operation, whether or not the suspects carry weapons, the quantities of crack being sold out of the house, and so on.

Tactical

Tactical intelligence targets areas of criminal activity of *immediate* concern to the law enforcement agency. It provides specifics regarding individuals and organizations, their activities, their methods of operation, and the areas in which they are active. Given the previous example, tactical intelligence would include information on the fortification of the residence, the existence of booby traps in the residence, and the location of drugs, business records, or weapons inside the residence.

Intelligence Gathering

Because so much sensitive information is learned through the intelligence gathering process, law enforcement agencies must be very cautious regarding (a) what information they collect, (b) how it is stored, (c) to whom it is disseminated, and (d) how long it is kept on file. Generally, a covert unit may collect intelligence information on individuals suspected of involvement in one or more of the following activities:

Violations of federal criminal law.

Violations of state criminal law.

Organizations who advocate the use of violence toward any goal.

Organizations who finance those who use violence against others.

Individuals who threaten, plan or commit acts of violence or other criminal acts.

Organizations who attempt to acquire weapons, firearms, explosives, or other dangerous devices for the purpose of commiting a criminal act.

In collecting information on individuals suspected of involvement in the above acts, a delicate balance must be effected between the constitutional rights afforded citizens and the goals and objectives of the law enforcement agency. In order to help ensure that this balance is maintained, the unit also should specify the acts for which the collection of intelligence is prohibited:

Data should not be collected on individuals solely based on sexual preferences, race, religion, or political beliefs.

Data should not be collected on an individuals or groups because they support an unpopular cause.

No unit personnel will violate the law for the purpose of collecting intelligence information.

No unit personnel will hire, contract or otherwise employ another to collect intelligence information unlawfully.

Electronic surveillance equipment will not be used improperly or illegally when gathering intelligence information.

Intelligence information will not be disseminated outside the department without first going through the proper channels and chain of command.

Under no circumstances will the Constitutional rights of citizens be violated by unit personnel while employed by the department.

The Procedural Flow of Criminal Intelligence Gathering

Target Selection

This is the first step in the collection process. It is usually a management decision because the entire intelligence collection mechanism begins here. Targets should be selected in an orderly and systematic manner, which should utilize the expertise and experience of officers and supervisors alike.

Factors to consider in this phase are: (a) Does this target conform to the objectives of the unit? (b) Does the unit possess the required resources for the operation? (c) How valuable is the target? (Is it worth the trouble?). It is pointless to consider targets that will not further the goals of the unit, or which are unobtainable due to insufficient resources (Fig. 9-8).

Data Collection

This function consists of both planning and collection of information. Before this process is initiated, it should be determined who is to collect what data, when, and where.

Data Collation and Analysis

This step organizes the information into coherent form. It is in this phase that information is filed and flow-charts depicting relationships and associations between suspects are created. Once the information is organized, it should then be interpreted for any particular significance in the operation.

Intelligence Files

Because intelligence reports are not normally used in court proceedings, the style of writing is somewhat more relaxed than in preparing a complaint or supplemental violation report. It is generally acceptable to write an intelligence report that contains speculation and hearsay in addition to any documented or verified facts. The reporting agent should, however, distinguish whether the remarks are based on opinion or fact in the body of the report, and he or she

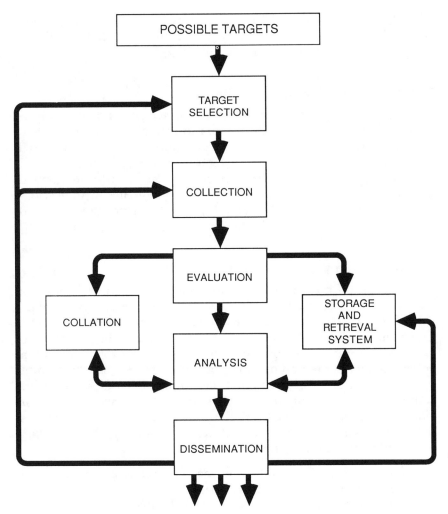

9-8 Chart of intelligence process

should try to structure the report to be concise and to the point. To catalog information that is considered reliable, it is also a good policy to require all agent personnel to verify any information contained in intelligence reports when possible.

The agent preparing the report should indicate the type of sources used (private citizen, criminal source, government agency, law enforcement officer).

It also should be indicated in the report how the source obtained the information (personal knowledge, documents, hearsay or rumor, hypothesis). Finally, the reporting officer should estimate the overall reliability of the source of information by marking an appropriate box on the face of the report: highly reliable, usually reliable, reliability questionable, unevaluated (see Fig. 9–9).

The Temporary Intelligence File

As indicated earlier, only certain types of activity should be documented by the unit, and such information should be verified whenever possible. In the event unverifiable information is considered important enough to document, a temporary intelligence file should be considered. The temporary file should catalog information on alleged activity for which there is no strong evidence or indication. The temporary file should hold information for no more than 90 days during which time it should have limited dissemination.

Auditing the Intelligence Files

All information maintained within the intelligence files should be accurate, or as accurate as possible. It is therefore necessary to establish a system whereby the files are purged of unwanted, inaccurate, irrelevant, or dated information that is of no use to the department. With this in mind, the host department should establish a written policy giving a set period of time (such as five years) at which point such information will be purged. The intelligence files should be audited at the beginning of each year. Information five years old or older should be removed from the system and the case numbers should be reassigned for future reference. Generally, the following information should be purged:

1. Information that is found to not have been disseminated, added to, or used during the last five years.
2. Information that is not or cannot be validated.
3. Information that, if retained, will not serve the goals and objectives of the department.
4. Information received from other agencies; actually, this should be purged sooner than every five years.

Charting

With the emergence of various groups of drug traffickers such as youth gangs, Jamaican gangs, and traditional organized crime groups, it is increasingly difficult for drug investigators to keep track of 1) the growing numbers of suspects in an investigation, 2) the important events that occur during the investigation, and 3) the different illicit commodities under investigation (ie, drugs, weapons, laundered money, chemical precursers, etc.).

| CITY POLICE DEPARTMENT
INTELLIGENCE REPORT | File:
Date: |

SUBJECT: (Name and any identifying numbers)

SOURCE IDENTIFICATION: (Name or Number) _____
  Private Citizen ☐
  Criminal Source ☐
  Govt. Agency ☐   Personal Knowledge☐ Documents☐ Hearsay/Rumor☐ Hypothesis☐
  Law officer ☐   Other_____

EVALUATION OF SOURCE:
  Highly Reliable☐   Usually Reliable☐   Reliability Questionable☐   Unevaluated☐

BY:

INFORMATION CONTENT: INFORMATION FILES CHECKED:
  Partially Verified☐   State Criminal Record☐   Similar Info.
  Unverified☐   State Drivers Licence☐   In File No._____
  Verified☐   NCIC☐
                      Other:_____

RECOMMENDED FOLLOWUP:
  Investigator to Verify☐   Source to Verify☐   Analyst to Research☐   File Only☐

DISSEMINATION:

9-9   Intelligence Report form

It is, therefore, necessary in many cases to organize investigations that involve large numbers of individuals, in a series of charts. These charts help investigators utilize both the information contained in the intelligence files as well as information learned in the course of the investigation.

Charting not only benefits the investigator but will also aid in the prosecution of the case by explaining complex organizations to prosecutors and jurors. Three of the most widely used charts in drug investigations are link analysis, event flow charting, and commodity flow charting.

Link Analysis

Link analysis is an extremely useful tool when investigating large groups of individuals or organizations. It is used to graphically illustrate relationships between individuals so their involvement in criminal activities can be more easily understood. Link analysis is also beneficial when many different individuals are alleged to belong to the same organization and are mentioned in numerous reports.

On the link analysis chart, persons are indicated by circles and businesses by rectangles. If a particular individual (or group of individuals) has ownership or control over a business the person is categorized as a business in the chart. (In Fig. 9–10 below, Hanson and Smith are the co-owners of Independent Investors Company, Inc.) When a person(s) has controlling interest in more than one business they are represented by overlapping rectangles. This is illustrated in Fig. 9–10, in which Johnson is the sole owner of both the After Five Bar and the Cloud Nine Tavern. A "confirmed" relationship is one that is known to exist and it is illustrated in the link analysis chart by a solid line between two suspects or organizations. For example, in the chart shown, there is a confirmed link between Willis and On-Line Productions. Suspected or unconfirmed relationships are shown by a dotted line.

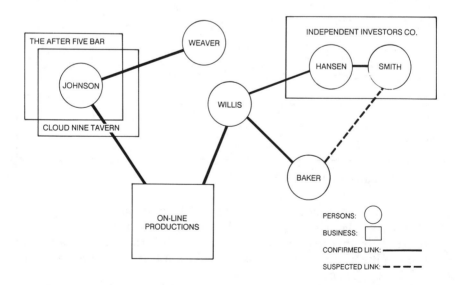

9–10 Hypothetical link analysis chart

Event Flow Charting

The event flow chart organizes events in a particular ongoing type of crime. Unlike the "frozen effect" of link analysis in which relationships between persons and businesses are only outlined, the flow chart shows a graphic flow of events and activities over a period of time. Additionally, it depicts events in the sequence in which they occurred. The event flow chart is normally used early in an investigation so that unorganized or fragmented pieces of information can be easily understood (Fig. 9–11).

In the event flow chart, each event is briefly described inside a circle, rectangle, or other symbolic area, and those events are then connected by arrows showing the direction and sequence of the occurrence. The hypothetical event flow chart shown in Figure 9–11 depicts a cocaine–crack conversion and a street distribution operation. The events that have either occurred or that will occur are shown in sequential order on one line. For example, it is logical that cocaine must be smuggled into the United States before it can be converted into crack (or packaged as powdered cocaine) and sold in street quantities. When events have already occurred, or might yet occur simultaneously, they are shown on parallel lines.

Commodity Flow Charting

This type of chart assists the intelligence analyst by clarifying the methods of operation and roles of individuals in a particular organization. It is especially advantageous in narcotics investigations in which drugs can be tracked down the organizational chain and revenue (money) can be tracked back up the organizational chain.

The example shown in Figure 9–12 depicts a methamphetamine manufacturing and distributing operation in which the flow of necessary precursors, shown by a white arrow is from the legitimate source through a "front" business to 123 North Oak Street where it is manufactured by Thomas. The finished methamphetamine product is shown by black arrows flowing from Thomas to two major dealers (Russell and Phillips) and from there to numerous street dealers.

The Information Dissemination Log

Dissemination is where the entire intelligence process breaks down most frequently. It has been said that good criminal intelligence is much like gold nuggets because everybody wants as much as they can get and no one is willing to share what they have. Intelligence,

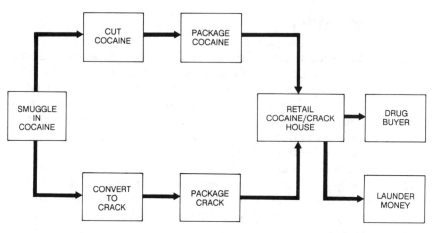

9-11   Hypothetical event flow chart

regardless of its accuracy, or how much time, money, or resources were used in collecting it, is worthless unless it is shared with organizations or persons who need it.

When disseminated, a dissemination log should be used. This should be a detailed list of information disseminated by the unit to other law enforcement agencies. Strict policy should be followed here to insure the protection of the Constitutional rights of those persons whose names are contained in the files, and to protect other types of sensitive information from unauthorized access. Usually, requests for information should be made in writing, but occasionally other departments make requests in person or over the phone. When responding to requests, the requesting agency should state the reason for needing the information and the nature of the investigation.

As a rule, copies of documents sent to other agencies should be stamped with the date of dissemination to deter further dissemination by those receiving agencies. In addition, the dissemination log should indicate the name of the person receiving the information and the date the request was honored. Disseminated material should also be stamped with an inscription, which should read:

This report is the property of the City Police Department and is loaned to your agency. It is not to be copied or distributed outside your agency and is to be destroyed after 60 days.

Intelligence information should not be disseminated to non-law enforcement agencies or to private individuals.

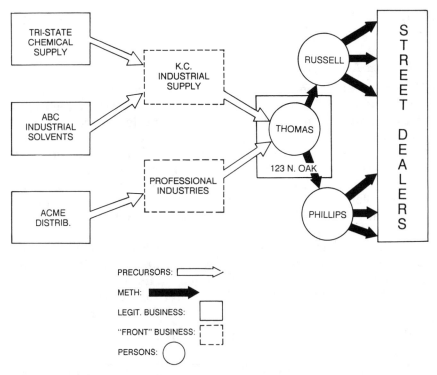

9-12 Hypothetical commodity flow chart

Special Information Files

Special information files may include anything of interest to the agency, such as the locations of high-crime areas within the unit's jurisdiction or perhaps an address file of known organized crime suspects. This file would index any and all addresses of suspects who appear in case or intelligence files. Although many drug dealers are considered highly transient, many addresses continue to show current locations of drug suspects and may benefit investigators in their work.

Another example of special information files would be an aviation file containing aircraft "N" numbers, or descriptions of any aircraft suspected in smuggling activities. In addition, pilots' names and other airport employees' names and descriptions could be entered in the file for future access (see Chapter 1). Other examples are suspects' nicknames, automobiles, establishments, etc.

The files should always be kept as simple as possible, making it easy to enter and retrieve information. A cross-reference system should also be used in order to allow easy access of related information on a given topic.

The Case Management Report

The task of case management rests with both the supervisor and the case agent alike. Case management is a system whereby each open case is monitored on a regular basis (e.g., monthly) for progress and a projected closing date. Once a case is opened, a case number will be assigned and an initial case complaint (front sheet) will be prepared (discussed above). After the initial complaint is written, all subsequent reports pertaining to the same defendants should be prepared on a supplemental report bearing the original case number of the complaint. This will insure that all paperwork and progress reports of the same case are placed in one central file.

A case management report system should always be maintained by each unit officer and regularly reviewed by supervisors. Basically the case management form is a single page containing a list of all open cases, their case numbers, the date the last report was written, any new investigative leads, and an anticipated closing date for the case.

- The list of open cases gives officers an at-a-glance review of their case loads.
- The list of case numbers allows agents immediate referral to all open cases for review, if needed.
- New investigative leads provide managers information on how much attention a particular case has been getting from the case agent.
- The anticipated closing date projects how much longer the case will stay open before suspects are arrested.

The case management system should require supervisors to review each open case with the subordinate. If an anticipated closing date has arrived or passed, a new one should be established with specific tasks to be carried out prior to the arrival of the next evaluation date.

The Weekly Activity Report

Because in many instances narcotics agents work excessive hours and maintain many different cases at the same time, their time and activities must be accurately accounted for (Fig. 9–13). The weekly activity report is one such method. Daily entries are made by each officer in the unit and submitted at the end of each week to the supervisor. The report is a daily accounting of each individual agent's performance and case progression. The report should include the following data:

Name of officer
Individual officer radio number
Hours worked
New cases opened (including case numbers)
Ongoing cases (updated with case numbers)

CITY POLICE DEPARTMENT
OFFICER'S ACTIVITY REPORT

AGENT _____   FROM _____ TO _____

SSN: _____ UNIT NO. _____

BEGINNING ODOMETER READING _____

ENDING ODOMETER READING _____

SUNDAY   ACTIVITY
Date _____ Hrs. Worked _____ O.T. Hours _____
Lodg. Expense _____ Other Expense _____
Travel Began _____ Travel Ended _____
Hrs. Taken: (Leave) Comp. _____ Annual _____
              Sick _____ Other _____

MONDAY   ACTIVITY
Date _____ Hrs. Worked _____ O.T. Hours _____
Lodg. Expense _____ Other Expense _____
Travel Began _____ Travel Ended _____
Hrs. Taken: (Leave) Comp. _____ Annual _____
              Sick _____ Other _____

TUESDAY   ACTIVITY
Date _____ Hrs. Worked _____ O.T. Hours _____
Lodg. Expense _____ Other Expense _____
Travel Began _____ Travel Ended _____
Hrs. Taken: (Leave) Comp. _____ Annual _____
              Sick _____ Other _____

WEDNESDAY   ACTIVITY
Date _____ Hrs. Worked _____ O.T. Hours _____
Lodg. Expense _____ Other Expense _____
Travel Began _____ Travel Ended _____
Hrs. Taken: (Leave) Comp. _____ Annual _____
              Sick _____ Other _____

THURSDAY   ACTIVITY
Date _____ Hrs. Worked _____ O.T. Hours _____
Lodg. Expense _____ Other Expense _____
Travel Began _____ Travel Ended _____
Hrs. Taken: (Leave) Comp. _____ Annual _____
              Sick _____ Other _____

FRIDAY   ACTIVITY
Date _____ Hrs. Worked _____ O.T. Hours _____
Lodg. Expense _____ Other Expense _____
Travel Began _____ Travel Ended _____
Hrs. Taken: (Leave) Comp. _____ Annual _____
              Sick _____ Other _____

SATURDAY   ACTIVITY
Date _____ Hrs. Worked _____ O.T. Hours _____
Lodg. Expense _____ Other Expense _____
Travel Began _____ Travel Ended _____
Hrs. Taken: (Leave) Comp. _____ Annual _____
              Sick _____ Other _____

Signature_____   Supervisor _____

9-13 Officer's Activity Report form

Overtime hours

Other law enforcement agencies contacted during the week

Assigned vehicle number, with beginning and ending mileage

Court appearances

Other significant activities

Manpower, hours, and vehicle use can be scrutinized through the reviewing of these reports along with providing the supervisor a handle on how many new cases each officer has opened and closed over a period of time.

Fiscal Management

Another particularly delicate area of any covert police operation is the handling of funds. Financial discrepancies in this area cause more potential problems than any other area of unit management and are a frequent cause for internal investigations. Unpleasant circumstances can be avoided if certain objectives and guidelines in fiscal management are established. The administration process may differ greatly from agency to agency due to the specific policy and legal requirements of each unit or agency, but certain standards should be observed, and four basic questions on how the overall fiscal system is set up should be answered:

1. Who maintain fiscal records?
2. Who are responsible for expenditures?
3. Who authorize the payment of bills?
4. Who actually pay the bills?

Each officer joining the unit should have a specific understanding of how the fiscal office works. This is accomplished by requiring each officer to read and initial the standard operating procedure for the fiscal office and keep that document on file.

The Confidential Funds Account

In addition to maintaining general fiscal records, the unit is also responsible for managing special or confidential funds.

The expenditures of confidential funds should be indexed as simply as possible to allow for retrieval of the records with little effort. Basically, there are three categories of expenditures within the drug unit: a) purchases of evidence; b) purchases of information; and c) purchases of services.

1. *Purchase of Evidence* (the P/E file). This category is for the pur-

chase of evidence such as controlled substances, illegal firearms, stolen property, etc., to be used as evidence in a criminal trial (Fig. 9 – 14).

2. *Purchase of Information* (the P/I file). This category includes the payment of monies to informants in exchange for information of criminal activity. All other informant expenses should probably

CITY POLICE DEPARTMENT
PURCHASE OF EVIDENCE RECEIPT

Date _____

Case no. _____

_____

Suspect: _____

Location: _____

_____

Substance: _____

Quantity: _____

Amount Expended: _____

_____

CERTIFICATION OF INFORMANT

I certify that I received $_____ from investigator _____
to purchase evidence as reflected above.

_____
(Informant)

CERTIFICATION OF INVESTIGATOR

I certify the expenditure of $_____ for the above described purpose.

_____
(Investigator)

9 – 14 Purchase of Evidence Receipt form

be made under the purchase of services (P/S) category and charged accordingly.

3. *Purchase of Services* (the P/S file). This category includes travel or transportation of nonfederal officer or informant; the leasing of an undercover apartment, business front, specialty automobiles, aircraft, etc.; meals, liquor purchases, entertainment and similar expenses for undercover purposes. It does not include the purchasing of items such as cameras, binoculars, weapons for the unit, etc.

The monitoring of these three accounts is beneficial for supervisory purposes as it can help determine the activity of a particular officer, as well as how effectively he or she is spending unit funds. Entries should include dates of expenditure, case numbers, and what was purchased. The proper maintenance of the confidential funds account will also benefit the officer in his own case management undertakings.

It is essential to keep files accurate because when officers are audited they will be expected to produce either the currency that they were initially issued or receipts showing where the funds were spent. It should also be established in writing exactly how long unit managers should maintain receipts for a particular year. This could vary from jurisdiction to jurisdiction, but likely will be from three to five years in duration. This figure can usually be established and authorized through the city, county, or state department of finance. Once established, the receipts gathered during a particular year are marked for destruction, which will eliminate the subsequent accumulation of mountains of reports and paper.

Drug Purchases (the P/E file)

Drug purchases become part of the confidential (P/E file) account and a system (preferably computerized for quick access) should be established where each drug purchase is logged with a corresponding case number to identify the expenditure. This could also be done manually in a card file/ledger system. Additional references should be made with regard to informant payments (the P/I file) and any other investigative expenses (the P/S file) deemed necessary during the course of any particular investigation. All confidential ledger information should include the following information:

1. Date of the expenditure
2. Amount of the expenditure
3. Purpose of the expenditure
4. Corresponding case number for the expenditure
5. Any reference numbers associated with the expenditure

Handling P/E Funds (Buy Money)

Although this area deals somewhat with enforcement policy, it should be discussed here because many agencies coordinate drug money expenditures through the fiscal office.

P/E funds for the purchasing of drugs, or so-called buy money, is currency issued to each undercover agent for the purpose of purchasing evidence. In most circumstances the evidence purchased is illicit drugs but there could be other types of cases encountered by undercover agents requiring the purchasing of different types of evidence such as stolen property, illegal weapons, etc. The manner and circumstances in which these special funds may be spent largely depend on the policy of each individual agency. Some agencies, for example, prohibit the expenditure of P/E funds for anything other than controlled substances. So in this case, expenses such as stolen property and illegal weapons would have to come from different funding sources.

It is important that written policy be established for the use of any confidential funds in order to avoid discrepancies in accounting for the money later on and to minimize the undercover officer's chances of being hijacked while undercover. It is common (although unauthorized), for example, for undercover officers to spend their confidential funds for personal use, thinking that they can easily reimburse themselves prior to an agency audit. In this circumstance, officers tend to spend more than they realize and if there is an unannounced audit, the shortage of official funds may be looked upon by auditors as embezzlement on the part of the officer. Avoidance of this situation can usually be accomplished by regular internal audits by the undercover officers themselves or their supervisors.

Policy must also be established regarding how much money any given officer is permitted to carry with him or spend on evidence. This will also vary greatly from department to department and is generally dictated by the structure of the unit.

For example, if the unit is structured such that undercover officers generally work alone with no support agents or partners, officers might be restricted as to the amount of P/E money they can spend without prior supervisor approval. For example, in the case where there is a limited budget, one gram of cocaine (costing approximately $100) may be considered an expensive purchase. Conversely, some agencies may authorize expenditures of up to $500 without prior supervisor approval. Approved amounts may be based on the officer's rank or time in grade. In either case, the undercover officer should only be authorized to carry money within the amount authorized by supervisors.

A hypothetical P/E authorization scale for drug purchases is outlined below:

1. Expenditures up to $500 with no surveillance or backup.
   A. Circumstances may arise where an undercover officer has an opportunity to purchase a small quantity of drugs to initiate a new case.
   B. In a first-buy situation, small quantities should be purchased so the drugs can be examined by police chemists to determine purity and whether they are actually controlled substances instead of non-controlled look-alikes.

2. Expenditures from $500 to $1,000 — telephone approval required from immediate supervisor prior to transaction (followed up by a written authorization after the transaction).
   A. Although the risk of a drug rip-off is present at any time during an undercover transaction, it is a good idea for supervisors to touch base with the undercover operative to ensure that the suspect is fully identified (name, address, other identifiers) and that a smaller drug purchased preceded this one and proved to produce an actual controlled substance rather than a look-alike.

3. Expenditures from $1,000 to $3,000 — must require written authorization from both supervisor and unit commander.
   A. In addition to precautions outlined in 2, other considerations should be noted. As stated, all drug transactions should have covert surveillance officers watching the undercover officer for safety purposes. Written authorization should, however, be required in agency policy for transactions in excess of $500. This is true even if there is a manpower shortage in the department. Policy should dictate that if surveillance is not available the deal is called off and rescheduled at a later time. In this case the likelihood for a "rip-off" or other type of set-up is great and should be prepared for.

4. Expenditures or flash-rolls over $3,000 — must be authorized in writing by the executive officer via the unit commander (see Chapter 7).
   A. Before agents and their supervisors attempt to acquire such large sums of cash, extensive investigation of the suspect, his or her associates, residence, and vehicles must be documented.
   B. Once the money is signed over to the agent, a minimum of three agents should accompany the cash at all times for security purposes.

Informant Payment Files (the P/I file)

In addition, there should also be an informant file maintained by the unit, which should be kept part of the confidential funds account.

This procedure may differ from agency to agency because some units allow individual officers to maintain independent informant files.

Generally speaking, the unit will usually pay for any and all informant expenses associated with the unit. Investigating officers would not have the informant in the first place if it were not for the agency, so the informant should belong to the unit as a whole and not to a particular officer. Unit managers and fellow investigators should, therefore, have access to who is being used as an informant to prevent informants from attempting to sell the same information to several officers within the agency (Fig. 9–15).

Included in each officer's P/I file should be the following information:

1. A completed cooperating individual agreement signed by the informant.
2. A full background information form of the informant including legal name, nicknames, addresses, POB, DOB, wife's and children's names, parents' names and address and former addresses.
3. Two photographs of the informant (front and side) updated every six months.
4. A completed fingerprint card.
5. A hard copy of a NCIC criminal check of the informer (updated every six months).
6. A copy of the informant's signature.
7. All copies of receipts of monies paid to the informant (signed in the informant's legal name).

Maintenance of these files is important in the event the informant must be contacted in an emergency situation and the control agent is unavailable (see Chapter 5).

Agent Identification Files

Drug enforcement supervisors should keep separate identification files for each officer in the unit in addition to any personnel files maintained by the personnel division. Specifically, information contained in the agent identification file should include:

1. Full name of officer (including nicknames and street names used).
2. All identifying information: DOB, POB, SS#, address, information on wife, children, and parents.
3. A record of the amount of P/E funds being carried by the officer.
4. A copy of the agent expenditures ledger.
5. A list of any and all equipment issued to the officer (including serial and identifying numbers).

CITY POLICE DEPARTMENT

PURCHASE OF INFORMATION RECEIPT

Date _____

Case no. _____

Investigator _____

Informant _____

_____

I certify that I received $_____ in payment for information and/or expenses incurred while cooperating with investigator _____.

_____
(Informant)

_____

I certify the expenditure of $_____ for the above described purpose.

_____
(Investigator)

9-15 Purchase of Information Receipt form

6. A special form signed by the individual officer stating that he has read and understood all agency policy and procedure.
7. Xeroxed copy of undercover officer driver's license and any other official undercover documentation which is being used on the street.
8. Assigned undercover officer vehicle description, VIN, and license plate number.

Dealing with Outside Agencies

In evaluating our past history in drug control strategies, it is evident that a single drug enforcement agency does not possess enough resources to effectively control the current drug trafficking problem in the Unites States. Although an onslaught of enforcement agencies is not necessarily an astute resolution either, those agencies charged with performing certain functions in the drug enforcement function must cooperate with one another for the most effective results. The premise of interagency cooperation poses certain concerns which, if not accounted for, may retard the overall success of any given enforcement effort.

Agencies possessing drug enforcement responsibilities exist on local, state, and federal levels. Because drug enforcement is a proactive law enforcement stratagem requiring enforcement personnel to seek would-be traffickers, a climate of case competition frequently develops between agencies. Admittedly, competition in many instances may prove to increase motivation, but in excess it tends to hamper investigations through an unwillingness to share information and resources.

> A narcotics agent was contacted by a long-time informant late one afternoon. The informant advised the officer that he had just learned of a transaction in which a group of suspects was going to trade two kilos of heroin for several fully automatic machine guns. The exchange, according to the informant, was to take place at 9:00 PM at a local tavern. Based on this information, the agent organized a surveillance team and arrest plan to observe the transaction and intervene to make any necessary arrests.
>
> The agent and informant posed undercover in the tavern at the time of the transaction to observe any suspects. At 8:45, the informant pointed out a group of four subjects who arrived at the tavern, claiming they were the ones with the heroin. The agent immediately recognized one of the subjects as an undercover ATF agent he had previously worked with, and through a concealed transmitter, advised the surveillance agents outside that the transaction was probably a reverse sting in which the ATF agents were using the heroin as bait to acquire automatic weapons.
>
> A few minutes later, one of the agent's partners entered the tavern and advised him that four additional subjects had just arrived outside the tavern, and that two of them had been identified by surveillance officers as undercover DEA agents. It then became clear that this whole transaction was turning out to be cops arresting cops. The DEA thought they could lure heroin

traffickers with weapons as bait, and the ATF was attempting to lure gun-runners by offering two kilos of heroin as bait. Neither agency had contacted each other regarding the transaction. Had the original narcotics agent not intervened, a firefight between the law enforcement agencies might have occurred.

Without a substantive drug enforcement policy that requires regular contact and interaction with other drug enforcement agencies, problems may occur where, for instance, one agency might arrest a suspect who is a player in another agencies' investigation. The arrest could in turn create a sense of panic or paranoia on the part of his criminal associates and might then impair the second agency's investigation. The result would be animosity between the two agencies, making future cooperation unlikely.

Another situation that has the potential for creating poor interagency relationships (as well as potential danger for undercover officers) is that of the drug raid. Different agencies have different missions. One agency might focus their efforts on a low-level dealer/ user while another agency, operating within the same jurisdiction, may be focusing on higher-level traffickers. In the event both groups of dealers are conducting business with one another and a raid takes place at a residence where an undercover officer is working, the potential exists for undercover officers to be shooting at other officers, each thinking the other is a drug suspect. Open lines of communication could circumvent these problems.

Multiagency Drug Enforcement Units

Many of the problems experienced by federal agencies in the early years of drug enforcement policy have now become a reality for local law enforcement agencies. Many of these problems present themselves while an enforcement alternative to this dilemma is considered. Some of these problems exist because drug traffickers are so transient that broad jurisdiction is necessary to follow up on investigative leads. Frequently, when concerned agencies without "in-house" drug enforcement personnel request assistance from outside agencies, no help is forthcoming because the agencies contacted must prioritize their own investigations because of shortages of manpower, and therefore concentrate on larger traffickers in other areas. In areas where more than one drug enforcement unit operate, there are problems of duplication of services. Drug buys are being made with the same defendant, the sharing of criminal intelligence is minimal, and sharing manpower and other resources are seldom reciprocated.

In the federal system, one response to this dilemma has been the federal task force concept, which was created to more effectively address the multijurisdictional problem. The federal government determined that money was being wasted because there were many different agencies working on drug trafficking, with so many different resources available to each one. The task force concept basically employs one or two agents from enforcement agencies such as the FBI, DEA, IRS, ATF, Customs, and the U.S. Marshals Service, and place those agents under the supervision of an assistant U.S. attorney. Each participating agent, although still employed by his or her host agency, works on the same investigative level with the other agents, permitting a closer working relationship between agencies. Additionally, each participating agency may have some unique contribution to make to the task force (equipment, manpower, money, records).

Many smaller departments in both urban and rural jurisdictions have considered organizing multiagency drug enforcement units designed to serve in all of the jurisdictions of participating agencies. This is not a new concept but until recently it has enjoyed a minimal degree of success.

Jurisdictions within a given area experience drug problems unique to that area. For example, in a large metropolitan area such as St. Louis (where 69 different police agencies operate), a Metropolitan Enforcement Group (MEG) unit was established to combine the talents and resources of seven local departments. Although investigative leads may in fact take agents out of their primary area of operation, a concentrated effort has been made to focus on drug traffickers within their particular area of jurisdiction and has been proven effective. The same results could also be achieved by forming multiagency task forces in rural areas. The agency administrators, in this case, are cognizant of many local offenders who are likely targets for undercover investigations.

State and federal drug enforcement agencies cannot always assist a local agency with their problems. A gram cocaine dealer in rural America may be viewed as big of a problem to the rural officer as a one-pound dealer is to an officer in a larger jurisdiction. In addition, the task of rural law enforcement presents many unique problems that are not normally considered in an urban environment. These problems include investigation of marijuana cultivators and clandestine laboratories, with their associated booby traps and survivalist tactics (see Chapter 7). Ideally, this concept would enable participating agencies to share valuable resources as well as to pursue investigative leads across jurisdictional boundaries. Problems arise, however, when several jurisdictions agree to form a multicounty task force and each contributing agency administrator wants to sit on an advisory board to "steer" the activities of the unit. When boards of this fashion are set up, there is seldom agreement as to the direction of the unit.

Multiagency units usually fall into three categories:

1. The Metropolitan Enforcement Group (MEG), which is mainly made up of officers from police departments from metropolitan areas.
2. The city/county concept, which is usually organized by a county sheriff's office or police department in cooperation with other officers from police departments within the county.
3. Civilian staffed units; an older concept in which drug units are comprised of hired agents (possibly hired on 90-day contracts), who may or may not have previous police experience. There are many administrative headaches associated with this type of arrangement, as some agents turn out to be untrustworthy, unreliable, unethical, and in many cases, drug users themselves. Because of the inherent pitfalls associated with this system it is the least recommended.

A multiagency unit should be considered if any of the following conditions exist in a given area:

1. Increased publicity regarding the increase of illicit drugs.
2. New illicit drugs becoming available with indications of local sources of supply.
3. The inability of patrol officers to effectively combat the problem.
4. Increasing frustrations of enforcement personnel over limited jurisdiction.
5. Minimal coordination among other law enforcement agencies.
6. Problems in acquiring equipment for communication and surveillance operations.
7. Insufficient manpower.
8. Inability of individual law enforcement agencies to acquire sufficient funding for investigations (such as informant payments and drug purchases).

The funding of such an unit poses the biggest hurdle in the organizational process. There are, in fact, many sources of revenue to finance the project:

1. *Federal block grants:* Requesting agencies usually are required to provide a percentage of the total funds requested as "match money." Under this plan programs will vary from state to state with some funding lasting for five years and other funding lasting as little as three years.

2. *Discretionary grants*: This source of income usually begins at a certain number, and over a designated period of time decreases in size, requiring the participating agencies to contribute a larger percentage of the funding as time goes by.
3. *Donations*: A law enforcement agency might solicit short-term funding from interested groups such as the Kiwanis Club, the Lions Club, or the Knights of Columbus. This source of funding might net the department anywhere from $5,000 to $10,000, which might fund a drug unit for a short period of time (three to six months). Although this is not a sufficient time to make any great impact on the local drug trade, if spent wisely, it could be the foundation to base a later approach to city and county leaders (based on the success of the agency) for additional, more substantial funding.

It is common for smaller units to disband after the funding period has expired because of other financial burdens for law enforcement in the area. Larger departments, however, seem to have an easier time in absorbing the cost of the multiagency unit through other financial sources within the department. Again, the biggest hurdle to overcome in this concept is the interference of administrators in the daily function of the drug unit.

Public Relations

As in all phases of police work, the public has a right to know where and how their law enforcement agencies are directing their efforts. It was the public, after all, who created the law enforcement component of government and who must continually provide financial support for its operations. In keeping with this premise, all law enforcement should strive to gain approval of the public through an honest and open exchange of information.

Community relations are important to all law enforcement agencies. It is the interaction between the public and the police that creates harmony within the community. Without this closeness, the police are only a watchdog-type agency, existing separate and apart from the people it serves. Good public relations can be achieved by focusing on the concerns of the public. By focusing investigations toward this goal, the law enforcement agency will find their task easier.

Because drug violations affect so many different segments of society, drug arrests will probably attract more public interest than any other criminal investigation (except perhaps, that of a death investigation). The news media and general public alike are traditionally intrigued by undercover work and the "seedy side" of our society. Many television series have focused episodes on the life and times of drug enforcement and undercover agents who infiltrate dangerous, organized criminal organizations. Even though the Hollywood stereotype is a far cry from the realities of actual undercover work, the mythology still exists.

Another segment of society feels that the role of an undercover agent and police techniques involving secrecy and subterfuge represent an infraction of the personal liberties guaranteed to citizens by the Constitution, and police agencies generally have too much freedom in their operations. This position usually stems from the proactive nature of drug enforcement (where there is no complaintant to initiate the case). Although unsubstantiated, much misunderstanding of the drug enforcement effort stems from this viewpoint. These two variables, however, create an atmosphere where much critical attention is given drug related investigations, seizures and arrests.

The Media

In coping with public scrutiny, policy administrators must adopt a policy of open and responsive communication between the agency and the media. It should be remembered that the media is the publics' primary information conduit for the activities of local law enforcement. Most of the public learn about the criminal justice process, criminal laws, and procedures through some component of the media (newspapers, magazines, radio, or television).

The question is sometimes raised, do motion picture companies, newspapers, magazines, and television stations have the right to proclaim publicly the findings of sensitive investigations involving ongoing operations, public figures, police corruption, or other critical issues? The answer is "yes," as the First Amendment to the Constitution guarantees a free press. Somewhat in contrast to this, however, the Sixth Amendment guarantees a person a fair and impartial trial. Is it possible that the media could jeopardize or hamper the outcome of criminal cases through sensationalized publications about them?

The media is an objective reporting entity who, generally speaking, owes no allegiance to law enforcement, and polices its own members. Unfortunately, when news accounts are reported incorrectly because of insufficient or unsubstantiated information, these stories may cause much public furor about the reported quality of police work and may undermine the public's confidence in the law enforcement agency's effectiveness. It is, therefore, the responsibility of each law enforcement agency to adopt a public information policy that will ensure that proper and accurate data is conveyed to the public in order to eliminate misunderstandings.

The Public Information Officer

A public information officer (PIO) should be assigned by the agency to disseminate information regarding the activities and accomplishments of the drug enforcement unit. The person in this position must work closely with the chief executive officer in deciding what information is released on any given investigation. The ability for the PIO to "jump command" and speak directly to the agency administrator is essential in emergency situations where the release of sensitive information might jeopardize an ongoing investigation or prove embarrassing for the agency. Specific duties of the PIO are

1. Establish a cohesive working relationship with members of all local media.
2. Identify reporters who are easiest to work with as well as those who have failed to accurately report information in the past.
3. Release information on agency policy.
4. Release information on agency activities.
5. Organize an interdepartment system for the relaying of information to the PIO.
6. Provide open news conferences to interested members of the media on topics of concern.
7. Maintain a current roster of all media and contact personnel (crime/action reporters, program directors, news producers), including day and night telephone numbers.

In 1971 the United States Department of Justice released recommended guidelines for press releases by local, state and federal law enforcement agencies. These guidelines, also called the Katzenbach Guidelines, are:

1. Permissible Releases
   A. The defendant's name, age, residence, employment, marital status, and similar background information.
   B. The substance of the charge (e.g., information, indictment, or complaint).
   C. The identity of law enforcement agencies assisting in the investigation or arrest of the suspect.
   D. The immediate circumstances surrounding the arrest, the time and place of arrest, the quantity and type of drugs seized, the estimated street value, resistance, pursuit, any possession or use of weapons and a list of items seized at the time of arrest.

When calculating a drug's street value, always do so according to a designated formula so as not to seem as though the department is inflating its figures. For example, if a pound of cocaine is seized and street value per pound is between $18,000 to $25,000, be careful not to overinflate the estimate of its street value by calculating the number of dosage units times a cutting process of 5, 10, or 15 times. This will result in an unrealistic figure and may reflect poorly on the unit's honesty and credibility.

2. Nonpermissible Releases
   A. Personal observations of the arrested person's character.
   B. Statements, admissions, confessions, or alibis pertaining to the defendant.
   C. Reference to investigative procedures such as fingerprints, polygraph examinations, laboratory results, etc.
   D. Statements concerning the identity of witnesses.
   E. Personal opinions relating the guilt or innocence of the arrestee.
   F. Information regarding prior arrest records of the accused.
   G. The number of drug buys on the suspect.
   H. The estimated distribution level of the suspect.
   I. At no time shall personnel furnish any statement or information for the purpose of influencing the outcome of a defendant's trial or an ongoing case, nor shall personnel furnish any statement or information that could reasonably be expected to influence the outcome of a pending trial or future trial.

At times it might be advantageous for the PIO to generate stories for the media that will reflect well on the department. These stories may not result from an arrest situation or investigation, but may instead address other areas of interest of the media and the public:

Announcements about results of the agency's semiannual or annual report. This is an excellent opportunity for the PIO to boast of the accomplishments of the agency over the preceding year, supporting any remarks with statistics of arrests, amount of drugs seized or purchased, and weapons and property seized.

Informative press releases addressing the dangers of various drugs of abuse on the street, and what the agency is doing to combat distribution of the drug.

In addition, the PIO should be aware of the benefits of public service announcements. The public service announcement is produced by one (or each) of the local television or radio stations in the area, and provides the PIO an opportunity to deliver a message, which may be

5 to 30 seconds long—sometimes as long as one minute. This no-cost service may be used to voice the department's concern for contemporary drug enforcement problems affecting the public (the dangers of crack, spotting and reporting marijuana fields, reporting suspected smuggling aircraft, driving under the influence of drugs, or crime stoppers programs).

Occasionally members of the news media will ask to accompany agents on drug buys or arrests. Generally, these instances can produce publicity beneficial to the section, which in turn may generate more public support. It should be remembered, however, that a drug transaction or raid might not proceed as planned or may result in a confrontational arrest or shooting situation, which leaves reporters to film and document officers in a deadly or possibly embarrassing situation. In addition, reporters on the scene may serve to inhibit officers to the point where their effectiveness is impaired, resulting in added confusion. It should also be remembered that reporters and cameramen injured during arrests may possibly sue the host agency.

Summary

The manner in which a police organization is structured will vary greatly from jurisdiction to jurisdiction. Organizational structure is sometimes mandated under law, and sometimes at the pleasure of the chief executive officer. In any event, its organization will play a large part in determining whether or not the establishment of a drug enforcement unit is feasible. Once established, the many organizational concerns affecting management include proper personnel administration, fiscal procedures office, filing systems, and specialized unit structures within the drug enforcement section. Fiscal management in police administration is always under the public microscope, and great care should be excercised to avoid any accidental or intentional mismanagement of funds.

Public relations play an important role in the general support of any police agency. After all, the police can do no more or no less than the public they serve will allow them to do. Therefore, once the police gain the respect of the general public, enforcement initiatives such as drug enforcement are more easily achieved. Because police work often involves confidentiality and secrecy, many questions will arise about how the police are conducting their responsibilities. This is especially true in the investigations of deaths or drugs because of the high visibility of the cases and arrests. The media is the main channel of communication between law enforcement and the general public, so it is politically necessary for a police agency to have a system to disseminate information to the media. This can be accomplished by the establishment of a public information office and a special chain of command that answers directly to the chief administrator. If implemented properly, this will serve to increase public support of and confidence in the agency.

Drug violators are extremely transient, and investigations frequently require the sharing of information and resources with other law enforcement agencies. This necessitates a public–relations-oriented attitude on the part of each agency. This is sometimes difficult because of interagency competition for case recognition and other petty political and personal jealousies. The federal task force concept has successfully addressed this problem, inasmuch as members of many agencies work on an equal footing toward a common investigative goal.

When good working relationships can be established among agencies of smaller jurisdictions or on limited budgets, city or county investigative groups may be considered. These groups are comprised of officers who represent all contributing agencies and are commissioned to work drug investigations within the area of all member jurisdictions. If structured properly, where advisory boards are not used and where the administrators of each participating agency permit the unit to be managed by one individual, it may prove to be successful.

Suggested Readings

"Fighting the War Against Drugs — The Word from the Trenches (10 drug enforcement administrator's writings)." *The Police Chief Magazine*, October, 1987.

Lawn, John C., "DEA Emphasizes Cooperation at International, National, State and Local Levels." *The Police Chief Magazine*, October, 1987.

More, *Critical Issues in Law Enforcement*, 4th ed. Cincinnati, OH: Anderson, 1985.

Schultz, Donald O., *Police Operational Intelligence*, 3rd. ed. Springfield, IL: Charles Thomas, 1973.

Souryl, Sam S., *Police Organization and Administration*. Cincinnati, OH: Anderson Publishing, 1985.

Stenzel, William W., *Police Work Scheduling: Management Issues and Practices*. U.S. Department of Justice, National Institute of Justice, 1983.

Swanson, Charles R., *Police Administration*, 2nd. ed. New York, NY: MacMillan Publishing, 1988.

Personnel Management 10

The selection of candidates for the police profession is generally a difficult one due to public expectations, agency policy and legal requirements, as well as other extenuating factors. The selection of personnel to staff a drug enforcement unit is further complicated by additional considerations such as the dangers inherent in undercover work (in some cases involving minimal supervision or protection), long hours, and the close associations with known criminals. The actual hiring of unit personnel will be discussed later in this chapter, but we should first examine how administrators can predict the initial number of officers that will be needed to staff the drug enforcement unit.

As briefly discussed in the last chapter, manpower requirements for each section within the unit may be assessed fairly easily. A time-per-case determination or "time budget" should be established so that cases can be effectively planned. Examination of officers' hours worked will provide administrators with a key as to how many officers are required for a given task. Case–time evaluation is usually based on how long it takes to complete an investigation after the basic phases of case initiation are completed (see Chapter 1). In addition, an estimate of clerical or secretarial assistance should be considered. Support staff should also have activity sheets regularly filled out so it can be determined how much time is spent on paperwork per case.

After a period of time, averages can be established as to how much time investigative personnel spend on a given investigation. The same evaluation period can be used by the agency to predict the volume of cases to be expected in the forthcoming year (or quarter, etc.). From the expected number of cases and the average number of staff hours per case administrators can project the number of personnel the agency needs. Allowances should be made for vacations, sick time, and compensatory leave. Although it is generally accepted that many narcotics investigations extend into lengthy operations, the time budget will give administrators direction as to the upcoming year.

Personnel Selection

The hiring process for drug enforcement personnel is crucial, and it will vary widely from agency to agency due to a number of reasons. First, civil service boards in county, city, and state governments may require applicants to successfully complete a general series of eligibility procedures before the specific law enforcement agency is permitted to evaluate the candidate for employment. Second, in the case of a larger department, drug enforcement candidates will probably already be employed by the agency, and their qualifications and capabilities will then be considered for transfer to the drug enforcement unit. Once candidates have passed initial testing procedures, character traits of prospective undercover agents should then be considered:

1. The ability to think in a logical and rational manner.
2. The ability to comprehend and understand complex masses of data.
3. Impeccable standards of honesty and integrity.
4. The ability to communicate and relate well with other members of the department.
5. An understanding of the concepts of organized crime, intelligence collection, and civil liberties.

Every attempt should be made by the agency administration to select candidates objectively rather than through favoritism. This would normally require an agency to select candidates through a semistructured or even a highly structured process. Such a process should drastically cut down on the likelihood of dissension and lowering morale within the agency. Moreover, a higher quality investigator can be selected through an objective selection process, which includes:

1. The initial job application.
2. The written examination.
3. The oral interview.
4. Investigation of background or evaluation of past performance.
5. The psychological evaluation.
6. The physical agility test results.

The Initial Job Application

In the case of a new job applicant, an initial application form will first be required. Before the candidate submits a formal application, however, he or she should be furnished with literature and information sufficient to understand the qualifications and duties of the position fully. Both (or either) the information and the application may be made available by mail or through a personal visit to the personnel department.

Some police agencies require applicants to take a written examination as a first step to weed out unqualified or otherwise unfit candidates. In other areas, civil service commissions handle police job applications instead of the police personnel department. In either case, a basic determination must be made as the applicant's credentials and ability to perform the job. Rejecting obviously unworthy candidates at this point saves hundreds of dollars in further processing, and expedites the overall hiring process.

The Written Examination

It should be recognized that many applicants may not have been in school of some time before applying to the unit, and may consequently experience a certain amount of apprehension at the thought of passing a written exam. This is one reason why the other three components to the selection process exist. However, it should also be noted by the hiring board that an applicant's ability to analyze and evaluate criteria under a stressful situation (such as taking a written exam) is a fundamental prerequisite for the position of criminal investigator. After all, the written testing procedure is one which evaluates a candidate's ability to retain, evaluate, and analyze facts. Academic ability is not being assessed here as much as the individual's ability to practice good common sense and to communicate in writing effectively.

The written examination should be structured for two different groups of candidates: the experienced policeman and the novice recruit. Specifically, examinations should evaluate the candidates knowledge in the following areas:

The Experienced Policeman

1. Criminal law.
2. Constitutional law.
3. Investigative procedure: arrests, interviews, etc.
4. Tactical knowledge; raids, shootings, etc.

The Novice Recruit

1. General skills: reading, writing, comprehension, etc.
2. Common sense scenarios.

The Interview

Another revealing component to the selection process is the interview. The purpose of the interview is to further evaluate candidates who have successfully passed the written exam and thereby warrant additional consideration. The interview should be conducted by a panel consisting of command staff, unit personnel, and a psychologist trained in the diagnosis and treatment of police stress and related problems. It might be best for the unit members of the interview panel to be tenured street agents; supervisory members should be familiar with all aspects of drug enforcement. If the candidate is being transferred from within the agency, it would be appropriate for the candidate's personnel files for the previous three years to be reviewed by panel members. Although questioning may vary from member to member, specific areas of interest need to be discussed. An officer's work history, for example, will often reveal much about his or her ability to carry out new assignments. The following are focal points to examine during the candidate oral interview:

Overall Attitude and Personality

As undercover agents must assume many different roles in the performance of their duties, the candidate should demonstrate certain versatility. If the subject has been employed as a uniformed police officer for any length of time, he or she may display characteristics in stance, walk, or attitude that may distinguish him or her as a police officer to outsiders.

Police officers tend to possess, for the most part, an aggressive personality. This must be avoided in an undercover agent. The desired personality must not be one that intimidates, but one that allows the officer to mingle and mix with a variety of different people on all levels of society.

Appearance

There is no particular type of appearance considered most suitable for the duties of an undercover agent. The agent should be able to blend in with a target group with as little trouble as possible. Investigations might require the subject to go undercover as a street-level dealer or a high-level financier. The candidate must be able to look the part in each case.

Personal Lifestyle

Although a controversial issue, the examination of a candidate's personal lifestyle will most likely give administrators insight as to the quality of the applicant. If, for example, the officer has experienced marital problems in the year or so just prior to his or her application, it is likely that required long hours and increased hazards will create additional tension at home. This may result in a separation or even divorce, both of which can drastically affect an officer's effectiveness and safety on the street.

It is difficult to judge whether or not the best candidate should be single, or if a stable family life is a more desirable quality. Some administrators believe a single officer may be more cooperative about working overtime and out of town assignments, but might prove to be less cautious in stressful and dangerous circumstances. A married officer may display a higher degree of maturity and caution when confronted with the same circumstances (see Background Investigation).

The Background Investigation or Evaluation of Performance

Upon successful completion of the written examination and interview, the candidate should undergo an extensive background investigation. This is usually the final phase of the hiring process and serves to disqualify many otherwise attractive candidates. An experienced investigator should be assigned this task and should investigate the following areas of concern:

Past Job Performance

An extensive review of the applicant's past work history should be conducted. This is true for both a transfer candidate and for a newcomer to the agency. The investigator should look for patterns of poor judgement and/or attitudinal changes over time. In addition, more positive signs should be identified, such as the officer's overall interest in his or her work, effective verbal skills, and a proven ability to conduct criminal investigations; the applicant's past supervisors will be the most valuable source of information in this area. A candidate's absenteeism rate and number of promotions will also prove beneficial when evaluating past job performance.

Affiliations and Accomplishments

Much of what is done in this phase is a follow-up from the oral interview. Again, it is somewhat difficult to determine an individual's personal habits and lifestyle, but some inquiry should be attempted. Does the applicant belong to any organizations or interest groups? If so, what is his or her involvement? Is the applicant a contributor to the community in any civic context? If the individual is not as outgoing, an examination should be made to identify any personal accomplishments or other interests. In particular every effort should be made at this point to ensure that the applicant is not involved in drug use, nor are any of his immediate family, friends or associates.

Financial Indebtedness

Recognizing that in narcotics work, a certain potential exists for officers to become corrupt, it is essential for an applicant's financial records to be examined. This will identify any officer who is living beyond his or her means and might fall victim to possible corruption later on. In addition, as discussed earlier, drug enforcement agents are required to carry large sums of money for varying periods of time (buy-money); if an officer is experiencing financial difficulty, the temptation of embezzlement of these funds could be harder to resist.

The Polygraph Examination

If authorized, the use of a polygraph (lie detector) may prove useful in establishing an applicant's honesty and integrity, but because the use of the polygraph is somewhat controversial, not all agencies may choose to use it. In many circumstances, however, it may be beneficial in identifying any detrimental personal habits or activities in which the applicant is currently, or was previously involved. (Note: As of the writing of this text, Congress is considering the legality of continued use of the polygraph in pre-employment proceedings; its use, therefore, may ultimately be severely restricted or even outlawed for continued use in this capacity.) Specific areas of examination should include:

1. Use of alcohol.
2. Use of illicit drugs.
3. Theft.
4. Any medical data.
5. Previous official corruption.
6. Financial discrepencies.
7. Past civil rights violations or police misconduct.

Psychological Evaluation

This phase of the hiring process is critical because it may demonstrate existing psychological problems being experienced by the applicant. Problems that are identified may or may not disqualify an candidate from appointment, but they also may give managers an indication of problems that may later become amplified as a result of employment in the drug unit. Psychological evaluations can reveal a lot about the applicant including psychological deviances, stress, deception, and an applicant's tendencies to be "liability prone."

One popular testing method for police candidates is the Psychological Stress Evaluator (PSE). Originally designed in 1970, it is being used with increasing frequency by law enforcement agencies. Basically, it is a machine that registers involuntary physiological changes that occur in response to stress by graphically displaying stress-related audible and inaudible modulations of the human voice. The PSE has been compared to the standard "lie detector," though it is a less complex machine to operate. The subject does not have to be present for the PSE test. A tape recording of the candidate's initial interview can be fed into the machine, which would then read and interpret the necessary data. The PSE can even make evaluations from "live" or taped telephone conversations. The comparative effectiveness of PSE and the polygraph is currently being studied. Agencies should consider the merits of both in the hiring process.

Written psychological tests are also commonly given to police applicants in order to provide administrators an early indication of possible problems. One of the most common tests of this nature is the Minnesota Multiphasic Personality Inventory (MMPI), which can be scored by computer but still requires a psychologist to review and interpret the results. Administrators should realize that MMPI scoring was designed on the premise that the test taker is a mental patient, therefore tending to emphasize negative psychological information about the applicant. These test results, when evaluated, must be done so by a psychologist knowledgeable about both MMPI evaluations and the law enforcement profession.

Profile of the Police Psychologist

Although employed full-time by many large metropolitan police departments, the police psychologist used by most departments is retained on a part-time basis. To be most effective, any psychologist used by a law enforcement agency should be familiar both with the interworkings of the particular agency with which they are working and with police work in general. Agencies utilizing nonqualified personnel in this capacity, who are not "police oriented," might be providing a grave disservice to the agency as a whole.

Those psychologists who possess adequate credentials but who lack sufficient police exposure should be considered as an intern who should become exposed to all aspects of the agency on a step-by-step basis. This will gradually indoctrinate the psychologist to the responsibilities, fears, motivations, and duties of all affected personnel. Once properly trained, the police psychologist, working in support of management, can augment the effectiveness of the officer selection process.

Interview with the Applicant's Spouse

During the background investigation it is imperative that investigators meet with the applicant's spouse and discuss those aspects of the job she or he should be aware of: long and irregular hours, close associations between agent and criminals in undercover situations, being required to assume an undercover identity, and the possibility of transfer (if applicable).

The Physical Agility Test

Drug enforcement is a profession which requires a lot of mental and physical exertion. In addition to testing a candidate's mental health and aptitude, his or her physical abilities must also be evaluated. The general physical condition of the applicant (in addition to the traditional weight/height ratio, which is no longer considered appropriate as a single disqualifier) should be assessed. Other indicators of existing physical conditions affecting the candidate's ability to perform required duties must also be considered: age, obesity, and circulatory and respiratory disorders. Five areas in particular are critical to the physical duties of the drug enforcement agent: (a) upper body strength, (b) overall coordination, (c) leg strength, (d) quick reactions, (e) grip strength.

Each candidate should undergo an actual physical agility test, which particularly focuses on the criteria named above. Candidates who are less than qualified physically may later prove to be a liability to the unit (both administratively and civilly).

An investigator must also possess other important qualities to ensure he or she will be effective in the field. Table 10–1 is a synopsis of a 1987 National Institute of Justice (NIJ) report (prepared by Bernard Cohen and Jan Chaiken) which discussed performance attributes and outlined several specific areas of candidate performance. These are "general" investigator duties and personal qualities sought by police administrators but they must also apply to the drug investigator as well.

Personnel Administration

When selection and hiring are complete, agency administrators are then confronted with the task of just how the drug enforcement unit will be managed. Considerations such as delegation of assignments

Table 10-1 Qualities for Investigative Performance

Gathering information
  crime scene management
  good communication skills
Field operations
  stake-outs
  patrol
  crime pattern analysis
  ability to develop informants
  good street knowledge
Arrests
  quantity
  quality
Public and victim satisfaction
  crime reduction
  diminution of fear
Personal traits
  motivation
  stability
  persistence
  perseverance
  intelligence
  initiative
  judgement
  teamwork
  involvement
  dedication
Qualifications
  education
  training
  previous assignments in department
Prosecutions
  quantity
  presentation of testimony in court
  percent leading to conviction
Personal performance
  low absenteeism
  minimal public complaints
  awards

for personnel, selection of supervisors and command staff, promotion and disciplinary procedures and case management will be discussed in this chapter.

The Line Supervisors

In most police organizations, the administration process (assignments, procedure, and policy) operates through a chain-of-command system. In larger police departments where the agency administrator is not running the unit, a line supervisor will have responsibility for

Table 10-2 Line Supervisor Duties

Field duties
  Overseeing drug transactions in which new agents are involved
  Overseeing drug transactions that are considered high-risk
  Supervising surveillance operations
  Overseeing raids and arrest situations
Administrative duties
  Review ongoing case files
  Supervising cases
  Assigning case loads
  Overseeing the field training of new agents
  Supervising unit financial expenditures
  Evaluating agent performance objectives
  Assisting agents in managing informants
  Assigning work schedules or shifts

line-level administration of the unit. The line supervisor function is a control function, which maintains the overall effectiveness of the unit, identifies weak links in the system, and takes measures to correct them through evaluation and development of the subordinate (Table 10-2).

The line supervisor is the manager who works closest to the street officers and the one who must set an example for subordinates, both as an administrator and field officer. The line supervisor must balance between the roles of administrator and field manager. This means that he or she cannot just read and approve written reports, but must also spend time in the field to develop or enhance officer performance or ensure the success of a case. This is not to say that the line supervisor must participate in an undercover capacity; he or she should not. The supervisor, however, should be on the scene to direct and make whatever command decisions are deemed necessary. The line supervisor must also monitor the daily performance of subordinates to make sure that all reports are up to date, financial records are properly maintained, and that each officer's caseload is being managed properly (see Chapter 9).

It is somewhat debatable as to just how many subordinates should be assigned to each line supervisor. This decision depends largely on the total size of the unit and the structure of the agency. Obviously, if there are more subordinates assigned to a line supervisor than they can effectively control, then the overall effectiveness of the unit will be diminished. The recommended number of subordinates that can be most effectively managed is five.

Work Schedules

When discussing work schedules, the subject of overtime automatically comes up. There are significant differences in overtime policy from one agency to the next. Some agencies pay officers time-and-a-half for time worked in excess of 40 hours per week. Others offer compensatory time in lieu of pay. Though "comp time" is considered an attractive fringe benefit of the job, many times officers are unable to use all accrued time because of hectic work schedules. This can result in many hours (sometimes well into the hundreds) of service with no compensation.

Part of the problem of scheduling and overtime lies in that some officers believe drug deals are more likely to transpire at night, eliminating the need to be in the office during early morning hours. Other officers are of the opinion that drug dealers will gladly take drug money any time of the day or night and may choose to work during more conventional hours. Although case agents should manage their drug buys so that transactions occur during regularly scheduled work hours, circumstances frequently present themselves where agents have little control over the time a particular transaction is arranged. Unplanned informant intervention, spur-of-the-moment surveillances, and other unforseen and uncontrollable variables on the trafficker's end of the transaction may create or aggravate a overtime problem.

The number of staff assigned to a unit will have a large impact on whether multiple shifts should be worked, or whether a unit should work on one regularly scheduled shift and then be on-call for special (overtime) situations. This latter arrangement, termed flex-time, may result in officers working 50 to 60 hours per week (or more) — a situation that raises the probability of low morale and dissension within the unit. In the case of a surveillance operation, the team approach is best suited for around-the-clock observation. In this case, each team works a 12-hour shift and the two teams meet at shift change to exchange information about any developments during the previous shift (see Chapter 6).

Regardless of which method is adopted, the supervisor must anticipate the likelihood for extended overtime and should arrange for additional manpower from other divisions within the agency to be on stand-by in the event a large-scale transaction or operation is planned. Even though more hours will be logged in this event, time-and-a-half compensation will be minimized.

Agent Responsibilities

Although the narcotics supervisor is accountable for the overall effectiveness of the drug enforcement unit, certain reports are required of the agent as a documentation of his or her activities. These include the weekly activity report, investigative and confidential expense funds account reports, and the case management report (see Chapter 9). The officers themselves bear most of the responsibility for completing and maintaining these documents, and supervisors should review them regularly.

Undercover agents report directly to the supervisor on a daily basis and must keep the supervisor apprised of any progress or problems in ongoing investigations. In addition, agents must be familiar with all section equipment: its capabilities, its proper use, and its maintenance. Other duties of the drug agent include:

1. To cultivate sources of information regarding drug trafficking and organized crime.
2. To maintain issued undercover vehicles.
3. To be alert to any problems within the community that would be considered a threat to public safety.
4. To conduct and assist in surveillance activities.
5. To make regular contacts with law enforcement agencies who are also involved in drug enforcement or related activities.
6. To thoroughly investigate all assigned cases in accordance with the goals and objectives of the section.
7. To apply sound investigative techniques to improve the effectiveness of the section.
8. To adhere to all orders and policy procedures.
9. To actively cooperate with members of all prosecutors offices, both state and federal.
10. To testify in criminal and civil court proceedings when required to do so.

Personnel Risk Management

Law enforcement is a dangerous job and drug law enforcement is probably the most dangerous duty within the profession. As discussed throughout this text, there is a multitude of circumstances that can evolve into a deadly situation for the investigator. This section looks at personnel risk management, a first line responsibility for not only the manager but for every agent involved in the investigation.

There is a high potential for violence in drug law enforcement. Two different types of violence should be recognized as prevalence in this line of work:

1. *Intermural Violence* — Between the drug/criminal community and the drug law enforcement community.
2. *Intramural Violence* — Between rival factions within the drug community.

Risk management considers when risks should be authorized, under what conditions, and with whom. Although risks are an everyday hazard of drug law enforcement, certain risks must be looked on as "going with the territory." Any risk, however, regardless of its degree, should be reasonable and justified with some benevolent purpose.

Ironically, studies have revealed that drug agents frequently seek careers in risk management because of the risk factor rather than some inherent need to serve the public. Narcs are by nature, *risk aggressive* people.

In drug law enforcement, there are four primary areas which contribute to the majority of high risks for drug agents. Each of these areas presents a possible threat to agents during their investigations, and each area is one that is dealt with on a fairly regular basis, increasing the risk potential. These areas are:

1. *Criminal Informants.* The criminal informant (as opposed to the civic minded civilian informant) is an individual who is A) criminally oriented, who B) generally displays a confused loyalty to the drug enforcement officer and mission, and who C) usually has questionable motives. Many investigations rely heavily on informants and the use of them should always be conducted in a cautious manner (see Chapter 3).

2. *Undercover.* The undercover technique has essentially become the hallmark of drug law enforcement, although it might be somewhat over used. It is a technique whereby the police officer is placed in direct personal contact with a drug criminal during ongoing comtemporaneous criminal activity, which increases physical risk for the officer. The undercover agent will ultimately elicit a strong emotional reaction from the defendant, which will oftentimes result in violence toward the officer (see Chapter 2).

3. *Raids.* This is an extraordinary police tactic routinely used by all drug law enforcement. The drug raid places the undercover officer in a highly volatile situation and because most defendants take overt actions to protect themselves from intrusions by other members of the criminal community, the police raid may be misinterpreted by the defendant as a rip-off (see Chapter 12).

4. *Arrests.* Most drug arrests occur when illicit drugs are seized from the defendant. As mentioned above, because of this the defendant is psychologically (and physically) prepared for an attack. So the arrest may be misinterpreted by the defendant as a rip-off or not carefully orchestrated (see Chapter 2).

The interplay between these four aspects of drug law enforcement are the factors that most greatly contribute to officer risk. To best combat this problem, the risk management process involves examining several critical areas in the decisions to enter into high-risk activity.

1. *Risk Assessment.* This is the identification and evaluation of risk factors. More specifically, it is the identification factors or warning signs which indicate that the investigation should change direction and must not be ignored. Examples include:
   A. When drugs and money are expected to be present at the same location at the same time.
   B. When an undercover operative (officer or informant) is present inside a structure during a raid or buy–bust.
   C. When the location of the drug deal changes *after* the deal is in progress.
   D. When the drug dealer expects the undercover officer to be in possession of large amounts of money.
2. *Justification of Risk Action.* Managers must recognize that an agent's willingness to enter into a dangerous situation is no justification for taking the risk. Risk action should be related to institutional mission and major risks in exchange for minor results are unjustifiable.
3. *Risk Compensation by Tactics.* When a risk is identified, a solution or method of dealing with the threat should then be decided on. This could include strategies on how either to eliminate risk or to reduce or control the dimensions of the risk factor itself. In this definition the term compensation refers to enhanced tactics (officer survival and safety techniques) used in all four of the above high-risk categories. When compensating for a high-risk variable, managers must keep basic investigative techniques in mind, as it is easy to complicate matters with excessive planning.
4. *Risk Evasion.* This is the step in the investigation when the investigators must be able to *stop* the course of events and literally *shut the deal down!* It is in this phase that the agents must be willing to try the deal at another time in spite of what appears to be progress in the transaction. Time is needed here to reevaluate the situation and consider any new developments in the case. It is likely that this phase is the most difficult for narcotics agents to master, as it 1) seems to delay the culmination of an investigation, and 2) tends to act against the proactive instincts of the drug investigator. It is the manager, in this case, who must realize that calling off the deal at this point and avoiding further risk might in fact be the only success achieved in the case.

Once the first three areas listed above have been identified in a given situation, it is then necessary to judge the relationship between each and attempt to diagnose a responsible course of action. In many cases where drug agents have been injured or killed in the line of duty, they were probably taking chances which were not justified or they failed to identify the risk. In some cases agents might even misread the risk factors that are present during a drug transaction. In

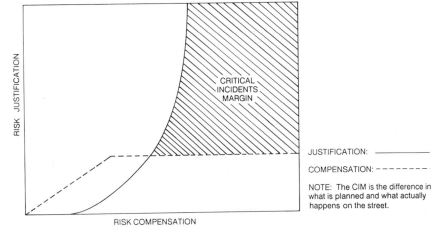

RISK MANAGEMENT INDEX

10-1 Relationship between the degree of risk and the number of risk factors in a given situation

any case, the hazards of the situation far exceed the tactical and logistical expectations of the agents and may result in a volatile outcome (Fig. 10-1).

Stress Management

Stress management has been only recently addressed by police personnel administrations. It is clear that a law enforcement career contains an overabundance of job-related stress: it requires that its members expose themselves to physical injury or death, and subjects them to the overwhelming grief and pain of others. Stress produces many different physiological and psychological problems, which if not properly identified and treated can result in an array of disorders for the officer. Recent studies show that three-quarters of the heart attacks experienced by officers are job-related. Moreover, the stress chronically experienced by officers may also manifest itself in emotional disorders that may impair the officer's safety, impair the safety of other officers, jeopardize ongoing investigations, and create intense family strife. Some of the most common stresses and stress-related problems include:

Marital problems

Post shooting trauma

Long hours

Peer pressure

Supervisory pressure

Erratic work schedules

Negative public image

Dangerous undercover work

Pressure for successful undercover performance

Poor eating habits

Misuse of substances (drugs or alcohol, or both)

Drug enforcement officers may exhibit stress symptoms in many ways other than physical impairments. For example, at the conclusion of a successful drug-buy or raid, agents will commonly get together for a meal or a drink. This could be an indicator of job-related stress and the officer's attempt to relieve it. Because undercover agents are frequently required to work in liquor-serving establishments, they may fall victim to alcohol abuse sooner than people who are not required to work in such an environment. Those who choose to resort to alcohol consumption sometimes find themselves borderline (and sometimes chronic) alcoholics after a relatively short period of time. At this point, the officer is experiencing problems with *both* stress *and* alcohol. Both can have devastating effects on family relationships and professional competence.

More and more police officers are now turning to illicit drugs rather than alcohol for stress relief (as well as for recreational use). Obviously, a drug agent's frequent association with drug dealers and the constant availability of illicit substances through those dealers poses a very real potential both for abuse and for subsequent corruption. The detection of these officers within the ranks is a constant administrative priority (see Officer Drug Testing, below).

Fifteen of the most prevalent stress warning signs in drug enforcement officers are:

1. Sudden changes in behavior
2. More gradual changes in behavior indicating deterioration of behavior
3. Eratic work habits
4. Increased sick leave
5. Inability to maintain train of thought
6. Excessive worrying
7. Grandiose behavior
8. Excessive use of alcohol or drugs
9. Fatigue
10. Peer complaints
11. Excessive citizen complaints
12. Consistency in complaint pattern
13. Sexual promiscuity

14. Excessive accidents
15. Manipulation of fellow officers

Other Poor Performance Indicators

In addition to the indicators listed above there are additional warning signs of stress which should not go unnoticed by the supervisor. These warning signs will manifest themselves in the undercover agent who fails to step out of his undercover role. Specific indicators include:

1. Using profanity and foul language when not necessary
2. Walking the "walk" of the drug dealer/user when not required
3. Projecting superior attitude toward other workers and supervisors

Alternatives

In dealing with such personality changes therapy might be considered as an alternative, and this is discussed later in this chapter. From an administrative standpoint, however, the unit manager should consider dealing with stress-related personality changes in the following manner:

1. *Transfer.* It may be necessary to remove the officer from the particular duties he is currently assigned. The transfer can be an effective tool in increasing unit cohesiveness and the individual motivation of the officer.
2. *Interview.* Oftentimes it is most beneficial to confront the officer with his problems. In doing so it is likely that the manager and the subordinate can identify workable solutions to problems.
3. *Document Activity.* Documenting the specific problems displayed by the subordinate may help the manager to identify patterns of stress before they evolve into major problems.
4. *Employee Assistance Programs.* As mentioned earlier, the agency's employee assistance program might be able to recommend a number of treatment alternatives.
5. *Time off.* Time off, if well spent, can reduce stress levels and enable the officer to identify and deal with personal problems.

The Personal Improvement Plan

Once the police manager identifies a problem and confronts the affected officer, a personal improvement plan should be outlined. It should be remembered that this program is designed to help the employee and not to punish him. The PIP should address five specific areas:

1. *Statement of the problem.* The employee cannot be held responsible for problems of which he or she may not even be aware. The statement of the problem identifies this area and gives direction to a solution.
2. *Specified minimal expected standard.* The employee must be aware of the minimal progress expected so his or her actions and behavior can be gauged.
3. *Retraining.* It might be necessary to retrain the officer in a number of critical areas to prevent future recurrences of the problem. In this case the officer's training record should be reviewed with the agency training officer and the officer's immediate supervisor for recommendations.
4. *Specified time period.* The personal improvement plan should include a specified time period in which the identified problems should be corrected.
5. *Consequences of noncompliance.* Punitive measures for noncompliance must be clearly articulated in the personal improvement plan. This clearly defines expected behavior and consequences of the officer's inability or unwillingness to correct the problem. Such consequences might include termination, transfer, suspension, and so forth.

To best deal with stress and stress-related problems, several avenues of therapy may be considered. If the officer's department does not offer an employee assistance program to assist in treatment of stress, the officer should consider other personal outlets for relief. First, a self-regulated, but structured program of diet and exercise is recommended for all agents, whether symptoms of stress exist or not. Experts recommend aerobic exercises, such as jogging, racquetball, or weightlifting, over other forms. When practiced in moderation, all exercise is beneficial: it not only improves one's physical and mental health, but increases job productivity as well.

Second, the officer should try to develop cognitive coping skills for dealing with confrontations and difficult persons. Obviously, spur-of-the-moment situations cannot be prepared for as well as those that can be anticipated, but the list provided in Table 10–3 should help agents in mental preparedness in many circumstances.

If a regularly scheduled, rigorous exercise program is not possible for unit personnel, then a method should be established where a partial reduction of stress can be realized. Table 10–4 lists several stress management techniques that help promote relaxation and ease mental and physical strain.

Table 10–3 Cognitive Coping Skills

Preparing for a difficult situation.
    What is it that must be accomplished?
    Is there a plan that can be worked out to deal with the situation?
    There won't be any need for an argument.
    Easy does it; keep your sense of humor.
Impact and confrontation.
    Stay in control. Keep your cool.
    Don't try to prove yourself.
    There is no point in getting mad.
    Try not to make more out of the situation than it already is.
Coping with your own arousal.
    When muscles tense up, it is time to relax and slow things down.
    It is not worth it to get angry.
    Although you have a right to be upset, try to keep a lid on the situation.
    Stand your ground, but try not to lose control either.
Reflecting on the provocation.
    When the situation has not gone well.
        Forget about the aggravation. Thinking about it will only upset you.
        Try to shake it off. Don't let it interfere with your job.
        Don't take it personally.
    When the conflict is successfully resolved.
        Feel good about the manner in which the situation was handled.
        Realize the problem wasn't as bad as it seemed.
        You could have gotten more upset than the situation was worth.

Officer Rotation

Here is an area that varies from agency to agency not only in terms of operations but also in terms of management philosophy. How long should an officer remain in the drug enforcement unit? Should he or she stay year after year if he or she is producing quality work — or should there be a set rotation time, after which the officer is transferred? If the officer does stay, should he or she remain undercover? Answers to these questions are difficult. They depend largely on the mission of the agency and the needs of other units within the department.

Skill and knowledge in narcotics investigation takes time to develop. It is not mastered in one or even two years. During the 1960s and 1970s, many agencies required officers to work undercover for only a year or so before being rotated out of the unit because managers felt that an officer's discipline would deteriorate and he or she would have difficulty in readjusting to plainclothes or uniform patrol work. Many administrators also felt that undercover officers would become known by drug dealers after a year or so on the street.

If the specific mission of the agency is drug enforcement, supervi-

Table 10–4 Stress Reduction Techniques

Exercise

Engage in endurance exercises for a minimum of 30 minutes, three times a week, up to your target heart rate. Check with a physician about an appropriate program for physical fitness.

Calf and hamstring stretches can relax and loosen legs after prolonged sitting.

Neck and shoulder rolls and touching your hands over your shoulder and behind your back can loosen these areas before headache or cramping arises.

Relaxation techniques

Progressive relaxation by gradually tensing and relaxing large groups of muscles from hand to head to foot. Initial training may take 20–30 minutes a day, but this may later be done almost immediately.

Facial and ear massage may tend to relax head and facial muscles, raise your energy level, and "take a break" from attending so much outside yourself.

Body scanning can be done quickly several times a day by quickly scanning the body from head to foot and letting go unnecessary tensions.

Cue breathing is a "cue to relax." It is done by inhaling deeply and holding it for about 2 seconds, then relaxing deeply with the exhalation.

Color breathing also involves the feeling of relaxed breathing while imagining deep breathing of a relaxing color (warm golden sunshine or cool blue water).

Mental methods

Permission words or phrases are statements you say to yourself as a reminder to take time to relax. These can be in conjunction with breathing: saying "I can" on inhalation and "feel relaxed" on exhalation.

Positive self-statements are words and statements you can repeat to yourself that build esteem and give encouragement rather than saying demeaning and self-critical things, which only adds to the stress already being experienced.

Mental imaging of a peaceful or comforting scene, such as a lake or island scene. For a few minutes explore what you felt, heard, and smelled; try to develop as complete a picture as possible.

Diet

A proper diet is essential for every officer working within the unit. There will be times when circumstances arise when proper eating is not possible, but a balanced diet should be maintained at all other times. Because a recommended diet will differ from one person to another (due to age, build, weight, height, etc.), a physician should be consulted. Generally, a diet may consist of a decrease in the intake of sugar, salt, and caffeine, and the use of supplements such as vitamin B complex and vitamin C. Again, a physician should always be consulted first.

Peer support

Support groups of one's peers, friends, or family may provide a source of strength during times of stress. Support may not only come from encouragement from others but from critical remarks from them regarding one's stressors.

(Note: For support groups to effectively aid one in stress reduction, they must first be educated as to the causes and problems of stress and what is required to reduce it.)

sors might still wish to consider rotating an agent out of a particular section (e.g., diversion or intelligence). This should be the case if the agent's productivity has fallen due to complacency in his or her current assignment. A new assignment can often generate new vigor and enthusiasm in a nonproductive employee.

In the case of a drug enforcement unit operating within a police department, other factors should be considered. For example, even though an officer's cover might eventually be exposed after a long period of undercover work, he or she could still be of service to the section in another capacity: surveillance officer, records officer, or intelligence analyst. It is costly to train new drug enforcement officers because so much is learned on the job. It is to the agency's advantage to retain personnel as long as possible (see Officer Evaluation).

Training Requirements

Regardless of what police duty is being discussed, ongoing training is one of the most important aspects of the profession. Training enhances an officer's chances of survival, techniques in criminal investigation, and knowledge of criminal law, and overall police effectiveness. Training should be a continuing feature of any officer's career.

In drug enforcement, training may be affected both internally and externally. It is up to the command staff to determine the training needs of the section. This can prove to be somewhat difficult, as these needs may vary greatly within the section. New officers must first be trained in the basics: drug identification, search and seizure procedures, and basic undercover operations. Experienced officers, on the other hand, may require specialized training in areas such as electronic surveillance or conspiracy investigations (Table 10-5).

Table 10-5 Drug Enforcement Training Needs

Basic training
Drug Identification
Drug street prices and packaging
Search and seizure
Fundamentals of undercover investigation
The handling of criminal informants
Preparing search warrants
Collection and preservation of evidence
Preparing investigative reports
Preparing for courtroom testimony
Advanced training
Surveillance techniques
Conspiracy investigations
Tactical training
Investigation of clandestine laboratories
Investigation of marijuana fields
Booby traps
Wire-tap investigations
Electronic surveillance techniques
Raid planning

In-House Training

In-house training (or in-service training) is that which is conducted within or by the unit. In-house training allows experienced officers to train less experienced officers about specific techniques and practices. In-house training may be conducted in a classroom setting, by using a more experienced officer, or even a field training officer (FTO) program in which the newcomer is assigned to a more experienced officer for a period of time and learns on the street (see Chapter 11).

Frequently, on-the-job-training (OJT) is offered to better acclimate an officer to street surroundings. The OJT method should never be used in place of formalized training, only as adjunct to such training for a better understanding of the agency's different policies, procedures, and tasks. OJT does, however, have its advantages:

1. It allows new officers the ability to observe more experienced officers in real-life situations.
2. It enables supervisors the chance to evaluate the newcomer as he or she makes mistakes.
3. The section can utilize new personnel as they are learning.
4. Problems can be recognized in the early phases of employment.
5. The officer can learn about local narcotics conditions in the area while learning.
6. The recruit is familiarized with unit policy and procedure.

In the OJT concept, the officer should experience as many new duties as possible for familiarization and to more rapidly become a more productive member of the unit.

External Training

This is the training offered by outside training sources, such as other law enforcement agencies or certified police training facilities. Training topics include everything possible in police work, but the specific training needs of each officer should be evaluated by the supervisor of the section. The courses offered in police training schools will probably range from one day to two weeks, and they occasionally require the officer to go out of town. In the latter case, the travel and expense of external training must be weighed for necessity and feasibility.

Unit supervisors should take care that officers who are sent to schools are getting the specific training needed by the unit. Although both basic and advanced training is offered in external training, the more experienced officers will probably learn more from a school offering practical problem-solving scenarios rather than strict classroom instruction.

Training for Outside Agencies

Training law enforcement officers who are not part of the drug enforcement agency has several advantages. Given the fact that narcotic enforcement personnel are often isolated from the mainstream of law enforcement, a training program to foster outside awareness of existing drug problems will serve as not only a good public relations tool, but also as a possible means to convince outside officers to more freely share investigative leads and resources with the drug enforcement agency.

All law enforcement officers are faced with the problems of drug use because drug users are involved in all categories of crime. Instruction in identifying the specific mental and physical state of an arrestee could mean the difference in a controlled arrest or a violent confrontation (see Chapter 4). Typically, training should be done in stages, where the basics are given first, then followed by more advanced sessions addressing more specific topics. The basic course should be as short as possible (one or two days), thus requiring road officers and detectives to be away from their duties as little as possible. Topics should include:

Basic drug identification: Patrol officers must be familiar with what drugs look like, how they are packaged, what they are cut with, and their street prices.

User identification: This acquaints the officer with the probable reactions of the drug user: the user's probable mental state at the time of arrest, and physical characteristics (size of pupils, nervousness, sweating, movements, etc.).

Drug concealment: Instruction on how and where drugs are commonly concealed so that street officers can look in the proper areas during vehicle stops.

Evidence collection: Instruction on how to collect and preserve drug and drug-related evidence for prosecution.

Profiling drug trafficking activity: This will inform officers as to the typical activity of different drug dealers (marijuana growers, clandestine laboratory operators, street dealers, and pedestrian traffic patterns).

Promotions

Promoting officers to a higher rank is somewhat of a double edged sword, and it may play an important role in determining the morale within the unit. Although promotions are a primary work incentive for the officer, the anticipation of the results of a promotional exam, or the psychological let-down of not being chosen for a promotion can create a negative incentive for the candidate.

Unfortunately, many police promotions are based on political influence or personal friendships with superiors, thereby creating a morale problem within the unit. Methods of promotion and candidate qualifications should be conducted in a manner of openness, fairness, and objectivity so that all qualified officers have an equal chance. Factors normally considered in a typical promotional process are:

1. *Basic qualifications:* This is a primary step used to weed out candidates who fail to meet basic employment requirements for the promotion.
2. *Officer seniority:* The number of years an officer has within the police agency. Seniority may play a significant role in the candidate's knowledge of the agency's policy, procedures, and investigative techniques. Administrators, however, should be careful not to attach too much weight to it as they may inadvertently pass up other better-qualified candidates with less time.
3. *Written examination:* In almost all circumstances promotional candidates should be required to take a written examination. The exam should provide administrators an insight as to the applicant's knowledge of the job and ability to express him- or herself clearly in writing. The written examination, however, should not be considered the major factor in the promotion process, when compared to a candidate's interview and past performance.
4. *Oral interview:* During the interview, the candidate should be questioned by a board of superiors or experts. Questions should be designed to probe the candidate's ability to think quickly and analytically.
5. *Other considerations:* Other factors to be considered are overall attitude, academic achievements, and the officer's general contribution to the agency.

Assessment Centers

An assessment center is not a place but a strategy used for interviewing applicants for promotions. Basically, it is a standardized evaluation of behavior based on multiple inputs or exercises, including job-oriented simulations, interviews, or tests. These are subsequently evaluated by several trained observers, who may include chiefs, sheriffs, or other administrative personnel from outside the candidate's agency. Typically, the assessment center will use any of the following job simulations as means by which to base their decisions:

Group discussions.

In-basket exercises (assuming the role of an administrator and working through a series of memos, letters, and other administrative material commonly found in an administrator's basket).

Management tasks.

Simulations of discussions with subordinates.

Oral presentations.

Written communication exercises.

Disciplinary Procedures

The internal affairs unit (IA) of the agency (or a designated manager) is charged with the administration of police discipline to officers who have violated agency policy, procedures, or provisions of criminal law. An unpleasant task, disciplinary procedures are essential in the effective control of the unit. Depending on what infraction is being addressed by the department, it is always preferable for the department to conduct its own internal investigation rather than let the situation escalate to the point that a civilian review board or grand jury is necessary.

According to Fifth and Fourteenth Amendments to the Constitution, no person shall be deprived of life, liberty or property without "due process" of law. The adjudication process in police work focuses on two areas: (a) when government actions jeopardize the rights of the officer, and (b) when the officer's property rights are jeopardized. The accused officer must be given formal notice of the charges against him or her, accompanied by a public hearing. The hearing is to determine whether the evidence against the officer supports the charge. In addition, the officer must be guaranteed the right to appeal. The process begins with an investigation, which is followed up by a hearing before a review board comprised of officers of varying ranks, but whose lowest rank must be that of the accused. The board should have the authority to make recommendations to the chief executive officer as to the fate of the accused, with considerations given to both procedural and substantive due process.

Police misconduct may fall into several general categories:

1. *Misconduct while off duty:* Although somewhat controversial, an officer must be held accountable for infractions of the agency's code of conduct when off duty. Such actions include: public drunkenness, failure to pay debts, etc.
2. *Infractions of conduct while on duty:* These violations may include drinking while on duty, insubordination, gross neglect of duty, and other conduct unbecoming to an officer.

3. *Criminal misconduct:* This includes activity that is in violation of the penal code of a particular state or locality: drug violations, assault, theft, etc.
4. *Other infractions:* These might include lesser infractions, such as tardiness or sloppy dressing.

Officer Drug Testing

Although an extremely controversial issue in the late 1980s, police officer drug testing has become a priority topic at executive police seminars. At present, there is no federal or state law either prohibiting or mandating drug testing of employees. Nonetheless, there is rising public concern about impaired public employees. Obviously, with police officers — a position where there is ample opportunity for abuse of authority and judgement — those under the influence of drugs should not be tolerated. Another reason police officers (and narcotics personnel in particular) have been singled out is because of the widespread availability of drugs and the police officers' close contact with the criminal element. Moreover, given that traumatic and stressful situations are the norm in police work, and they may be the foundation for substance abuse.

Narcotics agents deal regularly with sensitive information. However other positions within the police department may also be considered sensitive positions: supervisors, tactical (SWAT) team members, records and data processing personnel, and evidence technicians. Should employees holding these jobs also be tested? Many believe so. Many also believe that testing applicants for narcotic and probationary agent positions is necessary to determine fitness for employment (Fig. 10–2).

Although the argument of unreasonable search and seizure is commonly given by those opposed to drug testing, it has yet been undetermined whether or not such a practice (in police work) is either unreasonable or unconstitutional. Other skeptics of officer drug testing question the reliability of the tests. According to many experts in this area, to avoid incorrect test results and so-called false positives, the following procedures should be considered:

1. *The chain of custody:* Urine is evidence and should be treated as such. The initial collection should be observed to eliminate later charges of a false collection. Second, the urine vial should be labeled immediately to ensure proper identification of the sample. Once turned over to the laboratory, the chain of custody must then be maintained by laboratory personnel.
2. *The sample identification:* Each laboratory must have established sample identification procedures whereby urine samples do not get mixed up.

3. *Laboratory procedures:* This involves the standard operating procedures of the laboratory testing the sample. These procedures should be done in a manner consistent with established testing programs. Both the initial screening and confirmation procedures should indicate the level of sensitivity for all drugs tested. Laboratory techniques and procedures should also be available for examination.

4. *Test reliability:* Procedures should remain consistent from test to test. Differences in precision, sensitivity, and specificity may create differences in results from test to test. If a confirmatory test shows the presence of a controlled substance, then a second, but different, test should be performed. The second test also serves as a confirmatory test, and it also uses urine from the original urine sample.

5. *Trained personnel:* When contested, the competence of laboratory personnel will be at stake. City or state certification in this area will most likely substantiate the chemists' abilities.

6. *Methods of screening:* Three methods of screening are used at present: enzyme immunoassay (EIA), radioimmunoassay (RIA), and thin-layer chromatography (TLC). The methods used to confirm findings are gas–liquid chromatography, high-performance liquid chromatography, gas-chromatography mixed with mass spectroscopy (GC/MS), and special thin-layer chromatography methods.

7. *Accuracy:* The accuracy of the testing procedure described previously is from 99% to 100%.

A special problem exists with regard to undercover agents who are authorized to simulate the smoking of marijuana. Little is known about the possibility of cannabinoids to be absorbed through the membranes of the mouth (and then enter the bloodstream). It is, therefore, not known whether or not an agent simulating marijuana smoking might actually come under the influence of the drug. In addition, officers who are present in locations where marijuana smoke is prevalent may also come under the influence of the drug through ambient marijuana smoke (a "contact high"). Because so little hard data exists in this area, it can only be recommended that unit supervisors maintain close contact with laboratory personnel in order to establish whether or not there is any actual drug abuse on the part of the agent.

Some police agencies test only new applicants for employment. Other agencies have adopted a policy of random (unannounced) testing of employees. Given resistance from some police unions, departments such as the Miami Police Department have chosen not to conduct random testing for drugs per se, but instead require random physical examinations, which happens to include urinalysis for drugs. Problems have arisen, however, in police departments (such as in Washington D.C.) where allegations of gross mismanagement of the drug testing procedure have been reported. These claims include charges of harassment by supervisors (where only certain officers were required to be tested), and altering urine test scores to implicate innocent officers of drug abuse unfairly.

IACP Model
Drug Testing Policy

In October, 1986 the IACP Executive Committee approved a model drug testing policy designed to help law enforcement executives identify and deal with the use of illegal drugs by police officers in their agencies.

The policy recommends establishing a testing program, using urinalysis procedures, that are directed at all department employees who are believed to be using drugs illegally.

Police officers, like every other citizen in our society, can fall victim to the temptations and hazards associated with the use of narcotics and illegal drugs. Unlike many other citizens, however, the professional responsibilities of a police officer demand that he or she must remain free of drug dependence, illegal drug use and drug abuse. Police administrators must take every step necessary to ensure that their employees are meeting this drug-free requirement at all times.

GENERAL ORDER 86-

(____) POLICE DEPARTMENT (DATE)
OFFICE OF THE CHIEF OF POLICE

DRUG TESTING PROGRAM

I. PURPOSE OF DRUG TESTING PROGRAM NOTICE
  A. The Police Department has a legal responsibility and management obligation to ensure a safe work environment: as well as paramount interest in protecting the public by ensuring that its employees have the physical stamina and emotional stability to perform their assigned duties. A requirement for employment must be an employee who is free from drug dependence, illegal drug use, or drug abuse.
  B. Liability could be found against the Department and the employee if we fail to address and ensure that employees can perform their duties without endangering themselves or the public.
  C. There is sufficient evidence to conclude that use of illegal drugs, drug dependance, and drug abuse seriously impair an employee's performance and general physical and mental health. The illegal possession and use of drugs and narcotics by police employees is a crime in this jurisdiction, and clearly unacceptable. There are unique corruption hazards associated with drug possession and use by the police. Therefore, the Police Department has adopted this written policy to ensure an employee's fitness for duty as a condition of employment: to ensure drug tests are ordered based on a reasonable objective basis; and where the employee knows testing is a requirement of employment.

II. DEFINITIONS
  A. Employee--All personnel employed by a law enforcement agency, both sworn and civilian.
  B. Sworn employee--All sworn (commissioned) employees, including ranking officers.

C. Supervisor--Both sworn and civilian employees assigned to a position having day-to-day responsibility for supervising subordinates, or responsible for commanding a work element.
D. Drug Test--A urinalysis test administered under approved conditions and procedures to detect drugs.
E. Reasonable Objective Basis (select one)
  1. Having more evidence for than against.
  2. An apparent state of facts and/or circumstances found to exist upon inquiry by the supervisor, which would induce a reasonably intelligent and prudent person to believe the employee was under the influence or using drugs/narcotics.
  3. A reasonable ground for belief in the existence of facts or circumstances warranting an order to submit to a drug test.

III. GENERAL RULES (reference other rules that pertain to this subject)
  A. Department employees shall not take any narcotics or dangerous substance unless prescribed by a person licensed to practice medicine. Employees who are required to take prescription medicine shall notify their immediate supervisors of the medication prescribed and the nature of the illness or injury. Any statutory defined illegal use of drugs by an employee whether at or outside police employment, will not be tolerated.
  B. All property belonging to the Department is subject to inspection at any time without notice as there is no expectation of privacy.
    (Note: this statement should be a standing rule in all matters.)
  C. Police employees who have reasonable basis to believe that another employee is illegally using drugs or narcotics shall report the facts and circumstances immediately to their supervisor.
  D. Failure to comply with the intent or provisions of this general order may be used as grounds for disciplinary action. Refusal by a police employee to take the required drug test or follow this general order will result in immediate relief from police duties pending disposition of any administrative personnel action.

IV. POLICY--DRUG TESTING/URINALYSIS
  A. Applicants for the position of sworn police officer. Shall be routinely tested for drug or narcotic usage as a part of their pre-employment medical examination. The testing procedure and safeguards set forth in this order shall be followed by the examining physicians and others involved in the testing procedure.
    1. Refusal to take the test, or test results reporting a presence of illegal drugs or narcotics, or the use of nonprescription drugs, shall be the basis of discontinuing an applicant in the selection process. Any use or possession that constitutes a felony shall preclude any further consideration for employment.
    2. Applicants found to be involved in the illegal sale, manufacture or distributionp of any narcotic/drug will be permanently rejected.

Officer Evaluation

Narcotic enforcement personnel experience many unique conditions, which can create a substantial amount of on-the-job stress and problems in their personal lives. For example, an undercover officer's social life may be restricted by not being able to attend normal social events with other police officers: The risk is too great that he or she

---

3. Applicants demonstrating addiction to any narcotic/drug will be permanently rejected.
4. Any improper use of any narcotic/drug by an applicant after application will be grounds for permanent rejection.
5. After one year from the date of the above drug test, an applicant may reapply for the position of sworn police officer of use or possession did not constitute a felony. Applicants who previously refused the test are not eligible for further consideration.
6. The results of drug tests on applicants for the position of sworn police officer shall be kept confidential.
   (Note: These rules may be the prerogative of a civil service board or other hiring authority.)
B. *Current employees of the Department.* Shall be required to submit to a test for drug or narcotic usage as outlined below:
1. A supervisor may order a drug test when there is documentation that an employee is impaired or incapable of performing his/her assigned duties: reduced productivity, excessive vehicle accidents, high absenteeism, or other behavior inconsistent with previous performance. The contents of the documentation shall be made available to the employee.
2. Current employees may be ordered by a supervisor to take a drug test.
   a. Where the allegation involves the use, possession or sale of drugs or narcotics, or
   b. Where the allegation involves the actual use of force, or
   c. Where there is serious on-duty injury to the employee or another person.
   d. The purpose of the test is to determine if drug use affected the employee's actions or judgment. The employee shall be advised of the content and details of the allegation.
3. A supervisor who orders a dug test when there is a reasonable objective basis for suspecting usage shall forward a report containing the facts and circumstances directly to the Chief of Police.
4. A drug test shall be a part of each routine physical examination, and physical examination required for promotion or specialized assignment: i.e. pilot, bomb technician, vice squad, narcotics unit evidence control.
5. Test results reporting a presence of illegal drugs or narcotics, or the use of prescription drugs without a prescription, or the abuse of any over-the-counter drug, will be submitted as a part of a written complaint by the supervisor, consistent with Section IV-B-3 above, requesting departmental action. (Each Chief of Police adopting this model policy must decide the appropriate action depending upon the facts and circumstances.)
C. *Current sworn employees assigned to the drug/narcotic enforcement unit or vice unit.* Shall be required (in addition to Section B above) to submit to periodic unannounced drug tests at the direction of their supervisor.
1. Prior to accepting a special assignment, an employee shall execute a written agreement and

release stating that he/she fully consents to any medical, physical, psychiatric, pshychological or other testing, including urine and/or blood for drug or narcotic substances. In addition, the agreement or release shall give the Department permission to have access to all the employee's medical records.
2. The supervisor of the drug/narcotic enforcement unit or vice unit shall select the date and time when each employee assigned to the unit will be tested. The test may be administered randomly at least (times a year) without advance notice.
3. Sworn employees assigned to the drug/narcotic unit shall serve in this assignment for a period not to exceed _____ years. Extensions may be approved by the Chief of Police due to involvement in a major investigation or lengthy criminal trial.
D. The procedure for administering the urinalysis program is outlined in Appendix A of this general order.
E. Tenured employees who have been found to be using drugs or narcotics shall be provided with a hearing, where evidence is presented and preserved, before action taken against the employee becomes final. The accused employee shall have a right to explain the presence of drug in the urine.

By Order of

(Name)
Chief of Police

The IACP model drug screening policy is intended to serve as a guide to the police executive who is interested in establishing a method for testing for drug use in a department. It is not meant to stand alone as a complete agency policy. It may serve as a solid foundation for a final program design that must be shaped to the contour of the unique needs, legal requirements, case law, civil service regulations, state statutes, city ordinances, and existing collective bargaining agreements of the implementing jurisdiction.

The state of the law as it applies to mandatory drug screening is quite new and continually emerging. In recieving any drug screening policy, it is imperative to remember that the law enforcement community is dealing with a Fourth Amendment search issue. The Fourth Amendment, however, only prohibits unreasonably searches. According to the U.S. Supreme Court, a search is reasonable and therefore constitutionally sound if the need for the search outweighs its intrusion upon a person's rights. Since drug use among law enforcement personnel would clearly impact the public safety and public confidence in the integrity of law enforcement, the need for periodic drug testing of law enforcement officers can outweigh any privacy rights that are implicated, especially where there exists a reason to believe an individual is using drugs.

The implementation process of a drug testing program is critical. Before beginning a testing program, a law enforcement agency must develop clear procedures, based upon a fully articulated written policy for dealing with the testing process and for dealing with employees that test positive. These procedures must be communicated clearly to all employees, enforced consistently and applied fairly. They should be firmly based on the principal that drug abuse affects the health and safety of all law enforcement officers, employees, and the general public.

10-2 *(continued)*

will be recognized as associating with police officers and consequently lose his or her cover.

Even fellow police officers might look upon him or her as an outcast within the department. Because the job of drug investigation involves so many sensitive areas, great secrecy must be maintained within the unit. This secrecy creates an atmosphere of isolation for the unit members. Additional pressure may come from friends, relatives, and neighbors who think of drug agents as drug-using cops who are enforcing a double standard, not realizing the strict controls prohibiting drug use that are placed upon narcotics officers.

The wives and husbands of drug enforcement officers will also experience a sense of isolation because their spouses may not be at liberty to discuss details of each investigation. This can create tension in the officer's home life, which may ultimately affect the quality of their investigations.

To combat these problems, an evaluation process must be established within the unit. This process should be in addition to already established police officer evaluations, and it should focus on the officer's mental and emotional health. Through this evaluation, supervisors should be able to identify existing or future problems and formulate workable solutions. Narcotics officers should be evaluated in two critical areas: job performance and psychological well being. Other reasons for officer evaluations include:

1. *Organizational development:* This gives administrators an idea of the effectiveness and efficiency of the agency by examining information such as officer turnover, training needs assessments, the number of officers disciplined or promoted, etc.
2. *Patterns of disciplinary problems:* This is useful for identifying officers who are making the same mistakes repeatedly so corrective measures can be taken.
3. *Pay increases:* A running record of an officer's job performance can be an indicator of when merit or cost of living increases are due.

Job Performance

The unit supervisor has the responsibility of conducting a personal job performance evaluation for each member of the unit; though usually done quarterly or semiannually, they may also be performed monthly. The job performance evaluation is a checklist itemizing all performance objectives within the officer's job description. Through written reports and personal interviews, the supervisor should be able to identify areas of improvement. Two critical areas of evaluation include the quality and quantity of cases (see Table 10–6).

Table 10-6 Job Performance Evaluation

Quantity
Number of pending cases
Number of newly opened cases
Types of cases
Number of intelligence reports submitted
Number of working informants
Number of drug purchases and types of drugs
Amount of drug buy-money checked out
Amount of buy-money on hand
Number and type of arrests
Hours spent in court
Number of cases closed
Training received
Law enforcement agencies worked with
Number of regular and overtime hours worked
Number of absences
Quality
High level of violator
Type of drug dealt
Quantity of drug dealt
Size of distribution network
Estimated number of customers
Hours worked
Number of officers/hours used in the investigation

Psychological Well-Being

As discussed in the preceding section on stress, the quality of an officer's work (or lack thereof) could be a direct reflection on his mental health. Not only should managers observe and evaluate the officer's ability to deal effectively in an undercover capacity, but also his ability to get along with others with whom he or she works. Generally, a positive attitude, physical energy, and a sense of humor indicate that no psychological problems have surfaced. Should the telltale signs appear, managers should deal with the problem as soon as possible (see previous sections in this chapter on Poor Performance Indicators and The Personal Improvement Plan).

Summary

Because of the differences in jurisdiction, state and federal law, and local illicit drug problems, a variety of drug enforcement units exist throughout the United States. Although all such units serve more or less the same purpose, there are vast differences in their organizational structures. Regardless of how a unit or agency is structured, however, it should be capable of meeting certain investigative tasks in drug enforcement: street level enforcement, intelligence gathering and storage, high-level criminal investigations, and investigating drug diversion cases.

In the administration of drug units, managers must first concentrate on hiring the most qualified candidates for the position of drug enforcement agent. This is a unique position within the law enforcement community, and those selected as recruits must be scrupulously screened and trained. After training, a close relationship should be maintained between the officer and supervisor to maximize officer safety and unit productivity. If this can be done the unit should be productive, efficient, and operate with a high state of morale.

Suggested Readings

Bopp, William J., *Crises in Police Administration*. Springfield, IL: Charles C. Thomas, 1984.

Carver, John A.J.D., *Drugs and Crime: Controlling Use and Reducing Risk through Testing*. U.S. Department of Justice, National Institute of Justice, 1986.

Higgenbotham, Jeffery, *Urinalysis Drug Testing Programs for Law Enforcement*. FBI Law Enforcement Bulletin, October 1986.

Hurrell, Joseph J. Jr., *Stress Among Police Officers*. U.S. Department of Health and Human Services, October 1984.

Kuykendall, Jack L., *Community Police Administration*. Chicago, IL: Nelson Hall, 1975.

Munro, *Administrative Behavior and Police Organization*. Cincinnati, OH: Anderson Publishing, 1974.

Peirson, Gwynne, *Police Operations*. Chicago, IL: Nelson Hall, 1975.

Souryal, Sam S., *Police Organization and Administration*. Cincinnati, OH: Anderson Publishing, 1985.

Drug Enforcement Field Training 11

As far back as 1965, the President's Commission on Law Enforcement and Administration made recommendations on how to improve management in police departments — and it specified police field training as a priority. Since 1965 many agencies have adopted (and refined) such programs, which have generally been well received within the law enforcement community. The FTO (Field Training Officer) concept is one such program, which up until recently has been used primarily in training uniform police recruits. Drug enforcement personnel have largely been left out of FTO-type programs, and most of their training has been through on-the-job (OJT) programs.

Because of the specialized training needs of narcotics personnel (which are usually not addressed in basic academy training) a need has arisen for field training for drug enforcement personnel. Field training focuses on two types of recruits: those who are sworn officers, already employed by the department and in need of transitional training, and those who are newcomers to police work and require substantial training in the area of narcotics enforcement and general police procedure.

The Program

An agent field training program should be a structured process of ongoing education and information designed to minimize job-related risk, maximize officer safety, and increase unit productivity. The program's results are measured through verbal and written evaluations by an experienced field training officer (FTO), and through self-evaluations by the recruits (Figs. 11-1, 11-2, 11-3, pp. 345-350).

Field training is necessary because undercover agents sometimes operate with minimal supervision and therefore must be able to make many field decisions on their own. Decisions made in the field may affect the officers' own safety, the safety of others, and the overall effectiveness and integrity of the investigation. Second, undercover personnel must have sufficient training in the different types of evidence necessary to prosecute a drug case. Evidence must often be acquired by officers working undercover, out of touch with supervisors, and there may not be a second opportunity for evidence collection. Finally, there are many unforseen circumstances that arise during a covert operation; therefore an undercover agent must be as prepared as possible to deal with the unexpected.

Other benefits of the FTO program are (a) to minimize the likelihood of civil litigation by increasing agent effectiveness through a documented program of competency-oriented training; (b) to provide specialized training specifically suited to the needs of the drug unit; (c) to provide transitional-orientation training for officers new to narcotics enforcement and for department officers newly transferred into the unit; and (d) to reduce in-house grievances by agent personnel through job understanding and efficiency.

In this program, the new member of the unit will also learn much of the job by OJT. The program affords the host agency not only a learning process, but also the means to identify mistakes or bad habits before the recruit becomes "set" in his or her ways (Table 11-1).

Selection of a Field Training Officer

Because the field training program is critical in the training and development of recruits, it is imperative that only qualified individuals serve as FTOs in the unit. To select the highest quality candidates for the position of FTO,

the FTO position must be voluntary;

candidates for the FTO position must hold a senior rank within the unit;

candidates must appear before a selection board consisting of line and command staff, who will question each candidate;

criteria for selection should include past work performance (cases initiated, cases closed, conviction rate, absenteeism, and disciplinary actions), supervisor remarks, and other observations of the board.

Table 11–1 General Recommendations for Field Training Programs

The field training program should be required by policy for all recruits. This will standardize drug enforcement training and supplement training received in the basic police academy.

All field training should be established in a standard training format and in written policy to insure that all recruits receive equality in training. When reduced to writing, goals and objectives of the field training program can be fully understood by both trainees and each FTO.

More than one FTO should be used for each recruit if possible. Although some may argue that this might only confuse the recruit, it should offer different points of view from the field and give the recruit a diversity of opinions from experienced personnel.

Standardized evaluation methods should be used in all cases. In addition to the written field training program, if the same criteria is used to evaluate trainees, discrepancies will be minimized. Such evaluations should be made by the FTO weekly, identifying poor performance trends and making recommendations for improvement. Evaluations should be submitted promptly to the supervisor for evaluation.

All FTOs must receive a minimum of 40 hours training. This is a position that encompasses many of the same skills of the unit supervisor in terms of teaching, personnel motivation, and performance evaluation.

The FTOs' task responsibilities should be clearly defined to eliminate confusion.

Extra compensation should be offered to FTOs to attract the highest quality candidates for the job, and to build tenured FTOs over a period of time.

The overall program should be continually evaluated by agency managers. The program evaluation could be on an annual or even semiannual basis. Evaluations should include:

The number of trainees entering the program

The number of trainees disciplined during the training process

The number of trainees dismissed as a result of the program

The number of trainees who successfully complete the program

All training should be on-site and scheduled during the recruits regularly scheduled shift.

Role of the Field Training Officer

Field training officers should be officers who possess skills learned through time in grade and whose past work records speak well for both the individual and the agency he or she represents. All FTOs should be required to train new officers according to the agency's standard operating procedure (SOP), and should be proficient in all aspects of the drug investigation field.

The training and orientation program should cover all important aspects of the job in specific phases. Each of these phases should focus on a particular aspect of training, and should be completed in a specified period of time. Subsequent officer evaluations should be conducted by the FTO or the supervisor each week during the training phases (The Drug Enforcement Training Record). The results will then be reviewed by the FTO and the unit supervisor for a final determination as to the officer's suitability for continued service in the drug unit.

The success of a field training program relies heavily on the ability of the FTO to conduct an accurate evaluation of the recruit. Table 11–2 offers a proposed field training officer task analysis, which includes individual job specifications.

The administration of field training is critical, and officers new to the unit should be required to complete all phases successfully before being placed into service. This program, therefore, involves a constant process of evaluation of the new officer, which could take from 6 weeks to 90 days, depending on how extensively the program is structured.

Outlined below is a prototype agent field training program for the drug enforcement unit, which outlines specific tasks and goals for the new officer to complete in a three-month (90-day) period. Upon the completion of the program, the officer should be prepared for undercover work and assigned a case load.

It should again be stressed that the learning process through OJT is to be used in conjunction with the formalized training program and other drug enforcement training schools. Officers should be evaluated in the program during probation, and they should be proficient in all areas in order to complete the program successfully. In addition, the designated FTO will evaluate the progress of the new officer on a step-by-step basis.

Table 11–2 Field Training Officer Task Analysis

The FTO must maintain daily contact with the trainee and closely observe the trainee's job performance.

The FTO must explain and make clear all performance expectations to the trainee.

The FTO should expose the trainee (as an observer) to as many practical aspects of drug enforcement as possible.

Trainees should not be placed in tactical, sensitive, or potentially dangerous positions until they successfully complete all phases of the training program.

The FTO's responsibility includes a written weekly trainee evaluation, which is filled out by him or her and submitted to the unit supervisor for critique.

Once the evaluation is reviewed by the FTO and the unit supervisor, it is discussed with the trainee and any areas requiring improvement are identified with possible solutions.

The relationship between a FTO and the assigned recruit is that of teacher and student, not partners. As a student, the trainee is not in a position to back up the FTO on the street.

Proposed Program Structure

New recruits cannot be held responsible for on-duty or off-duty policy infractions if they have not been familiarized with the unit's policy requirements. In addition, any procedures not contained in policy guidelines should be made clear to recruits in order to avoid complications during investigations.

If administered properly, the field training program will avoid such problems and benefit the sponsoring agency. It will give the drug investigation unit a structured system to evaluate new members, and will also provide an administrative tool to lessen the likelihood of civil action (by either defendants or officers) against the agency because of lack of adequate training. Finally, it should give managers an indication of those who are not suited for undercover work.

Below is model drug agent field training program designed to offer the sponsoring agency optimum efficiency in training and evaluation of prospective candidates for the position of investigator. This 90-day program will acquaint the recruit with the workings of the agency, the unit, how drug traffickers operate, investigative techniques, criminal law and procedure, and agency policy.

During the program, the recruit should be exposed gradually to experiences that he or she will encounter on the street. When the recruit completes the program, he or she should be ready to manage a case load independently. During each phase of training, the recruit will be evaluated on performance through weekly observation reports and meetings with the FTO and unit supervisor. It is up to the FTO and supervisor to identify problems and seek solutions to them.

At the conclusion of the program (Phase 4), all reports and evaluations will be reviewed by the unit supervisor for a determination regarding the recruit's suitability for continued employment. The FTO will confer with the unit supervisor about the progress of the recruit and any other necessary issues during the field training program. The four phases are:

Phase 1: General orientation (3 weeks)
   This is an indoctrination phase that will familiarize the officer with all basic information needed by the officer: contact with the FTO, understanding agency regulations and policy, a drug identification. Each week's progress is summarized in a weekly observation report and in meetings between the FTO and unit supervisor.

Phase 2: Field performance (3 weeks)
   This phase deals with substance abuse, management of unit confidential funds for investigative expenses, and drug pur-

chases. In addition, reporting procedures and electronic surveillance techniques are discussed. Throughout this phase the recruit officer will be closely monitored by the FTO for his or her ability to apply what has been learned so far in the program. Each week's progress is summarized in a weekly observation report and in meetings between the FTO and unit supervisor.

Phase 3: Criminal investigation (4 weeks)

Fundamental techniques of criminal investigation will be taught at this stage, which will include instruction in working undercover, managing cases, and testifying in criminal court proceedings. Each week's progress will be summarized in a weekly observation report and in meetings between the FTO and unit supervisor.

Phase 4: Surveillance operations phase (2 weeks)

In this phase, the recruit will be familiarized with the various methods of surveillance and specific techniques considered most effective. Additional instruction will include dealing with drug-related crime and search warrant preparation. This phase involves the recruit applying what he or she has learned to the field. The recruit will be evaluated in a weekly observation report and in meetings between the FTO and unit supervisor.

Serving as a general example, the program below is organized into the four phases which address critical areas of officer orientation and development. Much of the information eluded to in the following training scenarios is discussed in the preceding chapters of the book and is referenced.

Phase 1: General Orientation

Week 1: Contact with the FTO

1. *Appropriate use of pager:* Because agents are on call 24 hours a day, every officer working within the unit should be furnished with a pager. This will allow him or her to be available to the unit whenever necessary.
2. *Home phone:* All unit personnel must have a home phone number where they can be contacted whenever they are not in an official vehicle or on their assigned pager.
3. *"Hello phone" procedure:* The "hello phone" is a telephone located at the police department that has a number unrelated to the department. This number is given to drug suspects as an agent's home or work phone so that contact between the two can be maintained. When answered, officers say "hello" and treat the call as if it were a personal call. All hello-phone calls should be recorded.

4. *Telephone check-in:* Methods of telephone check-in must be established: only authorized personnel should be contacted by the agent. This prevents the agent from calling in from the street and discussing sensitive operations with unauthorized personnel, increasing the risk of "burning" an investigation or the identity of the undercover officer. (*Note:* It is the officer's responsibility to maintain contact with the FTO and to report in regularly. The trainee must also acclimate him- or herself to the idea of being on call at all times.)

Understanding Rules and Regulations

5. *Standard operating procedures manual:* Every unit should have a written standard operating procedures manual that outlines what is expected of all unit personnel.
6. *Work schedule:* A structured work schedule should be adhered to by all officers within the unit. It should be remembered, however, that most drug enforcement work involves unscheduled overtime.
7. *Days off and overtime:* The scheduled work week should be kept to 40 hours with two days off. Some agencies use flex-time, where officers may take off "comp time" whenever they get caught up with their caseload. This program contributes greatly to the stress variable in the job and should not be considered as the best antedote to the overtime problem.
8. *Leave time (sick, disciplinary):* Established agency policy regarding time off should be understood by the new recruit.
9. *Transfers:* It should be understood early on whether a member of the unit is to be transferred after serving a designated period of time in the unit. Many agencies, for example, hire personnel from outside the unit to work undercover and then transfer them to the patrol division. The establishment of this policy should deter the attrition rate of officers who do not desire working in uniform after service in the drug section.
10. *Outside employment:* Because many undercover assignments require agents to work an outside job to maintain cover, policy should be established regarding accepted behavior on the undercover job and handling income derived from that job. It is recommended that the agent work under his or her fictitious social security number and that the extra income be absorbed by the agency. This will eliminate the officer's tax bracket being affected by the additional income.
11. *Contacts with police while undercover:* It is common for undercover agents to come into contact with uniformed police officers while officially associating with criminal suspects. It must be

established by the unit whether or not the undercover officer will identify him- or herself to the uniformed officer. If the officer is being accompanied by suspects or if there are circumstances that might otherwise jeopardize the investigation or the officer's safety, then the undercover officer should use his or her undercover identity (undercover driver's license). A full report must later be made to the officer's supervisor regarding the circumstances of the encounter. In all other circumstances, the officer should identify him- or herself properly.

12. *Drug simulation policy:* One method used by drug suspects to determine whether or not a potential buyer is a police officer is to observe the buyer using drugs. Unless an officer's life is in direct jeopardy, officers should not be authorized to consume illicit drugs. Drug use will ruin the credibility of the officer, the agency, and the investigation. It is possible, however, to train an officer to simulate the smoking of marijuana.

Most drug simulation involves marijuana. Because many diseases are associated with drug use and may be transmitted through saliva remaining on the marijuana cigarette, the agency may be open to liability. (Saliva-borne diseases include hepatitis A and B.)

If a simulation policy is adopted, the officer must be properly trained. Though it is not easy to simulate snorting, agents could be taught "slight-of-hand" techniques that might be used in emergency situations.

13. *Drug enforcement statutes:* Familiarity with applicable drug statutes is essential for all unit personnel. Agents must understand the elements of drug violations (possession, distribution and conspiracy) in order to collect evidence effectively.

Week 2: Drug Identification

The importance of drug identification cannot be overemphasized (see Chapter 4). Criminals, both professional and amateur, know what drugs are on the street and so should the recruit drug agent. In addition, recruits should have a thorough knowledge of their street terms, prices, and profit margins. Moreover, the effects of drugs on an individual must be understood. The trainee should be prepared for encounters with suspects who might be under the influence of drugs and be prone to violence. Minimum training should include:

1. General hazards and effects
2. Diluents
3. Marijuana
4. Cocaine

5. Heroin
6. PCP
7. LSD
8. Pharmaceuticals
9. Methamphetamine
10. Designer drugs

Week 3: Overview of Undercover Work

1. *Expelling the myths:* Undercover work is rarely as it is portrayed on television (see Chapter 2). It is interesting, but not glamourous; it is dangerous, and sometimes boring. During this phase of training, the officer must become acquainted with what realistically lies in store for him.
2. *The mission of the agency or unit:* The particular mission of the agency will relate to its jurisdiction and resources. If the mission is to address vice and property crimes, an understanding of the mission will give direction to the officers field decisions (see Chapter 9). (*Note:* Because so much misunderstanding exists regarding undercover work and the drug trade, new officers must understand their role in drug enforcement. Much of their role is directly related to the overall mission of the agency.)
3. *Responsibilities and expectations:* This addresses the general code of conduct for the agent; it should be read and signed by the recruit.

Phase 2: Field Performance Phase
Week 4: Substance Abuse

1. *Alcohol abuse:* Undercover work frequently involves extended contacts with suspects in liquor-serving establishments. These contacts may require officers to consume large quantities of alcohol to preserve their cover. To avoid complications, each department should, by policy, require each investigator to be aware of the legal state requirements for blood alcohol content (BAC), and stay under that limit at all times while on duty. This will avoid the problem of officers being under the influence of alcohol while working in an official capacity and while operating official vehicles (see Chapter 10).

    Additionally, an officer's personal use of alcohol should be kept in check when he or she is off duty so that the effects of excessive drinking will not intrude into his or her official duties.
2. *Drug dependency:* Officers should never be permitted to consume illicit drugs on or off duty. In addition, managers should be aware

of those officers who might acquire controlled substances legally (through prescription), and then abuse such drugs. To safeguard against drug abuse by unit officers, a sound and written drug testing policy must be established and made clear to recruits (see Chapter 9).

3. *Employee assistance and counseling services:* In the event unit officers experience job-related problems such as drug dependency, stress, or family problems, a structured assistance program should be available through which referrals can be made for the officer.

Management of Finances

5. *Paperwork:* As with any criminal investigation, a lot of paperwork is necessary for case documentation. All official forms such as complaints, intelligence, case management, investigative expenses, and daily activity reports should be completely understood by recruits.

6. *Requirements for receipts:* Because large sums of money changes hands and because investigations are so costly, expended funds must be accounted for according to prescribed agency policy. Misappropriated funds will create legal nightmares for case officers and managers alike. This is considered an extremely sensitive area.

7. *Acceptable and unacceptable expenditures:* Agents will be given official funds to spend on drugs, informant payments, investigative expenses, auto repairs, and related expenses. Authorized amounts for expenditures must be understood during training. The accuracy and legibility of these reports must be properly emphasized.

(*Note:* Competent management of paperwork and a thorough understanding of what is permitted in the way of expenditures is essential. Officer liability and the credibility of the agency is constantly under scrutiny when units spend as much money as drug investigations require.)

Week 5: Reporting Procedures

1. Drug–buy reports (complaint and supplemental)
2. Arrest reports
3. Intelligence reports

All of the above reports should be filled out accurately, legibly, and in uniform fashion (see Chapter 9).

Undercover Residences

1. Location
2. Set-up of residence
3. Security of residence
4. Utility hookups
5. Maintenance

Because undercover residences may be used for providing the agent substantiation of his or her cover story and to allow officers to equip the residence with special audiovisual equipment, the officer must be trained in the basic set-up of the equipment. In addition, the officer must be taught how to best position a suspect so that the image and sound will be clearly recorded, and how to ask specific (lead) questions to extract appropriate conversation from the suspect.

Knowledge of City or County (Jurisdiction)

1. *Other law enforcement agencies:* Because many drug offenders are transient, law enforcement agencies must frequently work together. During field training, the recruit must become familiar with all law enforcement agencies that might benefit future investigations.
2. *Hospitals:* In case the officer encounters victims of gunshot wounds or drug overdoses, recruits should know hospital locations and emergency routes.
3. *High-crime areas:* If the officer is not yet familiar with the jurisdiction, high-crime areas must be identified. Knowledge of these areas will benefit the officer when making arrangements for surveillances or undercover drug purchases.
4. *Other areas of interest*

Phase 3: Criminal Investigation
Week 6: Establishing an Undercover Identity

1. Undercover drivers license
2. Social security number
3. Cover story

This week involves understanding and establishing an undercover identity. This will prepare the trainee with credentials to conduct covert investigations and allow him or her to get used to a chosen undercover name (see Chapter 2).

Week 7: Case Development

1. *Case initiation:* One of the foremost responsibilities of a drug agent is to develop cases by proactive investigation. Officers will not always have informants at their disposal (nor is it desirable for an officer to become too reliant on them). An officer must have the ability to develop cases independently (see Chapter 1).
2. *Investigative leads:* Investigative leads are the clues investigators follow up to help develop cases.
3. *Testifying in court:* When an arrest has been made, an officer must anticipate providing testimony in criminal court. For those officers who have never been called upon to testify before, ground rules must be established. All officers must dress appropriately (coat and tie). If the agent has long hair or a beard, both should be trimmed as much as necessary to present a favorable image of the officer and the agency; it also adds credibility to the case. Officers must be reminded that it is acceptable to read police reports before appearing in court, but such reports will likely fall into the hands of the defense attorney who will attempt to find discrepancies in the report and the officer's testimony. Before making a court appearance, officers should communicate with other prosecution witnesses in the case (the police chemist or informant) in order to ensure that necessary evidence will be available for the proceeding.

Week 8: Use of Undercover Vehicles

1. *Types of vehicles:* Depending on the individual resources of the agency, different vehicles will be needed for various undercover assignments (drug buys, covert surveillance, and command-post vehicles). The recruit should be familiar with all unit vehicles (see Chapter 2).
2. *Preventive maintenance for assigned vehicle:* Each agent must assume responsibility for the official vehicle he or she is assigned. Maintenance includes scheduled oil changes, tune ups, and other necessary service.
3. *Use of undercover gas credit cards:* Each agent in the unit should be assigned undercover credit cards to use while working in a covert or undercover capacity. Every agency should establish policy regarding which expenditures are authorized with the credit card and which are not.
4. *Accidents:* In the event an agent has an automobile accident while on duty, it should be understood under which circumstances he or she will identify him- or herself. For instance, if accompanied by a

suspect, the officer should not jeopardize his or her cover by giving accident investigators the correct proper name. The undercover name and driver's license should be given at the scene of the accident, followed by a complete report to an immediate supervisor when not accompanied by the suspect.

5. *Concealment of radios:* Without exception, all radios and official gear must be concealed when working undercover.

The appropriate use of undercover vehicles can support an undercover investigation. All unit officers should be familiar with unit policy to minimize problems that may "burn" the officer's identity, the undercover vehicle, or the investigation.

Week 9: Covert Surveillance

1. *Objectives*
2. *Moving*
3. *Stationary*
4. *Electronic*
5. *Reconnaissance of surveillance locations*

Methods of surveillance must be understood by the recruit as well as knowing which method is most appropriate in a given investigation (see Chapter 4).

Undercover Employment

1. *Purpose*
2. *Target areas*
3. *Policy on undercover income*
4. *High-crime areas*
5. *Low-crime areas*

Officer Safety

1. *Use of deadly force*
2. *Legal aspects of shooting*
3. *Duty weapons*
4. *Firearms policy*
5. *Flashrolls*
6. *Confrontational situations*

Phase 4: Surveillance Operations

Week 10: Use of Equipment

1. *Visual equipment*
2. *Audio equipment*
3. *Tracking equipment*

Trainees should learn how to operate and maintain technical equipment. Policy should be established regarding the loan of equipment to other law enforcement agencies, and, if permitted, under what conditions will it be loaned (see Chapters 2 and 4).

Week 11: Agent Response to Drug-Related Crime

1. *Reporting procedure:* Two out of every three prisoners currently serving time had been under the influence of drugs when their crimes were committed. This is important to the investigator because he or she will occasionally be in circumstances where crimes other than drug dealing will be observed. When crimes are observed (such as assault, theft, forgery, child abuse), the officer must recall as many details of the crime as possible and report it to a supervisor as soon as possible. It is not a good idea for an undercover agent to intervene personally unless there is an immediate threat of death or severe bodily injury.
2. *Property offenses:* It is common for drug dealers to be involved with burglary and other property offenses to acquire revenue for the purchase of drugs. If an undercover agent discovers such activity, a complete report should be submitted to the *narcotics* supervisor; after evaluation, it may then be forwarded to the crimes against property unit for joint consultation. A similar policy should be maintained by the crimes against property unit in the event they discover activity involving drug dealing.

Week 12: Knowledge of Search Warrants

1. *Legal requirements*
2. *Forms*
3. *Procedure*
4. *Use of informants*
5. *Methods of searching*
6. *Packaging and handling evidence*

Knowledge of search and seizure must become second nature to the drug agent. Searches and seizures are common in criminal investigations, and it is an area in which there are many opportunities for civil rights violations.

CITY POLICE DEPARTMENT
RECRUIT OFFICER WEEKLY EVALUATION FORM

RECRUIT _____ FTO _____ WEEK _____ DATE _____

Codes: A= Not Observed B= Unacceptable C= Acceptable D= Above Average

CHARACTER TRAIT	A B C D	CHARACTER TRAIT	A B C D
GENERAL APPEARANCE	A B C D	ACCESSIBILITY	A B C D
ACCEPTANCE OF CRITICISM	A B C D	PROBLEM SOLVING DECISION MAKING ABILITY	A B C D
ATTITUDE TO POLICE WORK	A B C D	RELATIONSHIPS: U.C. CONTACTS	A B C D
KNOWLEDGE: DEPT. POLICY	A B C D	RELATIONSHIPS: SUPERVISORS/OFFICERS	A B C D
KNOWLEDGE OF RELATED STATE STATUTES	A B C D	STABILITY POLICE: U.C. IDENTITY	A B C D
KNOWLEDGE OF CITY	A B C D	FINANCES: RECORD KEEPING ACCURACY	A B C D
REPORT WRITING: ACCURACY DETAIL, ORGANIZATION	A B C D	INTERACTION WITH CONFIDENTIAL C-I'S	A B C D
REPORT WRITING: TIME USED	A B C D	DEVELOPMENT OF UNWITTING INFORMANTS	A B C D
REPORT WRITING: GRAMMAR, SPELLING	A B C D	USE OF EQUIPMENT: TAPE RECORDERS, BODY MIC	A B C D
FIELD PERFORMANCE: NON-STRESS PERFORMANCE	A B C D	USE OF VIDEO	A B C D
FIELD PERFORMANCE: STRESS CONDITIONS	A B C D	COURT PLANNING	A B C D
SELF-INITIATED ACTIVITY	A B C D		
OFFICER SAFETY	A B C D		

DATES OF TRAINING WEEK _____

11-1

UNDERCOVER OFFICER TRAINING RECORD

DATES

INSTRUCTION PERFORMANCE

PHASE I - GENERAL ORIENTATION

1. CONTACT WITH FBO

   a. Need for home phone _____

   b. "hello" phone procedure _____

   c. Telephone Check-in proc. _____

   d. Knowledge of SOP manual _____

   e. Work Schedule _____

   f. Days off/overtime _____

   g. Leave/sick time _____

   h. Transfers _____

   i. Outside employment _____

   j. UC police contacts _____

   k. Drug simulation policy _____

   l. Knowledge of drug laws _____

2. DRUG IDENTIFICATION

   a. Drug schedules _____

   b. Drug categories _____

   c. Physical effects of drugs _____

   d. Psychological effects _____

   e. Organic/synthetic drugs _____

   f. Drug sources _____

3. OVERVIEW OF UNDERCOVER WORK

   a. Expelling the myths _____

   b. The agency's mission _____

   c. Responsibilities/expectations _____

11-2 Undercover Officer Training Record

page 2

DATES

INSTRUCTION PERFORMANCE

4. PHASE II - FIELD PERFORMANCE

SUBSTANCE ABUSE

a. Alcohol abuse _____

b. Drug dependency _____

c. Employee assistance program _____

5. REPORTING PROCEDURES

a. Paper work _____

b. Requirements for receipts _____

c. Acceptable expenditures _____

d. Knowledge of city _____

e. Other law enforcement agencies _____

f. Hospitals _____

g. High crime areas _____

PHASE III - CRIMINAL INVESTIGATION

6. ESTABLISHING AN UNDERCOVER IDENTITY

a. UC drivers licence _____

b. Social Security Number _____

c. Cover story _____

7. CASE DEVELOPMENT

a. Case initiation _____

b. Investigative leads _____

c. Testifying in court _____

11–2 (continued)

DATES

INSTRUCTION PERFORMANCE

8. USE OF UC VEHICLES

    a. Types of vehicles   _____

    b. Preventive maintenance   _____

    c. Use of UC gas credit cards _____

    d. Handling of accidents   _____

    e. Concealment of radios   _____

9. COVERT SURVEILLANCE

    a. Moving surveillance   _____

    b. Stationary surveillance   _____

    c. Foot surveillance   _____

    d. Undercover employment   _____

    e. Officer safety   _____

    f. Use of deadly force   _____

    g. Flashrolls   _____

    h. Firearms policy   _____

PHASE IV - SURVEILLANCE OPERATIONS

10. USE OF EQUIPMENT

    a. Visual equipment   _____

    b. Audio equipment   _____

    c. Tracking equipment   _____

11-2   Undercover Officer Training Record (*continued*)

349

DATES

INSTRUCTION PERFORMANCE

12. AGENT RESPONSE TO
DRUG RELATED CRIME

a. Reporting procedure _____

b. Property offenses _____

c. Other types of crimes _____

13. KNOWLEDGE OF SEARCH WARRANTS

a. Legal requirements _____

b. Forms _____

c. Procedure _____

d. Use of informants _____

e. Searching methods _____

f. Packaging evidence _____

11-2 *(continued)*

CITY POLICE DEPARTMENT
RECRUIT WEEKLY EVALUATION FORM
COMMENTS

Name of Recruit _____   Date _____

Best performance of the week:

_____

_____

_____

_____

_____

Area(s) needing improvement:

_____

_____

_____

_____

_____

Has the recruit been counseled on his deficiencies?

                 YES   NO

Have these deficiencies required remedial training?

                 YES   NO

If yes describe the plan: _____

_____

_____

Recruit officer _____   FTO _____

Section Supervisor _____   Date _____

Summary

The importance of undercover agent field training cannot be overemphasized: the safety of the officer is directly related to the quality of field training he or she will receive. In addition, the success of an investigation may lie in the effectiveness of the investigator's field training. Moreover, because officers cannot be held responsible for infractions of policy and procedures that they do not know, prompt training in the department's standard operating procedures is imperative. Great responsibility lies with the field training officer and the unit manager, who must work together in evaluating recruits. It is in field training that the recruit is judged on his ability to become an effective member of the drug unit.

Suggested Readings

McCampbell, Michael S., *Field Training for Police Officers: State of the Art.* U.S. Department of Justice, National Institute of Justice: Research in Brief, 1986.

APPENDIX
A CHRONOLOGY OF FEDERAL
DRUG CONTROL POLICY

There seems to be no end to the country's illicit drug woes. There is also no apparent end to the controversy and debate as to how to best address the problem. When considering drug enforcement policy, the issue of supply and demand is always considered.

The current debates over supply and demand — and which should be dealt with first — are sources of confusion and frustration for concerned civilians and lawmakers alike. Much of the confusion stems from a failure to realize that both components are part of the same problem: one perpetuates the other. Regardless of which approach should be considered — attacking supplies or attacking demand — the fact remains that drug use perpetuates organized crime and vice versa. It is, therefore, the general opinion that federal drug control in this decade must develop a more sophisticated response to the problems at hand. The historic track record of federal drug laws has demonstrated that enforcement initiatives are, for the most part, on the offensive, resulting in a defensive reaction by drug users and members of established organized crime groups.

For the most part, the federal government has taken the approach of attacking the supply of drugs coming into the country. Although this philosophy has been practiced for over 75 years it is now thought that further understanding of the relationship between drug users and their suppliers be considered for a more comprehensive and effective federal policy. This recent philosophy has resulted in numerous programs aimed at drug prevention, research, treatment and education.

The early history of drug enforcement policies reflect a society that — though well meaning — was awash in misinformation about drugs, drug use, and their consequences. For decades a large segment of society viewed drug abuse as a medical problem rather than one of organized and violent crime. Many Americans looked on the drug abuser as one whose personal moral character had eroded, not a criminal. Interestingly enough most of today's laws to control illicit drug use and trafficking are of recent vintage.

last part

1875: The Anti-Opium Smoking Act (San Francisco)

This ordinance was passed in direct response to public outrage over the existence of opium dens, which were primarily operated by Chinese immigrants. The law was the model for at least twenty-five states laws the years that followed.

1887

Congress raised the tariff on smoking opium from $6 to $10 per pound. In 1887 Congress completely outlawed the importation of smoking opium (a mild form of opium) by Chinese importers. Despite these early legal controls, problems of drug addiction and smuggling continued to increase, along with general public concern. The drug problem at the turn of the century reflected the careless use of misinformation about drugs. During the Civil War, the indiscriminate use of morphine on bloody battlefields had created an enormous addict population. It is estimated that there were more than 400,000 addicts in the army alone by the end of the war; indeed, morphine addiction became known as "the soldiers disease." Much of this use was promoted by the newly developed hypodermic needle.

1898

Heroin, which was first considered a wonder drug—safe and nonaddicting—was commercially developed by the Bayer Company of Germany to cure morphine addiction.

1908

The American Opium Commission. An act of Congress established the American Opium Commission, which studied the problem of opium use in the United States. Based on the findings of the commission, Congress passed an act in 1909 to prohibit the importation and use of opium for other than medicinal purposes. Legal controls were limited: it did not regulate the interstate transfer of opium, nor did it outlaw domestic manufacture of the drug. Consequently, opium was widely available without a physician's prescription—through mail-order and retail outlets throughout the country.

1909

At the prompting of the United States, the International Opium Commission was formed, which consisted of delegates from 13 nations concerned about the problems of opium addiction. The meeting took place in Shanghai, and it is regarded as the first international response to the opium problem. This meeting (later dubbed the Shanghai Convention) unanimously adopted several resolutions to be considered by the participating nations. Three of the resolutions were:

> To consider the desirability of reviewing each country's system of regulation of the use of opium, in light of the discrepancies among countries' regulatory systems.

> To adopt measures to prevent the export of opium and its derivatives to countries that prohibit the importation of such items.

> To take measures for the gradual suppression of opium smoking in each country's own territories and possessions.

The success of the Shanghai Convention resulted in the signing of the International Opium Convention on January 23, 1912, which was ratified by the U.S. Senate a year later. The treaty committed nations to enact laws designed to reduce the use of opium, morphine, and cocaine (which was thought to be a narcotic at the time), along with other opiates.

1914: The Harrison Narcotic Act

The United States Congress passed the Harrison Narcotic Act on December 17, 1914. It became the model federal drug abuse policy for the next 56 years. Among the provisions of the Harrison Act:

> *Section 1:* Anyone legitimately dealing in the drugs regulated by the act must register annually and pay a special tax of one dollar.

> *Section 2:* Distribution of the drugs covered by the act was illegal without a written prescription issued by the Commissioner of Internal Revenue for the person obtaining them.

> *Section 4:* It was illegal to engage in interstate traffic in the covered drugs without first paying the special tax. Exceptions were patients and employees of physicians.

> *Section 8:* Possession of any of the covered drugs by any person who had not paid the special tax required by Section 1.

> *Section 9:* Stipulated a penalty of not more than $2000 or more than 5 years in prison be imposed against those in violation of the act. The Harrison Act was designed to regulate addiction and drug abuse through government taxation. Because the Act was basically a revenue measure, enforcement was made the responsibility of the Department of the Treasury and the Commis-

sioner of Internal Revenue. It was believed that distributors of covered drugs would be brought out into the open and a better handle on the problem could be achieved.

After the Harrison Act was passed, there were a series of Supreme Court decisions that addressed the constitutionality of different provisions of the law: *United States v. Doremus* questioned the taxing authority of Congress; and *Webb v. United States* disputed the exact definition of a "prescription" as opposed to an "order." Other, unintended consequences of the Harrison Act became apparent over the next few years. In 1915, 162 collectors and agents of the IRS were charged with restricting the sale of prescribed drugs (see next section).

1920: The Volstead Act

The enforcement of the National Prohibition Act (The Volstead Act) — sponsored by Minnesota Representative Andrew Volstead — was made the province of the Commissioner of Internal Revenue. In the context of the times, it seemed reasonable to place enforcement responsibilities for the Harrison Act within the Prohibition Unit; a narcotics unit, with 170 agents, was formed in 1919. The Prohibition Unit existed until 1927, when drug enforcement responsibilities were transferred to the Secretary of the Treasury. Between 1914 and 1929, enforcement practices were unstructured and controversial, though thousands of prosecutions were undertaken. It was estimated that 50,000 individuals, including physicians and others required to register under the Harrison Act, were charged with violations. The narcotics division next focused on closing clinics, which had been originally established for research and treatment of addicts who could not afford individual private care.

The American Medical Association, which had originally supported the Harrison Act, now looked on the policies of the Division of Narcotics as harassment. Subsequent pressure resulted in the Department of the Treasury encouraging its agents to focus on interdiction and sale of narcotics. Tragically, the ambiguities of the Harrison Act caused physicians to become so fearful of prosecution that they began refusing to treat addicts. The addict population, denied medical attention and treatment clinics, turned to illicit sources of supply. This is the probable foundation for the huge narcotics trafficking underground we see today.

The experiences of the Harrison Act serve to illustrate the principle of supply and demand: the demand for drugs will always find a source willing to supply it; where no source exists, a new one will be created. The Harrison Act failed because it did not include a demand-reduction or treatment component. Moreover, federal policy failed to pursue such a provision in its drug enforcement strategies for the next 50 years.

1930: The Federal Bureau of Narcotics

The reputation of the Narcotics Division was later tainted by allegations of falsification of arrest records, pay-offs, collusion with drug dealers, and a generally unfavorable association between the Narcotics Division and the country's defunct anti-liquor laws. In 1930 the Federal Bureau of Narcotics (FBN) was established under the Department of the Treasury, and it was given responsibility for federal drug enforcement. (It was here that the term "narcotics agent" was first associated with drug enforcement.) At this point, federal drug enforcement was divided: the FBN assumed enforcement responsibility for the Harrison Narcotic Act, and the Bureau of Customs dealt with interdiction and smuggling.

For the most part, marijuana was not considered an especially dangerous drug; the Harrison Act did not address marijuana use at all. Marijuana was generally considered a plant with practical social benefits to be used as hemp or rope, in veterinary medicines, and in other products. It was not necessarily associated with the problem of substance abuse. As awareness of its intoxicating effects became more widespread, so, too, did local and state laws to control its use. By 1931 most states had legislation prohibiting possession or use of the drug.

1937: The Marijuana Tax Act

Supported by the FBN, the Marijuana Tax Act was essentially a revenue stratagem closely resembling the Harrison Narcotic Act. At the time of its passage, there was an estimated 10,000 acres of marijuana being commercially grown in the country. The MTA effectively required any person whose business was related to marijuana to register and pay a special tax. Under the law, the transfer of marijuana had to be pursuant to a written order issued by the Secretary of the Treasury. The subject was then required to pay a tax of $1.00 per ounce if he or she was registered and $100.00 per ounce if not. Additional taxes were assessed for transferring marijuana without the proper paperwork.

1942: The Opium Control Act

Mexico was identified as a major source country for marijuana in 1942. The FBN recognized that crop eradication efforts should be considered in an effort to effectively suppress drug use in the United States. In that same year, the Opium Control Act of 1942 was passed, which controlled domestic production of opium poppies.

It was during this period that the FBN recognized its severe manpower shortages and made appeals to Congress for more money and personnel; it was soon apparent that drug enforcement then was by no means the national priority it is today. In efforts to shed earlier stains of corruption, the FBN became quite aggressive in their enforcement posture. In 1963 Mafia informer Joe Valachi testified that the FBN was so successful in infiltrating trafficking organizations that high-ranking Mafia bosses often had to shift their trafficking tactics to avoid detection. In 1948 Frank Costello, who was the acting boss of the Luciano family, reportedly ordered members involved in drug trafficking to stop because of FBN covert operations. Former La Cosa Nostra member James Fratianno, while testifying before the President's Commission on Organized Crime, gave the following account of the effectiveness of the FBN in the 1940s:

> Much more important . . . was the dogged harassment of the Bureau of Narcotics. The Cosa Nostra despised and feared the FBN. . . .
>
> The Narcotics Bureau, unlike the FBI, which tends to look down its nose at it, does not depend on the informant system for much of its intelligence but regularly engages its agents in dangerous undercover work; they are, as a result, . . . highly motivated, less disciplined, generally more daring and innovational, occasionally corruptable. Above all else, the [FBN] was the first to recognize the existence of the Cosa Nostra, and no other arm of the law has put more of a crimp in its operation.

1951: The Boggs Act

As the 1950s unfolded, public attitudes toward the overall drug problem began to change and an amendment to the Harrison Act was passed. The Boggs Act of 1951 increased the penalties in previously enacted marijuana and narcotics laws. The act was in response to public concern that existing laws were too lenient and provided little deterrent for violators. A factor contributing to the passage of the Boggs Act was that the recidivism rate among drug defendants had dramatically increased since 1935. In 1935 40% of those convicted of drug offenses had prior convictions; by 1950, recidivism had increased to 63%. Under the Boggs Act, marijuana and narcotics were lumped together under uniform penalties, which basically provided for a minimum sentence of two years for first-time offenders and up to 10 years for repeat offenders.

1956: The Narcotic Control Act

The Narcotic Control Act of 1956 further raised the penalties contained in the Boggs Amendment — in particular for those who were repeat offenders. The act also authorized FBN and Customs agents to carry firearms, make arrests, and serve search warrants. In passing this act, Congress maintained that "suppression of the illicit drug traffic" would be the most important contribution the federal government could make to the successful rehabilitation of drug addicts. In this philosophy, the government believed that the suppression of supply through enforcement would curb future drug demand.

1963: The Prettyman Commission

With the political and social unrest of the 1960s, public concern about illicit drugs intensified. Pressure for an effective federal public drug policy increased. As a result, the President's Advisory Commission on Narcotics and Drug Abuse (The Prettyman Commission) was formed on January 15, 1963. The final report, which was forwarded to President Kennedy in November 1963, contained 25 recommendations, including:

Transfer the enforcement and investigative functions of the FBN relating to illicit transactions in narcotic drugs and marijuana from the Department of Treasury to the Department of Justice.

Transfer the responsibilities of the FBN relating to regulation of the legitimate traffic in narcotic drugs and marijuana from the Department of the Treasury to the Department of Health, Education and Welfare.

Substantially increase the number of federal agents assigned to the investigation of the illicit importation of and trafficking in narcotic drugs, marijuana and dangerous drugs.

Transfer the responsibility for investigating the illicit traffic in dangerous drugs from the Department of Health, Education and Welfare to the Department of Justice.

Strictly control, by federal statute, all nonnarcotic drugs capable of producing serious psychotoxic effects when abused.

1965: The Drug Abuse Control Amendments

Resulting from the Commission's final report, Congress adopted the Drug Abuse Control Amendments of 1965, which authorized enforcement in drug diversion cases and included provisions for recordkeeping, and the inspection of stimulant and depressant drugs from the manufacturer to the consumer. These amendments were the result of the newly identified trafficking problem of legally made drugs which were being diverted from legal channels of distribution.

1966: The Bureau of Drug Abuse Control

Another result of the Drug Abuse Control Amendments was that yet another enforcement agency was created, the Bureau of Drug Abuse Control (BDAC), which was placed within the Food and Drug Administration. This ended the Treasury Department's long-standing statutory monopoly of federal drug enforcement. In legislation designed to follow up on the Drug Abuse Control Amendments of 1965, the Narcotic Addict Rehabilitation Act of 1966 was drafted and adopted by Congress. Three provisions of the act are worth noting: District courts were authorized to order the civil commitment of individuals who were addicts; individuals who were charged with certain offenses against the United States; and individuals who were addicts and who were in the custody of the Attorney General could be remanded to treatment and rehabilitation in lieu of prosecution.

Federal drug enforcement strategy during the 1960s was ultimately evaluated in 1979. It was found that most drug enforcement efforts of the decade had focused on the supply of illicit drugs through taxation, prohibition, and legal control. During the 1960s, it was generally believed that by reducing the supply of drugs, a reduction in demand would follow. (Again, the supply and demand dilemma.)

Also in 1966, President Lyndon B. Johnson established the President's Commission on Law Enforcement and Administration of Justice (the Katzenbach Commission). The Commission issued a report in 1967, which addressed the issue of drug abuse with regard to both supply and demand. The report made the following recommendations:

1. Substantially increase the enforcement staffs of FBN and the Bureau of Customs.
2. Permit courts and correctional authorities to deal flexibly with violators of the drug laws.
3. Undertake research to develop a sound and effective framework for regulatory and criminal laws relating to dangerous drugs.
4. The National Institute of Mental Health should develop a core of educational and informational materials relating to drugs.

1968: The Bureau of Narcotics and Dangerous Drugs

In 1968 President Johnson sent a reconstruction plan for federal drug law enforcement policy to Congress to consider; the plan became effective April 7, 1968. For the first time the Department of Justice was given the primary responsibility for federal drug law enforcement. In addition, it provided for the creation for a Bureau of Narcotics and Dangerous Drugs (BNDD) and the simultaneous abolition of the FBN and the BDAC. This move, it was thought, would eliminate duplicated efforts among agencies and departments, and it would reduce bureaucratic red tape in investigations.

This reorganization effort did not, however, significantly affect the tax collection functions of the Harrison Act or the Marijuana Tax Act, nor did it affect the duties of the Customs service in interdiction and smuggling. In an effort to keep the FBI and the BNDD separate, Congress placed the newly created BNDD within the Treasury Department instead of the Justice Department. This decision was also made based on the successful and effective history of the FBN and the BDAC.

During the 1968 Presidential campaign, the two main issues were crime and drugs. Newly elected President Richard Nixon almost immediately formed a special task force charged with identifying programs which would have an immediate effect on the country's drug problems. In particular, the task force was to address the issues of trafficking in heroin and other illegal drugs considered to be the most dangerous.

A major border interdiction program (Operation Intercept) was soon developed, which involved more than 2000 Customs, BNDD, and Border Patrol agents. It was soon realized, however, that the program was creating public relations problems with Mexico and that any significant solution to the United States drug problem would have to involve cooperation with source countries. Ultimately, Operation Intercept was transformed to Operation Cooperation, which provided for financial aid to Mexico for aircraft and troops to assist in interdiction efforts.

1970

President Nixon announced in 1970 that the BNDD had jurisdiction over all investigations involving all violations of U.S. narcotics laws. Later, the jurisdiction and authority of Customs and the Border Patrol was broadened to augment enforcement efforts.

1970: The Comprehensive Drug Abuse Prevention and Control Act (the Controlled Substances Act)

Probably the most significant development of 1970 was the Comprehensive Drug Abuse Prevention and Control Act. The act was passed in response to the welter of overlapping drug laws, which required many different federal agencies to enforce them. The Comprehensive Act was important because of its many provisions for organization and control:

Title I: Authorized the Department of Health Education and Welfare to increase its efforts in drug rehabilitation, drug treatment and prevention.

Title II: Specified the enforcement procedures and authority given to the BNDD. In this section, five schedules where established in which dangerous drugs were listed according to their dangerous effects and acceptability in medical treatment. In addition, there were nine control mechanisms, which set requirements for registrants, and a section dealing with prescribed penalties.

Title III: The Controlled Substances Import and Export Act, which established regulations for the importation and exportation of controlled substances.

As mentioned there were nine registrant control clauses also contained in the Controlled Substances Act. Because this act was considered a landmark in federal drug control policy, the requirements of legal handlers should be noted:

1. The registration of handlers: Any person who handles or intends to handle controlled substances must obtain a registration issued by the DEA. A unique number is assigned to legitimate handlers, importers, exporters, manufacturers, wholesalers, hospitals, pharmacies, physicians, and researchers. Prior to the purchase of a controlled substance, the number must be made available to the supplier by the customer, thus diminishing the opportunity for illegal transactions.
2. Recordkeeping requirements: Full records must be kept of all quantities manufactured, and of all purchases, sales, and inventories of all controlled substances regardless of the schedule in which they are placed. Limited exceptions are available to physicians and researchers. The system makes it possible to trace the flow of any drug from the time of manufacture or import to the time the end consumer receives it. It also serves as an international check for large corporations, who must be concerned about employee pilferage.
3. Quotas on manufacturing: The DEA limits the quantity of controlled substances listed in Schedules I and II, which may be produced during a calendar year. Certain other drugs listed in Schedules III, IV, and V may also be limited as derivatives from Schedule I and II drugs.
4. Restrictions on distribution: Recordkeeping is required for the distribution of a controlled substance from one manufacturer to

another, from manufacturer to wholesaler, and from importer to wholesaler to dispenser. In the case of Schedule I and II drugs, the supplier must have a special order form from the customer. This form is issued only by DEA (Form 222) to those who are properly registered, and the form is preprinted with the name of and address of the customer. According to this provision, the drugs must be sent *only* to that customer. For Schedule III, IV, and V drugs, no form is necessary, but the supplier is fully accountable for the drugs shipped to a purchaser who does not have a valid registration.

5. Restrictions on dispensing: There are additional restrictions on the dispensing or delivery of a controlled substance to the ultimate user (who may be a patient or research subject). Schedule I drugs may be used only in research situations, as they have no accepted medical use in the United States. A prescription order is required for Schedule II, III, and IV drugs under federal law. The decision to place drugs in a particular schedule lies with the Food and Drug Administration. Schedule V drugs include many over-the-counter (OTC) narcotic preparations (including antiperussives and antidiarrheals), and here, too, restrictions are imposed.

6. Limitations on Imports and Exports: International transactions involving any drug in Schedules I or II or a narcotic drug in Schedule III must have prior approval of the DEA. International transactions involving a nonnarcotic drug in Schedule III or any drug in Schedule IV or V do not need approval, but prior notice must be given to the DEA. Approval to import a Schedule I or II drug is not given unless the importer can show that there is an insufficient domestic supply with no adequate competition. The exportation requirements must show that the drug is going to a country where they will actually be used, and will not be re-exported.

7. Conditions for storage of drugs: The DEA sets requirements for the security of the premises where controlled substances will be stored. Among the requirements for Schedule I and II drugs are specially constructed vault and alarm systems. For Schedule III, IV, and V drugs, a vault is optional, but they must be segregated in a secure area under constant supervision. These requirements do not apply to qualified researchers, physicians, exporters, and wholesalers who handle small quantities of controlled substances.

8. Reports of transactions to the government: All manufacturing activities, importations, exportations, and all other distributions must be reported to the DEA.

9. Criminal, civil, and administrative penalties for illegal acts: The term "trafficking" is defined as unauthorized manufacture, dis-

tribution (delivery by sale, gift, or other means), or possession with intent to distribute any controlled substance. For narcotics in Schedules I and II, a first offense is punishable by up to 15 years in prison and a $25,000 fine. For trafficking in nonnarcotic Schedule I and II drugs or any Schedule III drug, the penalty is up to 5 years imprisonment and a $15,000 fine. Trafficking in a Schedule IV drug is punishable by a maximum of 3 years imprisonment and a $10,000 fine. Trafficking in a Schedule V drug is a misdemeanor and punishable by twice the penalty imposed for the first offense.

1970: The Organized Crime Control Act

Additional laws were passed in 1970 to help not only drug enforcement, but also to combat the escalating problem of organized crime in the United States. Among these were the Organized Crime Control Act of 1970. Title IX of this act was the Racketeer Influenced and Corrupt Organizations statute (RICO). Under this act, drug trafficking (along with many other criminal acts), referred to as "racketeering," were specified. Title IX enabled law enforcement to be better equipped to attack criminal organizations by imposing harsh sentences and the forfeiture of all property acquired during a criminal enterprise. If convicted under the RICO provisions, the penalty could range from a fine of not more than $25,000 to imprisonment of not more than 20 years, or both. Substantial civil sanctions were also set by the statute.

1971: The Special Action Office for Drug Abuse Prevention

The Special Action Office for Drug Abuse Prevention (SAODAP) was formed in 1971 as a result of the new antidrug philosophy of the government. This was considered a major step in organizing federal programs for training, education, research, rehabilitation, treatment, and prevention. In addition, the director of SAODAP was charged with formulating policy for domestic demand reduction through prevention.

The Nixon Administration also pursued the problem of supply reduction. In addition to the SAODAP, the Committee on International Narcotics Control (CCINC) and the Narcotics Traffickers Program (NTP) were formed. The CCINC was to develop a plan to regulate the illegal flow of drugs into the United States, and to coordinate efforts by federal agencies working with drug enforcement abroad. The NTP was to help the IRS focus on high-ranking drug dealers. The NTP, however, proved ineffective because the objective was not tax-related; it was disbanded in 1975.

1972: Office for Drug Abuse Law Enforcement

In 1972 the Office for Drug Abuse Law Enforcement (ODALE) was established and placed under the Department of Justice. The role of ODALE was to assist local law enforcement agencies in drug investigations. With SAODAP and ODALE in place, the total federal drug enforcement program was, at least theoretically, complete. It became the general consensus that the BNDD could not act swiftly enough on both large and small scale traffickers, so the ODALE was charged with concentrating on street-level drug dealers.

1972: The Office of National Narcotics Intelligence

Also formed in 1972 was the Office of National Narcotics Intelligence (ONNI) under the Department of Justice. ONNI was to provide intelligence to federal, state, and local law enforcement agencies who might have a legitimate need for the information. ONNI worked closely with ODALE in drug enforcement efforts.

1972: The Drug Abuse Office and Treatment Act

In 1972 another important measure was passed. The Drug Abuse Office and Treatment Act added intensive treatment and prevention components to existing federal enforcement policies. The act was passed because of a general agreement in Congress that the drug problem had reached epidemic proportions and that additional emphasis on the demand side of the problem was needed. This act provided for better planning and policy-making functions for all federal drug abuse prevention efforts and making recommendations for improvements in federal policy. The act also directed the Secretary of HEW and the Director of SAODAP to implement projects and plans for more effective prevention functions through private and public organizations.

1972: The National Institute of Drug Abuse

Finally, in 1972 the National Institute on Drug Abuse (NIDA) was established, which put the Secretary of HEW in charge of administering new programs for drug prevention and treatment. The NIDA is currently the primary source for current and reliable drug information on the effects of drug abuse. Currently, NIDA's top priority is to research, analyze, and disseminate new information about drug abuse, and to assist the private sector in community-based prevention and treatment programs.

The problem with the Drug Abuse Office Act, however, was that it

was established on the mistaken belief that the existing drug problem could be controlled in a relatively short period of time. With this in mind, Congress provided that SAODAP was to be abolished in June 1975. Statistics have shown that the momentum in cocaine use began to accelerate during the mid-1970s, just when the government was most optimistic about its success in the suppression of drug abuse.

It was soon observed that interagency competition and rivalry was growing to the point that it hampered the overall drug enforcement objective. The problem included agencies who were unwilling to share information and resources in ongoing investigations, and simple petty jealousies.

1973: The Drug Enforcement Administration

In response to this problem was a 1973 reorganization plan, which noted that no single agency was responsible for the overall drug enforcement effort. Therefore, the Drug Enforcement Administration (DEA) was created within the Department of Justice. The DEA was designated as the single federal agency within the Department of Justice to spearhead the nation's antidrug efforts. The Director of the DEA reports directly to the Attorney General with regard to enforcement functions, and the agency was further to absorb the personnel of ODALE, BNDD, and ONNI. Specific responsibilities of DEA are:

1. Development of overall federal drug law enforcement strategy, programs, planning, and evaluation.
2. Investigation and preparation of criminal prosecutions for violations of federal drug trafficking laws.
3. Investigation and preparation for prosecution of suspects connected with illicit drugs seized at ports of entry and borders.
4. Conducting relations with foreign drug law enforcement officials, under the guidance of the Cabinet Committee on International Narcotics Control.
5. Coordination and cooperation with state and local law enforcement personnel on joint drug enforcement efforts.
6. Regulation of the legal manufacture of other controlled substances.

The 1973 plan reaffirmed the jurisdiction of the Bureau of Customs to enforce interdiction of drugs at the ports of entry, but it restricted their authority away from the ports of entry where they have no investigative authority. It also mandated that the Attorney General ensure maximum cooperation between the FBI, DEA, and other enforcement divisions within the Justice Department.

1974: The El Paso Intelligence Center

With the establishment of the DEA, other advances were implemented to further federal drug enforcement. Among them was the establishment of the El Paso Intelligence Center (EPIC) in 1974 as a border intelligence unit, operating 24 hours a day. EPIC has the capabilities to collect, process, and disseminate information on drug trafficking, weapons trafficking, and smuggling of illegal aliens on an international scale.

A second system developed under the DEA was the Narcotics and Dangerous Drugs Information System. This system was to provide law enforcement officials access to DEA's investigative records as well as the records of other state and local drug enforcement units.

The DEA task force enforcement concept was also adopted in 1974, and has acquired the name of Central Tactical Units (CENTAC). CENTAC pooled the manpower and resources of DEA, IRS, Customs, and state and local agencies, and it received special funding so that investigations could be undertaken against high-level traffickers. This program was generally considered a success: it accounted for about 12% of the total DEA arrests made between 1976 and 1979 while using less than 3% of DEA's personnel.

1974: The Narcotic Addict Treatment Act

The year 1974 proved to be a busy one for drug legislation. The Narcotic Addict Treatment Act of 1974 amended the 1970 Controlled Substances Act to require annual registration by practitioners dispensing narcotic drugs, including methadone. The act was passed because increased awareness about diversion of methadone, which is used in the treatment of heroin addicts. Another law passed was the 1974 Alcohol and Drug Abuse Education Act Amendments, which focused on potential users rather than those who were already addicted on drugs. These programs were offered by the Department of HEW, which promised to endorse only programs containing factual information.

1974: The Alcohol and Drug Abuse Education Act

Another law, originally opposed by the Nixon administration, was called the Alcohol and Drug Abuse Education Act Amendments of 1974. This law provided for considerably more money ($90 million over three years) to be spent on programs aimed at early intervention, and specifically dealt with factors that might affect a person's involvement in drugs: peer pressure, schools, and family.

1975: The Office of Drug Abuse Policy

With the abolition of SAODAP in 1975, policymaking responsibilities rested with a new agency called the Office of Drug Abuse Policy (ODAP). The ODAP was created in 1976 because (a) there had been no real indication of a reduction in drug abuse in the country, and (b) the drug problem was recognized as much more than had been in the early 1970s. Similar to SAODAP, the director of ODAP was charged with coordinating all federal drug abuse programs. Specifically, ODAP was to oversee the performance of functions by federal agencies and to prioritize objectives for drug abuse and trafficking efforts on the federal level. Although the ODAP was established during the Ford Administration, it was not staffed until March 1977, under President Jimmy Carter.

Two months after the initiation of ODAP, the Carter Administration proposed a reconstruction plan that altered the structure of the Executive Office of President, and basically abolished ODAP. The responsibilities of ODAP fell under the direct control of the President, who would then delegate specific functions.

Several members of Congress became concerned that ODAP's functions would not be carried out in the new Executive Office of the President. President Carter assured them that all necessary functions would be undertaken by the new office.

1979: The Treatment and Rehabilitation Amendments Act

This act provided for authorization for NIDA's state formula grants and specific grant and contract programs for drug education and prevention. In this, Congress prevented the President from combining alcohol and mental health programs with drug abuse programs because they feared that funds might be misapplied or mischanneled and that the direction of the total drug abuse mission might be lost.

The 1970s proved to be significant in the evolution of federal drug abuse policy. There was a comprehensive reorganization of federal drug laws and drug law enforcement agencies. Policies were implemented to cut down on interagency competition and promote efficiency. It also became widely recognized and accepted that efforts to reduce drug demand must remain one of the foremost federal priorities and that "quick-fix" solutions to the country's drug problems were unlikely to have significant effects. Additionally, new drug enforcement approaches to locate, identify, and apprehend drug traffickers were tried at the end of the decade. However, there was still debate over the supply and demand issue, as well as ongoing reorganization within the government.

1981

In the 1980s the Reagan Administration has taken many initiatives aimed at improving the effectiveness of federal drug policy. One major policy shift occurred in January 1981 when the FBI was given concurrent jurisdiction with the DEA for drug law enforcement. In conjunction with this change, the administrator of DEA was required to report directly to the Director of the FBI, who was given responsibility for overseeing federal drug enforcement efforts. This was designed to increase FBI and DEA coordination in drug investigations. Although at first this appeared to be a consolidation, the DEA was still permitted to act independently as a federal enforcement agency.

The President also issued an executive order entitled "United States Intelligence Activities," which authorizes agencies within the law enforcement community to collect, catalog, and disseminate intelligence throughout the federal government. In addition, as drug trafficking could be considered a threat to national security, the order established provisions for distributing information about the conduct and development of foreign drug suspects.

1981: The Omnibus Crime Bill

In 1981, the President issued an executive order instructing the Office of Policy Development to undertake coordination and oversight of all executive international and domestic drug abuse functions. Although this was passed under authority of the Drug Abuse Prevention, Treatment and Rehabilitation Act, Congress was still not convinced that coordination between all such functions was being accomplished. The Omnibus Crime Bill (H.R. 3963) established an Office of Director of National and International Policy. This, again, was similar to SAODAP but was to oversee and coordinate Federal law enforcement operations. President Reagan pocket-vetoed the bill, claiming that another layer of bureaucracy would only produce friction and disrupt the effectiveness of law enforcement.

1982

Faced with a continuing decline in the quality of life in southern Florida, in 1981 concerned citizens began demanding prompt action by all law enforcement agencies. In January 1982, the federal government implemented the South Florida Task Force (Operation Florida), chaired by Vice-President Bush, to assist and coordinate federal efforts with local law enforcement agencies in the area. Participating federal agencies were the DEA, IRS, ATF, the U.S. Marshals Service, the Department of Defense, and the Coast Guard. This program was very similar to the earlier CENTAC program in 1974, and its focus was on the prosecution of smugglers and interdiction.

The strategy proved successful in that it forced traffickers to cut back on their activities in Florida and/or establish new smuggling routes elsewhere. The Attorney General appointed a committee to evaluate the success of the program. It was the general consensus of the Committee that the program was a success, but that no single law enforcement agency could control the existing drug problem.

1983: Organized Crime Task Force

A second multiagency approach was adopted in 1983. This was the formation of the 12 regional Organized Crime Task Forces (OCDETF), which operated much like the South Florida Task Force program, although with some differences. The focus of the Florida program had been interdiction; the focus of the OCDETF was the leaders of drug distribution organizations. Participating in the task force were the DEA, the FBI, the IRS, Customs, the U.S. Marshals Service, and the Coast Guard. After the OCDETF program was established the Reagan Administration created the National Narcotics Border Interdiction System (NNBIS), which was headed by Vice-President Bush. The organization was developed to coordinate interdiction efforts of other organizations, but had no interdiction authority of its own.

1984: The Comprehensive Crime Control Act

The Comprehensive Crime Control Act of 1984 has been generally believed to be one of the most significant drug laws to date. Among other things its provisions are:

1. *The Bail Reform Act:* This act provided that in narcotics cases where there is a penalty of 10 years or more, a special hearing must be held to ensure that the accused will not jump bail, and that the accused must show that there are conditions where the community's safety is guaranteed if he or she is released on bail.
2. *The Comprehensive Forfeiture Act:* This act revised civil and criminal forfeiture laws. In particular it held that a defendant's ill-gotten profits were forfeitable if the government establishes by a preponderance of the evidence that the defendant acquired the property during a period of violation or a reasonably short period thereafter.
3. *The Controlled Substances Penalties Amendments Act:* This enhanced the penalties of the Controlled Substances Act. Included

were specific penalties for trafficking in large amounts of LSD, PCP, narcotics or Schedule I and II drugs. Fines were also substantially raised along with special provisions for repeat offenders and those convicted in foreign countries.

4. *Dangerous Drug Diversion Control Act:* This provision again updated the Controlled Substances Act. Under this act registration may be denied to practitioners if it were against the public interest. In addition the act gave the Attorney General emergency scheduling authority.

5. *Currency and Foreign Transactions Reporting Act Amendments:* This law was designed to fine tune currency reporting requirements to fight the nation's money laundering problem. One of the changes increased the civil penalties from $1,000 to $10,000 per transaction and from 1 year to 5 years imprisonment.

In addition to the Comprehensive Crime Control Act, the National Drug Enforcement Policy Board was established. The Policy Board was created because it was found that drug trafficking was estimated at an $80 billion a year industry. It was also noted that only 5% to 15% of the illicit drugs entering the country were being interdicted, and that controlling the supply of drugs was thought to be a key to reducing the drug related crime epidemic. The Policy Board was to impose coordination of federal supply and demand strategies.

The 1980s were extremely active for federal drug legislation. In addition to the Comprehensive Crime Control Act of 1984, the Department of Defense Authorization Act of 1982 provided for military cooperation with civilian law enforcement officials. Specific responsibility was outlined for what equipment could be used and what command personnel were authorized to do in assisting civilian law enforcement agencies. Other laws included The Controlled Substance Registrant Protection Act, which made it illegal to steal any quantity of controlled substances from a registrant, and The Aviation Drug Trafficking Control Act, which revokes airman certificates and registrations of those convicted of violating state or federal law regarding controlled substances.

1986: The Anti-Drug Abuse Act

In October 1986, President Reagan's proposed Anti-Drug Abuse Act was passed. It was thought to be the most far-reaching antidrug act to date. Like past legislation, the act was designed to fine-tune existing drug trafficking laws. In Title I, for example, there are the following provisions:

Penalties: Creates mandatory minimum terms of 5 to 10 years for certain violations of the CSA;

CCE (Continuing Criminal Enterprise) Penalties: Creates life sentences for certain CCE violations;

Money laundering: Creates new offense for the laundering of monetary instruments;

Career criminals: Expands predicate offenses to include serious drug offenses;

Clandestine laboratories: Prohibits using any place for the purpose of manufacture, distribution or use of controlled substances.

Summary

Federal drug policy began with the attempts of state and federal lawmakers to control drug abuse through restrictive laws, many of which proved difficult to enforce. A more effective form of drug control was the antidrug tax laws of 1914 and 1937. Although the intent of these laws was well meaning, many problems still existed with the use of illicit drugs in the country.

Concerted drug enforcement efforts began with the establishment of the Federal Bureau of Narcotics in 1930. At this time, strategies of supply and demand began to be considered. Although the initial emphasis was on controlling domestic handlers of drugs, the focus ultimately shifted to interdiction and supply. From then on the federal government has reinforced its drug enforcement efforts through a number of sweeping changes, which basically shifted manpower from one organization to another.

After it was realized that a quick solution to the country's drug problem was unlikely, government strategies tended to focus on the establishment of governing or policy-making committees within the government. Again the mission of these policy-making bodies of government varied from administration to administration.

At the present time, most of the federal budget earmarked for the suppression of illicit drugs focuses on supply rather than demand. Supply strategies include enforcement actions such as eradication, interdiction, domestic enforcement, and foreign liaison programs. Although these strategies have fallen victim to much criticism because of a lack of fast results, the long-term goals of the federal programs might yet prove to be successful.

Many proponents of the legalization of drugs believe that if drugs were legalized, the supply would then subside. (The President's Commission on Organized Crime in fact considered such an alternative, which was published in March 1986.) It should be generally understood that the potential for huge profits are the driving force behind drug trafficking. In most cases, the traffickers feel that monetary gains outweigh the risks. If drugs were legalized, some argue, the high profits would be removed from drug activities. Although on the surface this may seem to have some merit, it does not account for the health risks at stake in drug use. This, by itself, is a fundamental issue.

Aside from the damage drugs can do to a user's health, educational potential, and productivity, the likelihood for criminal activity might very well increase should drugs be more readily available. In addition, it is also believed that organized crime would not abandon its involvement in smuggling because there would still be an illicit market in newly developed and chemically enhanced drugs.

Glossary

Abstinence Refraining from drug use.

Abuse Use of an illicit substance or incorrect or excessive use of any drug.

Abuse potential A drug's susceptibility to abuse or abuse patterns.

Acapulco gold An especially high potency marijuana grown in Mexico.

Acetone A solvent commonly found in cements and nail polish removers, which may produce a euphoric effect when inhaled.

Acid Street name for LSD.

Acquired immune deficiency syndrome (AIDS) A little-understood disease that attacks the body's immune system. The indiscriminate shared use of hypodermic needles by drug addicts has greatly contributed to the spread of this disease.

Acute A term that describes a condition that quickly develops into a crisis.

Addict subculture An alternative lifestyle that centers around the knowledge and use of drugs.

Addiction A state of periodic or chronic intoxication produced by repeated consumption of a drug, which in turn produces an overpowering desire or need to continue use of the drug, a tendency to increase the dosage, and renewed psychic and physical dependence.

Adverse drug reaction A negative psychological or physical reaction to drug taking.

Alkaloids A diverse group of more than 5,000 bitter compounds of plant origin that contain nitrogen in their molecules, as well as carbon, oxygen, and hydrogen.

Amobarbital An intermediate-acting barbiturate.

Amotivational syndrome A condition associated with marijuana use, characterized by a loss of effectiveness, apathy, and reduced capacity to carry out long-range plans.

Amphetamines Stimulants that act on the central nervous system. Their effects resemble those of the naturally occurring substance, adrenaline.

Amyl nitrate An inhalant used to lower blood pressure, which is used occasionally in the treatment of asthma. It is thought of by drug users to produce sexual stimulation.

Angel dust Street name for powdered PCP.

Aphrodisiac A substance that enhances sexual arousal or sensitivity.

Army disease A term used during and just after the Civil War for morphine addiction.

Bad A term referring to drugs that are especially potent.

Bad trip An unpleasant experience resulting from the use of LSD.

Bag Normally, a one-ounce quantity of marijuana.

Bag man A term for a person who handles the money in a drug transaction.

Balloon Approximately one gram of powder (for example, of heroin).

Barbiturates Calming and sleep-inducing drugs that act as central nervous system depressants.

Barrels Small LSD tablets.

Bazooka Unrefined cocaine.

Bennies Benzedrine.

Benzine A volatile petroleum distillate used in motor fuels and many cleaning fluids. It produces an intoxicating effect when inhaled.

Bindle (druggist fold) A small paper packet containing approximately one gram of a powdered illicit substance.

Black beauties Biphetamines.

Black mollies Biphetamines.

Blackout A memory lapse associated with the injesting of drugs and/or alcohol over a relatively short period of time.

Black tar Unrefined, smokable heroin.

Blond hash A light-colored, less potent form of hash.

Blotter acid LSD.

Blow Street name for cocaine.

Blues Amytal sodium.

Bong A water pipe used to smoke marijuana.

Boost To steal.

Bowl A small pipe used to smoke marijuana.

Boy Street name for heroin.

Brick Normally, one kilogram of marijuana.

Brown sugar Mexican brown heroin.

Buds The flower tops of the female marijuana plant.

Bummer A bad experience while under the influence of drugs.

Burn Being cheated in a drug deal.

Burn-out A term given to those who have ingested large quantities of drugs over a long period of time, and as a result, have difficulty distinguishing reality from illusion.

Bust A police arrest on drug charges.

Buttons Peyote cactus (sylicyben).

Butyl nitrate An inhalant similar to amyl nitrate.

Buzz To feel the effects of a drug.

Cactus The peyote cactus; also a street name for mescaline.

Caffeine A naturally occurring alkaloid found in many plants around the world. It acts as a central nervous system stimulant.

Candy Street name for cocaine.

Cannabinoids Derivatives of marijuana (*Cannabis*). Marijuana contains more than 60 cannabinoids.

Cannabis Marijuana containing Δ9-tetrahydrocannabinol.

Capital with codeine A narcotic opiate used for mild-to-moderate pain.

Central nervous system The network of nerve cells, concentrated in the brain and spinal cord, which conduct sensory and motor electrical impulses to and from all parts of the body.

Channel To inject drugs.

Chasing the dragon Smoking raw opium.

Chromatography A technique used for testing for drugs in urine.

Chronic A condition characterized by slowly progressing symptoms, which continue for a long time.

Coca Erthroxylon coca, a bush that grows in South America. The alkaloid cocaine is found in its leaves.

Coca paste The first extract produced during the manufacture of cocaine from coca leaves.

Cocaine An alkaloid found in the leaves of the coca plant.

Cocaine freebase A liquid solution made by mixing cocaine powder and a volatile liquid such as ether.

Codeine A narcotic analgesic that appears in the juices of the unripe opium poppy pod.

Coke Street name for cocaine.

Cola Street name for cocaine.

Cold turkey To stop taking drugs suddenly, with no gradual reduction of dosage.

Collapsed veins A common condition among heroin addicts, caused by frequent injections over a long period of time.

Coma A state of profound unconsciousness.

Come down To come off the effects of a drug.

Compulsion A psychological term referring to a force that compels a person to act against his or her own will.

Collar An arrest.

Confidentiality The assured anonymity of participants in an agreement.

Connection A supplier of illicit drugs.

Consumption The ingestion of a substance.

Contact A supplier of illicit drugs.

Controlled drugs Drugs that are strictly controlled by the Controlled Substances Act.

Controlled Substances Act (CSA) The Comprehensive Drug Abuse Prevention and Control Act of 1970.

Convulsions Involuntary spasmatic contractions of muscles.

Cooker One who sets up an illegal drug laboratory.

Cop To purchase drugs.

Cough medicine A medication for coughs, which commonly contain narcotic drugs and have a propensity for addiction.

Crack Freebase cocaine in crystal ("rock") form.

Crank Street name for methamphetamine powder.

Crash To come down from a drug-induced high quickly.

Craving An overwhelming desire or need for a drug, which can be either physical or psychological.

Crossroads Street name for amphetamines.

Crystal Street name for methamphetamine.

Crime, drug related The National Institute of Drug Abuse has reported that addicted drug users commit several kinds of crimes to support their drug habits: theft, robbery, drug dealing, prostitution, and gambling.

Crime, organized Diverse organizations of individuals working in concert to commit crimes for profit.

Cross-addiction A person who is addicted to one drug will most likely be addicted to other drugs within the same category.

Cross-dependence Similar to cross-addiction in that dependence on drugs within the same category is interchangeable.

Cross-tolerance If tolerance has developed to one drug, it will carry over to others in the same category.

Cut Term describing substances used to dilute drugs.

Darvocet-N A mild analgesic related to narcotics, but which is far less potent.

DAWN The Drug Abuse Warning Network.

DEA The Drug Enforcement Administration.

Decriminalization Removing or relaxing the criminal penalties in drug control legislation.

Delirium A mental disturbance characterized by confusion, disorded speech, disorientation, and a general clouding of consciousness.

Demerol Brand name of a narcotic used as an analgesic for moderate to severe pain.

Dependence A term meaning either physical or psychological addiction.

Depressants Drugs that act on and slow down the central nervous system.

Depression A feeling of inadequacy, pessimism, and apathy.

Desoxyn Brand name of a central nervous system stimulant containing methamphetamine hydrochloride.

Detoxification A treatment process that allows a patient to withdraw from drug addiction under controlled medical conditions.

Dexedrine Brand name for an amphetamine usually taken for weight control.

Diacetylmorphine Heroin.

Diazepam The active ingredient in Valium.

Didrex A central nervous system stimulant similar to amphetamine.

Dilaudid Brand name of a narcotic analgesic similar to morphine.

D-Lysergic acid diethylamide LSD.

Dime bag A ten-dollar quantity of drugs.

Dips Liquid PCP.

Dirty In possession of illicit drugs.

DMT A fast-acting hallucinogen similar to LSD.

Dopamine A neurotransmitter important in the action of cocaine and amphetamines.

Dope Illicit drugs.

Downers Drugs that have a depressant effect on the central nervous system.

Drop To consume a drug, usually in tablet form.

Duby A marijuana cigarette.

Dust (angel dust) Powdered PCP.

Eighth A term usually referring to a one-eighth quantity of powdered drugs.

Elbow A one-pound (i.e., lb.) quantity of drugs.

Empirin Compound with Codeine A brand-name prescription drug sometimes diverted for recreational use.

Employee assistance program An in-house, employer-financed program to aid employees with personal problems, including drug dependancy, family counseling, etc.

Endorphins A compound produced by the body, resembling opiates, with the ability to produce a general sense of well-being.

EMIT Enzyme Multiplied Immunoassay Test (urine testing).

Erthroxylon coca The coca plant.

Ether A volatile and highly flammable anesthetic.

Euphoria A feeling of extreme well-being.

Fake coke A cocaine substitute or look-alike.

False negative or false positive A term used to describe the incorrect reading of a test for drug use.

FBI The Federal Bureau of Investigation.

Fentanyl A narcotic analgesic and opium derivative. It is between 100 and 1000 times more potent than morphine.

Fire To inject drugs intravenously.

Fix To inject drugs or to relieve the pain of withdrawal.

Flake Street name for cocaine.

Flashback A recurrence of a previous LSD "trip."

Flower top The buds made by the female marijuana plant.

Freebase cocaine A smokeable cocaine solution.

French connection A major heroin pipeline from France to New York, which functioned from the 1930s to the early 1970s.

Ganja A street term for marijuana; it is most commonly used in Jamaica.

Get off To feel the effects of a drug.

Glue sniffing Inhaling glue for the intoxicating effects.

Golden Crescent The opium-producing countries in Southwest Asia: Pakistan, Afghanistan, and Iran.

Golden Triangle The opium-producing countries in Southeast Asia: Laos, Burma, and Thailand.

Gram A common street quantity of powdered illicit drugs.

Grass A street name for marijuana.

Gum opium Raw opium.

Habit Physical addiction.

Half-life The amount of time it takes the body to remove one-half of a drug dose from the system.

Halfway house A home for formerly institutionalized individuals.

Hallucinogens Drugs that act on the central nervous system and produce mood and perceptual changes, and hallucinations.

Hard drugs A term given to drugs that may cause physical dependency such as heroin and cocaine.

Hashish An extract of the hemp plant (marijuana), many times more potent than marijuana.

Hash oil A resin or fluid extracted from the hemp plant containing a high concentration of THC.

Head shop Stores that sell drug-use paraphernalia.

Hemp Marijuana.

Hepatitis B An inflammation of the liver, which can occur when addicts use dirty hypodermic needles.

Herb A street name for marijuana.

Heroin A narcotic derived from morphine.

High A euphoric feeling.

Hit One dose of a drug.

Hog PCP.

Holding In possession of illicit drugs.

Homicide Murder.

Hooked Addicted.

Horse A street name for heroin.

Hype A hoax.

Illusions Hallucinations.

Impairment Reduction of an individual's ability to perform due to drug use.

Indian hemp A wild-growing, low-quality form of marijuana.

Infection A term commonly associated with addicts who use dirty needles. The most common infections are hepatitis, tetanus, and AIDS.

Inhalants Anesthetic gases and volatile hydrocarbons, which are absorbed through the lungs to create a certain effect.

Intravenous injection Using syringes to inject drugs (mainlining).

Intramuscular injection Injecting a drug into the muscle.

Joint A street name for a marijuana cigarette.

Junk A street name for heroin.

Junkie Addict.

Killer drugs High-potency drugs that are considered good.

Kilo A kilogram; 2.2 pounds.

Kit Apparatus for injecting drugs.

L.B. A one-pound quantity.

Lebanese Hashish from Lebanon.

Librium Brand name for a sedative-tranquilizer used to reduce tension, anxiety, and fear.

Lid One ounce of marijuana.

Lidocaine A synthethic local anesthetic with little potential for abuse.

Liquid hashish Hash oil.

LSD D-Lysergic acid diethylamide; a semisynthetic hallucinogen found in ergot fungus.

Ludes Quaaludes.

Mainlining Intravenous injection of drugs.

Marijuana A plant that, when consumed, produces a mild hallucino-genic effect; the active agent is Δ9-tetrahydrocannabinol.

MDA 3,4-Methylenedioxyamphetamine A hallucinogenic drug combining some of the properties of amphetamine and mescaline.

Meperidine Generic name for the drug found in Demerol.

Mescaline The principal hallucinogenic alkaloid found in the peyote cactus.

Meth Street name for methamphetamine.

Methadone A synthetic form of heroin.

Methamphetamine A synthetic form of amphetamine.

Methaqualone A powerful central nervous system depressant.

Microdots A street name for LSD tablets.

Milk sugar (lactose) A harmless substance commonly used to dilute (or "cut") cocaine and heroin.

Minor tranquilizer A depressant commonly used in the treatment of anxiety and tension.

MMDA A derivative of myristicin (found in nutmeg) with psyche-delic properties.

Morning glory seeds An organic hallucinogen similar to LSD.

Morphine A narcotic analgesic and the principal alkaloid agent in opium.

Narc An undercover police officer or police informer.

Narcotics Central nervous system depressants with analgesic and sedative properties.

Narcotic antagonist A drug that blocks the effects of opiate nar-cotics; it is used in drug treatment.

National Institute on Drug Abuse (NIDA) Established in 1972, NIDA provides public information and programs to fight drug abuse.

NORMAL The National Organization for the Reform of Marijuana Laws.

National Prohibition Act (the Volstead Act) Passed in 1920, it re-stricted the manufacture and sale of alcoholic beverages.

Needle freak One who uses illicit drug by injection.

Nembutal Brand name for barbiturate sedative containing pentobarbital.

Nickel bag A $5-quantity of drugs.

Nicotine A potent oily alkaloid found in tobacco.

Nitrous oxide A general anesthesic normally used in dentistry.

Nose candy A street name for cocaine.

O.D. Overdose.

Oil A street name for hashish oil.

Opiates Alkaloids derived from the opium poppy such as heroin, codeine, and morphine.

Opium A narcotic that acts as a depressant on the central nervous system.

Overdose An ingestion of a drug in an amount larger than the body's system can cope with; it often results in death.

Over-the-counter medications Drugs that may be purchased without a prescription.

Oxycodone A semisynthetic morphine derivative.

O.Z. One ounce.

Papaver somniferum The opium poppy plant.

Papers Rolling papers for marijuana cigarettes.

Paranoia Obsessive and excessive actions.

Paraquat A herbicide that has been used by the Drug Enforcement Administration to eradicate marijuana plants.

Paraphernalia Apparatus used in the administration of illicit drugs.

Passive inhalation Small amounts of smoke entering the lungs of nonsmokers.

Pasta Unrefined cocaine.

PCP An easily manufactured hallucinogen.

Peer pressure The desire and need to belong to a particular group.

Percodan A semisynthetic narcotic containing oxycodone.

Peyote A spineless cactus whose buds contain hallucinogenic agent mescaline.

Pharmaceuticals Drugs with medical uses.

Phenobarbital A long-acting barbiturate.

Physician's Desk Reference (PDR) An annual volume listing pharmaceutical drug preparations.

Physiological Physical, or acting on the body.

Placidyl Brand name of a sedative-hypnotic commonly used for insomnia.

Pot A street name for marijuana.

Preludin A common, brand-name weight control medicine similar to amphetamine.

Procaine A local anesthetic similar to cocaine.

Psilocybin The active hallucinogenic agent in the mushroom *Psilocybe mexicana*.

Psychedelic Mind altering.

Psychological Mental; of the mind.

Pusher A street dealer.

Quaalude Methaquaalone; nonbarbiturate sedative-hypnotic.

Quarter One-fourth (gram, ounce, pound, etc.).

Quarter bag Normally, a one-quarter ounce quantity.

Quarter paper One-quarter gram of powder.

Reggae Music popularized by the Rastafarians.

Rag weed Low-quality. Indian hemp marijuana.

Reefer A street name for marijuana.

Rastafarians A religious group who worship former Emperor Ras Tafari of Ethiopia; they are centered in Jamaica.

Rat To inform for the police.

Receptor sites Sites within the body where chemical substances interact to produce certain physiological or psychological effects.

Recreational drug use Drug use in a social setting among friends or acquaintances.

Rehabilitation Techniques used to help rid drug users of their habit.

Resin The oily substance secreted by the *Cannabis* plant.

Reverse tolerance A condition in which the response to a particular dosage of a drug increases with repeated use.

Rig A street name for a hypodermic needle.

Ritalin Brand name for a central nervous system stimulant.

Roach Street name for a partially used marijuana cigarette.

Roach clip An instrument used for holding a partially used marijuana cigarette (a roach).

Rush To feel the effects of a drug suddenly.

Scheduled drugs Drugs specified in the Controlled Substances Act of 1970.

Schizophrenia A mental disorder characterized by a withdrawal from reality.

Script A street name for a prescription for drugs.

Score To purchase a quantity of drugs.

Seconal A sedative-hypnotic containing Secobarbital.

Sedative A drug that relaxes and calms.

Sedative-hypnotic A sleep-inducing drug.

Seizures Convulsions.

Shit A street name for drugs.

Shroom A street name for magic mushrooms.

Sinsemilla Seedless marijuana flower tops.

Skag Street name for heroin.

Skin popping The subcutaneous injection of a narcotic.

Smack A street name for heroin

Smoke A street term for a quantity of marijuana, or to smoke marijuana.

Smuggling The covert transportation of contraband.

Snort To inhale (e.g., cocaine) a drug.

Snow A street name for cocaine.

Speedball A combination of heroin and cocaine.

Speed freak One who uses large quantities of methamphetamine.

Spoon A small quantity of heroin.

Stash A hiding place for drugs.

Stepped on Diluted.

Steroids Drugs used to increase body mass by improving the body's nitrogen utilization.

Stimulants Drugs that stimulate the central nervous system.

Stoned Feeling the effects of marijuana.

Straight One who does not use drugs.

Sublimaze Brand name for a narcotic analgesic containing fentanyl.

Substance abuse The improper use of drugs.

Sudden death A fatal condition recently associated with the use of cocaine.

Sunshine A street name for LSD.

Syndrome X A flooding of the lungs with fluid, resulting in sudden death; a result of heroin use.

Synergy A condition in which, when two or more drugs are taken together, the combined action increases the normal effect of each drug.

Synthetic narcotics Narcotics that are produced entirely within a laboratory as opposed to those directly or indirectly derived from nature.

Synthetic marijuana A drug (Maranol) which acts on the body in the same manner as THC. It is used in the treatment of cancer patients.

"T" PCP.

Tabs Tablets.

Talwin Brand name for a potent analgesic containing pentazocine; its effects are equivalent to those produced by codeine.

Tar Raw gum opium.

Taste A small sample of drugs.

Tetrahydrocannabinol (THC) The active agent in marijuana that produces euphoria.

Thai sticks Potent, seedless marijuana grown in Thailand and Vietnam; it is packaged in bundles resembling sticks.

THC (tetrahydrocannabinol) The active agent in marijuana.

Theraputic community A halfway house.

Thorazine A very potent tranquilizer often used in cases of extreme or violent psychosis.

Tobacco A plant containing nicotine, a major drug of abuse.

Toke To smoke marijuana.

Tolerance A state of acquired resistance to the effects of a drug.

Toot A street name for cocaine.

Tops The flowering part of the female marijuana plant.

Toxic Poisonous.

Tracks Scars caused by injecting drugs.

Trafficking Selling large quantities of drugs.

Tranquilizers A group of depressant drugs that act selectively on the brain and spinal cord.

Trip The effects of LSD.

Tuinal Brand name for a short-acting barbiturate.

Turn on To introduce one to drug use.

Tylenol with Codeine A brand-name analgesic that contains acetaminophen and codeine.

U.C. A term for an undercover police officer.

Uppers Stimulant drugs.

Valium Brand name for a minor tranquilizer and sedative-hypnotic containing diazepam.

Volstead Act The popular name for the National Prohibition Act of 1920, which enforced the Eighteenth Amendment.

Wack Street name for liquid PCP.

Waste To use drugs, or to commit a murder.

Wasted A term referring to one who is murdered, or one who is heavily under the influence of drugs.

Water A street name for liquid PCP.

Window pane A street name for LSD.

Wired Under the influence of stimulants.

Withdrawal A physical and psychological syndrome that appears when a drug on which the user is physically dependant is abruptly stopped or reduced.

Wood alcohol Methanol.

Works Apparatus for injecting drugs.

Zigzag Brandname of cigarette papers commonly used to smoke marijuana.

Index

A

ABC method. *See* Surveillance
Abandoned property. *See United States v. Oliver*
Aerocommander aircraft, 179
Affiant, 64
Affidavit. *See* Searches
Afghanistan, 108, 172
Agent Identification File, 287–288
AIDS, 111
Aircraft "N" numbers, 279
Alcohol
  use, 31, 314–315, 339
Amphetamines, 93, 113
Analogs, 122
"Angel dust." *See* Phencyclidine
Arizona v. Hicks, 76
Armstrong's mixture. *See* Booby traps
Arrest records, 9
Arrest situations, 311
  self-defense, 39
Assessment centers, 322–323
Audio surveillance. *See* Surveillance, electronic
Auditing intelligence files. *See* Intelligence
Automobile searches. *See Carroll v. United States*

B

Bahamas, 179
Banks, 13
Barbiturates, 93, 119
Bartering materials, 81
Bayer Company, 108
Beat package. *See* "Dummy bag"
Behavioral systems theory, 247–249
"Black tar" heroin. *See* Heroin

Bladder tanks, 179
Blake and Mouton's managerial grid, 252–253
Body transmitters. *See* Surveillance, electronic
Bolivia, 104, 123
Bolt gun, 219
Booby traps, 176, 209–221
Bridging theories, 238, 250
Bumper beepers, 160–161. *See also* Surveillance, electronic
Burma, 108
Buy-bust, 38, 39, 40. *See also* Drug buys
Buy-walk, 38, 41, 42. *See also* Drug buys

C

Caffeine, 96, 120
Cameras. *See* Evidence
Cannabis *See* Marijuana
Caribbean groups, 263
Carroll v. United States, 76
"Cells" (crack houses), 208
Cessna aircraft, 179
Chain conspiracy. *See* Conspiracy
Chain of custody. *See* Evidence
Charting, flow, 194, 274–278
Chimel v. California, 61
"China White" heroin. *See* Designer drugs
Clash of Pyramids, 246
Cloning. *See* Cultivation, marijuana
Closed systems theories, 239
Clothespin bomb. *See* Booby traps
Coca leaves, 123
Cocaine, 71, 80–81, 93–94, 103–105, 113, 176, 179, 197
Co-conspirator, 49

Codeine, 115–116, 197
Coffee, 96
Colombia, 98, 104, 123, 174
Combined vehicle-foot surveillance. *See* Surveillance
Commercial aircraft, 184
Commercial marijuana. *See* Marijuana
Commodity flow charting. *See* Charting, flow
Comprehensive Crime Control Act, 53
Comprehensive Forfeiture Act, 52
Conspiracy investigations, 35, 47–48
  agreement, 48
  chain conspiracy, 50
  enterprise conspiracy, 51
  overt act, 49
  wheel conspiracy, 50
"Contact high," 325
Contraband, 62
Controlled drug purchase, 145–146
Controlled Substances Act, 52, 108, 120, 191, 197
Conversion labs, 199
Corruption, 189
Cover story, 18, 28, 30, 139
Crack. *See* Cocaine
Crack houses, 206–209
Credit, sources of, 13
Cuba, 179
Cultivation, marijuana, 171–175. *See also* Marijuana
Cyalume lightsticks. *See* Infrared light sources

D
Data collection/collation. *See* Intelligence
Data plates, aircraft, 181–182
Decentralization, 256–257
Deep cover assignments. *See* Undercover
Delivering, 79
Demerol, 84, 96, 117, 127, 194, 196
Dentists, 196–197
Designer drugs, 94, 122–123
Desoxyn, 120
Diacetylmorphine. *See* Heroin
Didrex, 98, 196
Dilaudid, 96, 97, 117, 127, 196–197
Disciplinary problems, 328
Discretionary grants, 293
Dissemination, intelligence, 265, 277–278
Distribution, 79
Documents, 82
Dogs, detection, 190
Dolophine, 197
Dominion and control, proving, 71, 85
Donations, financial, 293
Drug buys, 35, 37, 42–44, 138, 140–141

Drug enforcement myths, 339
Drug Enforcement Training Record, 334, 345–350
Drug identification, 338–339
Drug quality, 80, 84, 104, 110, 112, 114, 125
Drug quantity, 79, 84, 110, 112, 114, 125, 127
Drug records, 82
Drug-related crime, 3, 67, 344
Drug simulation, 338
Drug testing, 314, 324–327
Drug tolerance, 95, 104–105
Drug treatment, 94
Drug use, agent, 339. *See also* Drug simulation; Alcohol use
Drug withdrawal, 95
Drugs, value of, 80
"Dummy bag," 37

E
Eavesdropping. *See* Surveillance, electronic
Education, Department of, 10
Education, drug, 94
"Elephant in a matchbox" theory, 69
Emergency Ordinance Disposal (EOD), 210–211, 218–219
Employee assistance programs, 315, 340
Employment, outside, 337
Enterprise conspiracy. *See* Conspiracy investigations
Entrapment, 47
Enzyme immunoassay test. *See* Drug testing
EPIC, 9
Equipment
  investigative, 8, 23
  special, 27
  standard issue, 26
Eradication, 99, 175–176
Erthroxylon coca. *See* Cocaine
Ether, 204–205
Event flow charting. *See* Charting, flow
Evidence. *See also* Searches
  audiovisual tapes as, 86–87
  chain of custody of, 86, 324
  collection of, 83–84, 321
  liquids as, 84
  photographs as, 86–87, 164–166
  plant material as, 84
  powders as, 84
  preservation of, 83–84
  statements as, 87–88, 140
  tablets as, 84
  video tapes as, 164–166
Exclusionary rule, 163
Exigent circumstances. *See* Searches
Expert testimony, 83

External control methods. *See* Tactical
operations
Extraction labs, 199

F

"Fatal funnel," 229
Federal Aviation Administration,
177–178
Federal block grants, 292
Federal Bureau of Investigation, 9
Field interview, 8
Field training officer
program, 331–332
selection of, 332–333
the role of, 333–334
Fingerprints, 9, 84
Flash fire bomb. *See* Booby traps
Flashbacks, 113
Flower tops, 98
Food and Drug Act, 108
Foot breaker trap. *See* Booby traps
Forfeiture sanctions
automobile, 51–52, 59
money, 72, 86
records 72
Fortification, residence, 82, 206–208
Freebasing, 104–105
Fronting drugs. *See* Drug buys
Fronting money. *See* Drug buys
Funds
confidential, 137
informant, 137

G

Gang unit, 209
Gas liquid chromatography. *See* Drug
testing
Gas masks, 205
Golden Crescent, 108, 198
Golden Triangle, 108, 198
Good faith seizures. *See United States
v. Leon*
Grid search pattern, 73. *See also* Searches
Ground crew, 178–179
Growing marijuana. *See* Cultivation,
marijuana
Guerilla warfare, 173

H

Hallucinogens, 97
Harrison Narcotics Act, 103, 109
Harvesting marijuana. *See* Cultivation,
marijuana
Hawthorne effects. *See* Hawthorne
Studies
Hawthorne Studies, 242–243
Health Department, 11
Heroin, 80, 84, 93, 95, 97, 108–110,
122, 190

Hepatitis, 111
High crime areas, 341, 343
Highway Department, 11
Hospitals, 192–195, 198, 263, 341
Hot light bomb. *See* Booby traps
Human relations theory, 242
Human resources management, 238
Hydroponics. *See* Cultivation, marijuana

I

Infiltration, 31–33
Informant payment file, 286–287
Informants
contracting, 137, 140, 142–143, 311
egotistical motive of, 134
fear motive of, 133
mercenary motive of, 134
payments, 139
perverse motive of, 133
repentance motive of, 134
revenge motive of, 133
unwitting motive of, 134
working with, 5, 33, 36, 269
Information, receiving, 4–5
Infrared light sources, 161–162,
164–166, 178
Initial job application. *See* Personnel
issues
Initiation, case, 342
Instrumentation of the crime, 62
Intelligence, criminal, 8, 14, 17
Intelligence, narcotics, 258–259, 262,
264, 265, 270–279
Intermural violence, 310–311
Internal affairs (IA), 323
Internal control methods. *See* Tactical
operations
Internal Revenue Service, 10
Interviews, informant, 135. *See also*
Personnel issues
Intramural violence, 310–311
Iran, 108

J

Jamaica, 98, 176
Job performance, past, 303
Justification of risk action, 312–313

K

Katz v. United States, 163
Katzenbach Guidelines, 295–296

L

Laboratories, clandestine, 107, 124
Laboratory fees, 38
La Cosa Nostra, 263
Laos, 108
Law enforcement transponder, 178

Leap-frog method. *See* Surveillance
Legalizing drugs, 93, 100–101
Legislation, drug, 17
Librium, 97, 98
Licensing, 10
Link analysis. *See* Charting, flow
Lithium aluminum hydride, 204
LSD (d-lysergic acid diethylamide), 84,
    93, 97, 112–113, 198

M

McGregor, Douglas, 247, 248
Magazine bomb. *See* Booby traps
Magic mushrooms. *See* Psilocybin
Mainlining, 110
Management by Objectives (MBO),
    250–252
Manpower, 7–8
Marijuana, 80–81, 83–84, 98–103, 174,
    commercial, 172
    sinsemilla, 98–99, 172–173
Maslow, Abraham, 244–245
Mass spectroscopy test. *See* Drug testing
Mayo, Elton. *See* Hawthorne studies
MDMA
    (methylenedioxymethamphetamine),
    122
Media. *See* Public relations
MEG units, 291
Mercuric chloride (Bromide), 202
Methamphetamine, 84, 113–114, 130,
    197–198, 200–201, 205
Mexico, 98, 108, 110, 172, 176, 198
Minimizing. *See* Surveillance, electronic
Minnesota Multiphasic Personality
    Inventory (MMPI), 305
Miranda v. Arizona, 87
Money, 81
Mononucleosis, 111
Morphine, 93, 97, 115, 194
Mother ships. *See* Vessels
Motives, informant's, 5
Motor Vehicles, Department of, 11
Motorcycle gangs, outlaw, 113, 263
Mouse trap. *See* Booby traps
"Murphy's Law," 220

N

Narcotics, 96, 115
National Forest Service, 172
National Guard, 176
National Institute of Justice, 93, 306
New York v. Belton, 75
NCIC, 8, 67, 270
Nicotine, 120
Nighttime warrant service. *See* Searches
No-knock warrant. *See* Searches
Nurses, 191–195

O

On-the-job training. *See* Field training
    officer
Open fields doctrine, 14
Open systems theory, 238, 242–245
Opium, 96, 109–110
Organizational law enforcement charts,
    258–261
Organizational pyramid. *See* Williams,
    J.D.
Ostrich effect, 47
Over-the-counter drugs, 96, 115, 121
Overt act. *See* Conspiracy investigations

P

Pager, use of, 336
Pakistan, 108
Panama, 176
Paraphernalia, 81, 90
Parkinson's disease, 123
Patrol maneuvers, 209
Patterns, search. *See* Searches
Peel, Sir Robert, 237
Pen register, 8, 12
Percaset, 194
Percodan, 194, 197
Performance management, 250–253,
    315–316
Personal improvement plan, 315
Personal lifestyle, agent's, 302–303
Personnel Issues, 300–305, 311–316
Peru, 123
Peyote, 84, 93, 198
Pharmaceutical drugs, 108, 115,
    191–193
Pharmacies, 191, 198, 263
Phencyclidine (PCP), 80–81, 84, 97,
    107–108, 198–200, 205
Photographs, as evidence. *See* Evidence
Physicians, 190–193, 198, 263
Physiological dependence, 94–95
Pilots, aircraft, 184–185
Plain view doctrine. *See* Searches
Polygraph examinations, 304–305
Possession
    actual, 71
    constructive, 71
    definition of, 79
    with intent to distribute, 79
Potassium cyanide, 204
Precursors, 202–203
Preludin, 120, 197
Prescriptions, 191–196
President's Commission on Law
    Enforcement and Administration,
    331
Prevention, drug, 94

Prison gangs, 189
Proactive investigations, 3
Probable cause, 54, 67
Probation and parole, 10
Promotions, 321–322
Proof, methods of, 78–79
Property offenses, 344
Prosecution, 5, 10, 47–48, 193, 262
   strategies, 78–79, 146
Prostitution, 31, 262
Psilocybin, 84, 198
Psychological dependence, 94, 96–97,
   115–116
Psychological stress evaluator, 305
Psychological well-being, 329
Psylisyben, 84, 198
Public information officer. *See* Public
   relations
Public relations, 293–297
Public utility companies, 13
Puerto Rico, 179
Punji Pit. *See* Booby traps
Purchase of evidence file, 282–283
Purchase of services file, 284–286
Purity, drug. *See* Drug quality

Q
Quality circles, 248–250

R
"RF" signals, 86
Radioimmunoassay test. *See* Drug
   testing
Radios, 22–23, 343
Raids. *See* Tactical operations
Reagents, 202–203
Records, court, 10
Resources, 7
Rip-offs. *See* Tactical operations
Risk assessment, 312–313
Risk compensation by tactics, 312–313
Risk evasion, 312–313
RISS Project, 264
Ritalin, 97, 120, 194, 197
Rock cocaine. *See* Cocaine
Rotation, officer, 317–318

S
Sanitation Department, 10
Scamming, 195–196
Schedules, drug, 97–98
Schedules, work, 308–309
Scientific management, theory of. *See*
   Taylor, Fredrick
Scramblers, 24
Searches
   automobile, 76
   body cavity, 77–78

consent, 74–75
exigent circumstances, 74
function of recorder in, 70
function of searcher in, 70
incident to arrest, 74
location of, 62
nighttime warrant service, 67
no-knock warrant, 66
obtaining warrants for, 34, 60, 151
   the affidavit, 60, 62, 65
   the application, 61, 68
   the execution of, 66
   the mechanics of, 61
   the return, 67, 69
patterns of, 73–74
plain view, 76
strip, 77–78
warrantless, 59
Seconal, 197
Sedatives, 96
Seizures. *See* Forfeiture sanctions
Sharing provisions. *See* Forfeiture
   sanctions
Sinsemilla. *See* Marijuana
Skin popping, 110
Smuggling, 109
Social pyramid. *See* Williams, J.D.
Social Security Administration (SSA),
   25, 266, 341
Sodium, 204
Solvents, 202–203
Southeast Asia. *See* Golden Triangle
Southwest Asia. *See* Golden Crescent
Speedball, 197
"Speed-Freak," 113
Spouse, agent's, 306
Standard operating procedure, 331–333,
   337
Starlight scope, 166
Statements, as evidence. *See* Evidence
Stimulants, 96, 120
Sting operations, 201
Stress, 313–318
Subpoenas, 13
Superglue fuming, 84
Supervisors, line, 307–308
Support officers, 20
Supra-addictive. *See* Synergy
Surveillance
   electronic, 5, 7, 40, 82, 151–153,
      159, 160, 163–164, 167–170,
      263, 336, 343–344
   moving, 151–155, 269, 310, 343–344
   stationary, 42, 151, 157–158,
      343–344
SWAT, 26, 222, 324
Synergism. *See* Synergy
Synergy, 95

Synthesis labs, 199
Synthetic drugs, 95, 122

T

Tactical operations
  drug rip-offs, 37, 45-47, 124
  raids, 223-232, 311
Talwin, 98, 197
Tape recorders, 24
Task force, drug, 290-293
Target selection, 4, 7, 272
Taverns, 33
Taylor, Fredrick, 239-240
Tax departments, 11
Telegraph companies, 13-14
Telephone calls, 336-337
  pretext, 42
  recording, 162
Telephone company, 12, 201
Testifying in court, 342
Tetrahydrocannabinol. See Marijuana
Texas v. Brown, 76
Thailand, 108, 172
Third-party interceptions, 162, 163. See
  also Surveillance, electronic
Traditional organizational theories,
  238-242
Traffic accidents, agent, 342-343
Traffic citations, 8
Training, 18
  external, 320-321
  field, 41, 319-320
  in-service, 26, 319-321
Transfers, employee, 315, 337
Transmitters, body. See Surveillance,
  electronic
Trashing, 14, 202
Trot line trap. See Booby traps
Tylenol III with codeine, 194, 197

U

Undercover, 167-168
  apartments, 337
  contacts (police), 21
  equipment, 24, 341
  identification, 6, 14, 17-18, 28,
    38-39, 255
  procedure, 21-22, 342
  vehicles, 262, 311, 314, 341-343
United States Bureau of Alcohol,
    Tobacco and Firearms, 9, 10,
    290-291
United States Customs Service, 9,
    177-178, 238

United States Department of Justice,
    53, 264, 295
United States Drug Enforcement
    Administration, 9, 115, 131, 191,
    238
United States Marshals Service, 10
United States Postal Service, 174,
    200-201
United States v. Chadwick, 75
United States v. Diaz, 76
United States v. Leon, 60
United States v. Oliver, 14
United States v. Ross, 76
Uppers. See Stimulants

V

Valium, 97-98, 119, 130, 194, 196
Vehicles, 21
  drone, 158
Vehicle indemnity form, 54
Venus fly trap. See Booby traps
Vessels, 187-189
Victimless crime, 3
Victims, crime, 3
Videotaping, 87. See also Evidence
Vollmer, August, 237
Voluntary statements. See Evidence

W

Waiver of rights, 88
Warrant file, 9
Warrant return. See Searches
Warrantless searches. See Searches
Weapons, 25-26, 62
Weber, Max, 240-241
Weeks v. United States, 60
Wheel conspiracy. See Conspiracy
  investigations
Williams, J.D., 245-246
Wiretaps, 161-162. See also
  Surveillance, electronic
Written examination. See Personnel
  issues

X

"X" theory. See McGregor, Douglas

Y

"Y" theory. See McGregor, Douglas

Z

Zone search pattern, 73. See also
  Searches